Lecture Notes in Artificial Intelligence

Edited by R. Goebel, J. Siekmann, and W. Wahlster

Subseries of Lecture Notes in Computer Science

Koen V. Hindriks   Alexander Pokahr
Sebastian Sardina (Eds.)

Programming Multi-Agent Systems

6th International Workshop, ProMAS 2008
Estoril, Portugal, May 13, 2008
Revised Invited and Selected Papers

 Springer

Volume Editors

Koen V. Hindriks
EEMCS, Delft University of Technology
Delft, The Netherlands
E-mail: k.v.hindriks@tudelft.nl

Alexander Pokahr
Distributed Systems and Information Systems
University of Hamburg
Hamburg, Germany
E-mail: pokahr@informatik.uni-hamburg.de

Sebastian Sardina
School of Computer Science and Information Technology
RMIT University
Melbourne, Australia
E-mail: sebastian.sardina@rmit.edu.au

Library of Congress Control Number: Applied for

CR Subject Classification (1998): I.2.11, I.2, C.2.4, D.2, F.3, D.3

LNCS Sublibrary: SL 7 – Artificial Intelligence

ISSN   0302-9743
ISBN-10   3-642-03277-X Springer Berlin Heidelberg New York
ISBN-13   978-3-642-03277-6 Springer Berlin Heidelberg New York

Typesetting: Camera-ready by author, data conversion by Scientific Publishing Services, Chennai, India
Printed on acid-free paper   SPIN: 12626137   06/3180   5 4 3 2 1 0

Preface

These are the proceedings of the International Workshop on Programming Multi-Agent Systems (ProMAS 2008), the sixth of a series of workshops that is aimed at discussing and providing an overview of current state-of-the-art technology for programming multi-agent systems.

The aim of the ProMAS workshop series is to promote research on programming technologies and tools that can effectively contribute to the development and deployment of multi-agent systems. In particular, the workshop promotes the discussion and exchange of ideas concerning the techniques, concepts, requirements, and principles that are important for establishing multi-agent programming platforms that are useful in practice and have a theoretically sound basis. Topics addressed include but are not limited to the theory and applications of agent programming languages, the verification and analysis of agent systems, as well as the implementation of social structure in agent-based systems (e.g., roles within organizations, coordination and communication in multi-agent systems).

In its previous editions, ProMAS constituted an invaluable occasion bringing together leading researchers from both academia and industry to discuss issues on the design of programming languages and tools for multi-agent systems. We were very pleased to be able to again present a range of high-quality papers at ProMAS 2008. After five successful editions of the ProMAS workshop series, which took place during AAMAS 2003 (Melbourne, Australia), AAMAS 2004 (New York, USA), AAMAS 2005 (Utrecht, The Netherlands), AAMAS 2006 (Hakodate, Japan), and AAMAS 2007 (Honolulu, Hawai'i), the sixth edition took place on May 13 in Estoril, Portugal, in conjunction with AAMAS 2008, the main international conference on autonomous agents and MAS. ProMAS 2008 received 27 submissions. These were reviewed by members of the Program Committee, and 12 papers were accepted for presentation.

At the workshop, in addition to the regular papers that were presented, Dana Nau (University of Maryland) gave an invited talk about planning and multi-agent systems. There are many interesting links between planning and agent programming languages for multi-agent systems. We believe that the agent programming community can learn from the progress made in the planning community, and, vice versa, may have potential to contribute to relatively new topics addressed in the planning community such as real-time and multi-agent planning. For this reason, we are also happy that Dana Nau provided an invited paper for this ProMAS proceedings-volume.

In his paper, Nau throws some light on how to cope with the intrinsic complexity that an automated planner would face in the context of multi-agent settings. Now that the field of *automated planning* has recently experienced tremendous progress and planners are able to deal with complex and reasonably sized problems, enhancing agent systems with explicit planning capabilities becomes appealing. However, planning in multi-agent settings is much more complex than the classical planning setting: "the actions of the other agents can induce a combinatorial explosion in the number of contingencies that the planner will need to consider, making both the search space and the solution size exponentially larger." Nau describes three promising approaches to tackle such complexity, namely, state abstraction, explicit use of procedural domain information, and adequate frameworks for interleaving planning and execution. Although interesting work has already been done, both in the agent and planning communities, we believe integrating planning into multi-agent frameworks is an open challenge that will receive increasing research attention in the upcoming years.

As at previous editions, the themes addressed in the accepted papers included in this Volume range from technical topics related to, for example, security issues to conceptual issues related to, for instance, incorporating norms in multi-agent systems. More specifically, new contributions are included related to extensions and innovations of agent programming languages, contributions related to social dimensions of multi-agent systems, and contributions related to tools and environments in which agents operate.

Agent Programming Languages

The paper by Hindriks et al. presents an extension of the agent-programming language GOAL with a utility-based lookahead planning capability. The idea is that quantitative heuristics added to a GOAL agent program may be used to prune some of the options for action derived by the qualitative action selection mechanism of such an agent. The paper thus allows for a mechanism to optimize agent behavior based on costs and rewards that may be associated with an agent's actions.

The paper by Dennis and Fisher introduces an agent infrastructure layer (AIL) that supports multiple, heterogeneous agent frameworks. AIL is a Java toolkit to support the implementation of a variety of agent programming languages including Gwendolen, SAAPL, and GOAL by implementing a set of transition rules that support these languages. AIL is proposed as a step toward formal verification of heterogeneous multi-agent systems that consist of agents written in a variety of agent languages.

The paper by Tinnemeier et al. introduces organizations and norms as an extension of agent programming. The programming language proposed is designed to implement multi-agent organizations. Various normative aspects of organizations including monitoring of behavior, regimenting behavior, and sanctioning are discussed.

The paper by Novak discusses the agent-programming language Jazzyk as a means for programming agents that use heterogeneous knowledge representations in order to achieve their objectives. The basic idea is that different tasks require different knowledge representation techniques and a principled approach is needed to allow for this. The semantics based on behavioral state machines is discussed as well as an implementation of an interpreter for Jazzyk.

Multi-Agent Systems Frameworks

The paper by Neville and Pitt describes a programming and simulation environment for prototyping and testing *societies of agents*, called PRESAGE. The Java-based environment is designed to allow developers to investigate properties that emerge from long-term, global system behavior. The idea then is to use the PRESAGE platform for prototyping to investigate system-wide performance and emergent behaviors before frameworks such as JADE or AgentBuilder are used to implement the multi-agent system.

The work by Gaud et al. presents JANUS, a platform that allows the development of *holonic* multi-agent systems. Thus, the idea behind the platform is the modeling of multi-agent systems as recursive entities. JANUS deals with an explicit representation of roles and organizations as first-class entities, and provides a direct implementation of part of the CRIO metamodel. The paper provides a complete description of the platform and describes an example of a market-like community.

The paper by Magarinop et al. proposes a complete computerized process of the Delphi protocol by which expert humans/agents can come to an agreement using iterative question–answer sessions. A model of the Delphi process using the INGENIAS methodology is first developed; the resulting INGENIAS model is a high-level, domain-independent description of the goals and tasks involved in the Delphi method. The paper then goes on to implement and evaluate the approach by providing the details for one domain-specific instance, showing an improvement over the Delphi process without the use of the INGENIAS model.

Agent Environments and Tools

The paper by Acay et al. argues that a suitable modeling of the environment would help agents to learn, understand, and adapt to it at run time. To that end, the paper explores the relation between the agent reasoning and the availability of tools and artifacts populating the agent's situated environment. The authors coined the term *extrospection* to refer to the act of an agent reasoning about the tools that become available at run time.

Bade et al. deal with how information about potentially highly dynamic environments can be collected and made available to interested agents in an efficient and effective way across multiple agent platforms. In this respect an abstract model of an infrastructure for resource-aware agents is proposed that allows providing generic as well as application-dependent information channels which agents can use. The authors present an implementation of the infrastructure and argue that exchangeable discovery and distribution protocols as well as exchangeable query and representation languages simplify the development of agent applications based on reusable components.

The work of Serrano et al. focusses on the analysis of an implemented multi-agent system based on message exchanges recorded during actual execution runs. Concretely, the authors use aspect-oriented programming to obtain information about sent and received messages from arbitrary running agent platforms. Moreover an algorithm for achieving a logical ordering of messages sent across agents running on distributed hosts is presented. The approach is implemented in a generic tool for debugging and testing of distributed multi-agent-based software systems.

The paper of Erdene-Ochir et al. is also about multi-agent tools and presents Toolipse, an integrated development environment (IDE) for building applications based on the JIAC agent platform. Interestingly, JIAC and its corresponding tools have originally been developed as closed, commercial software and have only recently been released to the public. This means that, although the presented IDE is a more recent development, it is based on many years of experience in building multi-agent systems for real industrial applications.

In the paper of Such et al. it is argued that security features are an important aspect of agent platforms, but that such features also usually tend to degrade performance. Therefore an evaluation of different security protocols has been made and a new secure platform design is proposed based on the Kerberos security protocol and on Linux access control mechanisms. The design is realized in the Magentix platform, which the authors evaluate with respect to performance.

Agent Contest

This volume also includes short papers related to the Agent Contest 2008 (http://cig.in.tu-clausthal.de/agentcontest2008/). The Agent Contest has been organized since 2006 in conjunction with ProMAS. This year's contest was organized by Tristan M. Behrens, Jürgen Dix, and Peter Novák from Clausthal University of Technology, Germany and Mehdi Dastani from Utrecht University, The Netherlands. The challenge for the participants was driving herds of cows into a corral by designing and implementing strategies for controlling cowboy agents. This scenario puts much more emphasis on the coordination between agents than in previous years. The actual contest took place in May 2008. Like last year, the winner of this year's contest was the JIAC team from the Technische Universität Berlin, Germany. Six of the participant teams of the Agent Contest 2008 contributed a short paper that briefly describes the design and implementation of the multi-agent system developed by the team.

As for previous editions, we hope that the work described in these proceedings will contribute to the overall goal of stimulating the uptake of agent programming languages and the creation of industrial-strength programming languages and software tools that facilitate the development of multi-agent systems.

December 2008

Koen Hindriks
Alexander Pokahr
Sebastian Sardina

Organization

The ProMAS 2008 workshop was held on May 13 2008, in Estoril, Portugal. The workshop was part of the AAMAS 2008 Workshop Program.

Organizing Committee

Koen V. Hindriks	Delft University of Technology, The Netherlands
Alexander Pokahr	University of Hamburg, Germany
Sebastian Sardina	RMIT University, Australia

Steering Committee

Rafael H. Bordini	University of Durham, UK
Mehdi Dastani	Utrecht University, The Netherlands
Jürgen Dix	Clausthal University of Technology, Germany
Amal El Fallah Seghrouchni	University of Paris VI, France

Program Committee

Matteo Baldoni	Università degli Studi di Torino, Italy
Juan A. Botia Blaya	Universidad de Murcia, Spain
Lars Braubach	University of Hamburg, Germany
Jean-Pierre Briot	University of Paris 6, France
Keith Clark	Imperial College, UK
Rem Collier	University College Dublin, Ireland
Yves Demazeau	Institut IMAG - Grenoble, France
Frank Dignum	Utrecht University, The Netherlands
Michael Fisher	University of Liverpool, UK
Jorge Gómez-Sanz	Universidad Complutense Madrid, Spain
Vladimir Gorodetsky	Russian Academy of Sciences, Russia
Dominic Greenwood	Whitestein Technologies, Switzerland
Benjamin Hirsch	TU-Berlin, Germany
Shinichi Honiden	NII, Tokyo, Japan
Jomi Hübner	Universidade Regional de Blumenau, Brazil
Michael Huhns	University of South Carolina, USA
Yves Lespérance	York University, Canada
João Leite	Universidade Nova de Lisboa, Portugal
John-Jules Meyer	Utrecht University, The Netherlands
Jörg Müller	Clausthal University of Technology, Germany
David Morley	SRI, USA
Oliver Obst	CSIRO, Australia
Andrea Omicini	University of Bologna, Italy
Agostino Poggi	Università degli Studi di Parma, Italy

Alessandro Ricci	DEIS, Università di Bologna, Italy
Birna van Riemsdijk	Ludwig-Maximilians-Universität, Germany
Ralph Rönnquist	Intendico, Australia
Ichiro Satoh	NII, Kyoto, Japan
Kostas Stathis	City University London, UK
Paolo Torroni	University of Bologna, Italy
Tran Cao Son	New Mexico State University, USA
Gerhard Weiß	Software Competence Center Hagenberg, Austria
Michael Winikoff	RMIT University, Melbourne, Australia
Wayne Wobke	University of New South Wales, Australia

Additional Referees

Cristina Baroglio	Jean-Daniel Kant
Joris Deguet	Shakil Khan
Roberto Ghizzioli	Guillaume Piolle

Table of Contents

Agent Contest

Planning for Interactions among Autonomous Agents

Tsz-Chiu Au, Ugur Kuter, and Dana Nau

University of Maryland, College Park, MD 20742, USA

Abstract. AI planning research has traditionally focused on offline planning for static single-agent environments. In environments where an agent needs to plan its interactions with other autonomous agents, planning is much more complicated, because the actions of the other agents can induce a combinatorial explosion in the number of contingencies that the planner will need to consider. This paper discusses several ways to alleviate the combinatorial explosion, and illustrates their use in several different kinds of multi-agent planning domains.

1 Introduction

AI planning research has traditionally focused on offline planning for static single-agent environments. In environments where an agent needs to plan its interactions with other autonomous agents, planning is much more complex computationally: the actions of the other agents can induce a combinatorial explosion in the number of contingencies that the planner will need to consider, making both the search space and the solution size exponentially larger.

This paper discusses several techniques for reducing the computational complexity of planning interactions with other agents. These include:

- Partitioning states into equivalence classes, so that planning can be done over these equivalence classes rather than the individual states. In some cases this can greatly reduce both the size of the search space and the size of the solution.
- Pruning unpromising parts of the search space, to avoid searching them. This can reduce complexity by reducing how much of the search space is actually searched.
- Online planning, i.e., interleaving planning and execution. This can enable the planner to avoid planning for contingencies that do not arise during plan execution.

Each of these techniques has strengths and drawbacks. To illustrate these, the paper includes case-studies of two different multi-agent planning domains: the Hunter-and-Prey domain, and a noisy version of the Iterated Prisoner's Dilemma.

K.V. Hindriks, A. Pokahr, and S. Sardina (Eds.): ProMAS 2008, LNAI 5442, pp. 1–23, 2009.

2   Background

This section very briefly describes some relevant concepts from AI planning. For a much more detailed description, see [1].

2.1   AI Planning in General

Figure 1 shows a conceptual model of AI planning. The three components include (1) the *planner*, (2) the *plan-execution agent*, and (3) the *world* Σ in which the plans are to be executed.

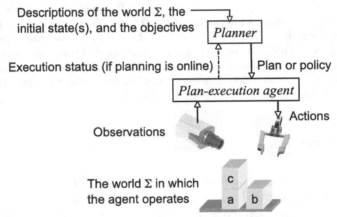

Fig. 1. Conceptual model of AI planning

The planner's input includes descriptions of Σ, the *initial* state(s) that Σ might be in before the plan-execution agent performs any actions, and the desired objectives (e.g., to reach a set of states that satisfies a given *goal condition*, or to perform a specified task, or a set of states that the world should be kept in or kept out of, or a partially ordered set of states that we might want the world to go through). If the planning is being done online (i.e., if planning and plan execution are going on at the same time), the planner's input will also include feedback about the current execution status of the plan or policy.

The planner's output consists of either a *plan* (a linear sequence of actions for the agent to perform) or a *policy* (a set of state-action pairs with at most one action for each state).

2.2   Classical Planning

Historically, most AI planning research has focused on *classical* planning problems. A classical planning problem is one that satisfies a very restrictive set of assumptions:

1. **State-transition model.** The world is a finite state-transition system, i.e., a triple $\Sigma = (S, A, \gamma)$, where S is a finite set of states, A is a finite set of actions, $\gamma : S \times A \rightarrow 2^S$ is a state-transition function. If $\gamma(s, a) \neq \emptyset$ then we say that a is *applicable* to s or *executable* in s.
2. **Full observability.** Σ's current state is always completely knowable.
3. **Determinism.** For every s and a, $|\gamma(s, a)| \leq 1$. In other words, if a is applicable to s, then there is exactly one possible outcome, namely the state in $\gamma(s, a)$. Furthermore, there is exactly one *initial state* s_0 that will be Σ's current state before plan-execution begins.
4. **Single agency.** The plan-execution agent is the only agent capable of making any changes in the world. If it were not for this agent's actions, the world would be static.
5. **Achievement goals and sequential plans.** The planner's objective is to produce a plan (i.e., a linearly ordered finite sequence of actions) that puts Σ into any one of some finite set of states S_g.
6. **Implicit time.** Actions have no duration; they are instantaneous state transitions.
7. **Offline planning.** The planner produces a complete plan for the given initial and goal states prior to any execution of its plan by the plan-execution agent.

In multi-agent systems, Assumption 4 does not hold, and several of the other assumptions may not necessarily hold. Sections 3 and 4 describe two generalizations of classical planning that can be used to represent certain kinds of multi-agent planning problems.

2.3   Classical Representation

A classical planning problem is conventionally represented as a triple $P = (O, s_0, g)$, where:

- s_0 and g, the *initial state* and *goal condition*, are sets of ground atoms in some first-order language L.
- O is a set of *planning operators*, each of which represents a class of actions that the plan-execution agent may perform. An operator is conventionally represented as a triple

$$o = (\text{head}(o), \text{precond}(o), \text{effects}(o)),$$

  where $\text{precond}(o)$ is a collection of literals called *preconditions*, $\text{effects}(o)$ is a collection of literals called *effects*, and $\text{head}(o)$ is a syntactic expression of the form $name(x_1, \ldots, x_n)$, where $name$ is a symbol called o's *name*, and $x_1, \ldots, x_n$ are all of the variables that appear anywhere in $\text{precond}(o)$ or $\text{effects}(o)$. We will let $\text{effects}^+(o)$ be the set of all non-negated atoms in $\text{effects}(o)$, and $\text{effects}^-(o)$ be the set of all atoms whose negations are in $\text{effects}(o)$.

A *state* is any set s of ground atoms of L. An atom l is *true* in s if $l \in s$; otherwise l is *false* in s. The set of goal states is $S_g = \{s : s \text{ is a state and } g \text{ is true in } s\}$.

An *action* is any ground instance of a planning operator. An action a is *applicable* to a state s if a's preconditions are true in s, i.e., if $l \in s$ for every positive literal $l \in \text{precond}(a)$ and $l \notin s$ for every negated literal $\neg l \in \text{precond}(a)$. If a is applicable to s, then the *result* of applying it is the state $\gamma(s,a)$ produced by removing from s all negated atoms in effects(a), and adding all non-negated atoms in effects(a). Formally,

$$\gamma(s,a) = (s - \text{effects}^-(a)) \cup \text{effects}^+(a).$$

A *plan* is a linear sequence of actions $\pi = \langle a_1, \dots, a_n \rangle$. The plan π is *executable* in a state s_0 if there is a sequence of states $\langle s_0, s_1, \dots, s_n \rangle$ such that for $i = 1, \dots, n$, $s_i = \gamma(s_{i-1}, a_2)$. In this case we say that $\langle s_0, s_1, \dots, s_n \rangle$ is π's *execution trace* from s_0, and we define $\gamma(s_0, \pi) = s_n$. If s_n satisfies the goal g, then we say that π is a *solution* for the planning problem $P = (O, s_0, g)$.

3   Nondeterministic Planning Problems and Multi-agency

A *nondeterministic* planning problem is one in which Assumption 3 does not hold. Each action may have more than one possible state-transition; and instead of a single initial state s_0, there is a set S_0 of possible initial states.

The classical representation scheme can be extended to model nondeterministic planning problems, by redefining a *nondeterministic operator* to be a tuple

$$o = (\text{head}(o), \text{precond}(o), \text{effects}_1(o), \text{effects}_2(o), \dots, \text{effects}_n(o)),$$

where each effects$_i(o)$ is a set of literals. If a is a ground instance of o and precond(a) is true in a state s, then the result of executing a in s may be any of the states in the following set:

$$\begin{aligned}
\gamma(s,a) = \{&(s - \text{effects}_1^-(a)) \cup \text{effects}_1^+(a), \\
&(s - \text{effects}_2^-(a)) \cup \text{effects}_2^+(a), \\
&\dots, \\
&(s - \text{effects}_n^-(a)) \cup \text{effects}_n^+(a)\}.
\end{aligned}$$

A nondeterministic planning problem can be represented as a triple $P = (O, S_0, g)$, where O is a set of nondeterministic planning operators, S_0 is the set of initial states, and g is the goal condition.

3.1   Representing Other Agents' Actions

Multi-agent planning problems can sometimes be translated into nondeterministic single-agent planning problems by modifying the plan-execution agent's actions to incorporate the effects of the other agents' possible responses to those actions. For example, suppose an agent α is going down a hallway and runs into another agent β going in the opposite direction. Suppose that to get past them, α moves to its right. Then β may either move right (in which case the agents can pass each other) or left (in which case neither agent can pass). As shown in

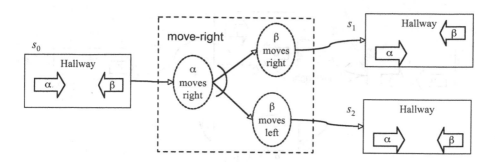

Fig. 2. Two possible outcomes of moving to the right in a hallway

Figure 2, β's two possible actions can be modeled as nondeterministic outcomes of α's move-right action.

3.2   Policies and Execution Structures

Most nondeterministic planning problems violate not only Assumption 3 but also Assumption 5, for if an action a can lead to more than one possible state, then we will need a way to provide conditional execution of subsequent actions depending on what state a takes us to. Hence for nondeterministic planning problems, solutions are typically defined to be *policies* rather than plans. A policy is a set π of state-action pairs such that for each state there is at most one action. In other words, π is a partial function from S into A.

Given a policy π, the *execution structure* Σ_π is a graph of all possible execution traces of π in the system Σ. For example, the policy

$$\pi_0 = \{(s_0, \text{move-right}), (s_1, \text{pass}), (s_2, \text{wait})\}$$

has the execution structure depicted in Figure 3.

3.3   Solutions

Recall that in a classical planning problem, the execution of a plan π in a state s always terminates at a single state $\gamma(s, \pi)$, and π is a solution to the planning problem if $\gamma(s, \pi)$ is a goal state. In nondeterministic planning problems, the execution of a policy π in a state s may terminate at any of several different states or might not terminate at all. Hence we can define several different kinds of solutions to nondeterministic planning problems, depending on which of the executions terminate at goal states [2]:

- **Weak solutions.** π is a *weak solution* for P if for every state $s \in S_0$ there is at least one execution trace of π that takes us to a goal state, i.e., if for every $s \in S_0$, there is at least one path in Σ_π from s to a state in S_g. For example, if the set of possible initial states in Figure 3 is $S_0 = \{s_0\}$ and if

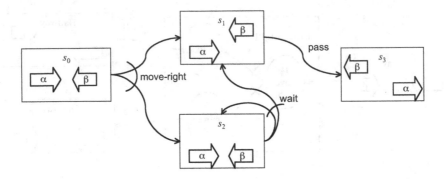

Fig. 3. Execution structure for the policy $\pi_0 = \{(s_0, \text{move-right}), (s_1, \text{pass}), (s_2, \text{wait})\}$

α's goal is to get to the state s_3 in the hallway, then the policy π_0 given earlier is a weak solution, because there exists an execution trace of π_0 that produces s_3. The same is true for the policy

$$\pi_1 = \{(s_0, \text{move-right}), (s_1, \text{pass})\}.$$

- **Strong solutions.** π is a *strong solution* for P if every execution trace of π produces a goal state, i.e., every leaf node of Σ_π is in S_g. For example, consider a modified version of the hallway problem in which β will *always* move to the right in the state s_2. In this version of the hallway problem, the execution structure for π_0 is not the one shown in Figure 3, but instead is the one shown in Figure 4. Hence π_0 is a strong solution.
- **Strong-cyclic solutions.** π is a *strong-cyclic solution* for P if every *fair* execution trace of π takes us to a goal state. A fair execution trace is one such that for every cycle C in which there is an action having more than one outcome, the execution trace will traverse C at most finitely many times before exiting C.

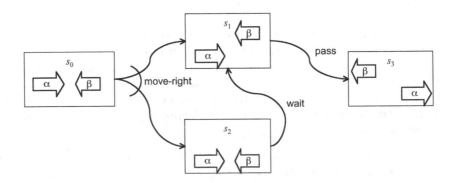

Fig. 4. π_0's execution structure if β *always* moves to the right in s_2

The concept of a fair execution trace can be understood intuitively as follows. Even though we are not attaching probabilities to the outcomes of an action, we would not normally say that a state s' is a possible outcome of executing a in s unless there is a nonzero probability that a will take us to s'. For example, in Figure 3, the wait action has two possible outcomes s_1 and s_2, so it is fair to assume that both of these outcomes have nonzero probability of occurring. Consequently, if C is a cycle in Σ_π (e.g., the wait action's outcome s_2) and if one or more of the actions in C has another possible outcome (e.g., the wait action's outcome s_1), then the probability of remaining in C forever is 0, so any execution trace that remains in C forever is unfair.

3.4   Partitioning States into Equivalence Classes

To illustrate how combinatorial explosion can occur in multi-agent planning, we now consider a multi-agent planning domain called the Robot Navigation domain [3,4,2]. In this problem domain, a robot is supposed to move around a building such as the one shown in Figure 5, picking up packages and delivering them to their destinations. There is another agent in the building, a "kid," who is running around and opening and closing doors. The kid can move much faster than the robot, hence the kid may open or close each of the n doors in between each of the robot's actions.[1]

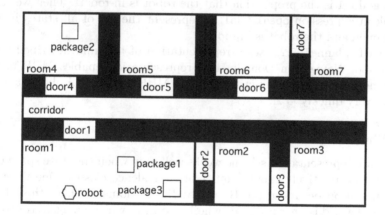

Fig. 5. A state in a Robot Navigation problem

If the building contains n doors and we model the kid's actions as nondeterministic outcomes of the robot's actions, then each of the robot's actions has 2^n possible outcomes: one for each possible combination of open and closed doors. If we represent each of an action's 2^n outcomes explicitly, then for every policy π and every state-action pair $(s, a) \in \pi$, the execution structure Σ_π will have 2^n

---

[1] Equivalently, one could assume that there are n kids, each of whom is playing with a different door.

successor states. In general, a solution policy will have exponential size and will take doubly exponential time to generate. This is not very good!

In the Robot Navigation domain, the size of the search space can be reduced by constructing policies over sets of states rather than individual states. For example, if the robot is in room room1 and wants to go into the hallway, then it matters whether door door1 is open but it does not matter whether any of the other $n - 1$ doors is open or closed. To go through door1, we only need to plan for two sets of states: the set S of all states in the robot is in room1 and door1 is open, (in which case the robot should move through the door), and the set of states S' in which the robot is in room1 and door1 is closed (in which case the robot should try to open the door).

More generally, we will want to represent π not as a set of pairs

$$\pi = \{(s_1, a_1), \ldots, (s_n, a_n)\},$$

where $s_1, \ldots, s_n$ are distinct states, but instead as a set of pairs

$$\pi = \{(S_1, a_1), \ldots, (S_k, a_k)\},$$

where $\{S_1, \ldots, S_k\}$ is a partition of $\{s_1, \ldots, s_n\}$. We'll call this a *partition-based* representation of π.

To represent a set of states, we can use a boolean formula that is satisfied by every state in the set. For example, suppose open1 is the proposition that door1 is open, and in1 is the proposition that the robot is in room1. Then we can use the boolean expression open1 $\wedge$ in1 to represent the set of all states in which door1 is open and the robot is in room1.

The MBP planner [5,2] uses a representation of the kind described above.[2] In the Robot Navigation Domain, this representation enables MBP to avoid the exponential explosion described above: MBP can solve Robot Navigation problems very quickly [5,2].

3.5   When the States Are Not Equivalent

MBP's state-representation scheme works well only when the state space can be divided into a relatively small number of equivalence classes. One illustration of this limitation occurs in the Hunter-and-Prey domain [7]. In this planning domain, the world is an $n \times n$ grid (where $n \geq 2$) in which an agent α called the *hunter* that is trying to catch one or more agents $\beta_1, \ldots, \beta_k$ called *prey*.

The hunter has five possible actions: move-north, move-south, move-east, or move-west, and catch. Each of the first four actions has the effect of moving the hunter in the stated direction, and is applicable if the hunter can move that direction without going outside the grid. The catch action has the effect of catching a prey, and is applicable only when the hunter and the prey are in the same location. For example, Figure 6(a) shows a situation in which the hunter has three applicable actions: move-north, move-west, and move-south.

---

[2] More specifically, the boolean formulas are represented as Binary Decision Diagrams (BDDs) [6].

Each prey has also five actions: a stay-still action which keeps the prey in the same square it was already in, and move-north, move-south, move-east, and move-west actions. These actions are similar to the hunter's actions described above, but with an additional restriction: at most one prey occupy a square at any one time, so it is not possible for two or more prey to perform movements that put them into the same square.

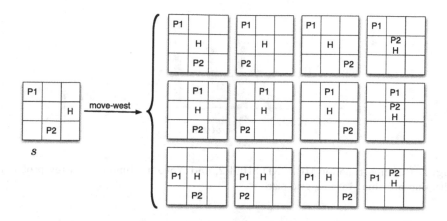

Fig. 6. A Hunter-and-Prey problem with two prey on a 3×3 grid. H represents the hunter's location, and P1 and P2 represent the locations of the two prey. In the state s shown at left, there are three possible moves for P1 and four for P2, hence twelve possible states that may be produced if the hunter moves west.

We can represent the possible actions of the prey as nondeterministic outcomes of the hunter's actions; Figure 6 gives an example. If there are m prey, any one of the hunter's actions may have up to 5^k outcomes; the exact number depends on the locations of the prey. A state's total number of predecessors or successors can be even larger.

On one hand, MBP can handle increases in grid size quite easily if there is just one prey (see Figure 7). This is because MBP can classify the locations of the hunter and prey into a small number of sets (e.g., in the set of all locations where the prey's x coordinate is 5 and the hunter's x coordinate is below 5, MBP might plan for the hunter to move East).

On the other hand, MBP's running time increases dramatically if we increase the number of prey (Figure 8). What causes MBP problems is the restriction that no two prey can be at the same place at the same time. This restriction means that unlike the doors' open/closed status in Robot Navigation problems, the prey's locations in Hunter-and-Prey problems are not independent of each other. When reasoning about the set of states in which prey p_i is in square (x, y), MBP cannot ignore the locations of the other prey because p_i's presence at (x, y) means that the other $m - 1$ prey must be in squares other than (x, y). MBP's

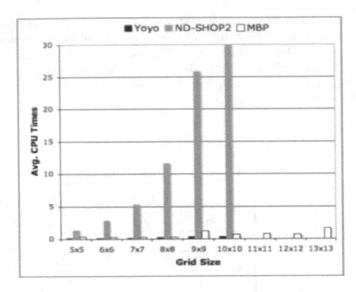

Fig. 7. Running time for MBP, ND-SHOP2, and Yoyo in Hunter-and-Prey problems with one prey and varying grid size

running time grows because there are many different states in which this can happen and MBP cannot represent them as a small number of sets of states.

3.6   Maintaining Focus on the Current Task

Another way of avoiding combinatorial explosion is to focus on one task t at a time, ignoring all actions except for those relevant for performing t. In the Hunter-and-Prey problem with a large number of prey, this means focusing on one prey at a time, and ignoring all of the other prey until this one has been caught.

In order to maintain focus on a particular task, we need a way to specify what the tasks are, and what actions are relevant to each task. One way to accomplish this is to use Hierarchical Task Network (HTN) planning [8,9,10]. In HTN planning, the objective of a planning problem is not expressed as a goal to be achieved, but instead as a task to be performed. Tasks are represented as syntactic entities that look like logical atoms, but their semantics is different: they represent activities (e.g., actions or collections of actions) rather than conditions on states of the world.

In HTN planning, the description of a planning domain includes not only the planning operators for the domain but also a collection of *HTN methods*, which are prescriptions for how to carry out various tasks by performing collections of subtasks. Planning is done by applying methods to tasks to decompose them into smaller and smaller subtasks, until *primitive* tasks are reached that

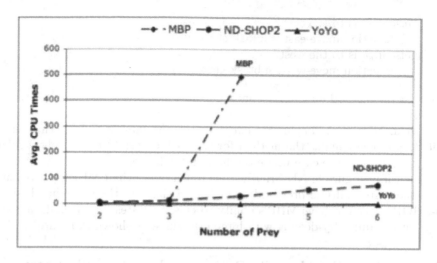

Fig. 8. Running time for MBP, ND-SHOP2, and Yoyo in Hunter-and-Prey problems with varying numbers of prey on a 4×4 grid

correspond directly to actions. If the actions are executable, the resulting plan is (by definition) a solution to the planning problem.[3]

ND-SHOP2 [13] is an HTN planning algorithm for nondeterministic domains. To solve Hunter-and-Prey problems with k prey, we can run ND-SHOP2 using methods that say basically the following:

- Method for the task catch-all-uncaught-prey
      if there are no uncaught prey, do nothing.
      else
            do subtask chase(β_i) for an arbitrarily selected uncaught prey β_i
            do subtask catch-all-uncaught-prey

- Method for the task chase(β_i)
      if β_i is at the hunter's location, do action catch(β_i)
      else if β_i is to the north
            do action move-north, subtask chase(β_i)
      else if β_i is to the south
            do action move-south, subtask chase(β_i)

---

[3] The status of HTN planning is somewhat controversial in the AI planning research community [11,12]. AI planning theorists have a preference for "domain-independent" planning, in which the planner is given no specific knowledge about a domain other than the definitions of the planning operators for that domain. In contrast, HTN planning is quite popular among people who do practical applications of AI planning, because they want to be able to use the knowledge they have about the problems they are trying to solve, and HTN methods provide a way to encode such knowledge.

      else if β_i is to the east
         do action move-east, subtask chase(β_i)
      else if β_i is to the west
         do action move-west, subtask chase(β_i)

Note that the method for catch-all-uncaught-prey recursively invokes itself whenever any uncaught prey remain. This tells the hunter to keep chasing prey until all of them have been caught. Similarly, to tell the hunter to keep chasing β_i until β_i has been caught, the method for the task chase(β_i) recursively invokes chase(β_i) except in the case where the hunter catches β_i.

As shown in Figure 8, ND-SHOP2 runs much faster than MBP on problems where there are multiple prey and a small grid size. On the other hand, since ND-SHOP2 does not have MBP's ability to classify states into a small number of sets, it has difficulty dealing with large grid sizes, as shown in Figure 7.

3.7   Combining Focusing with Reasoning about Equivalent States

To plan for a large number of prey on a large grid, we would like to combine MBP's ability to reason about sets of states with ND-SHOP2's ability to focus on individual tasks. There is a planner called Yoyo that does this. The details are complicated and we will not describe them here, but the basic idea is as follows: Yoyo does ND-SHOP2's HTN decomposition, but instead of doing it over individual states, Yoyo does it over sets of states represented as BDDs. As shown in Figures 7 and 8, Yoyo outperforms both MBP and ND-SHOP2 on Hunter-and-Prey problems; and it also has been shown to outperform MBP and ND-SHOP2 in several other problem domains [14,15].

3.8   Interleaving Planning and Acting

One of the biggest sources of difficulty in solving the Robot Navigation and Hunter-and-Prey problems is that we were trying to solve them *offline*, i.e., to generate the entire policy before executing it. The problems with exponential blowup in the size of the policy occurred because of the need to deal with all of the possible contingencies.

One of the reasons why AI planning research has traditionally focused on offline planning is that many planning problems contain *unsolvable* states, i.e, states from which it is impossible to reach any of the goal states. In such planning problems, it is important for the plan executor to avoid executing actions that will take it to unsolvable states. One way to avoid such actions is to generate an entire solution plan before the plan executor starts executing.

Neither the Robot Navigation and Hunter-and-Prey domains contain unsolvable states, hence they can be solved via *online* planning, in which the plan executor executes each action as soon as the planner generates it. In these two domains, online planning is much easier to do than offline planning, because the planner only needs to plan for one of the possible outcomes of each action, namely the outcome that the plan executor encounters when executing the action.

As an example, here is a simple online-planning algorithm for solving Hunter-and-Prey problems:

> **while** there are no uncaught prey **do**
>   **if** there is a prey β_i in the same location as the hunter
>   **then** execute catch(β_i)
>   **else** select a prey β_i arbitrarily, and move toward it

It is easy to prove that if the actions of the prey satisfy the fairness assumption discussed in Section 3.3, then the above algorithm is guaranteed to eventually catch all of the prey. In the Hunter-Prey domain, the fairness assumption means that if we keep coming back to the same state sufficiently many times, the prey will eventually do something different.

One could accomplish much the same thing by using a real-time search algorithm such as RTA* (real-time A*) [16,7]. Furthermore, one could take almost any forward-search planner for deterministic planning problems (e.g., FastForward [17], TLPlan [18], or SHOP2 [19]), and modify it so that action selection is replaced with action execution: rather than appending an action to its plan and inferring the next state, the planner would immediately execute the action and observe the state directly.

The idea of modifying a classical planner to interleave planning and execution is somewhat similar to A-SHOP [20], but A-SHOP did not interleave planning and execution in the way that we are discussing here. Its objective was to generate a plan, not to execute it; and its interactions with other agents were purely for information-gathering. On the other hand, the idea has more in common with agent systems based on the BDI model [21], such as PRS [22], AgentSpeak [23], or RAP [24]. A recent system, CanPlan [25,26], explicitly combines BDI reasoning with HTN planning.

4   Using Predictive Agent Models

One of limitation of the translation scheme in Section 3.1 is that the model of the other agents is trivial: it tells what actions the other agents *might* perform in different situations, but provides no way to help us predict how likely the agent will be to perform these actions. For good decision-making, it can sometimes be quite important to have such predictions.

As an example, consider the game of roshambo (rock-paper-scissors). The Nash equilibrium strategy for this game is to choose randomly among rock, paper, and scissors, with a probability of 1/3 for each choice; and the expected utility of this strategy is 0 regardless of what strategy the opponent uses. But in a series of international competitions among computer agents that played roshambo, some of the programs did much better than the equilibrium strategy [27,28,29]. They did so by building predictive models of the opponent's likely moves, and using these models to aid in choosing their own moves.

Another example is the game of kriegspiel [30,31]. This game is an imperfect-information version of chess, and its strategies are much more complicated than the strategies for roshambo—in fact, the game was used during the 19th century by several European countries as a training exercise for their military officers. It has been shown experimentally [32] that better play can be obtained by an opponent model that assumes the opponent will make moves at random, instead of using the minimax opponent model that is conventionally used in chess programs.

If β is an agent, we will define a *predictive model* of β to be a function $\hat\beta$ such that for each state s, $\hat\beta(s)$ is a probability distribution over the set of actions that β can perform in s. $\hat\beta$ need not necessarily be an accurate predictor of β's moves (although an accurate model is obviously preferable to an inaccurate one).

If we are playing a game G with β and we have a predictive model $\hat\beta$, then we can use $\hat\beta$ to translate the game into a Markov Decision Process (MDP). Sections 4.1 and 4.2 give quick summaries of what an MDP planning problem is and how the translation process works, Section 4.3 discusses how to partition states into equivalence classes, and Section 4.4 gives a case study on a game called the Noisy Iterated Prisoner's Dilemma (Noisy IPD).

4.1   MDP Planning Problems

A *Markov Decision Process (MDP)* planning problem is like a nondeterministic planning problem, but with the following changes:

- For state $s \in S_0$, there is a probability $P(s)$ that the initial state is s.
- If the set of possible outcomes for action a in state s is $\gamma(s, a) = \{s_1, \ldots, s_j\}$, then each of them has a probability $P(s, a, s_i)$, with $\sum_{i=1}^{j} P(s, a, s_i) = 1$.
- For each action a there is a numeric cost $c(a) \in \mathcal{R}$.
- For each state s there is a a numeric reward $r(s) \in \mathcal{R}$.
- There is a numeric *discount factor* δ, with $0 < \delta \leq 1$.[4]
- In most formulations of MDPs there is no explicit "goal states," but the same effect can be accomplished by giving these states a high reward and making them terminal states (i.e., states with no applicable actions) [33].

Given a policy π and an execution trace $T = \langle s_0, s_1, \ldots \rangle$, we can compute T's probability by multiplying the probabilities of the actions' outcomes:

$$P(T|\pi) = P(s_0)P(s_0, \pi(s_0), s_1), P(s_1, \pi(s_1), s_2), \ldots .$$

The *utility* of the execution trace is the cumulative discounted difference between the rewards and costs:

$$U(T) = \sum_i \delta^i r(s_i) - \sum_i \delta^i c(\pi(s_i)).$$

The objective is to find a policy π having the highest *expected utility*

$$E(\pi) = \sum_T P(T|\pi)U(T).$$

---

[4] In the MDP literature, the the discount factor is usually represented as γ, but that conflicts with our use of γ to represent the state-transition function.

Section 3.1 discussed how to extend the classical planning representation to represent nondeterministic planning problems. A similar approach can be used to represent MDPs, by including in the action representation the action's cost and the state-transition probabilities.

4.2   Translating Games into MDPs

Suppose two agents α and β are playing a game G, and let $\hat{\beta}$ be a predictive model for β's actions. Then we can use this model to translate G into an MDP planning problem $M(G, \hat{\beta})$. The translation is similar to the one described in Section 3.1, with the following additions:

- Each state in the game is a state in the MDP.
- As before, we represent β's possible actions as nondeterministic outcomes of α's actions—but this time we use $\hat{\beta}$ to compute probabilities for each of the outcomes. For example, suppose that in Figure 2, $\hat{\beta}$ says there is a probability of 3/4 that β will move right and a probability of 1/4 that β will move left. Then we would assign $P(s_0, \text{move-right}, s_1) = 3/4$ and $P(s_0, \text{move-right}, s_2) = 1/4$.
- We can obtain the actions' costs and the states' rewards directly from the definition of the game. For example, in chess the cost of each action would be 0, the reward associated with each nonterminal state would be 0, and the reward associated with each terminal state would be 1, -1, or 0, depending on whether the state is a win, loss, or draw.

4.3   Partitioning States into Equivalence Classes

Section 3.4 discussed how to decrease the size of the search space in a nondeterministic planning problem, by partitioning the set of states $\{s_1, \ldots, s_n\}$ into a set of equivalence classes $\{S_1, \ldots, S_k\}$ such that for each equivalence class S_i, the plan-execution agent will do the same action a_i at every state in S_i. Something similar can sometimes be done in MDPs, if an additional requirement can be met: every state in S_i must have the same expected utility.

As an example, consider the Iterated Prisoner's Dilemma (IPD). This is a well-known non-zero-sum game in which two players play n iterations (for some n) of the Prisoner's Dilemma, a non-zero-sum game having the payoff matrix shown in Table 1.

Table 1. Payoff matrix for the Prisoner's Dilemma. Each matrix entry (u_1, u_2) gives the payoffs for agents α and β, respectively.

		β's move:	
		Cooperate	Defect
	Cooperate	(3,3)	(0,5)
α's move:	Defect	(5,0)	(1,1)

In the Prisoner's Dilemma, the dominant strategy for each agent is to defect; and in the Iterated Prisoner's Dilemma, the Nash equilibrium is for both agents to defect in every iteration. But the iterations give each agent the opportunity to "punish" the other agent for previous defections, thus providing an incentive for cooperation [34,35]. Consequently, there are empirical results (e.g., [35]) showing that several non-equilibrium strategies do better in general then the Nash equilibrium strategy. The best-known of these is Tit For Tat (TFT), a strategy that works as follows:

- On the first iteration, cooperate.
- On the i'th iteration (for $i > 1$), make the move that the other agent made on the $i - 1$'th iteration.

Suppose our predictive model $\hat{\beta}$ is the following approximation of TFT:

- On the first iteration, cooperate with probability 0.9.
- On the i'th iteration (for $i > 1$), with probability 0.9 make the same move that α made on the $i - 1$'th iteration.

In the IPD, each history (i.e., each sequence of interactions among the two players) is a different state, hence after i iterations we may be within any of 4^i different states. But since $\hat{\beta}(s)$ depends solely on what happened at the previous iteration, we can partition the states at iteration i into four equivalence classes such that $\hat{\beta}$ is invariant over each equivalence class:

- $S_{i,C,C} = \{$all states in which the pair of actions at iteration i was $(C,C)\}$;
- $S_{i,C,D} = \{$all states in which the pair of actions at iteration i was $(C,D)\}$;
- $S_{i,D,C} = \{$all states in which the pair of actions at iteration i was $(D,C)\}$;
- $S_{i,D,D} = \{$all states in which the pair of actions at iteration i was $(D,D)\}$.

This gives us the MDP shown in Figure 9, in which each state (i, a_1, a_2) corresponds to the equivalence class S_{i,a_1,a_2}.

The two main problems are (1) how to obtain an appropriate predictive model, and (2) how to use the MDP to plan our moves. As a case study, we now discuss these problems in the context of a program called DBS [36,37] that plays a game called the *Noisy IPD*.

4.4   The Noisy Iterated Prisoner's Dilemma

The Noisy IPD is a variant of the IPD in which there is a small probability, called the *noise level*, that accidents will occur. In other words, the noise level is the probability of executing "cooperate" when "defect" was the intended move, or vice versa.

Accidents can cause difficulty in cooperating with others in real life, and the same is true in the Noisy IPD. Strategies that do quite well in the ordinary (non-noisy) IPD may do quite badly in the Noisy IPD [38,39,40,41,42,43]. For example, if both α and β use TFT, then one accidental defection may cause a long series of defections by both agents as each of them retaliates for the other's defections.

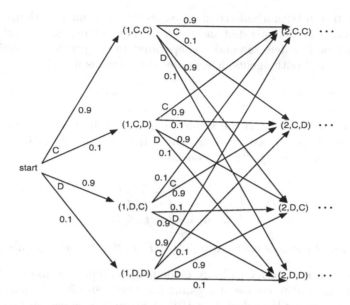

Fig. 9. An MDP in which each state is a set of equivalent game states

One way to deal with noise is to be more forgiving in the face of apparent misbehavior. For example, a strategy called Tit For Two Tats, which defects only when the other agent has defected twice in a row, can usually avoid the mutual-retaliation problem described above. One problem with such a strategy is that other agents can take advantage of it by occasionally defecting on purpose, without being punished for doing so.

Another way to deal with noise is to use a predictive model of other agent's behavior to filter out the noise, as discussed later in this section.

Modeling the other Agent's Behavior. As the game proceeds, DBS uses its observations of β's behavior to build a predictive model $\hat{\beta}$ that will give probabilistic predictions of β's future behavior. DBS's predictive model is a set of rules of the form

$$\hat{\beta} = \{C_1(s) \rightarrow P_1, \quad C_2(s) \rightarrow P_2, \quad \ldots, \quad C_m(s) \rightarrow P_m\},$$

where $C_1(s), \ldots, C_m(s)$ are mutually exclusive conditions (i.e., at most one of them is true in s), and P_i is the predicted probability that β will cooperate in a state that satisfies $C_i(s)$.

In principle, $\{C_1(s), \ldots, C_n(s)\}$ may be any set of mutually exclusive conditions, but which conditions should we use? If the conditions are too simple, then they will be incapable of accurately representing β's behavior, but if a condition $C_i(s)$ is too complicated, then it may be infeasible to learn an accurate value for P_i. DBS uses the following set of four very simple conditions:

- $C_1(s)$ is true if both agents cooperated on the previous iteration;
- $C_2(s)$ is true if α cooperated and β defected on the previous iteration;
- $C_3(s)$ is true if α defected and β cooperated on the previous iteration;
- $C_4(s)$ is true if both agents defected on the previous iteration.

One way to compute P_i is as follows (this is not exactly how DBS does it, but is an approximation). Let $0 < t < 1$ be a constant called the *threshold*, and $k > 0$ be an integer constant called the *window size*. Let S_i be the set of all states in the last k iterations that satisfy $C_i(s)$, Q_i be the set of all states in S_i in which β cooperated, and $r_i = |Q_i|/|S_i|$. Then we can set

$$P_i = \begin{cases} 0, & \text{if} \quad 0 \le r_i \le t, \\ r_i, & \text{if} \quad t < r_i < 1 - t, \\ 1, & \text{if} \quad 1 - t \le r_i \le 1. \end{cases}$$

Here are some of the reasons for computing P_i in the manner specified above:

- The conditions C_1, C_2, C_3, C_4 are inadequate to represent most IPD strategies over the entire course of a game, but they can often do well at representing the *recent* behavior of an IPD strategy. Hence we only compute P_i over the last k iterations rather than the entire history of the game.
- Clarity of behavior is an important ingredient of long-term cooperation, hence most successful IPD agents exhibit behavior that is at least partly deterministic, and we would like to model this. In the ordinary IPD, if β always cooperates when C_i is satisfied, then the ratio $r_i = 1$ will model this deterministic behavior. But consider the Noisy IPD with a noise level of, say, 10%. If β always cooperates when C_i is satisfied, then noise will transform 10% of these into defections. Hence $r_i = 0.9$ on average, which fails to model β's deterministic behavior. Hence in cases where r_i is close to 0 or close to 1, we'll want to hypothesize that β is actually behaving deterministically. The threshold t accomplishes this.

DBS computes its P_i values in a manner that is similar but not identical to the one described above. The main difference is that instead of using the ratio r_i, DBS uses a weighted ratio in which recent iterations are weighted more heavily than less recent iterations. For details, see [36].

Filtering Noise. In cases where $\hat{\beta}$ predicts deterministic behavior (i.e., it predicts the probability of cooperation to be either 0 or 1), DBS can use this deterministic prediction to detect anomalies that may be due either to noise or a genuine change in the other agent's behavior. If a move is different from a deterministic prediction, this inconsistency triggers an *evidence collection process* that will monitor the persistence of the inconsistency in the next few iterations of the game. The purpose of the evidence-collection process is to try to decide whether the violation is due to noise or to a change in the other player's policy.

Until the evidence-collection process finishes, DBS assumes that the other player's behavior is the behavior predicted by $\hat{\beta}$, rather than the behavior that was actually observed. Once the evidence collection process has finished, DBS decides whether to believe that the other player's behavior has changed, and updates $\hat{\beta}$ accordingly.

Planning DBS's Moves. Since the MDP in Figure 9 is infinite, DBS cannot generate the entire MDP. Instead, DBS plans its moves by generating and solving a truncated version of the MDP that ends at an arbitrary cutoff depth d (DBS uses $d = 60$). It is easy to compute an optimal policy π for the truncated MDP, using dynamic programming.

In an ordinary offline-planning problem, once the planner had found π, the plan executor would simply run π to completion. But this approach would not work well for DBS, because the predictive model $\hat{\beta}$ is only an approximation. By generating π, DBS may be able to make a good move for DBS in the current state, but we cannot be sure whether π will specify good moves in all of the subsequent states. Hence, instead of running π to completion, DBS executes only the first action of π, and recomputes π at every turn. Since the size of the MDP is polynomial in d, this does not require very much computation.

Performance. The 20th Anniversary Iterated Prisoner's Dilemma Competition [44] was actually a set of four competitions, each for a different version of the IPD. One of the categories was the Noisy IPD, which consisted of five runs of 200 iterations each, with a noise level of 0.1. 165 agents participated. Nine of them were different versions of DBS. As shown in Table 2, seven of these were among the top ten. Only two programs that did better: BWIN and IMM01.

BWIN and IMM01 both used the *master-and-slaves* strategy, which worked as follows: Each participant in the competition was allowed to submit up to 20 agents, and some of the participants submitted a group of 20 agents that could recognize each other by exchanging a pre-arranged sequence of Cooperate and Defect moves. Once the agents recognized each other, they worked together as a team in which 19 "slave" agents fed points to a single "master" program: every time a slave played with its master, the master would defect and the slave would cooperate, so that the master gained 5 points and the slave got nothing. Every

Table 2. Scores of the top 10 programs, averaged over the five runs

Rank	Program	Avg. score
1	BWIN	433.8
2	IMM01	414.1
3	DBSz	408.0
4	DBSy	408.0
5	DBSpl	407.5
6	DBSx	406.6
7	DBSf	402.0
8	DBStft	401.8
9	DBSd	400.9
10	lowESTFT_classic	397.2

time a slave played with a program not on its team, the slave would defect, to minimize the number of points gained by that program. BWIN and IMM01 were the "master" agents in two different master-and-slave teams.

DBS, in contrast, did not use a master-slave strategy, nor did it conspire with other agents in any other way. Despite this, DBS remained competitive with the masters in the master-and-slaves teams, and performed much better than the average score of a master and all of its slaves. A more extensive analysis [45] shows that if the size of each master-and-slaves team had been limited to less than 10, DBSz would have placed first.

5   Discussion and Conclusions

In general, planning gets very complicated when there are other autonomous agents to deal with. In order to accomplish this, it is essential to have a way to reduce the size of the search space. A variety of techniques have been developed in the AI planning literature for reducing search-space size in single-agent planning problems, and this paper has discussed how to utilize these techniques in multi-agent planning problems by translating the multi-agent planning problems into equivalent single-agent planning problems. In particular, we discussed two cases: one in which we wanted to achieve a given set of goals regardless of what the other agents might do, and one in which we wanted to maximize a utility function.

When the objective was to achieve a given set of goals regardless of the other agents' actions, the only model we needed of the other agents was what actions they were capable of performing in each state of the world. In this case, the approach was to model the other agents' actions as nondeterministic outcomes of the plan-execution agent's actions, and solve the problem offline in order to produce a policy for the plan-execution agent to use.

When the objective was to maximize a utility function, it mattered a great deal how likely or unlikely the other agent's actions might be. Hence, the approach in this case was to translate the multi-agent problem into an MDP in which the other agents' actions were represented as probabilistic outcomes of the plan-execution agent's actions. The probabilities of the outcomes were taken from a predictive model that was built by observing the other agent's behavior. This predictive model required updating as the game progressed; hence it was necessary to do the planning *online*: at each move of the game, the planner constructed a new MDP based on the updated model, and solved this MDP to decide what move the plan-execution agent should make next.

In both cases, an important technique for making the problem feasible to solve was to *partition states into equivalence classes*. In the nondeterministic planning problems in Section 3.4, the equivalence classes were based on what action we wanted to do in each state. In the MDP planning problems in Section 4.2, the equivalence classes were based not only on the action to be performed but also on the state's expected utility.

In Section 3.6 we used HTN methods to achieve additional reduction in the size of the search space by pruning unpromising paths. This approach was not used in Section 4.2, because the simple structure of a repeated game like the IPD does not lend itself to this approach. However, HTN methods have been used successfully to prune parts of the search space in more complicated games, such as bridge [46].

Although the state-aggregation and HTN pruning techniques were quite successful in the cases discussed in this paper, they each have limitations that may cause difficulty in more complex problem domains. Here are two examples:

– Section 3.5 showed that there are relatively simple classes of problems in which state aggregation does not work well. In Section 3.8 we pointed out that the problem becomes much easier to solve if the planning is done online rather than offline—and we believe one promising avenue for further work is to develop techniques for deciding when to do the planning offline and when to do it online.
– Our opponent-modeling technique for the Noisy IPD is a relatively simple one, and more complex games require more sophisticated opponent models. We believe that the development of techniques for generating good opponent models will be a very important task.

Acknowledgments. This work has been supported in part by AFOSR grants FA95500510298, FA95500610405, and FA95500610295, DARPA's Transfer Learning and Integrated Learning programs, and NSF grant IIS0412812. The opinions in this paper are those of the authors and do not necessarily reflect the opinions of the funders.

References

1. Ghallab, M., Nau, D., Traverso, P.: Automated Planning: Theory and Practice. Morgan Kaufmann, San Francisco (2004)
2. Cimatti, A., Pistore, M., Roveri, M., Traverso, P.: Weak, strong, and strong cyclic planning via symbolic model checking. Artificial Intelligence 147(1-2), 35–84 (2003)
3. Pistore, M., Bettin, R., Traverso, P.: Symbolic techniques for planning with extended goals in non-deterministic domains. In: Proceedings of the European Conference on Planning (ECP) (2001)
4. Pistore, M., Traverso, P.: Planning as model checking for extended goals in non-deterministic domains. In: Proceedings of the International Joint Conference on Artificial Intelligence (IJCAI), Seattle, USA, pp. 479–484. Morgan Kaufmann, San Francisco (2001)
5. Bertoli, P., Cimatti, A., Pistore, M., Roveri, M., Traverso, P.: MBP: a model based planner. In: Proceeding of ICAI 2001 workshop on Planning under Uncertainty and Incomplete Information, Seattle, USA, pp. 93–97 (August 2001)
6. Bryant, R.E.: Symbolic boolean manipulation with ordered binary-decision diagrams. ACM Computing Surveys 24(3), 293–318 (1992)
7. Koenig, S., Simmons, R.G.: Real-time search in non-deterministic domains. In: IJCAI 1995 (1995)
8. Tate, A.: Project planning using a hierarchic non-linear planner. Technical Report 25, Department of Artificial Intelligence, University of Edinburgh (1976)

9. Sacerdoti, E.: A Structure for Plans and Behavior. American Elsevier, Amsterdam (1977)
10. Erol, K., Hendler, J., Nau, D.S.: Complexity results for hierarchical task-network planning. Annals of Mathematics and Artificial Intelligence 18, 69–93 (1996)
11. Kambhampati, S.: Are we comparing Dana and Fahiem or SHOP and TLPlan? a critique of the knowledge-based planning track at ICP (2003), http://rakaposhi.eas.asu.edu/kbplan.pdf
12. Nau, D.: Current trends in automated planning. AI Magazine 28(4), 43–58 (2007)
13. Kuter, U., Nau, D.: Forward-chaining planning in nondeterministic domains. In: Proceedings of the National Conference on Artificial Intelligence (AAAI), pp. 513–518 (July 2004)
14. Kuter, U., Nau, D., Pistore, M., Traverso, P.: A hierarchical task-network planner based on symbolic model checking. In: Proceedings of the International Conference on Automated Planning and Scheduling (ICAPS), pp. 300–309 (June 2005)
15. Kuter, U., Nau, D., Pistore, M., Traverso, P.: Task decomposition on abstract states, for planning under nondeterminism. Artificial Intelligence (to appear, 2008)
16. Korf, R.: Real-time heuristic search. Artificial Intelligence 42(2–3), 189–211 (1990)
17. Hoffmann, J., Nebel, B.: The FF planning system: Fast plan generation through heuristic search. Journal of Artificial Intelligence Research 14, 253–302 (2001)
18. Bacchus, F., Kabanza, F.: Using temporal logics to express search control knowledge for planning. Artificial Intelligence 116(1-2), 123–191 (2000)
19. Nau, D.S., Muñoz-Avila, H., Cao, Y., Lotem, A., Mitchell, S.: Total-order planning with partially ordered subtasks. In: Proceedings of the International Joint Conference on Artificial Intelligence (IJCAI), Seattle (August 2001)
20. Dix, J., Muñoz-Avila, H., Nau, D.S., Zhang, L.: IMPACTing SHOP: Planning in a multi-agent environment. In: Sadri, F., Satoh, K. (eds.) Proc. Second Workshop on Computational Logic and Multi-Agent Systems (CLIMA), London, Imperial College, pp. 30–42 (July 2000)
21. Bratman, M.E.: Intentions, Plans, and Practical Reason. Harvard University Press (1987)
22. Georgeff, M.P., Lansky, A.L.: Reactive reasoning and planning. In: Proceedings of the National Conference on Artificial Intelligence (AAAI), pp. 677–682 (1987); reprinted in [47], pp. 729–734
23. Rao, A.S.: AgentSpeak(L): BDI agents speak out in a logical computable language. In: van Hoe, R. (ed.) Seventh European Workshop on Modelling Autonomous Agents in a Multi-Agent World, Eindhoven, The Netherlands (1996)
24. Firby, R.J.: Adaptive execution in complex dynamic worlds. PhD thesis 672, Yale University (1989)
25. Sardiña, S., de Silva, L., Padgham, L.: Hierarchical planning in BDI agent programming languages: A formal approach. In: AAMAS, Hakodate, Japan, pp. 1001–1008 (May 2006)
26. Sardiña, S., Padgham, L.: Goals in the context of BDI plan failure and planning. In: AAMAS, Honolulu, HI, pp. 16–24 (May 2007)
27. Billings, D.: The first international RoShamBo programming competition. ICGA Journal 23(1), 42–50 (2000)
28. Billings, D.: Thoughts on RoShamBo. ICGA Journal 23(1), 3–8 (2000)
29. Billings, D.: The second international roshambo programming competition (2001), http://www.cs.ualberta.ca/~darse/rsbpc.html
30. Li, D.: Kriegspiel: Chess Under Uncertainty. Premier (1994)
31. Li, D.: Chess Detective: Kriegspiel Strategies, Endgames and Problems. Premier (1995)

32. Parker, A., Nau, D., Subrahmanian, V.: Overconfidence or paranoia? search in imperfect-information games. In: Proceedings of the National Conference on Artificial Intelligence (AAAI) (July 2006)
33. Boutilier, C., Dean, T.L., Hanks, S.: Decision-theoretic planning: Structural assumptions and computational leverage. Journal of Artificial Intelligence Research 11, 1–94 (1999)
34. Aumann, R.: Acceptable points in general cooperative n-person games. In: Luce, R.D., Tucker, A.W. (eds.) Contributions to the Theory of Games, vol. 4. Princeton University Press, Princeton (1959)
35. Axelrod, R.: The Evolution of Cooperation. Basic Books (1984)
36. Au, T.C., Nau, D.: Accident or intention: That is the question (in the iterated prisoner's dilemma). In: International Joint Conference on Autonomous Agents and Multiagent Systems (AAMAS) (2006)
37. Au, T.C., Nau, D.: Is it accidental or intentional? a symbolic approach to the noisy iterated prisoner's dilemma. In: Kendall, G., Yao, X., Chong, S.Y. (eds.) The Iterated Prisoners Dilemma: 20 Years On, pp. 231–262. World Scientific, Singapore (2007)
38. Axelrod, R., Dion, D.: The further evolution of cooperation. Science 242(4884), 1385–1390 (1988)
39. Bendor, J.: In good times and bad: Reciprocity in an uncertain world. American Journal of Politicial Science 31(3), 531–558 (1987)
40. Bendor, J., Kramer, R.M., Stout, S.: When in doubt.. cooperation in a noisy prisoner's dilemma. The Jour. of Conflict Resolution 35(4), 691–719 (1991)
41. Molander, P.: The optimal level of generosity in a selfish, uncertain environment. The Journal of Conflict Resolution 29(4), 611–618 (1985)
42. Mueller, U.: Optimal retaliation for optimal cooperation. The Journal of Conflict Resolution 31(4), 692–724 (1987)
43. Nowak, M., Sigmund, K.: The evolution of stochastic strategies in the prisoner's dilemma. Acta Applicandae Mathematicae 20, 247–265 (1990)
44. Kendall, G., Yao, X., Chong, S.Y.: The Iterated Prisoner's Dilemma: 20 Years On. World Scientific, Singapore (2007)
45. Au, T.C., Nau, D.: An analysis of derived belief strategy's performance in the 2005 iterated prisoner's dilemma competition. Technical Report CSTR-4756/UMIACS-TR-2005-59, University of Maryland, College Park (2005)
46. Smith, S.J.J., Nau, D.S., Throop, T.: A planning approach to declarer play in contract bridge. Computational Intelligence 12(1), 106–130 (1996)
47. Allen, J.F., Hendler, J., Tate, A. (eds.): Readings in Planning. Morgan Kaufmann, San Francisco (1990)

Exploring Heuristic Action Selection
in Agent Programming

Koen V. Hindriks, Catholijn M. Jonker, and Wouter Pasman

EEMCS, Delft University of Technology, Delft, The Netherlands
{k.v.hindriks,c.m.jonker,w.pasman}@tudelft.nl

Abstract. Rational agents programmed in agent programming languages derive their choice of action from their beliefs and goals. One of the main benefits of such programming languages is that they facilitate a high-level and conceptually elegant specification of agent behaviour. Qualitative concepts alone, however, are not sufficient to specify that this behaviour is also nearly optimal, a quality typically also associated with rational agents. Optimality in this context refers to the costs and rewards associated with action execution. It thus would be useful to extend agent programming languages with primitives that allow the specification of near-optimal behaviour. The idea is that quantitative heuristics added to an agent program prune some of the options generated by the qualitative action selection mechanism. In this paper, we explore the expressivity needed to specify such behaviour in the Blocks World domain. The programming constructs that we introduce allow for a high-level specification of such heuristics due to the fact that these can be defined by (re)using the qualitative notions of the basic agent programming language again. We illustrate the use of these constructs by extending a GOAL Blocks World agent with various strategies to optimize its behaviour.

1 Introduction

In this paper, we use the well-known Blocks World domain [1] to explore and present evidence for the usefulness of adding expressive programming constructs that allow the specification of utility-based heuristic strategies for action selection to the agent programming language GOAL [2]. By means of various examples we illustrate that the new constructs introduced allow for an elegant specification of such strategies. Additionally, we present some experimental results that demonstrate the usefulness of the programming constructs introduced and confirm and slightly extend earlier results available in the literature [1,3,4].

Our objectives are twofold: (i) The first objective is to extend GOAL with programming constructs to define a heuristic or utility-based decision capability as an additional action selection mechanism. Such constructs allow the optimization of agent behaviour as well as reduce the amount of nondeterminism present in an agent program. (ii) The second objective is to assess the usefulness of the mechanism by comparing the behaviour of a GOAL agent which does not use the mechanism with various instantiations of GOAL agents that do use it.

K.V. Hindriks, A. Pokahr, and S. Sardina (Eds.): ProMAS 2008, LNAI 5442, pp. 24–39, 2009.

Although some related work on adding quantitative heuristics based on e.g. resource costs or other decision-theoretic extensions has been done, see e.g. [5,6], as far as we know little research has been done on programming constructs for specifying heuristic action selection in the area of agent programming. [5] allows for defining such decision-theoretic capabilities by means of arbitrary programming languages instead of introducing primitives that reuse the basic concepts of a rational agent programming language as we propose. Moreover, the work extending Golog with decision-theoretic capabilities in e.g. [7] relies on the situation calculus and cannot straightforwardly be incorporated into rational agents that derive their choice of action from their beliefs and goals.

The paper is organized as follows. In Section 2 the Blocks World is briefly introduced and a GOAL agent is presented that is able to effectively deal with Blocks World problems. In Section 3 some issues to improve the behaviour of this agent are discussed and a general framework for adding (utility-based) heuristics to an agent programming language is outlined. In Section 4 various heuristics for the Blocks World are presented and it is shown how these can be implemented using the primitives introduced. Section 5 concludes the paper.

2   Designing a Goal Agent for the Blocks World

In this Section, we design a GOAL agent that is able to effectively solve Blocks World problems. The Blocks World has been labelled the "Hello World" example for planning [1]. One reason why it is still being used is that it is computationally hard and moreover has some similarities with other, more realistic domains, e.g., it is related to freight operations [1]. Another reason why this domain is still interesting is that it is relatively simple and can be analyzed in detail to gain an understanding of the capabilities needed to deal with it effectively [1,3]. Since, historically, agent programming languages were motivated in part by ideas from reactive planning (see in particular [8,9]), it is interesting to start with this domain for analyzing whether the right features for fine-grained control of action needed to generate near-optimal behaviour are present in agent programming languages.

The Blocks World consist of a finite number of blocks of equal size that are stacked into towers on a table of unlimited size. Each block has a unique name $a, b, c, \ldots$ representing the fact that different blocks cannot be used interchangeably (which would be the case if only the colour of blocks would be relevant). Some basic axioms of the Blocks World are that no block is on more than one block, no more than one block is on a given block, and every block is either on the table or on another block (see e.g. axiom 4 and 5 in [10], which provides a complete axiomatization of the Blocks World). More realistic versions of this domain have been investigated (e.g., limited table size, varying sizes of blocks; cf. [4]). However, as argued in [1] the elementary Blocks World domain can support systematic experiments and, at least as important for our purposes, allows features relevant to various kinds of reasoning to be abstracted and studied. The Blocks World domain in particular allows for a precise study of various heuristics to ensure that an agent's choice of action generates near-optimal behaviour. Artificial domains such as the Blocks World moreover are hard for general purpose AI systems (e.g. planners), and it is only to be expected that this also holds for programming languages to build rational agents which provide abstract semantic primitives derived from common sense to do so [11]. In this paper some of these difficulties will be explored and discussed. In addition, Blocks World problems allow us to illustrate that programming languages for rational agents provide the expressiveness to construct elegant agent programs that solve such problems, though admittedly the domain is too simple to be convincing by itself.

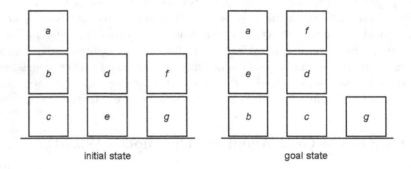

initial state   goal state

Fig. 1. Example Blocks World problem taken from [1]

The Blocks World planning problem is to transform an initial configuration of towers into a goal configuration, by means of moving one block on the top of a tower onto another tower or to the table; see Figure 1 for an example problem. A block on top of a tower, i.e. without any block on top of it, is said to be *clear*. By definition, there is always room to move a clear block onto the table and therefore the table is also said to be clear. The positioning of towers on the table is irrelevant in a Blocks World problem. The main task of an agent in this domain thus is to restack the blocks on the table according to its given goals. The main choice such an agent faces is which action (moving a block) to select. The performance of a Blocks World agent can be measured by means of the number of moves it needs to turn an initial state or configuration into a goal state. An agent performs optimally if it is not possible to improve on the number of moves it uses to reach a goal state. The problem of finding a minimal number of moves to a goal state is also called the *optimal* Blocks World planning problem. This problem is NP-hard [4], an indication that the problem is not trivial.[1]

Several basic insights help simplify the solving of a Blocks World problem. A block is said to be *in position* if the block in the current state is on top of a block or on the table and should be so according to the goal state, and all blocks (if any) below it are also in position; a block that is not in position is said to be *misplaced*.

---

[1] It is not within the scope of this paper to discuss the complexity of various proposed Blocks World heuristics for near-optimal planning; see [1,4] on this topic.

In Figure 1 all blocks except block c and g are misplaced. Only misplaced blocks have to be moved in order to solve a problem. A move of block X onto another block or onto the table is called *constructive* if in the resulting state block X is in position. In the elementary Blocks World with unlimited table size moving a block onto another block should only be done if the move is constructive, i.e., it moves the block in position. A constructive move always decreases the number of misplaced blocks. If in a state no constructive move can be made, we say that the state is in a *deadlock* (see [1] for a detailed explanation). A block is said to be a *self-deadlock* if it is misplaced and above another block which it is also above in the goal state; for example, block a is a self-deadlock in Figure 1. The concept of self-deadlocks, also called singleton deadlocks, is important because on average nearly 40% of the blocks are self-deadlocks [1].

Representing Knowledge and Goals. In the remainder of this paper, we will use Prolog notation to define and specify knowledge and goals. The basic facts and goals to be achieved in the Blocks World can be expressed by means of the predicate on(X,Y). on(X,Y) denotes that a block X is on Y, where Y may refer to either another block or the table. We use a predicate block(X) to denote that X is a block. The predicate clear(table) is used to denote that the table is clear, i.e. it is always possible to move blocks onto the table. Using the on predicate it is possible to formally define a Blocks World planning problem as a pair $\langle I, G \rangle$ where I denotes the initial state and G denotes the goal state. A state is defined as a set of facts of the form on(X,Y) that is consistent with the basic axioms of the Blocks World. A state is *complete* if for each block X it contains exactly one fact of the form on(X,Y); from now on, we only consider complete states.

In the agent program, all blocks are enumerated to make it clear how many blocks there are. The predicate above(X,Y) expresses that block X is above *block* Y and predicate tower([X|T]) expresses that the list of blocks [X|T] is a tower grounded on the table. We do not require that block X is clear, so e.g., tower([b,c]) holds in the initial state of Figure 1. The Prolog definitions of these concepts are given in the **beliefs** section in Table 1, which is called the *belief base* of the agent. The initial state of Figure 1 is represented in the agent's belief base, which is updated after every action that is performed.

In the **goals** section in Table 1, called the *goal base*, the goal state of Figure 1 is represented. (The clauses for above(X,Y) and tower(T) are repeated in the goal base. In the current version of GOAL, repetition of such clauses is necessary when they are needed in derivations that use the goal base.) One important difference between the belief and goal base is that individual goals need to be represented as a single conjunction instead of several clauses since it represents a *single* goal. The reason for the distinction is that a goal upon completion, i.e., when it is completely achieved, is removed from the goal base. Achieved goals are removed to satisfy the rationality constraint that an agent does not have any goals it believes to be achieved; the fact that this only happens when the goal has been completely achieved implements a blind commitment strategy.

Table 1. GOAL Agent Program for Solving the Blocks World Problem of Figure 1

```
 1  :main stackBuilder
 2  { % This agent solves the Blocks World problem of Figure 1.
 3      :beliefs{
 4          block(a), block(b), block(c), block(d), block(e), block(f), block(g).
 5          on(a,b), on(b,c), on(c,table), on(d,e), on(e,table), on(f,g), on(g,table).
 6          clear(table).
 7          clear(X) :- block(X), not(on(Y,X)).
 8          above(X,Y) :- on(X,Y), block(Y).
 9          above(X,Y) :- on(X,Z), above(Z,Y).
10          tower([X]) :- on(X,table).
11          tower([X,Y|T]) :- on(X,Y), tower([Y|T]).
12      }
13      :goals{
14          block(a), block(b), block(c), block(d), block(e), block(f), block(g),
15          on(a,e), on(e,b), on(b,table), on(f,d), on(d,c), on(c,table), on(g,table),
16          above(X,Y) :- (on(X,Y), block(Y)),
17          above(X,Y) :- (on(X,Z), above(Z,Y)),
18          tower([X]) :- (on(X,table)),
19          tower([X,Y|S]) :- (on(X,Y), tower([Y|S])).
20      }
21      :program{
22          if bel(tower([Y|T])), a-goal(tower([X,Y|T])) then move(X,Y).
23          if a-goal(tower([X|T])) then move(X,table).
24      }
25      :action-spec{
26          move(X,Y) {
27              :pre{ clear(X), clear(Y), on(X,Z) }
28              :post{ not(on(X,Z)), on(X,Y) }
29          }
30      }
31  }
```

Actions. Actions of a GOAL agent are specified in the **action-spec** section by means of a STRIPS-like specification of a precondition and add/delete lists, see e.g., Table 1. Add/delete lists are specified here as a single list of literals, where a positive literal denotes an add and a negative literal denotes a delete. Note that the precondition in Table 1 allows moving a block X on top of another block Y even if block X initially already is on top of Y. Such redundant actions, however, are never generated given the action rules in the **program** section; therefore it is unnecessary to add conditions preventing such moves to the precondition. For the same reason, it is not necessary to add the precondition not(X=Y).

GOAL *agent design.* The basic parts of a GOAL agent have now been specified. The belief and goal base together are called the mental state of the agent, typically denoted by $m = \langle \Sigma, \Gamma \rangle$. A mental state needs to satisfy some basic rationality constraints: (i) beliefs need to be consistent, (ii) individual goals need to be consistent, and (iii) individual goals in the goal base are not believed to be the case. Actions are executed in GOAL by checking whether the preconditions of an action follow from the agent's beliefs and, if so, by updating the beliefs in line with the action's postcondition after executing it. In addition, if as a result of action execution a goal in the goal base has been completely achieved, then this goal is removed from the goal base.

The **program** section specifies the *strategy for action selection* by means of so-called *action rules*. These rules consist of a mental state condition and an action and specify which actions an agent may consider for execution. The mental state condition determines which actions may be executed. In order to express such conditions a belief operator bel(...) and a goal operator goal(...) are available, which can be combined using conjunction , and prefixed with negation not. For example, bel(block(a)) expresses that the agent believes that a is a block whereas bel(on(a,b)), goal(on(a,e)) expresses that the agent believes it has not yet achieved its goal on(a,e) (since it believes a to be on top of b).

The semantics of the belief operator bel(φ) is that φ follows from the belief base (i.e. $\Sigma \models \varphi$ where $\models$ denotes the classical first order consequence operator; since we use Prolog, additionally the Closed World Assumption is used in practice). The semantics of the goal operator goal(φ) is slightly different from that of the belief operator; goal(φ) holds if φ follows from some goal in the goal base (i.e. $\exists \gamma \in \Gamma : \gamma \models \varphi$).[2] It is useful and necessary to have access to the belief base as well as the goal base of an agent. For example, without either of these operators it is not possible to specify that a block is in position, i.e. that its current position is in correspondence with its positions in the goal state. Using both operators, we can express that block X is in position by means of bel(tower([X|T])), goal(tower([X|T])) for some tower T. We call such a (sub)goal a *goal achieved* and introduce the new operator goal-a(...) as an abbreviation to denote this fact, i.e.,

$$\text{goal-a}(\varphi) \stackrel{df}{=} \text{bel}(\varphi), \text{goal}(\varphi)$$

The notion of an *achievement goal*, i.e., a goal not yet believed to be achieved, can also be defined using the belief and goal operator (cf. [12]). We introduce the new operator a-goal(...) to denote such goals as an abbreviation for:

$$\text{a-goal}(\varphi) \stackrel{df}{=} \text{bel}(\text{not}(\varphi)), \text{goal}(\varphi)$$

Using the achievement goal operator we can represent the fact that block X is not in position in the initial state by a-goal(tower([X|T])) for T a tower. a-goal(tower([X|T])) means that in the goal state block X must be on top of the tower T but in the current state the agent does not believe that this is already the case; a-goal(tower([X|T])) thus expresses that X is misplaced. This is an important concept in defining any strategy since only misplaced blocks should be moved to solve a Blocks World problem. The definition of a self-deadlocked block also requires the inspection of both the belief as well as the goal base. The concept of a self-deadlock can be quite naturally defined by a-goal(tower([X|T])), goal-a(above(X,Y)) where the first conjunct expresses that X is misplaced and the second conjunct expresses that X is above some

---

[2] This is different from definitions of the goal operator in previous work [2] where the goal operator was used to denote *achievement goals*, which additionally require that the agent does not believe φ. We need the more basic **goal** operator however to express that a block is in position.

block Y in both the current state as well as in the goal state. This concept is just as important for solving Blocks World problems since any self-deadlocked block needs to be moved at least twice to reach the goal state. Moving such a block to the table thus will be a necessary move in every plan.

The two action rules in the **program** section of Table 1 implements a simple strategy for a Blocks World agent. As explained, an action rule consists of a mental state condition φ and an action a. If the condition φ holds, the action a is said to be *enabled*. The first rule generates constructive move options the agent can choose from. The second rule allows a move of block X to the table if it is misplaced. The condition of this rule is weaker than the first implying that whenever the first rule is applicable the second is applicable as well, meaning that the actions of these rules are enabled. Then the agent *arbitrarily* chooses an enabled action. Note that this agent will never move a block that is in position.

Summarizing, a GOAL agent program consists of four sections: a belief base consisting of the agent's beliefs, a goal base with the agent's goals, a program section defining the agent's action selection strategy, and an action specification section with STRIPS-like action specifications. The GOAL Blocks World agent contains a specification of the initial state of the Blocks World problem in its belief base, a specification of the goal state in its goal base, a specification of the **move** action in its action specification section, and two action rules that define its strategy for performing either a constructive move in case such a move brings a block in position, or a move to the table if a block is misplaced.

3   Heuristic Action Selection in Agent Programming

Research in planning has shown that in order to plan effectively and be able to generate near-optimal plans for the Blocks World it must be possible to specify various domain-dependent heuristics [11]. The specification of these heuristics in domain-independent planning systems requires the right concepts to express and implement them. If agent programming languages are to match these capabilities, programming constructs with similar expressive power need to be available to program rational agents that use heuristics to improve performance. We argue that in programming languages for rational agents such programming constructs would be most useful if they allow for the specification of such heuristics in terms of the core concepts of beliefs and goals present in these languages.

In this Section we introduce a generic extension of the GOAL agent programming language that can be incorporated into other agent languages based on concepts of belief and goal, and add a capability for specifying heuristic selection strategies by means of utility functions. We first briefly introduce the basic concepts needed and discuss the semantics of the extension of GOAL with a utility-based action selection mechanism. Then we introduce a programming construct for specifying utility values. In Section 4 we show that the programming constructs we introduce allow for an elegant specification of behaviour that shows improved performance compared with a GOAL agent that does not make use of the utility-based selection mechanism.

3.1   Associating Utility Values with Action Execution

The idea is to associate a quantitative number with the execution of an action a in a state m, i.e., to associate a real valued number $U(m, a, m')$ with executing a in state m resulting in a new state m'. A number associated with an action in this way can be perceived of in two different ways. One perspective, the more principled view on what this number represents, is to suggest that the number is a utility value that represents how much value is to be gained from executing the action. It is standard to further decompose such a utility value into two components, a *cost component* that is associated with taking an action in the starting state and a *reward component* that associates a reward with getting to the resulting state (cf. [13]). Alternatively, such a number can be perceived of as a heuristic that only provides an estimation of e.g. the costs of executing an action. Since these different views do not conflict, and in practice it is very intuitive to use concepts such as costs and rewards, in the remainder we will freely use either terminology.

Formally, a utility function can be introduced which is defined in terms of costs and rewards by: $U(m, a, m') = R(m') - C(m, a)$. Here, the *reward function* R should be thought of as representing the *utility* of being in state m'. For example, an agent gains more utility for getting to a state with more blocks in position than to a state with less blocks in position. Likewise, the *cost function* C represents the costs associated with the resources spent. However, a cost function can also be used to indicate that performing an action is a good thing.

3.2   Semantics

Agent programming languages in general, and GOAL in particular, quite naturally lead to writing programs that are underspecified (i.e. such programs do not determine a unique action to perform next and thus may underspecify the actual behaviour of an agent).[3] The operational semantics of these languages leaves room for various alternatives as to how to implement the action selection mechanism of an agent. One of the benefits of underspecification is that it facilitates and simplifies the design and programming of an agent, but it may also give rise to suboptimal behaviour (due to ad hoc suboptimal choices). The basic idea now is to introduce another, utility-based mechanism for action selection on top of the qualitative selection mechanism already present in GOAL that can be used to further limit the number of choices.

Ideally an agent optimizes the sum of all utility gains over an entire execution run. The set of such runs of an agent with which we would like to associate utility values is given by the qualitative action selection mechanism. A run can

---

[3] The language GOAL does not have constructs to specify complex plans such as sequential composition that could be used to further reduce the choices left open by an agent at any particular moment. The action rules in a GOAL program thus naturally lead to more underspecification than is typical of other agent programming languages. The only construct available in GOAL to reduce this type of underspecification is the module-construct, see [14].

be formally specified as an infinite sequence of computation steps. Very briefly, a computation step written as $m \xrightarrow{a} m'$ denotes that action a can be performed in state m (i.e. action a is enabled: the precondition of a holds in state m and the condition of the corresponding action rule for a also holds) and results in state m'. A *run* r then can be defined as an infinite sequence $m_0, a_0, m_1, a_1, m_2, \ldots$ such that $m_i \xrightarrow{a_i} m_{i+1}$ (for details, we refer the interested reader to [2]). The set of all such runs is denoted by R_A for agent program A.

The main idea is to associate a utility value with each possible run of an agent and to actually execute that run which maximizes utility. In this setup, an agent first (pre)selects possible actions which it may execute in each state using its action selection mechanism based on qualitative action rules. In other words, action rules define the search space in which the agent needs to find an optimal run. The benefit is that this search space typically is significantly reduced compared to the search space induced by the set of all enabled actions in a state, i.e. actions whose preconditions hold.

Given a utility function U it is easy to extend this function to a run. We use m_i^r to denote the ith mental state in run r and similarly a_i^r denotes the ith action in run r. A utility value can be associated with a run r then as follows:

$$U_\delta(r) = \sum_{i=0}^{\infty} \delta^i \cdot U(m_i^r, a_i^r, m_{i+1}^r)$$

where δ is a discount factor in the range $\langle 0, 1]$, intuitively accounting for the fact that utility realized now is more valuable than utility in the future. The meaning of a GOAL agent A that uses the utility-based action selection mechanism on top of the qualitative one then can be defined as the set of runs r that maximize the associated utility $U(r)$, i.e., the meaning of a utility-based GOAL agent is defined by:

$$U_A = \max_{U(r)} \{r \mid r \in R_A\}$$

The semantics of a utility-based GOAL agent as defined above requires *infinite look-ahead*. That is, to select an action in any state requires the agent to compute the utility of all possible runs before performing that action to ensure utility is maximized over the complete computation. Computationally, such a requirement is not feasible and, therefore, we associate a *finite horizon* h with the computation of a utility. In case $h = 0$, the agent does not perform any look ahead at all. For $h > 0$, an agent would require a lookahead facility before taking action, of depth h. Formally, this finite horizon constraint can be defined on an arbitrary computation r at time point i by:

$$U(r, i, h) = \sum_{j=i}^{i+h-1} \delta^{j-i} \cdot U(m_j^r, a_j^r, m_{j+1}^r)$$

Here, $U(r, i, h)$ denotes the (discounted) utility associated with the actions performed from time point i to $i + h$. Using this definition, the meaning U_A^h of a utility-based GOAL agent with a finite horizon h is defined by $U_A^h = \sigma_A^h(\infty)$, where σ_A^h is defined by the following inductive definition:

$$\sigma_A^h(-1) = R_A,$$
$$\sigma_A^h(i) = \max_{U(r,i,h)} \{r \mid r \in \sigma_A^h(i-1)\} \text{ if } i \geq 0.$$
$$\sigma_A^h(\infty) = \bigcap_{i=0}^{\infty} \sigma_A^h(i).$$

The operator $\sigma_A^h(i)$ for $i \in \mathbb{N}$ selects those runs that have highest utility over the next h steps from time point i on, where the runs inspected are those runs that have survived the same selection using a horizon h at earlier time points $j < i$. At time point $i = 0$ the latter set coincides with the set of all possible runs R_A of agent A. An inductive definition is needed here to reflect the fact that an agent performs a look-ahead again after each step it performs. The limit $\sigma_A^h(\infty)$ defines the new meaning of a GOAL agent that uses a look-ahead h to filter runs.

The following proposition partly justifies the definition of σ.

Proposition 1

$$R_A = U_A^0 \tag{1}$$
$$U_A = \sigma_A^\infty(0) \tag{2}$$
$$U_A \supseteq U_A^\infty, \text{ i.e., } \max_{U(r)}\{r \mid r \in R_A\} \supseteq \sigma_A^\infty(\infty) \tag{3}$$

The first item of Proposition 1, $R_A = U_A^0$, expresses that the utility-based semantics with a horizon $h = 0$, i.e. no look-ahead, coincides with that of the original semantics that does not take utility into account. The second item $U_A = \sigma_A^\infty(0)$ shows that infinite look-ahead can be defined by means of the σ-operator; simply do infinite look-ahead at time point 0. It is easy to see that $U_A^\infty \subseteq U_A$, since $U_A^\infty \subseteq \sigma_A^\infty(0)$. The fact that U_A is not the same as $U_A^\infty = \sigma_A^\infty(\infty)$ is due to the fact that σ_A^h defines a step by step process and evaluates maximum continuations in each state and does not just once evaluate a global property of a run. Proposition 1 thus shows that in the limit case the semantics defined by the σ-operator approximates that of U_A. The advantage of the σ_A^h-operator over the infinite-lookahead U_A is that for finite horizons h it can implemented. Finally, we do not necessarily have that $U_A^h \subseteq U_A$ for a finite h, since σ_A^h may select runs that have high utility on initial prefixes of length h of the run but over the complete run do worse than other runs with low utility on initial prefixes of length h.

3.3   Specifying Quantitative Utility Values

In order to incorporate the assignment of quantitative values to transitions of a GOAL program, such programs are extended with a new **utility** section and the following notation is introduced for representing utility:

```
value(<initial-state-cond>, <action-descr>, <successor-state-cond>) = <utility-expr>
```

The `initial-state-cond` as well as the `successor-state-cond` refer to arbitrary mental state conditions, i.e., conditions that are combinations of goal(...) and `bel(...)` operators. In addition, the constant `true` - which holds in any mental state - may be used here as well. The `action-descr` part refers to any action description that is allowed in GOAL, e.g., in the Blocks World `move(X,Y)`. Variables are allowed in both mental state conditions used to characterize the initial or resulting state, as well as in the action description. The same holds for the `utility-expr` part, which denotes a numerical expression which may involve basic arithmetic operators such as addition and multiplication. The action description part may also be filled with a special don't care label `any`.

In the **utility** section of a GOAL program, multiple lines of value statements are allowed that apply to the same transition. In case multiple value statements apply to the same transition the multiple values assigned to that transition are added together by taking the sum of the values. As a simple example, the statements `value(true,move(X,table),true)=1` and `value(bel(on(X,Y)),any,true)=2` are both applicable to a transition that starts in a state where `bel(on(a,b))` holds and in which action `move(a,table)` is taken, and therefore the values 1 and 2 need to be added to give a total value of 3. Using the `value` construct we can define various useful abbreviations for reward and cost components as follows:

$$\texttt{cost(<initial-state-cond>, <action>)} \overset{df}{=} \texttt{-1·value(<initial-state-cond>, <action>, true)}$$
$$\texttt{reward(<successor-state-cond>)} \overset{df}{=} \texttt{value(true, any, <successor-state-cond>)}$$

Note that according to these definitions both costs and rewards are conditional on the beliefs as well as the goals of an agent.

For practical reasons, it is useful to introduce a `case` statement to define a complex value function based on case distinctions. Inside a `case` statement conditional expressions of the form `<state-cond>:cost(<action-descr>)=<utility-expr>` and `<state-cond>:reward=<utility-expr>` are allowed. By using a `case`-statement, costs and/or rewards are assigned to a transition using the *first* case that applies, i.e., that value is returned associated with the first condition `<state-cond>` that holds (assuming, of course that an action description, if present, matches as well). Various examples of the use of this statement are provided below.

In the extension of GOAL quantative values are assigned only to actions that an agent has preselected given its current goals. This reflects the fact that qualitative goals have priority over any quantitative preferences. That is, the first priority of a GOAL agent is to achieve its qualitative goals, whereas its second priority then becomes to do this such that utility is maximized.

4   Heuristic Action Selection in the Blocks World

As explained above, the GOAL Blocks World agent never moves a block that is in position. The agent will only move a misplaced block to the table or move a block onto another block. Note that the agent will only move a block X onto another block Y if this move puts X in position, and such a move thus is constructive. Also note that if a block can be moved onto another block the second action rule of the agent also allows to move this block to the table. In almost all Blocks World states multiple actions are feasible and in line with the semantics of GOAL an action then is selected randomly. The semantics thus allows for various strategies of action selection and does not enforce any of these strategies.

A number of alternative heuristics or strategies have been proposed in the literature [1,3,4]. We explore several of these to illustrate the use of utility values to guide the action selection mechanism of an agent. One of the most straightforward strategies for solving a Blocks World problem is to first unstack all (misplaced) blocks and then to move all blocks in position. This strategy has been called the Unstack-Stack (US) strategy [1]. It is clear that this strategy is compatible with the GOAL agent program presented in Table 1. Note that this strategy will only worsen the behaviour of the agent by never making a constructive move during the unstack phase even if such moves are available. We have implemented and experimented with it mainly for reasons of comparison. The following code needs to be added to the utility section:

```
case{
    bel(Y=table):  cost(move(X,Y)) = 1.          % unstack has priority
    true:          cost(move(X,Y)) = 2.          % otherwise
}
```

USG Heuristic

A first idea to improve the behaviour of the agent is to give priority to *constructive* moves over other moves. The reason that this may improve behaviour is simple: the move has to be made anyway, brings the current state closer to the goal state, and may make it possible to perform another constructive move next. Using the `cost` construct to assign costs to actions we have to make sure that a constructive move always has an associated cost less than that for other types of moves. Since as we noted above, any block that satisfies `bel(tower([X|T]))`, `a-goal(tower([X,Y|T]))` can be constructively moved, the cost function can be defined as follows:

```
case{
    bel(tower([Y|T]), a-goal(tower([X,Y|T]))):  cost(move(X,Y)) = 1.  % a constructive move
    true:                                       cost(move(X,Y)) = 2.  % otherwise
}
```

GN1G Heuristic

A second heuristic to get closer to near-optimal behaviour is to prefer moving a block that is *self-deadlocked* over moving other blocks when no constructive move is available. As explained above, a self-deadlocked block is a misplaced block above a block it has to be above in the goal state as well. As a result, such a block has to be moved twice (once to the table, and once in position) and it makes sense to do this first when no constructive move is available.[4] The addition of this heuristic to the program requires the more complex conceptual condition that defines a self-deadlock identified above. Here we can slightly simplify, however, because costs of an action are only computed if the action is enabled, i.e. the corresponding action rule condition is satisfied. This means that a block X in an enabled action move(X,Y) is misplaced and we do not need to repeat it; the part

---

[4] It does not make any difference whether a constructive or self-deadlocked move is made first; we follow [3,1,4] in preferring to make a constructive move here.

of the definition still required then is `goal-a(above(X,Z))`. For the same reason we also do not need to check whether the block to be moved is clear.

```
case{
   bel(tower([Y|T]), a-goal(tower([X,Y|T])): cost(move(X,Y)) = 1. % a constructive move
   goal-a(above(X,Z)):                       cost(move(X,Y)) = 2. % X is a self-deadlock
   true:                                     cost(move(X,Y)) = 3. % otherwise
}
```
SDG Heuristic

Although the heuristic costs associated with move actions above is quite natural, not quite the same behaviour but similar performance could have been achieved quite elegantly also by using the reward function instead of the cost function by making use of the counting operator #.

```
reward(true) = #T^goal-a(tower([X|T])-#T^Y^[a-goal(tower([X|T])),goal-a(above(X,Y))]
```

The first term in the utility expression `#T^goal-a(tower([X|T]))` counts the number of blocks in position in a state, whereas the second term

$$\texttt{\#T\textasciicircum Y\textasciicircum [a-goal(tower([X|T])),goal-a(above(X,Y))]}$$

counts the number of self-deadlocks in a state. Also note the use of the abstraction operators `T^` and `Y^` which, as in Prolog, existentially quantify variables T ($\exists$T) and Y ($\exists$Y) to ensure that we do not count variation over these variables. In the Blocks World domain the abstraction over T is not strictly necessary since in any state a block can be present at most in one tower, but the abstraction over Y is required since a block may be above multiple other blocks in both the belief as well as goal state. Rewards increase by either increasing the number of blocks in position or by decreasing the number of self-deadlocks in a state. The heuristic values associated by the **reward** function with performing a constructive move or breaking a self-deadlock are identical. This is different from the **cost** function introduced earlier which always prefers to perform a constructive move first if possible. As noted above, however, since a self-deadlock has to be moved twice in any optimal plan anyway this preference does not result in behaviour that is closer to optimal behaviour.

A third heuristic is adapted from a proposal in [3], and focuses on those cases where neither a constructive nor any self-deadlock move can be made. In that case some block has to be moved to the table, and we pick the block on the tower that has the lowest number of blocks that are neither in position nor self-deadlocked. This number is called the *deficiency* of the tower and is added as an additional third case to the previous cost function defined above.

```
case{
   bel(tower([Y|T]), a-goal(tower([X,Y|T])): cost(move(X,Y))=1. % a constructive move
   goal-a(above(X,Z)):                       cost(move(X,Y))=2. % X is a self-deadlock
   bel(tower([X|T]),length([X|T],H),last(T,B)), goal-a(on(B,table)): % compute deficiency
         cost(move(X,Y)) = H-#[bel(member(Y,T)), goal-a(tower[Y|U])]]
            -#Z^[bel(member(Y,T)), a-goal(tower([Y|U])), goal-a(above(Y,Z))].
   true:                                     cost(move(X,Y)) = #bel(block(X))+1. % otherwise.
}
```
DSG Heuristic

Results. Although our main aim has been to introduce expressive programming primitives for defining (utility-based) heuristics, it is interesting to briefly discuss the results of running the heuristics discussed. The various heuristics defined above were implemented in our prototype GOAL implementation. This prototype is implemented in Java and SWI-prolog. The default goal behaviour (RSG), which selects one of the applicable actions at random instead of picking the one that has maximum utility, was also measured.

To generate random start and end states in the blocks world, the BWSTATES algorithm of [1,15] was used, whereas the BWOPT algorithm of [1,15] was used to determine the optimal plan length. To run the experiments, 100 problems were generated, each consisting of a random start and end state, for worlds of size 10 up to 120 blocks with step size 10. Each problem was solved using the various utility heuristics. The agents used a horizon of 1. The performance is then computed as the number of steps it took to solve that problem divided by the optimal plan length.

Figure 4 shows the average performance as a function of the number of blocks. The standard deviations on the performance are all in the order of 0.04 and have been left out to improve readability of the Figure. The dashed lines show the results that were found by Slaney [1], the labels ending with G refer to heuristics defined in GOAL.

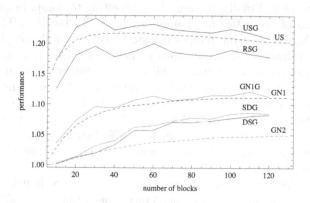

Fig. 2. Performance results

Given the relatively large standard deviations on our measurements, the USG and GN1G heuristics match Slaney's results for the US and GN1 heuristics. The various utility functions USG, GN1G, SDG and DSG were claimed to be a set of incremental improvements on the basic heuristic USG, which is confirmed by the performance results. At 120 blocks and with respect to the optimal performance of 1.0, the GN1G performs twice as good as USG, and the SDG and DSG adds another 37% to the performance of GN1G. The standard goal RSG also performs as expected: better than the USG algorithm but worse than GN1G as it still can do non-constructive moves when a constructive move is possible. The DSG heuristic is only a marginal improvement over the SDG heuristic. Even though the improvement is small, our results confirm the claim in [3] that the deficiency heuristic optimizes performance and adds some new evidence that this improvement is consistent at least for worlds of up to size 120 blocks.

5   Conclusion

We have introduced new programming constructs that add expressiveness to the GOAL programming language and allows to specify utility-based heuristics using high-level concepts such as beliefs and goals. The construct can be added to any programming language that is based on these agent concepts. Thus, high-level agent programming concepts are combined naturally with a utility-based action selection capability.

Similar ideas have been proposed in [5,7]. [7] discusses an extension of Golog with a decision-theoretic component called DTGolog. Since Golog is an extension of the situation calculus there are many differences between our work and that of [7]; one of the more important ones is that heuristics in the programming language GOAL can be defined using the concepts of belief and goal, which gives additional expressive power not present in [7]. [5] extends the AgentSpeak(L) language with a decision-theoretic capability but allows the use of arbitrary programming languages to do so instead of adding a new programming construct to the language itself. Finally, it would be interesting to compare our work with the specification of heuristics in planners such as TLPlan [11]. TLPlan allows for specifying heuristics using temporal logic to guide search for planning from scratch. The extension of GOAL in contrast assumes this search space has been predefined by means of action rules, which may be further pruned by means of the utility-based action selection capability introduced in this paper. It remains for future work to compare the expressiveness of both approaches.

Several example heuristics and related results were presented which show that the addition of a construct to specify quantitative heuristics for action selection may significantly improve performance which cannot be achieved as elegantly without it or not at all.

The action selection mechanism based on quantitative heuristics we introduced in this paper assumes a look-ahead mechanism that is not always applicable in dynamic environments. As argued in [16], however, it is useful to combine look-ahead or planning with action execution. By combining the concept of a module introduced in [14] and the look-ahead action selection mechanism discussed here we can achieve a similar "local" planning mechanism in GOAL that is performed within the context of such a module. We leave discussion of this combination for future work.

The extension of GOAL proposed here does not allow the use of probabilistic concepts which are available in decision-theoretic approaches. Future work could be to include these as well, but a proper integration of probabilistic concepts into GOAL would require an extension of the basic language as well to be able to execute actions with probabilistic effects. Another interesting idea is to allow agents to *learn* the priorities they should associate with actions. For example, reinforcement learning techniques could be deployed within GOAL to learn optimal policies.

References

1. Slaney, J., Thiébaux, S.: Blocks World revisited. Artificial Intelligence 125, 119–153 (2001)
2. de Boer, F., Hindriks, K., van der Hoek, W., Meyer, J.J.: A Verification Framework for Agent Programming with Declarative Goals. Journal of Applied Logic 5(2), 277–302 (2007)
3. Romero, A.G., Alquézar, R.: To block or not to block? In: Lemaître, C., Reyes, C.A., González, J.A. (eds.) IBERAMIA 2004. LNCS, vol. 3315, pp. 134–143. Springer, Heidelberg (2004)
4. Gupta, N., Nau, D.S.: On the Complexity of Blocks-World Planning. Artificial Intelligence 56(2-3), 223–254 (1992)
5. Bordini, R., Bazzan, A., Jannone, R., Basso, D., Vicari, R., Lesser, V.: AgentSpeak(XL): Efficient Intention Selection in BDI agents via Decision-Theoretic Task Scheduling. In: Proc. of the 1st Int. Joint Conference on Autonomous Agents and Multi-Agent Systems (AAMAS 2002), pp. 1294–1302 (2002)
6. Thangarajah, J., Padgham, L., Winikoff, M.: Detecting and avoiding interference between goals in intelligent agents. In: Proceedings of the 18th International Joint Conference on Artificial Intelligence (IJCAI 2003) (2003)
7. Boutilier, C., Reiter, R., Soutchanski, M., Thrun, S.: Decision-Theoretic, High-level Agent Programming in the Situation Calculus. In: Proc. of the 17th National Conference on Artificial Intelligence (AAAI 2000), pp. 355–362 (2000)
8. Ingrand, F., Georgeff, M., Rao, A.: An architecture for real-time reasoning and system control. IEEE Expert 7(6) (1992)
9. Rao, A.S.: AgentSpeak(L): BDI Agents Speak Out in a Logical Computable Language. In: Perram, J., Van de Velde, W. (eds.) MAAMAW 1996. LNCS, vol. 1038, pp. 42–55. Springer, Heidelberg (1996)
10. Cook, S., Liu, Y.: A Complete Axiomatization for Blocks World. Journal of Logic and Computation 13(4), 581–594 (2002)
11. Bacchus, F., Kabanza, F.: Using Temporal Logics to Express Search Control Knowledge for Planning. Artificial Intelligence 116(1-2), 123–191 (2000)
12. Cohen, P.R., Levesque, H.J.: Intention Is Choice with Commitment. Artificial Intelligence 42, 213–261 (1990)
13. Boutilier, C., Dean, T., Hanks, S.: Decision-theoretic planning: Structural assumptions and computational leverage. Journal of AI Research 11, 1–94 (1999)
14. Hindriks, K.: Modules as policy-based intentions: Modular agent programming in goal. In: Dastani, M., El Fallah Seghrouchni, A., Ricci, A., Winikoff, M. (eds.) ProMAS 2007. LNCS, vol. 4908, pp. 156–171. Springer, Heidelberg (2008)
15. http://users.rsise.anu.edu.au/~jks/bwstates.html (January 2008)
16. de Giacomo, G., Levesque, H.J.: An incremental interpreter for high-level programs with sensing. Technical report, Department of Computer Science, University of Toronto (1998)

Programming Verifiable Heterogeneous Agent Systems*

Louise A. Dennis** and Michael Fisher

Department of Computer Science, University of Liverpool, Liverpool, United Kingdom
L.A.Dennis@liverpool.ac.uk

Abstract. Our overall aim is to provide a verification framework for practical multi-agent systems. To achieve practicality, we must be able to describe and implement *heterogeneous* multi-agent systems. To achieve verifiability, we must define semantics appropriately for use in formal verification. In this paper, we tackle the problem of implementing heterogeneous multi-agent systems in a semantically clear, and appropriate, way.

1 Introduction

The construction of multi-agent systems has become relatively straightforward as more high-level agent programming frameworks have become available [8, 28, 6, 1]. Quite sophisticated systems have been developed and, in some cases, deployed. However, there still remain a number of problems, particularly regarding the *flexibility* and *reliability* of multi-agent systems. The particular aspect of flexibility we are interested in here concerns systems of *heterogeneous* agents. Thus, while we might construct a multi-agent system in one language, a more realistic scenario is that a practical multi-agent system will comprise agents implemented in a number of distinct languages. Several approaches already exist supporting heterogeneous agents, e.g:

- communication at a common level can be achieved if the agents are based on extensions of standard languages such as Java or Java Agent Services [19], or comprise standard distribution mechanisms such as CORBA [20] or .COM [27];
- if all agents are implemented within a common underlying framework [1, 17], then this provides a layer through which communication and ontologies can be handled;
- if the heterogeneous agents are embedded in an appropriate *wrapper* that handles communication and coordination, such as that utilised within the IMPACT framework [25, 13], then effective heterogeneous multi-agent systems can be built; and
- if all agents subscribe to a general interaction protocol, for example the FIPA [15] speech act approach, communicative aspects are taken care of within the protocol.

We are also interested in developing systems whose *reliability* and *trustworthiness* can be (automatically) assessed. Specifically, we aim to apply *formal verification techniques* to agents [4], by developing *model checking* [7, 18] techniques. For some of the above, formal analysis has been carried out; for others, no definitive formal semantics is available. However, those systems where formal analysis has been considered, notably IMPACT [25] and FIPA-ACL [21, 22], have only considered interaction aspects of agents,

---

* Supported by EPSRC grant EP/D052548.

** Corresponding author.

K.V. Hindriks, A. Pokahr, and S. Sardina (Eds.): ProMAS 2008, LNAI 5442, pp. 40–55, 2009.

not their full internal behaviour. This can cause problems if the mental states of the agents are inconsistent, even if the communication aspects are homogenised [26].

In our work, we have aimed to develop techniques for analysing implemented multi-agent systems. Beginning with model-checking techniques for AgentSpeak [5], we are extending these now to other languages such as 3APL [8] and SAAPL [29]. Until now we have only considered systems of agents implemented using the same language, i.e. homogeneous multi-agent systems. Our overall aim within this paper is to describe our approach for handling *heterogeneous multi-agent systems*. Thus, we aim to show: (1) how our Agent Infrastructure Layer (AIL) [12] provides an effective, high-level, basis for implementing operational semantics for BDI-like programming languages; (2) how the AIL supports heterogeneous agent computation, and to provide an example of this — the example is a simplified *Contract Net* [24] and the system comprises three agents, each implemented in a different language[1]; and (3) how formal verification can be carried out, using the agent verification system under development [10, 3].

2   The AIL

The AIL [12, 10] is a toolkit of Java classes designed to support the implementation of BDI programming languages and the model checking of programs implemented in these languages. Our previous approaches to model checking agent programs showed that encoding agent concepts, such as goals and beliefs, into the state machine of the model checker was a complex and time-consuming task. It was also necessary to adapt the property specification language of a model checker to express properties in these terms; the natural terminology for reasoning about an agent-based program. Our approach is to encode the relevant concepts from the AIL into the model checker just once and then allow multiple languages to benefit from the encoding by utilising the AIL classes in their implementation. The AIL therefore consists of data structures for representing agents, beliefs, plans, etc., which can be adapted to the operational semantics of individual languages. A language implemented in the AIL sub-classes the AIL's agent class and then specifies a *reasoning cycle*. The reasoning cycle consists of a transition system which defines a number of stages and specifies the changes to the agent structure that occur as it passes from one stage to the next. The AIL agent data structure contains a place holder for the current stage of the reasoning cycle which is instantiated in interpreted agents. To aid the implementation of interpreters the AIL also contains an *operational semantics package* (OSRules) containing sample transition rules.

In [12], the AIL is described as a customisable language with its own operational semantics and reasoning cycle. This proved too inflexible to accommodate the language features found in implementations of the major agent programming languages. In particular, the reasoning cycle became an obstacle. Hence our current implementation of the AIL is a *collection* of data structures. The AIL's most complex data structure is that representing an *intention*. BDI languages use intentions to store the *intended means* for achieving goals – this is generally represented as some form of *deed stack* (a deed may be an action, a belief update or the commitment to a goal). Intention structures in BDI languages may also maintain information about the (sub-)goal they are intended

---

[1] GOAL [9], SAAPL [29] and Gwendolen [11], a BDI language developed by the first author.

to achieve or the event that triggered them. In the AIL, we aggregate this information. Most importantly for the discussion here an intention becomes a stack of pairs of an event and a deed, Individual pairs associate a deed with the event that has caused the deed to be placed on the intention. New events are associated with an empty deed, ϵ.

The AIL's basic plan data structure associates some matching information, a guard and a deed stack. The AIL includes operations for using plans to modify intentions. In these the plan is "matched" to the intention; the plan's guard is checked; and the plan's body (a deed stack) is added to the deed stack of the intention. Since some BDI languages trigger plans by matching the prefix of the deed stack and some by matching a *trigger event*, the AIL plan matching information contains both a trigger event (which must match the top event of the intention) and a deed stack prefix (which must match the prefix of the intention's deed stack). The matched prefix is replaced by the plan's body. By way of example, consider the following AIL plan for cleaning rooms.

trigger	prefix	guard	body
+!$_a$clean()	ϵ	dirty(Room)	+!$_a$Goto(Room) +!$_a$Vacuum(Room)

We use the syntax +!$_a g$ to indicate the commitment to an *achievement goal*. The AIL allows several different goal types. In this paper we will be interested in *achievement* (or declarative) goals representing a belief the agent desires to have; and *perform goals* (syntax +!$_p g$), which need not lead to a belief. The following shows the operation of the AIL's default planning operation on an intention, given the plan above.

trigger	deed
+!$_a$ clean()	ϵ

$\rightarrow$

trigger	deed
+!$_a$clean()	+!$_a$Goto(Room)
+!$_a$clean()	+!$_a$Vacuum(Room)

The plan's trigger matched the top event of this intention and its prefix matched the deed stack prefix. We assume the guard was believed. The top row of the intention (matching the prefix) was removed and replaced with two rows representing the body of the plan. The AIL can also handle *reactive plans* which become applicable whenever the guard is satisfied, but do not match a specific intention. We have omitted discussion of unification as handling unifiers obscures the presentation.

The AIL provides an environment interface which it expects systems implemented using it to satisfy. An environment, ξ, is expected to implement the following: $\mathbf{do}(a)$ executes the action, a. It is assumed that this handles any external effects of an agent's actions. *newpercepts*(ag) returns any new perceptions from the environment since the agent (ag) last checked and *oldpercepts*(ag) returns a list of things that can no longer be perceived. *getmessages*(ag) returns a list of messages. When one of these interface functions is called we write it, for instance, as $\xi.\mathbf{do}(a)$.

3   The AIL as an Environment for Heterogeneous Agents

The AIL view of the world is shown in Fig. 1. The AIL is implemented in Java and, in turn, a variety of languages can be implemented in the AIL. The AIL comes with interfaces and default classes for composing multi-agent systems, these classes handle agents at the level of the underlying AIL data structures and so can be used with agents

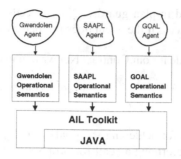

Fig. 1. Architecture of Heterogeneous Multi-Agent System

in any language that builds upon those structures. This makes it straightforward to build a heterogeneous multi-agent system using the AIL once the implementations of the target semantics are in place. In the subsequent sections, we will describe the three agent languages we use, namely: Gwendolen (Section 4); SAAPL (Section 5); and GOAL (Section 6). Our aim was to use not only the AIL data structures but as many of the pre-written AIL transition rules as possible in order to assess their breadth and utility. We also provide code fragments, both to give the reader some concrete syntax, and to introduce our heterogeneous scenario. Thus, we will code agents in each of these languages to take part in a *Contract Net* scenario [24], a well-known, and widely used, model of coordination in distributed problem-solvers. Essentially, a particular agent (the *manager*) broadcasts tasks (goals) to be achieved, and then agents capable of achieving these tasks bid for the contract. In real scenarios, the bidding, allocation and sub-contracting are all complex. However, we consider a *very* simple version: the manager does not broadcast to all the agents in the system at once but instead contacts them in turn; there is no bidding process nor sub-contracting; agents volunteer for a task if, and only if, they can perform it; and the manager simply accepts the first proposal it receives.

4   Gwendolen

Gwendolen [11] is based on the language presented in [12] now abstracted away from the AIL. Gwendolen uses the AIL's planning mechanisms "off the shelf" with both achievement and perform goals, event triggered, reactive and prefix matching plans. In this paper we only look at plans which match the prefix ϵ and so omit that from our plan presentation. We therefore represent Gwendolen's version of the plan

trigger	$+!_a\texttt{clean()}$
prefix	$[\epsilon]$
guard	$\texttt{dirty(Room)}$
body	$+!_a\texttt{Goto(Room)}$
	$+!_a\texttt{Vacuum(Room)}$

as $+!_a clean() : dirty(Room)$ <-
$$+!_a Goto(Room); +!_a Vacuum(Room)$$

Throughout this paper, we will use ';' to indicate concatenation of deeds on a stack and $\uparrow^a m$ to indicate the sending of a message m to agent a and $\downarrow^a m$ to indicate the receipt of a message m from an agent a (as in [29]). Gwendolen has two negation symbols which can be used in plan guards. $\neg gu$ succeeds if the agent believes $\neg gu$ (strong negation), $\sim gu$ success if the agent does not believe gu (weak negation).

Contract Net Code. The code for our Contract Net written in Gwendolen is as follows:

$$+!_a g : cando(g) \ \texttt{<-} \ a \qquad\qquad +!_a g' : cando(g') \ \texttt{<-} \ a'$$
$$+!_a g : \neg cando(g) \ \texttt{<-} \ +!_p cfp(g) \qquad +!_a g' : \neg cando(g') \ \texttt{<-} \ +!_p cfp(g')$$

These are four basic plans for achieving the goals g and g' either by performing an action or committing to performing a "call for proposals". Our Contract Net protocol assumes a message semantics consisting of a performative and a ground formula. The **perform** performative expects the agent to perform an action and the **tell** performative expects the receiving agent to update its belief base. So, Gwendolen has a plan for asking an agent to respond to a request to perform a goal, together with a number of plans for how to perform a 'respond' action and how to act if an agent has a proposal or is awarded a contract. $ag(A)$ is the belief that A is the name of another agent and $name(N)$ is the belief that N is the agent's own name.

$$+!_p cfp(T) : ag(A) \wedge name(N) \wedge \sim \uparrow^A (\textbf{perform}, respond(T, N)) \ \texttt{<-}$$
$$\uparrow^A (\textbf{perform}, respond(T, N)); \texttt{wait}$$

$$+!_p cfp(T) : proposal(T, A) \ \texttt{<-} \ \texttt{wait}$$
$$+!_p respond(T, A) : cando(T) \wedge name(N) \ \texttt{<-} \ \uparrow^A (\textbf{tell}, proposal(T, N))$$
$$+!_p respond(T, A) : \neg cando(T) \wedge name(N) \ \texttt{<-} \ \uparrow^A (\textbf{tell}, sorry(T, N))$$
$$+proposal(T, A) : \top \ \texttt{<-} \ \uparrow^A (\textbf{tell}, award(T))$$
$$+award(T) : \top \ \texttt{<-} \ +!_a T$$

5 SAAPL

SAAPL (Simple Abstract Agent Programming Language) [29] is an abstraction of languages such as Jason [6], 3APL [8], and CAN [30]. In [29] SAAPL is used to drive the discussion of *commitment machines*. We ignore this issue and focus instead on SAAPL's semantics as a simple, yet typical, language. The semantics of SAAPL [29], are shown in Fig. 2 where Q is the environment (a message queue), N the agent's name, B the belief base, Γ the intentions, Π the plan base, and Δ the applicable plans.

SAAPL *implemented with AIL.* SAAPL's semantics has three stages: Basic (which acts on a single intention); Agent which acts on a set of intentions; and MAS which acts on a set of Agents. SAAPL's semantics handles transitions between stages by treating a transition in one stage as a precondition to a rule for the next (e.g., rule (8) in Fig. 2), while the AIL expects a "chaining" style where an agent's reasoning cycle decides when to change stage. We include the current stage as part of the agent data structure.

Let us consider the Basic stage first. Although our agent data structure contains all the intentions, it also distinguishes a "current intention" so in the Basic stage we work

$$\frac{}{\langle Q, N, B, +b\rangle \underline{\text{ Basic }}_\rightarrow \langle Q, N, B \cup \{b\}, \epsilon\rangle} \tag{1}$$

$$\frac{}{\langle Q, N, B, -b\rangle \underline{\text{ Basic }}_\rightarrow \langle Q, N, B \backslash \{b\}, \epsilon\rangle} \tag{2}$$

$$\frac{\Delta = \{P_i\theta \mid (t_i : c_i \leftarrow P_i) \in \Pi \wedge t_i\theta = e \wedge B \models c_i\theta\}}{\langle Q, N, B, e\rangle \underline{\text{ Basic }}_\rightarrow \langle Q, N, B, \mathcal{S}_\mathcal{O}(\Delta)\rangle} \tag{3}$$

$$\frac{\langle Q, N, B, P_1\rangle \underline{\text{ Basic }}_\rightarrow \langle Q', N, B', P'\rangle}{\langle Q, N, B, P_1; P_2\rangle \underline{\text{ Basic }}_\rightarrow \langle Q, N, B, P_1; P_2\rangle} \tag{4}$$

$$\frac{}{\langle Q, N, B, \epsilon; P\rangle \underline{\text{ Basic }}_\rightarrow \langle Q, N, B, P\rangle} \tag{5}$$

$$\frac{}{\langle Q, N, B, \uparrow^{N_B} m\rangle \underline{\text{ Basic }}_\rightarrow \langle Q + N : N_B : m, N, B, \epsilon\rangle} \tag{6}$$

$$\frac{Q = N_A : N : m + Q'}{\langle Q, N, B, \Gamma\rangle \underline{\text{ Agent }}_\rightarrow \langle Q', N, B, \Gamma \cup \{\downarrow^{N_A} m\}\rangle} \tag{7}$$

$$\frac{P = \mathcal{S}_\mathcal{I}(\Gamma) \quad \langle Q, N, B, P\rangle \underline{\text{ Basic }}_\rightarrow \langle Q', N, B', P'\rangle}{\langle Q, N, B, \Gamma\rangle \underline{\text{ Agent }}_\rightarrow \langle Q', N, B', (\Gamma \backslash \{P\}) \cup \{P'\}\rangle} \tag{8}$$

$$\frac{P = \mathcal{S}_\mathcal{I}(\Gamma) \quad P = \epsilon}{\langle Q, N, B, \Gamma\rangle \underline{\text{ Agent }}_\rightarrow \langle Q', N, B', \Gamma \backslash \{P\}\rangle} \tag{9}$$

$$\frac{\langle N, B, \Gamma\rangle = \mathcal{S}_A(As) \quad \langle Q, N, B, \Gamma\rangle \underline{\text{ Agent }}_\rightarrow \langle Q', N, B', \Gamma'\rangle}{\langle Q, As\rangle \underline{\text{ MAS }}_\rightarrow \langle Q', (As \cup \{\langle N, B', \Gamma'\rangle\}) \backslash \{\langle N, B, \Gamma\rangle\}\rangle} \tag{10}$$

Fig. 2. Operational Semantics for **SAAPL**

on this intention. **SAAPL**'s intentions are stacks of belief modifications, send message actions or events, while the AIL has a more complex structure of events and deeds. In general we will be interested in the AIL's deed stack. Only when planning will we be interested in the AIL's event stack. We will look at rule (1) in detail. We discovered, while performing this case study, that many of the operational rules in OSRules were *over complex* and still specialised towards what is now the **Gwendolen** language. In particular they contained pre-conditions and effects that were unnecessary in many cases. As a case in point, there is a belief addition rule in OSRules which, excluding unifiers and irrelevant parts of the Agent data structure, was:

$$\frac{\mathbf{consistent}(B \cup \{b\})}{< ag, (E, +b); i, I, B, \mathbf{?} > \rightarrow < ag, i, [(+b, \epsilon)]; I, B \cup \{b\}, \mathbf{?} >} \tag{11}$$

In this transition rule, and in all others in the paper, we will include in the agent data-structure $< \ldots >$ only those parts affected by the rule. Throughout this paper we will use ';' to indicate concatenation of the rows in our intention data structure so $(E, +b); i$ is the intention whose top row has event, E and deed, $+b$. '**?**' indicates the placeholder for the stage of the agent's reasoning cycle. We replaced (11) with

$$\frac{\mathbf{consistent}(B \cup \{b\})}{< ag, (E, +b); i, I, B, \mathbf{?} > \rightarrow < ag, i, I, B \cup \{b\}, \mathbf{?} >} \tag{12}$$

which does not now issue a new intention $(+b, \epsilon)$. **consistent** defaults to $\top$ in the AIL, but can be over-ridden in language implementations. We keep the default and again that pre-condition is trivial. Changing the presentation of the rule to use SAAPL syntax (B for belief base, P the current intention, Γ the intentions, N agent name) gives:

$$< N, (E, +b); P, \Gamma, B, \textbf{Basic} > \to < N, P, \Gamma, B \cup \{b\}, \textbf{Agent} > \qquad (13)$$

which is in most respects identical to (1) and (4), then returning to the **Agent** stage as specified by (8). The AIL's default "drop belief" rule (combining (2) and (4)) becomes:

$$< N, (E, -b); P, \Gamma, B, \textbf{Basic} > \to < N, P, \Gamma, B \backslash \{b'\}, \textbf{Agent} > \qquad (14)$$

We now look at plan selection; rule (3). This rule combines two operations that are separated in OSRules. Firstly a set, Δ, of applicable plans is determined and then one of these is selected $\mathcal{S}_\mathcal{O}(\Delta)$ using a selection function. Since we had two rules to represent this we introduced a new stage **BasicPlanning** to chain them together:

$$\frac{\Delta = \{(t_i, P_i) \mid t_i : c_i \leftarrow P_i \in \Pi \wedge (t_i \theta = e) \wedge B \models c_i \theta\} \quad \Delta \neq \emptyset}{< N, [], (e, \epsilon); P, B, \textbf{Basic} > \to < N, \Delta, (e, \epsilon); P, B, \textbf{BasicPlanning} >} \qquad (15)$$

$$\frac{\mathcal{S}_\mathcal{O}(\Delta, i) = (e, P_i)}{< N, (e, \epsilon); P, \Delta, \textbf{BasicPlanning} > \to < N, (e, P_i); P, [], \textbf{Agent} >} \qquad (16)$$

$(e, P_i); P$ is a shorthand for adding a row (e, p_i) to the intention P for each deed, $p_i \in P_i$. SAAPL has a mechanism for posting events, e. These are placed on the intention stack and picked up immediately for planning. In the AIL data structures they get placed on the deed stack and need to be moved to the event stack before planning can take place. This step requires us to introduce a new rule from OSRules into SAAPL:

$$< N, (E, +!_p g); P, \textbf{Agent} > \to < N, (+!_p g, \epsilon); P, \textbf{Agent} > \qquad (17)$$

The SAAPL semantics requires the use of a new distinguished symbol 'ϵ' to represent a "done" update. Since we have integrated (4) into our rules for individual steps we no longer need this marker nor (5) to handle it.

We now look at sending messages. SAAPL assumes a message queue, while AIL assumes a more adhoc arrangement where an agent can access all its messages at once. Therefore we implemented two new rules for (6) and (7):

$$\frac{\xi.enqueue(N : N_B : m)}{< N, \xi, \uparrow^{N_B} m; P, B, \textbf{Basic} > \to < N, \xi, P, B \cup \{\uparrow^{N_B} m\} \textbf{Agent} >} \qquad (18)$$

$$\frac{N_A : N : m = \xi.dequeue}{< N, \Gamma, \textbf{Agent} > \to < N, (\downarrow^{N_A} m, \epsilon); \Gamma, \textbf{Agent} >} \qquad (19)$$

ξ is the agent environment. The SAAPL implementation therefore specifies two operations (*enqueue* and *dequeue*) that any environment in which it runs must implement. We treat the receipt of a new message as the acquisition of a belief that the message has been received (so in the AIL this is modelled as a belief change event). Rules (8) and (9) handle the selection of intentions. Although we are not using the SAAPL "do nothing" symbol we can have empty intentions all of whose deeds have been performed. There were "select intention" rules within the AIL but, again, were simplified.

$$\frac{P = \mathcal{S}_{\mathcal{I}}(\Gamma \cup \{P_o\}) \quad \neg \text{empty}(P)}{< N, P_o, \Gamma, \textbf{Agent} > \rightarrow < N, P, \Gamma \backslash \{P\} \cup \{P_o\}, \textbf{Basic} >} \tag{20}$$

$\mathcal{S}_{\mathcal{I}}$ is a function for selecting intentions. Since AIL's default rules expect a separate distinguished current intention the equivalent of Γ in rules (8) and (9) is $\Gamma \cup P_o$ in AIL, where P_o is the "old" current intention. This is not a complete representation of (8) we have to assume the correct operation of the **Basic** stage to complete the rule.

$$\frac{P = \mathcal{S}_{\mathcal{I}}(\Gamma \cup \{P_o\}) \quad \text{empty}(P)}{< N, P_o, \Gamma, \textbf{Agent} > \rightarrow < N, null, \Gamma \backslash \{P\} \cup \{P_o\}, \textbf{Agent}\} >} \tag{21}$$

We also introduced a rule that put an agent's thread to sleep should its intention set Γ become empty (as opposed to letting it continuously run, checking for an applicable rule). Rule (10) implicitly assumes a single threaded environment. In a multi-threaded Java implementation it seemed sensible not to implement this rule in the semantics but allow the Java scheduling algorithm to handle interleaving of agent execution.

Since we were interested in an example which required agents to perform actions beyond simply sending messages, we also introduced one further rule from OSRules:

$$\frac{a \neq \uparrow^{NA} m \quad \xi.\textbf{do}(a)}{< N, \xi, (E, a); P, \textbf{Basic} > \rightarrow < N, \xi, P, \textbf{Agent} >} \tag{22}$$

Recall that **do** is an interface requirement for all environments that support the AIL. It is assumed that an environment for **SAAPL** would fulfil the basic AIL requirements (implementing **do** etc.) as well as those specific to **SAAPL** (*enqueue* and *dequeue*).

Faithfulness of the Implementation. Any claim to have implemented the operational semantics of a language is faced with correctness issues involved in transferring a transition system to, in this case, a set of Java classes. Verifying implementations is a complex undertaking. Such a verification effort would be a significant task and falls outside the scope of this work. However, that aside, it is also the case that we have not directly implemented the transition system presented in [29] but the one shown above and so the question arises "Are these two transition systems equivalent"? In fact they are not. For instance we have included a new rule for action execution and have interleaved agent execution. But nevertheless it would clearly be desirable to produce a theorem demonstrating the extent to which the two transition systems match and so providing a clear idea of the extent to which we can claim to have implemented SAAPL with the AIL. We have offered above an informal discussion of the relationship between the semantics but leave a proper (formal) proof to ongoing work [14]. We anticipate that the production of such a proof will refine the implementation of SAAPL in the AIL.

Contract Net Code. The contract net code in **SAAPL** is similar to that for Gwendolen. The major difference is the inability to trigger plans by general belief updates. We create a special "react" event, r, used to trigger reactions to messages. The react event is posted when **tell** messages are received (see section 7).

$$g : cando(g) \leftarrow a \qquad\qquad g' : cando(g') \leftarrow a'$$
$$g : \neg cando(g) \leftarrow cfp(g) \qquad\qquad g' : \neg cando(g') \leftarrow cfp(g')$$

$$cfp(T) : ag(A) \wedge name(N) \wedge \sim\uparrow^A (\textbf{perform}, respond(T, N))$$
$$\leftarrow \uparrow^A (\textbf{perform}, respond(T, N)); \texttt{wait}$$

$$respond(T, A) : cando(T) \wedge name(N) \leftarrow \uparrow^A (\textbf{tell}, proposal(T, N))$$
$$respond(T, A) : \neg cando(T) \wedge name(N) \leftarrow \uparrow^A (\textbf{tell}, sorry(T, N))$$

$$r : proposal(P, Ag) \leftarrow \uparrow^{Ag} (\textbf{tell}, award(P)) \qquad r : award(T) \leftarrow T$$

6 GOAL

GOAL [9] is a BDI language introduced by de Boer et. al to illustrate the use of purely declarative goals in agent programming. It is clearly a BDI language but is quite different in style to many other agent languages. In particular it does not use the concepts of event or intention explicitly in its semantics. An agent is defined by its mental state: two sets of formulas Σ for the agent's beliefs and Γ for the agent's goals. In this sense, it is closer in style to the original AOP proposal [23] or to MetateM [16]. GOAL assumes an underlying logic on its formula language, $\mathcal{L}$, with an entailment relation $\models_C$ and defines entailment for mental states as in Definition 1 below. An agent's behaviour is governed by its *capabilities* and *conditional actions*. *Capabilities* are associated with a partial function $\mathcal{T} : Bcap \times \wp(\mathcal{L}) \to \wp(\mathcal{L})$. $\mathcal{T}$ operates on the belief base Σ to alter it. Capabilities may be *enabled* or not for an agent in a particular configuration. If the capability is not enabled then $\mathcal{T}$ is undefined. $\mathcal{T}$ is used by the mental state transformation function $\mathcal{M}$ to alter the agent state as in Definition 2.

Definition 1. *Let* $\langle \Sigma, \Gamma \rangle$ *be a mental state:*
- $\langle \Sigma, \Gamma \rangle \models_M \mathbf{B}\phi$ *iff* $\Sigma \models_C \phi$, $\qquad\qquad\qquad\qquad$ $\langle \Sigma, \Gamma \rangle \models_M \mathbf{G}\psi$ *iff* $\psi \in \Gamma$
- $\langle \Sigma, \Gamma \rangle \models_M \neg\phi$ *iff* $\langle \Sigma, \Gamma \rangle \not\models_M \phi$,
- $\langle \Sigma, \Gamma \rangle \models_M \phi_1 \wedge \phi_2$ *iff* $\langle \Sigma, \Gamma \rangle \models_M \phi_1$ *and* $\langle \Sigma, \Gamma \rangle \models_M \phi_2$.

Definition 2. *Let* $\langle \Sigma, \Gamma \rangle$ *be a mental state, and* $\mathcal{T}$ *be a partial function that associates belief updates with agent capabilities. Then the partial function* $\mathcal{M}$ *is defined by:*

$$\mathcal{M}(\mathbf{a}, \langle \Sigma, \Gamma \rangle) = \begin{cases} \langle \mathcal{T}(\mathbf{a}, \Sigma), & \text{if } \mathcal{T}(\mathbf{a}, \Sigma) \\ \Gamma \setminus \{\psi \in \Gamma \mid \mathcal{T}(\mathbf{a}, \Sigma) \models_C \psi\} \rangle & \text{is defined,} \\ & \text{if } \mathcal{T}(\mathbf{a}, \Sigma) \\ \text{is undefined for } \mathbf{a} \in Bcap & \text{is undefined} \end{cases} \qquad (23)$$

$$\mathcal{M}(\mathbf{drop}(\phi), \langle \Sigma, \Gamma \rangle) = \langle \Sigma, \Gamma \setminus \{\psi \in \Gamma \mid \psi \models_C \phi\} \rangle \qquad (24)$$

$$\mathcal{M}(\mathbf{adopt}(\phi), \langle \Sigma, \Gamma \rangle) = \begin{cases} \langle \Sigma, & \text{if } \not\models_C \neg\phi \text{ and} \\ \Gamma \cup \{\phi' \mid \Sigma \not\models_M \phi', \models_C \phi \to \phi'\} \rangle & \Sigma \not\models_C \phi \\ & \text{if } \Sigma \models_C \neg\phi \text{ or} \\ \text{is undefined} & \models_C \neg\phi \end{cases} \qquad (25)$$

Lastly, conditional actions and a *commitment strategy* provide a mechanism for selecting which capability to apply next.

Definition 3. *Let* $\langle \Sigma, \Gamma \rangle$ *be a mental state with* $b = \phi \triangleright \mathbf{do}(\mathbf{a}) \in \Pi$. *Then, as a rule, we have: If*

- *the mental condition* ϕ *holds in* $\langle \Sigma, \Gamma \rangle$, *i.e.* $\langle \Sigma, \Gamma \rangle \models_M \phi$, *and*
- $\mathbf{a}$ *is enabled in* $\langle \Sigma, \Gamma \rangle$ *i.e.,* $\mathcal{M}(\mathbf{a}, \langle \Sigma, \Gamma \rangle)$ *is defined.*

then $\langle \Sigma, \Gamma \rangle \xrightarrow{b} \mathcal{M}(\mathbf{a}, \langle \Sigma, \Gamma \rangle)$ *is a possible computation step. The relation* $\longrightarrow$ *is the smallest relation closed under this rule.*

The commitment strategy determines how conditional actions are selected when several apply and is not specified directly by the **GOAL** semantics.

GOAL *implemented with AIL.* To model **GOAL**'s mental states we treated the AIL belief base as the **GOAL** belief base, Σ. AIL already had an operation to extract the "goals" of a agent – interpreted as the set of AIL achieve goals appearing in the event stacks of intentions. **GOAL**'s goal set, Γ, became the AIL's goal set.

Implementation of $\models_M$ was simple. The formulas $\mathbf{B}(\phi)$ etc. are equivalent to the AIL's guard formulas and the AIL logical consequence relation, $\models$, is allowed to inspect not just AIL's belief base but also its intentions, mailboxes, plans[2] and goals. The AIL interpreted $\mathbf{G}(\phi)$ as $\phi \in \Gamma$ as required by **GOAL**. Therefore the AIL's $\models$ relation was equivalent to **GOAL**'s $\models_M$ except that the current implementation of $\models$, in the AIL, only allows for unification with the belief base. This therefore limits reasoning about **GOAL** mental states. (We intend to build in **Prolog** style reasoning in the future.)

Next we turn to capabilities. Inherent in the description of a capability is the idea that the agent performs an action associated with the capability. Also inherent in the description and in the semantics of mental state transformers is the idea that all the belief updates associated with a capability are performed before the agent does anything else (like planning a different intention). The AIL's pre-existing transition rules only allowed for one belief update at a time. There was nothing to prevent us from writing a new rule that would perform all the tasks in $\mathcal{T}(\mathbf{a}, \Sigma)$ at once, but since we were interested in re-using the AIL's pre-existing rules where possible we assigned a reasoning cycle stage, **Capability**, for performing all the updates required by $\mathcal{T}(\mathbf{a}, \Sigma)$. We treat capabilities as *perform* goals because they function as steps/sub-goals an agent *should* perform yet they are not declarative. The AIL requires the execution of actions to be triggered explicitly so we decided to treat $\mathcal{T}(\mathbf{a}, \Sigma)$ as a function on the belief base paired with an optional action. We write this as $\mathcal{T}(\mathbf{a}, \Sigma) = \mathbf{do}(a) + f(\Sigma)$ and represent it in the AIL as a plan, where the range of f is a deed stack of belief updates. The enabledness of a capability is governed by the plan guard. When $\mathcal{T}$ is executed it first performs the action (if appropriate) and then modifies the belief base. Lastly, it removes any achieved goals. This breaks down the execution of $\mathcal{T}$ into several transition rules. First we modify the deed stack of the intention in accordance with $\mathcal{T}$

---

[2] This allows us to model communication performatives such as *Jason*'s **askHow**.

$$\Delta = \{< \mathbf{a}, a'; f'(\Sigma) >| \ \mathbf{a} \in Bcap \wedge enabled(\mathbf{a}) \wedge \mathcal{T}(\mathbf{a}, \Sigma) = \mathbf{do}(a') + f'(\Sigma)\}$$

$$\frac{\mathcal{S}_{\mathrm{plan}}(\Delta) =< \mathbf{a}, a; f(\Sigma) >}{< ag, (\mathbf{a}, \epsilon); i, I, \mathbf{Main} >\rightarrow< ag, (\mathbf{a}, a; f(\Sigma)); i', I\backslash\{i'\} \cup \{i\}, \mathbf{Capability} >} \tag{26}$$

where $\mathcal{S}_{\mathrm{plan}}$ is an application specific function for selecting a plan from a set. This was a new rule but made use of pre-existing AIL operations, particularly the built-in functions for matching plans to intentions. After applying this rule the system is in the **Capability** stage which ensures that all the changes associated with $\mathcal{T}$ take place before the agent does anything else. We used four pre-existing transitions to handle most of $\mathcal{T}$, three of which (13), (14) and (22) we have already shown leaving us only to provide a special case for when the action to be performed involves sending a message:

$$\frac{\xi.\mathbf{do}(\uparrow^{ag'} m)}{< ag, (E, \uparrow^{ag'} m); i, Out, \mathbf{Capability} >\rightarrow< ag, i, Out \cup \{\uparrow^{ag'} m\}, \mathbf{Capability} >} \tag{27}$$

Note here how $\uparrow^{ag'} m$ is added to the agent's outbox, Out. This functions as part of the belief base, from now on the agent will believe it has sent the message.

Only deeds associated with a capability have a perform goal as their event. Since a capability can not invoke another capability there will never be two consecutive capabilities on the event stack of an intention. So we trigger the end of capability processing by detecting the event is no longer a perform goal. At this point we need to remove any goals already achieved.

$$\frac{e \neq \mathbf{a} \quad \mathcal{G} = \{g \in \Gamma \mid B \models g\} \quad i' = map(\lambda g. \, \mathbf{drop}(g, (e, d); i), \mathcal{G})}{I' = \{i \mid i = map(\lambda g. \, \mathbf{drop}(g, i')) \wedge i' \in I\}}{< ag, (e, d); i, I, \mathbf{Capability} >\rightarrow< ag, i', I', \mathbf{Perception} >} \tag{28}$$

Just as our implementation of $\models$ does not include anything equivalent to Prolog style reasoning, this rule also avoids dropping goals which follow from goals already achieved. **drop** is a built in AIL operation on intentions which removes a goal from the event stack and all subgoals subsequently placed there. GOAL had no semantics for perception or message handling which we needed for our example scenario. We assumed that these should directly update an agent's belief base. We therefore introduced two new stages to control these with simple new rules (which again are now a part of OSRules) using AIL's environment interface:

$$\frac{B_1 = \xi.newPercepts(ag) \quad B_2 = \xi.oldPercepts(ag)}{< ag, \xi, \Sigma, \mathbf{Perception} >\rightarrow< ag, \xi, \Sigma\backslash\{B_2\} \cup \{B_1\}, \mathbf{Messages} >} \tag{29}$$

$$\frac{M = \xi.getMessages(ag) \quad B' = \{\downarrow^A m \mid m \in M\}}{< ag, \xi, \Sigma, \mathbf{Messages} >\rightarrow< ag, \xi, \Sigma \cup B', \mathbf{Main} >} \tag{30}$$

We now need to deal with the selection and application of conditional actions and capabilities, and the mental state transformers for **adopt** and **drop**.

GOAL has no concept of multiple intentions (using multiple goals instead) however AIL has these goals distributed among intentions. Part of the process of planning with a conditional action must therefore include selecting the appropriate intention. We chose to first find all the plans that were applicable, no matter which intention, and then chose one of those plans, implicitly choosing (or creating) a new intention in the process. Naturally we chose to represent GOAL's conditional actions as AIL plans. We had a choice here as the AIL can have plans which are not triggered by an event but it was more natural within the AIL to use event triggers. We decided therefore that where a condition of a conditional action referred to a goal this would be treated as the event trigger for the plan. We created two new rules for reactive plans and triggered plans:

$$\frac{\Delta = \{ap \mid ap = \phi \rhd \mathbf{do}(a) \wedge ag \models \phi\} \quad \mathcal{S}_{\mathrm{plan}}(\Delta) = \phi' \rhd \mathbf{do}(a') \quad \mathbf{G}(\phi'') \not\subseteq \phi'}{< ag, i, I, \mathbf{Main} > \rightarrow < ag, (+\phi', a), i \cup I, \mathbf{Goal}\} >}$$
(31)

We use the absence of any goals in the plan's mental condition ($\mathbf{G}(\phi'') \not\subseteq \phi'$) to tell that this is a reactive plan. This rule starts a new intention when a reactive plan applies.

$$\frac{\Delta = \{ap \mid ap = \phi \rhd \mathbf{do}(a) \wedge ag \models \phi\} \quad \mathcal{S}_{\mathrm{plan}}(\Delta) = \phi' \rhd \mathbf{do}(a') \quad \mathbf{G}(\phi'') \in \phi'}{(\mathbf{adopt}(\phi'), \epsilon); i' \in \{I \cup i\}} \\ \overline{< ag, i, I, \mathbf{Main} > \rightarrow < ag, (\phi'', a'); i', I\backslash\{i'\} \cup \{i\}, \mathbf{Goal}\} >}$$
(32)

For triggered plans we modify the intention that triggered the plan. We overrode the AIL's default $\mathcal{S}_{\mathrm{plan}}$ function to prevent continuous firing of reactive rules once they became applicable. This was done by keeping track of how many times a conditional action had been used and, where there was a choice, opting for ones less frequently applied. We also needed to amend $\mathcal{S}_{\mathrm{plan}}$ to distinguish between plans representing capabilities and plans representing conditional actions and to ensure that the correct type of plan was used with the correct transition rule.

We have added a new **Goal** stage because the AIL needs to shift goals between deeds and events. We need rules for both perform and achieve goals. The rule for perform goals was a GOAL equivalent of (17). Similar rules were used to move **adopt** deeds and **drop** deeds to the event stack. Once back to the **Main** stage, we either plan with a capability, if that is now the event (as above), or handle the **adopt** (moving an achieve goal to the event stack, above) or **drop** event:

$$\frac{i' = \mathbf{drop}(\phi, i) \quad I' = \{i'_1 \mid i_1 \in I \wedge i'_1 = \mathbf{drop}(\phi, i_1)\}}{< ag, (\mathbf{drop}(\phi), \epsilon); i, I, \mathbf{Main} > \rightarrow < ag, i', I', \mathbf{Main} >}$$
(33)

We also added a rule to the language to sleep the agent when it had nothing to do.

Faithfulness of the Implementation. We have implemented GOAL with a commitment strategy based on planning *recent* goals (i.e., those goals at the top of an intention's event stack). Our semantics for **drop** are different because AIL's 'drop' function removes subgoals (which may not be explicitly represented as deducible from the dropped goal) – in retrospect an easy way to avoid this would have been to arrange for **adopt** deeds to start new intentions rather than being stacked as sub-goals on existing intentions. We would like to re-implement the example in this fashion before attempting a correctness proof of the equivalence of the two semantics.

Contract Net Code. We needed to split our plans for the contract net between capabilities and conditional actions. The requirement that *all* goals be declarative has caused the introduction of capabilities whose purpose is to add the belief that a goal is achieved.

Conditional Actions:

$$\mathbf{G}(g) \wedge \mathbf{B}(cando(g)) \triangleright g \qquad \mathbf{G}(g) \wedge \neg\mathbf{B}(cando(g)) \triangleright \mathbf{adopt}(cfp(g))$$
$$\mathbf{G}(g') \wedge \mathbf{B}(cando(g')) \triangleright g' \qquad \mathbf{G}(g') \wedge \neg\mathbf{B}(cando(g')) \triangleright \mathbf{adopt}(cfp(g'))$$

$$\mathbf{G}(cfp(T)) \wedge \mathbf{B}(ag(A)) \wedge \mathbf{B}(name(N)) \wedge \neg\mathbf{B}(send_p(A, respond(T, N))) \triangleright$$
$$\mathbf{do}(\mathbf{adopt}(send_p(A, respond(T, N))))$$

$$\mathbf{G}(cfp(T)) \wedge \mathbf{B}(ag(A)) \wedge \mathbf{B}(name(N)) \wedge \mathbf{B}(send_p(A, respond(T, N))) \triangleright$$
$$\mathbf{do}(cfp\_done(T))$$

$$\mathbf{B}(respond(T, A)) \wedge \neg\mathbf{B}(cando(T)) \wedge \mathbf{B}(name(N)) \triangleright \mathbf{do}(send_t(A, sorry(T, N)))$$
$$\mathbf{B}(respond(T, A)) \wedge \mathbf{B}(name(N)) \triangleright send_t(A, proposal(T, N)$$
$$\mathbf{B}(respond(T, A)) \wedge \mathbf{B}(send_t(A, sorry(T, N))) \triangleright believe(respond(T, A))$$
$$\mathbf{B}(proposal(P, Ag)) \triangleright send_t(Ag, award(P))$$
$$\mathbf{B}(award(T) \wedge \neg T \triangleright \mathbf{adopt}(T)$$

Capabilities:

$$\mathcal{T}(g, \Sigma) = \mathbf{do}(a) + \Sigma \qquad\qquad \mathcal{T}(g', \Sigma) = \mathbf{do}(a') + \Sigma$$
$$\mathcal{T}(cfp\_done(T), \Sigma) = \Sigma \cup (cfp(T)) \qquad \mathcal{T}(cfp\_done(T), \Sigma) = \Sigma \cup (cfp(T))$$

$$\mathcal{T}(send_p(A, G), \Sigma) = \mathbf{do}(\uparrow^A (\mathbf{perform}, G)) + \Sigma \cup send_p(A, G)$$
$$\mathcal{T}(send_t(A, G), \Sigma) = \mathbf{do}(\uparrow^A (\mathbf{tell}, G)) + \Sigma \cup send_t(A, G)$$

7 Execution and Verification of the Contract Net Scenario

The Environment. For the Gwendolen and GOAL agents we were able to use the
default environment for the AIL, but for SAAPL we needed to implement a message
queue on top of this. This involved sub-classing the default environment and implementing *enqueue* and *dequeue*. We also needed to define **do** for sending messages
(already present in the AIL's default environment) and the actions a, a' and wait. For
wait we simply slept the agent for a short time. a and a' introduce new perceptions g
and g' into the environment which agents would subsequently detect.

Communication Semantics. Our Contract Net assumed an agreed communication semantics between the agents. In this semantics messages were paired with a performative
(either **perform** or **tell**). The semantics of **tell** was simple: on receiving a **tell** message
an agent was to update its belief base with the body of the message. The semantics of
perform was more complex, especially since GOAL did not have perform goals. Its
semantics was simply that the agent should commit to that goal (irrespective of whether

it was a perform or achieve goal). In the AIL the semantics of communication is supposed to be determined by plans triggered by the receipt (or, where applicable, sending) of messages. This gave us the following additional plans in our environment.

Gwendolen Code

$$+\downarrow^{Ag} (\textbf{perform}, G) : \top \ <- \ +!_p G \qquad\qquad +\downarrow^{Ag} (\textbf{tell}, B) : \top \ <- \ +B$$

SAAPL Code

$$\downarrow^{Ag} (\textbf{perform}, G) : \top \leftarrow G \qquad\qquad\qquad \downarrow^{Ag} (\textbf{tell}, B) : \top \leftarrow +B : r$$

GOAL Code

$$\textbf{B}(\downarrow^{Ag} (\textbf{perform}, G)) \wedge \neg \textbf{B}(G) \triangleright \textbf{adopt}(G)$$
$$\textbf{B}(\downarrow^{Ag} (\textbf{tell}, B)) \wedge \neg \textbf{B}(B) \triangleright believe(B)$$
$$\mathcal{T}(believe(B), \Sigma) = \Sigma \cup \{B\}$$

Execution. Fig. 3 shows the message sequence (running from top to bottom) for a typical run of our scenario. The Gwendolen agent acts as the manager and GOAL and SAAPL agents bid for contracts. We show the more important goals and beliefs as they are added to, and removed from (represented by striking through) the agents' structure. The Gwendolen agent has two goals g and g'. It sends a message to the SAAPL agent with the content $respond(g')$. This becomes a goal of the SAAPL agent who responds with $sorry(g')$ which at some point later becomes a belief of the Gwendolen agent. Interaction with the environment (actions a and a') and perception are shown by arrows terminating or originating outside of an agent.

Verification. The AIL toolkit comes equipped with an LTL based property specification language. This language has some special predicates for agent-specific properties. We used this language to specify the property $\Diamond(\mathcal{B}(ag_1, g) \wedge \mathcal{B}(ag_1, g'))$ where $\mathcal{B}(ag, \phi)$ means ϕ is in the belief base of the agent with name ag and $\Diamond$ means "at some point in the future". ag_1 was the name of the coordinating Gwendolen agent in the Contract Net execution described above. So the property states that that eventually the Gwendolen agent will eventually believe both its goals, g and g', have been achieved in any

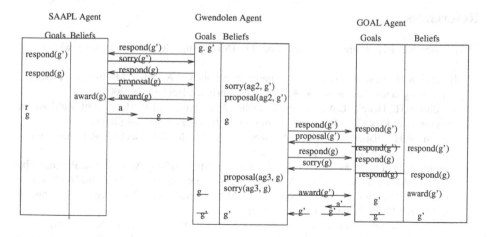

Fig. 3. Typical Execution of the Contract Net Scenario

possible execution of the program. We successfully verified that the Contract Net we had implemented satisfied this property using the AIL based model checking tools [3].

8   Conclusions

One of clearest conclusions we drew from our work was that the AIL data structures are sufficiently expressive to represent the concepts in (at least) the languages we had chosen. However our package of pre-existing transition rules was not well designed. This was not perhaps surprising since the transitions in this package were originally intended for a catch-all language. Fortunately, from a model checking perspective, the data structures are the crucial element needed for reasoning about an agent and we have been able to model check simple programs in our three languages even though the AIL classes are not yet optimised for the model checker. The transition rules were provided as a convenience, and in the hope that some might prove amenable for optimisation. However, it became clear, that the transition rule package needed to be redesigned to provide simple rules with better options for customisation. Yet, even with the burden of more customisation of the transition rules than we had originally anticipated we were able to implement interpreters for SAAPL and GOAL with relative ease. The SAAPL interpreter took about a week to implement and debug while the GOAL interpreter took about two weeks. Once correctly implemented it was simple to incorporate and run a heterogeneous multi-agent system. This, together with the (designed) ability to implement languages such as 3APL and AgentSpeak [12] confirms that the AIL provides a suitable level for implementing most BDI programming language semantics,

In the immediate future we intend to revisit the AIL implementation, and rework the OSRules in the light of this work. We also intend to improve the model checking aspects of the framework and to address larger, more complex languages, in particular the *Jason* implementation of AgentSpeak and 3APL and provide full AIL based implementations of these.

References

1. Bellifemine, F.L., Caire, G., Greenwood, D.: Developing MultiAgent Systems with JADE (2007)
2. Bordini, R.H., Dastani, M., Dix, J., El Fallah Seghrouchni, A. (eds.): Multi-Agent Programming: Languages, Platforms and Applications. Springer, Heidelberg (2005)
3. Bordini, R.H., Dennis, L.A., Farwer, B., Fisher, M.: Automated Verification of Multi-Agent Programs. In: Proc. 23rd Int. Conf. Automated Software Engineering (2008)
4. Bordini, R.H., Fisher, M., Visser, W., Wooldridge, M.: Model Checking Rational Agents. IEEE Intelligent Systems 19(5), 46–52 (2004)
5. Bordini, R.H., Fisher, M., Visser, W., Wooldridge, M.: Verifying Multi-Agent Programs by Model Checking. J. Autonomous Agents & Multi-Agent Systems 12(2), 239–256 (2006)
6. Bordini, R.H., Hübner, J.F., Wooldridge, M.: Programming Multi-agent Systems in AgentSpeak Using Jason. Wiley, Chichester (2007)
7. Clarke, E., Grumberg, O., Peled, D.: Model Checking. MIT Press, Cambridge (1999)
8. Dastani, M., van Riemsdijk, M.B., Meyer, J.-J.C.: Programming Multi-Agent Systems in 3APL. In: Bordini, et al. (eds.) [2], ch. 2, pp. 39–67

9. de Boer, F.S., Hindriks, K.V., van der Hoek, W., Meyer, J.-J.C.: A Verification Framework for Agent Programming with Declarative Goals. J. Applied Logic 5(2), 277–302 (2007)
10. Dennis, L.A., Farwer, B., Bordini, R.H., Fisher, M.: A Flexible Framework for Verifying Agent Programs. In: Proc. Int. Conf. Autonomous Agents & Multiagent Systems. ACM, New York (2008) (Short paper)
11. Dennis, L.A.: Gwendolen: A BDI Language for Verifiable Agents In Logic and the Simulation of Interaction and Reasoning. AISB Convention, University of Aberdeen (2008)
12. Dennis, L.A., Farwer, B., Bordini, R.H., Fisher, M., Wooldridge, M.: A Common Semantic Basis for BDI Languages. In: Proc. 7th Int. Workshop on Programming Multiagent Systems (2007)
13. Dix, J., Zhang, Y.: IMPACT: A Multi-Agent Framework with Declarative Semantics. In: Bordini, et al. (eds.) [2], ch. 3, pp. 69–94
14. Farwer, B., Dennis, L.A.: Translating into an Intermediate Agent Layer: A prototype in Maude. In: Proc. Concurrency, Specification, & Programming (2007)
15. FIPA: Foundation for Intelligent Physical Agents, http://www.fipa.org
16. Fisher, M.: METATEM: The Story so Far. In: Bordini, R.H., Dastani, M., Dix, J., El Fallah Seghrouchni, A. (eds.) ProMAS 2005. LNCS (LNAI), vol. 3862, pp. 3–22. Springer, Heidelberg (2006)
17. Gungui, I., Mascardi, V.: Integrating tuProlog into DCaseLP to Engineer Heterogeneous Agent Systems. In: Proc. Italian Conf. Computational Logic, Univ. Parma (2004)
18. Holzmann, G.J.: The Spin Model Checker. Addison-Wesley, Reading (2003)
19. Java Agent Services, http://www.java-agent.org
20. OMG: Object Management Group, http://www.omg.org
21. Paurobally, S., Cunningham, J., Jennings, N.: Verifying the Contract Net Protocol: A Case Study in Interaction Protocol and Agent Communication Language Semantics. In: Proc. 2nd Int. Workshop on Logic and Communication in Multi-Agent Systems (2004)
22. Paurobally, S., Cunningham, J., Jennings, N.R.: A Formal Framework for Agent Interaction Semantics. In: Proc. 4th Int. Conf. Autonomous Agents & Multiagent Systems, pp. 91–98 (2005)
23. Shoham, Y.: Agent-Oriented Programming. Artificial Intelligence 60(1), 51–92 (1993)
24. Smith, R.G., Davis, R.: Frameworks for Cooperation in Distributed Problem Solving. IEEE Trans. Systems, Man, & Cybernetics 11(1) (1980)
25. Subrahmanian, V.S., Bonatti, P., Dix, J., Eiter, T., Kraus, S., Ozcan, F., Ross, R.: Heterogeneous Agent Systems: Theory and Implementation. MIT Press, Cambridge (2000)
26. Suguri, H., Kodama, E., Miyazaki, M.: Assuring Interoperability in Heterogeneous, Autonomous and Decentralized Multi-Agent Systems. In: Proc. 6th Int. Symp. Autonomous Decentralized Systems, pp. 17–24. IEEE, Los Alamitos (2003)
27. Tan, X., Wang, S.: Implementation of Multi-Agent System Based on CORBA and COM. In: Proc. 6th Int. Conf. Computer Supported Coop. Work in Design, pp. 299–302 (2001)
28. Winikoff, M.: JACK^{TM} Intelligent Agents. In: Bordini, et al. (eds.) [2], ch. 7, pp. 175–193
29. Winikoff, M.: Implementing Commitment-Based Interactions. In: Proc. 6th Int. Conf. Autonomous Agents & Multiagent Systems, pp. 1–8. ACM, New York (2007)
30. Winikoff, M., Padgham, L., Harland, J., Thangarajah, J.: Declarative and Procedural Goals in Intelligent Agent Systems. In: Proc. Int. Conf. Principles of Knowledge Representation & Reasoning (2002)

Orwell's Nightmare for Agents?
Programming Multi-agent Organisations

Nick A.M. Tinnemeier, Mehdi Dastani, and John-Jules Ch. Meyer

Utrecht University, The Netherlands

Abstract. This paper presents a programming language that is designed to implement multi-agent organisations. These organisations are developed as separate entities regulating the behaviour of individual agents that interact with the organisation. The focus is on the normative aspect of organisations that are specified in terms of norms being enforced by monitoring, regimenting and sanctioning mechanisms.

1 Introduction

One of the greatest challenges in the development of multi-agent systems (MAS) is to cope with the large complexity that is caused by the interaction between agents that autonomously pursue their *own* goals. Using an *organisation-centred* approach (as opposed to an *agent-centred* one) is conceived as a way to decrease this complexity and make the development of MAS easier to manage [1,2]. In this approach the organisation is developed as separate entity in terms of organisational concepts (e.g. roles, groups, and norms). From the organisation perspective, the internal state of the agents is not observable, only the actions to be performed in external environments are. That the advantage of using an organisation-centred approach is widely recognised is displayed by the numerous agent methodologies (e.g. Gaia [3]), models (e.g. OperA [4], $\mathcal{M}$oise$^+$ [5], E-Institutions [6], AGR [7]) and frameworks (e.g. AMELI [8], $\mathcal{S}$-$\mathcal{M}$oise$^+$ [5]) that adopt (at least some) organisational concepts.

Normative elements constitute an important aspect in developing organisations. Since no assumptions are made about the inner workings of agents participating in the organisation, also no assumptions can be made about the behaviour they will exhibit. Norms provide the agents with some behavioural guideline, thereby ensuring that the objectives of the organisation are not endangered. Normative elements thus specify the rules of behaviour (norms) the agents ought to obey when participating in the organisation. These norms are often specified by means of concepts like permissions, obligations, and prohibitions.

To fully exploit the results of MAS research in the development of complex software systems, sophisticated programming languages are needed to put theory to practice. Such a programming language must satisfy the fundamental requirement that it is *"reasonably natural for solving problems, at least problems within its intended application area"* [9]. A language is considered reasonably natural if

K.V. Hindriks, A. Pokahr, and S. Sardina (Eds.): ProMAS 2008, LNAI 5442, pp. 56–71, 2009.

we are able to keep the concepts used in analysis and design alive in the implementation. Without this, the concepts used in specification and design need to be implemented in an ad-hoc manner, making the implementation a burdensome task prone to errors, having negative impact on the product's maintainability.

Although we acknowledge that a multi-agent organisation encompasses more than the normative element only (see section 2), the focus of this paper is on the normative element of multi-agent organisations. We aim at operationalization of the normative elements based on which we design a programming language to implement organisations. In the literature there is related work on electronic institutions for regulating agents according to certain norms. In particular, ISLANDER[6] is a formal framework for specifying norms in institutions, and is used in the AMELI platform[8] for executing electronic institutions based on rules provided in it. A difference with our work is that ISLANDER/AMELI is primarily aimed at very concrete norms in the form of procedures, typically in the form of "ought-to-do's" on speech acts, while in our approach we are primarily concerned with more abstract, declarative norms ("ought-to-be's", cf. [10,11]). Another difference is that in contrast to our approach, in ISLANDER/AMELI norms can never be violated by agents.

Another work that is concerned with the operationalization of multi-agent systems using organisational concepts is the work of S-$\mathcal{M}oise^+$[5]. S-$\mathcal{M}oise^+$ is an organisational middleware, in which also more abstract, declarative norms are used. In this approach, however, norms merely serve as guidelines of proper behavior for the agents in the system. It lacks a mechanism to detect whether an agent has actually fulfilled its obligations, let alone a sanctioning mechanism. In our approach, however, programming MAS means to program detection and sanctioning mechanisms since these determine the type of coordination put into place by the system.

A different approach of regulating the external behavior of individual agents is that of using coordination artefacts [12]. Just like these artefacts, we propose to develop an organisation as a separate entity with the goal of coordinating external agents. In our work, however, coordination is achieved by means of high-level constructs such as norms, more closely relating to the models in which MAS are usually designed, and not so much as low-level coordination concepts such as synchronization of processes coordination artefacts are based on.

Closely related to this work is [13] in which a simplified version of a programming language that is designed to implement norm-based artefacts is proposed, along with a logic that can be used to specify and verify properties of programs developed in this language. In this paper the programming language is enriched with temporal aspects, constructs to refer to actions and roles. A logic to reason about programs implemented in our language is omitted, however.

Section 2 explains the key concepts of normative MAS and organisations reasearch that are of importance in this paper. Section 3 presents the syntax and semantics of our programming language. Section 4 explains how normative multi-agent organisations can be implemented by this language, and section 5 concludes this paper and hints at some directions for future research.

2   Key Concepts of Multi-agent Organisations

Our approach of designing a normative multi-agent programming language is based on ideas from research in normative systems and research in multi-agent organisations. Therefore, this section introduces some of the key concepts that we use from this area.

In general, the organisations which we aim to implement with our programming language consist of the following components. Part of the organisation is the *environment* which state can be modified by the external actions of *agents* that interact with the organisation. No assumptions are made about the inner workings of these agents. We assume that the organisation is able to determine the effects of these external actions. Also part of the organisation is a *detectioning mechanism* that normatively assesses the organisation and a *sanctioning mechanism* imposing sanctions as a result of this normative assessment. The organisation thus becomes a Big Brother monitor the agents' behaviour and imposing sanctions accordingly, thereby embodying Orwell's nightmare for agents. It should be emphasised that in our approach the organisation is a passive entity merely reacting to the actions that external agents perform within the environment.

To illustrate these components as well as some other concepts that are of importance in our approach, we use a simple example of a software simulation of a railway system. In this simulation software agents play the role of passengers that travel by train. The conditions of using the transport system are captured as norms. Other examples of applications we are targeting at are, for instance, a financial administration database, a conference management system, or an online marketplace.

2.1   The Normative Aspect of Organisations

Norms often find their representation in deontic logic, a logic for reasoning about ideal and actual behaviour. Many different deontic logics have been developed introducing operators for permission, obligation and prohibition (see [14] for an overview). In this work norms are represented as elementary counts-as statements as motivated and developed in [15].

Counts-as statements are used to classify or make a judgment about the organisation. Herewith, a distinction is made between between brute and normative/institutional facts as first advanced in [16]. The environment is described by means of brute facts, e.g. *"agent a is in the train without a valid ticket"*. The value judgment of this situation is expressed by means of normative facts, e.g. a classification as good (desirable), ugly (undesirable, but tolerated) or bad (extremely undiserable, and not tolerated). For instance, to say that for agent i it is forbidden to be in the train without a ticket is to say in terms of counts-as statements that being in the train without a ticket counts as a violation for i:

$$\text{in\_train}(i) \wedge -\text{ticket}(i) \Rightarrow \text{viol}(i) \tag{1}$$

Counts-as statements thus label the situation as expressed by brute facts with normative facts, thereby normatively assessing the organisation.

Deontic notions like prohobition, obligation, and permission can be expressed as counts-as statements. Intuitively (see [15] for a thorough analysis), the deontic notion of being prohibited to be in a (brute or normative) state characterised by p can be modelled in terms of counts-as statements by stating that p counts-as a violation. If it is permitted to be in a situation in which p holds then being in a situation in which p holds does not necessarily count as a violation[1]. An obligation to be in a (brute or normative) state in which p holds means that being in a state in which p does *not* hold necessarily counts as a violation.

To validate the norm described by the counts-as statement as specified by formula 1 only the current state of the system needs to be judged, because the act of being in the train without a ticket can be detected at the very moment the agent is in the train without a ticket. There are also norms, however, which need a time line to be validated. For instance, in order to validate a norm like: *"A passenger ought to buy a ticket while on the train."*, requires an assessment of the whole period in which the passenger travels by train. To be able to also express this kind of norms, which have temporal character, we enrich the language of counts-as statements with temporal operators.

In order to motivate the agents that participate in the organisation to obey the rules of behaviour, besides a representation of the norms also a mechanism is needed for letting the agents abide by the norms. One way of assuring that the agents comply with the norms is to *rule out* all the actions that will lead to a violation state, such that a violation will never happen. This way of carrying out the norms is referred to as regimentation. The organisation can somehow prevent an agent from performing an external action that causes a violation. This presupposes the organisation to have the ability to determine the effect of the actions that can be performed by the agents. An example of a case in which this presumption holds is an operating system that can disable certain operations for users that do not have the right permissions. Note that this presumption does not imply that the system has control over the internals of the agent, it can still try to perform the operation, but the result is simply not effectuated by the operating system.

As alternative to regimentation an enforcement mechanism can be used. Enforcement is based on the idea of responding after a violation of the norms has occurred. Following the old Roman saying "ubi lex ibi poena" (where there is a law, there is a sanction), we also define rules that specify the sanction that should be imposed as a consequence of this violation. For example, the sanction belonging to the violation caused by agent i travelling without a ticket is a fine of 10 credits, written as:

$$\mathtt{viol}(i) \Rightarrow \mathtt{fined10}(i) \tag{2}$$

---

[1] In [15] also a more strong notion of obligation is defined in which p is permitted iff p necessarily counts as $-viol$. In this paper, we use the weak notion, however.

These rules are in fact the inversion of the counts-as rules. Instead of stating which normative terms apply as a consequence of brute facts, sanctioning rules associate new brute facts with certain normative facts. An enforcement mechanism is especially useful in case the system cannot determine the effects of certain actions. However, even when the organisation is able to apply regimentation, enforcement might still be fruitful, because allowing for violations contributes to the flexibility and autonomy of the agent's behaviour [17].

2.2   Other Organisational Aspects

As already mentioned, an organisation consists of more than normative aspects only. Besides the normative aspects, in [18] three other major organisational aspects were identified. *Functional elements* refer to the functioning of the organisation by stating its main objectives, and how they can be achieved. For instance, by specifying global plans that prescribe the steps that should be taken to reach the objectives (cf. functional specification of $\mathcal{M}oise^+$ [5]). *Structural elements* define the specific structure of the organisation that is used to reach these objectives, and is usually defined by means of the roles that should be fulfilled along with the relations between these roles, such as power, coordination, and control (cf. [15]). *Dialogical elements* deal with the communicative aspects of the organisation ensuring efficient communication between agents, an important prerequisite in reaching the organisational objectives. They specify, for instance, communication protocols (cf. [6]) specifying the possible dialogic interaction between roles.

Roles form an important concept in all organisational aspects. In [19] a role is described as "...*a class that defines a normative behavioral repertoire of an agent.*". In this work we will treat roles as being labels denoting the name of the roles agents can play within an organisation. Special facts $\mathtt{rea}(i, \rho)$ then model that agent i has enacted a role typified by the label ρ. Moreover, we will introduce actions for enacting and de-enacting (deact from now on) roles that allow agents to enact and/or deact roles dynamically. Later on, we will show that this simple view on roles in combination with the normative aspect of the organisation allows to already handle some structural aspects of an organisation.

3   A Normative Multi-agent Programming Language

This section presents the relevant parts of the syntax and semantics of a programming language that is designed to implement organisations.

3.1   Syntax of Programming Language

Agents that interact with the organisation can perform actions to change the organisation. In particular, these actions allow agents to change the environment (brute state of the organisation), to enact and deact roles, and to communicate with each other. In defining the action language (and in the following), we assume a set *RoleName* with typical element ρ as the set of labels identifying the roles that agents can play within the organisation, and we assume a set of agents that will be uniquely identified by $i, j, \ldots$

Definition 1 (actions). *Let $\rho \in RoleName$, let $ExtAct$ with typical element α be the set of external actions, and let $ComAct$ be the set of communicative actions with typical element γ_j in which γ is the identifier of the illocutionary act, and j the identifier of the receiving agent. Then the set of actions Act with typical element β is defined as:*

$$Act = ExtAct \cup ComAct \cup \{enact(\rho), deact(\rho)\}$$

The state of the organisation is built of brute facts specifying the environment and normative facts specifying the judgment about the organisation. This same distinction between brute and normative facts is made for the logical language for expressing the facts representing the organisation: brute facts are modelled in the propositional language L_b, whereas normative facts are modelled in the propositional language L_n. Although a first-order language is much more expressive, in this paper a propositional one is used for the sake of readability.

The special propositions of the form $\mathbf{rea}(i, \rho)$ are used to model the fact that agent i has enacted role ρ. Propositions of the form $\mathbf{done}(i, \beta)$ are used to denote that agent i has *just* performed action β. This allows to refer to actions in expressing the norms. The special proposition $\mathbf{viol}_\perp$ is used to mark those situations that are so undesirable that they are *strongly* forbidden in the sense that the system assures that never such a state is reached. These propositions thus pertain to the norms that are to be regimented.

The normative properties that are used for an assessment of the organisation are expressed in L, a language of propositional linear time logic (PLTL) (see [20] for an introduction). Norms can thus have a temporal character. In particular, the operators X (neXt), G (Globally), F (Eventually), and U (Until) are introduced. Some norms might also refer to normative facts, for instance, a violation an agent has committed at some moment in the past. Therefore, the language for expressing the norms can range over both brute and normative facts.

Definition 2 (logical languages). *Given the set of atomic propositions P, special propositions $\mathbf{done}(i, \beta)$ for all $\beta \in Act$ and all agents i, special propositions $\mathbf{rea}(i, \rho)$ for all $\rho \in RoleName$ and all agents i, the language L (norms), L_b (brute), and L_n (normative) are defined as:*

- *if $p \in P$ then $p, -p \in L_b$*
- *$\mathbf{done}(i, \beta) \in L_b$*
- *if $q \in P$ then $q, -q \in L_n$*
- *$\mathbf{rea}(i, \rho) \in L_n$*
- *$\mathbf{viol}_\perp \in L_n$*
- *if $\phi_1, \phi_2 \in (L_b \cup L_n)$ then $\phi_1, \phi_2 \in L$*
- *if $\phi_1, \phi_2 \in L$ then $\phi_1 \wedge \phi_2, \neg\phi_1 \in L$*
- *if $\varphi_1, \varphi_2 \in L$ then $X\varphi_1, G\varphi_1, F\varphi_1, \varphi_1 U\varphi_2 \in L$*

It is assumed that the brute and normative language are mutually exclusive, more formally $L_b \cap L_n = \emptyset$.

The performance of external actions by agents changes the state of the environment. Brute effects specify how the organisation can advance in its computation by stating which brute facts are changed after the execution of the external action, i.e. they determine the brute effect of the action execution. The specific effect of performing an external action depends on the current state of the environment. A brute effect is thus a triple consisting of a pre-condition specifying when the action can be executed, the action name that is to be executed, and a post-condition listing the brute facts that hold after execution.

Definition 3 (brute effects). *Let ExtAct be the set of external actions and ComAct be the set of communicative actions an agent can perform. The set of brute effects $\mathcal{R}_b$ is defined in the following manner:*

$$\mathcal{R}_b = \{(p_1, \ldots, p_k) \, \beta \, (p_{k+1}, \ldots, p_n) \lfloor p_1, \ldots, p_n \in L_b \text{ and } \beta \in (ExtAct)\}$$

Normative rules are used to normatively assess the organisation. Recall that norms are expressed as elementary counts-as rules associating normative facts with a certain situation the organisation is in. This situation is described by the antecedent by means of a temporal formula ranging over brute and normative facts. The consequent then specifies which normative facts are to be associated with this situation.

Definition 4 (normative rules). *The set of normative rules $\mathcal{R}_n$ is defined as follows:*

$$\mathcal{R}_n = \{(\varphi_1, \ldots, \varphi_n) \Rightarrow (q_1, \ldots, q_m) \mid \varphi_1, \ldots, \varphi_n \in L \text{ and } q_1, \ldots, q_m \in L_n\}$$

It is possible that the system ends up in a less desirable state, for instance, because some agent violated a norm. Sanctioning rules can then be used to indicate the punishments that are imposed as consequence of this violation. This mechanism thus pertains to enforcement of the norms. It should be noted that the verdicts raised by the normative rules are not necessarily always of an unfavorable nature. Sanctions can thus either be positive (rewards) or negative (punishments). Just like normative rules, sanctioning rules have an antecedent and a consequent, with the antecedent referring to the normative judgment of a particular state and the consequent being the sanction that should be imposed.

Definition 5 (sanctioning rules). *The set of sanction rules $\mathcal{R}_s$ is defined as:*

$$\mathcal{R}_s = \{(q_1, \ldots, q_n) \Rightarrow (p_1, \ldots, p_m) \mid q_1, \ldots, q_n \in L_n \text{ and } p_1, \ldots, p_m \in L_b\}$$

Note that the antecedent of a sanctioning rule refers to the normative judgment about a state and can only contain normative facts. The intuitive meaning is that given a normative judgment of a certain state the consequent states the sanction in terms of brute facts that are to be imposed on this state.

In the following, for each normative or sanctioning rule r we refer to its condition by $cond(r)$, and to its consequence by $cons(r)$.

3.2   Semantics of Programming Language

Having defined the syntax for specifying an organisation, next we define the operational semantics by means of a transition system [21]. Each transition corresponds to a single computation step describing the transformation of one configuration (program state) into another. Before defining the notion of organisational configuration, we first define the notion of organisational state and history and some necessary functions operating on them.

As explained before, an organisation is characterised by brute facts and normative facts. An organisational state, describing the state of the organisation at a certain moment, is therefore defined as a tuple consisting of a set of brute and a set of normative facts. Seeing that the organisational state evolves due to the execution of actions by agents, and the application of normative and sanctioning rules, we define a consistency preserving operator for updating the organisational state.

Definition 6 (organisational state). *Given a consistent set of brute facts* $\mathcal{B} \subseteq L_b$ *and a consistent set of normative facts* $\mathcal{N} \subseteq L_n$, *an organisational state* Ω *is defined as a tuple* $\langle \mathcal{B}, \mathcal{N} \rangle$.

Further let $\overline{X}$, *the complement of a set of (brute or normative) facts* X *be the set* $\{\phi \mid -\phi \in X\} \cup \{-\phi \mid \phi \in X\}$, *then the functions* $\oplus_b$ *and* $\oplus_n$ *for updating an organisational state are defined as:*

$$\langle \mathcal{B}, \mathcal{N} \rangle \oplus_b X_b = \langle X_b \cup \{\mathcal{B} \setminus \overline{X}_b\}, \mathcal{N} \rangle$$
$$\langle \mathcal{B}, \mathcal{N} \rangle \oplus_n X_n = \langle \mathcal{B}, X_n \cup \{\mathcal{N} \setminus \overline{X}_n\} \rangle$$

The performance of actions by agents changes the organisational state. The brute effects are used in determining the effects of external action performance. Not only external actions change the organisational state, however. For example, when an agent i performs an **enact** action the agent has enacted a role ρ, which is being modelled by the normative fact $\text{rea}(i, \rho)$. Given an organisational state, an action and an agent i, we define the effects function *effect* in order to determine the new organisational state as a consequence of the performance of the action by agent i.

Definition 7 (effects function). *Given brute effect* $b = (\Phi \; \alpha \; \Psi)$, *organisational states* $\Omega = \langle \mathcal{B}, \mathcal{N} \rangle$ *and* $\Omega' = \langle \mathcal{B}', \mathcal{N}' \rangle$ *such that* $\mathcal{B}' = \mathcal{B} \setminus \{\text{done}(i, \beta) \mid \beta \in Act\}$ *and such that* $\mathcal{N}' = \{\text{rea}(i, \rho) \mid \text{rea}(i, \rho) \in \mathcal{N}\}$, *functions* $effect(i, \beta, \Omega)$ *and* $effect(i, b, \Omega)$ *determine the effect of the performance of* β *or application of* b *(corresponding to performance of* α*) in organisational state* Ω *by agent* i:

$$
\begin{aligned}
effect(i, b, \Omega) &= \Omega' \oplus_b (\{\text{done}(i, \alpha)\} \cup \Psi) \\
effect(i, enact(\rho), \Omega) &= (\Omega' \oplus_b \{\text{done}(i, enact(\rho))\}) \oplus_n \{\text{rea}(i, \rho)\} \\
effect(i, deact(\rho), \Omega) &= (\Omega' \oplus_b \{\text{done}(i, deact(\rho))\}) \oplus_n \{-\text{rea}(i, \rho)\} \\
effect(i, \gamma_j, \Omega) &= \Omega' \oplus_b \{\text{done}(i, \gamma_j)\}
\end{aligned}
$$

After the performance of each action, the brute state is updated with the fact that the agent has performed that action. In particular, the fact $\text{done}(i, \beta)$ is designed to mean that the previous state has been transformed in a new state, *because* agent i has just performed action β. Therefore any previous **done** fact is removed from $\mathcal{B}$. As we shall see later on, only one agent can perform an action per computation step, conforming to an interleaved action execution strategy.

In each state the brute facts change as a result of the agents' actions, leading to a new state. Normative facts directly depend on the current situation of the system, i.e. a normative assessment needs to be done for each newly reached state. Therefore, in determining the effects of an action, all normative facts of the preceding state ($\mathcal{N}$) are removed in the subsequent state ($\mathcal{N}'$), such that this fresh state can be normatively assessed after the brute effects have been determined. Note that the **rea** propositions are not removed, because once an agent has enacted a role it will keep doing so until it performs a deact.

Recall that with the norms of the organisation we cannot only reason about the present situation, but can also reason about things that happened in the past. Therefore, we also need to remember the situations that occurred in the past, and introduce the concept of an organisational history.

Definition 8 (organisational history). *An (organisational) history σ is defined as a finite trace $\Omega_0 \Omega_1 \cdots \Omega_n$ with $\Omega_i = \langle \mathcal{B}_i, \mathcal{N}_i \rangle$ being an organisational state for all $i \leq n$. The concatenation operator $\circ$ on traces is defined in the usual way. Moreover, given a history $\sigma = \Omega_0 \Omega_1 \cdots \Omega_i \cdots \Omega_n$, the suffix of σ from i, denoted as (σ, i), is defined as the history $\Omega_i \cdots \Omega_n$.*

To illustrate the intuitive meaning of a history, consider an organsitational history $\Omega_0 \cdots \Omega_n$. Then the first state Ω_0 models the initial state of the organisation. The last state Ω_n then models the most recent state that has been reached due to the performance of an action by some agent. In case a new action is performed by an agent, a new state Ω_{n+1} is added, denoting the new organisational history as consequence of carrying out this action. The whole trace $\Omega_0 \cdots \Omega_n$ thus models the present and the past of the organisation at a certain moment. We emphasise that we use histories as snapshots pertaining to the execution thus far, and not so much as possible executions such traces usually pertain to.

The satisfaction relation $\models$ is defined on such organisational histories, making it slightly different from the standard satisfaction relation for PLTL. Firstly, in contrast to the traces on which PLTL formulae are evaluated an organisational history is finite. Secondly, the states a trace is composed of now consist of a tuple of sets of propositions instead of a single set. Since norms often refer to the current situation, the macro *now* is defined to facilitate the notation.

Definition 9 (logical entailment). *Let $\varphi, \psi \in L$ and let $p \in L_b$ and $q \in L_n$. Also let σ be a history of length $n + 1$ with $\Omega_i = \langle \mathcal{B}_i, \mathcal{N}_i \rangle$ for each $0 \leq i \leq n$. Then the entailment relation $\models$ w.r.t. trace σ is defined as:*

1) $(\sigma, i) \models (-)p$ iff $(-)p \in \mathcal{B}_i$

2) $(\sigma, i) \models (-)q$ iff $(-)q \in \mathcal{N}_i$

3) $(\sigma, i) \models \neg\varphi$ iff $(\sigma, i) \not\models \varphi$

4) $(\sigma, i) \models \varphi_1 \wedge \varphi_2$ iff $(\sigma, i) \models \varphi_1$ *and* $(\sigma, i) \models \varphi_2$

5) $(\sigma, i) \models X\varphi$ iff $i < n$ *and* $(\sigma, i+1) \models \varphi$

6) $(\sigma, i) \models \varphi_1 U \varphi_2$ iff $\exists j \geq i. \, ((\sigma, j) \models \varphi_2$ *and* $(\forall i \leq k < j. \, (\sigma, k) \models \varphi_1))$

The auxiliary operators F *and* G *are defined in terms of the already existing operators, such that* $F\varphi \equiv \top U\varphi$ *and* $G\varphi \equiv \neg F\neg\varphi$. *Further the macro now for discerning the last state of a trace is defined as:* $now(\varphi) \equiv F(\varphi \wedge X\bot)$

Each organisational state Ω that has just been reached needs to be assessed by the normative rules, and sanctions need to be imposed accordingly. This is a matter of adding the consequences of the (normative or sanctioning) rules of which the premises is satisfied to Ω. For this purpose, we define the applicability of rules given a certain history, and the closure of a last state of a history under a set of rules (being either normative or sanctioning rules). As the premises of a normative rule is a temporal formula, it needs to be evaluated on the whole history Ω is part of. The premises of sanctioning rules, on the other hand, refers to the assessment of the most recent state and needs to be evaluated on Ω.

Definition 10 (applicable rules and closure under rules). *Given a set of rules* R *(either* R_n *or* R_s*) and a trace* $\sigma = \Omega_0\Omega_1\cdots\Omega_{n-1}\Omega_n$, *the set of applicable rules w.r.t.* σ *is defined as:*

$$Appl(R_n, \sigma) = \{r \mid r \in R_n \text{ and } (\sigma, 0) \models cond(r)\}$$
$$Appl(R_s, \sigma) = \{r \mid r \in R_s \text{ and } (\sigma, n) \models cond(r)\}$$

Let $\oplus$ *be either* $\oplus_b$ *or* $\oplus_n$ *and let*

$$Cl_0^R(\sigma, \Omega_n, \oplus) = \Omega_n \oplus \left(\bigcup\nolimits_{r \in Appl(R,\sigma)} cons(r)\right)$$
$$Cl_{k+1}^R(\sigma, \Omega_n, \oplus) = \Omega_n' \oplus \left(\bigcup\nolimits_{r \in Appl(R,\Omega_0\Omega_1\cdots\Omega_{n-1}\circ\Omega_n')} cons(r)\right)$$
$$\text{s.t. } \Omega_n' = Cl_k^R(\sigma, \Omega_n, \oplus)$$

then the closure of Ω_n *under* R *is defined as* $Cl_k^R(\sigma, \Omega_n, \oplus)$ *for the minimal* k *such that* $Cl_{k+1}^R(\sigma, \Omega_n, \oplus) = Cl_k^R(\sigma, \Omega_n, \oplus)$.

It should be noted that such a closure only exists under certain conditions for the set of rules R (see [13] for what these conditions are).

Having defined all the necessary ingredients for defining the transition rules, we are now able to define the organisational configuration. An organisational configuration is a tuple composed of a set of agents that act in the organisation and a history, modelling the situation of the organisation.

Definition 11 (organisational configuration). *Let* $\mathcal{A} = \{A_1, \ldots, A_n\}$ *be the set of agents with each* A_i *the configuration of individual agent* i, *and let* σ *be an organizational trace. The configuration of an organization is defined as* $\langle \mathcal{A}, \sigma \rangle$.

Before defining the transition rules specifying how one organisational configuration can evolve into another, we first define possible transitions individual agents can make, without making any assumptions about their configuration.

Definition 12 (agent transitions). *The agent transitions are defined as:*

$$\text{ACT}_s : A_i \xrightarrow{\beta} A_i' \qquad \text{SEND}_s : A_i \xrightarrow{\gamma_j!} A_i' \qquad \text{REC}_s : A_i \xrightarrow{\gamma_i?} A_i'$$

Transition ACT_s states that an individual agent is capable of performing external actions, role enactment and deactment. Transition $SEND_s$ indicates that agents can always perform communicative acts, and REC_s indicates that the agent can always receive communicative acts sent by other agents.

The actual effect of individual agents' actions is determined by the organisation. The transition rules at the multi-agent level are therefore defined in terms of the single agent transitions, and define what it means to execute an action in the organisation. In particular, the transitions rules defined below specify what happens at the multi-agent level when an agent performs an external action (EXT_m), a deact or an enact (ROL_m), and a communicative action (COM_m). For an external action to be executed the pre-condition of the brute effect specifying the effect should be satisfied by the current state of the organisation. Moreover, the execution of a communicative action synchronises the sender and receiver.

The detection and sanctioning mechanism as discussed in section 2 is the same for all three types of actions. To start with a new state Ω as result of the action execution is determined by means of the effects function. The new situation of the organisation is normatively assessed by closing off the former history σ with Ω appended as last state under the normative rules. State Ω' is the result of this assessment. The sanctions that need to be imposed are determined similarly, that is by closing off Ω' under the sanctioning rules, resulting in Ω''. State Ω'' thus corresponds to the normatively assessed state with sanctions imposed accordingly, the organisation would reach after performance of the action.

Whether the action to be performed is tolerated depends on the normative judgment. That is to say, when Ω'' entails $\mathtt{viol}_\perp$, this means that the organisation would end up in a strongly forbidden situation. In this case the action is blocked, conforming to regimentation. If this is not the case, the organisation can advance in its computation; the history is updated with the new agent configurations and newly reached state Ω''. It should thus be noted that both enforcement and regimentation are captured in each of these separate transitions.

Definition 13 (multi-agent transitions). *Let R_n be the set of normative rules, R_s the set of sanctioning rules, $\alpha \in ExtAct$, $\beta \in \{enact(\rho), deact(\rho)\}$, $\gamma_j \in ComAct$, $b = (\Phi \, \alpha \, \Psi)$ s.t. $b \in \mathcal{R}_b$, and let $\langle \mathcal{A}, \sigma \rangle$ be a multi-agent system with $\sigma = \Omega_0 \ldots \Omega_n$. The multi-agent transitions are defined as:*

$$EXT_m : \frac{\begin{array}{c} A_i \xrightarrow{\alpha} A_i' \quad \Omega_n \models \Phi \quad \Omega = effect(i, b, \Omega_n) \\ \Omega' = Cl^{R_n}(\sigma \circ \Omega, \Omega, \oplus_n) \quad \Omega'' = Cl^{R_s}(\sigma \circ \Omega', \Omega', \oplus_b) \\ (\sigma \circ \Omega'', n+1) \not\models \mathtt{viol}_\perp \end{array}}{\langle \mathcal{A}, \sigma \rangle \longrightarrow \langle (\mathcal{A} \setminus \{A_i\}) \cup \{A_i'\}, \sigma \circ \Omega'' \rangle}$$

$$ROL_m : \frac{\begin{array}{c} A_i \xrightarrow{\beta} A_i' \quad \Omega = effect(i, \beta, \Omega_n) \\ \Omega' = Cl^{R_n}(\sigma \circ \Omega, \Omega, \oplus_n) \quad \Omega'' = Cl^{R_s}(\sigma \circ \Omega', \Omega', \oplus_b) \\ (\sigma \circ \Omega'', n+1) \not\models \mathtt{viol}_\perp \end{array}}{\langle \mathcal{A}, \sigma \rangle \longrightarrow \langle (\mathcal{A} \setminus \{A_i\}) \cup \{A_i'\}, \sigma \circ \Omega'' \rangle}$$

$$A_i \xrightarrow{\gamma_j !} A'_i \quad A_j \xrightarrow{\gamma_j ?} A'_j \quad \Omega = \mathit{effect}(i, \gamma_j, \Omega_n)$$
$$\Omega' = Cl^{R_n}(\sigma \circ \Omega, \Omega, \oplus_n) \quad \Omega'' = Cl^{R_s}(\sigma \circ \Omega', \Omega', \oplus_b)$$

$$\text{COM}_m : \frac{(\sigma \circ \Omega'', n+1) \not\models \texttt{viol}_\perp}{\langle \mathcal{A}, \sigma \rangle \longrightarrow \langle (\mathcal{A} \setminus \{A_i, A_j\}) \cup \{A'_i, A'_j\}, \sigma \circ \Omega'' \rangle}$$

Recall that, due to the construction of the effects function (Def. 7) the performance of a communicative action, deact and enact does not change the brute facts of the system except for the addition of the **done** proposition. Tolerated execution of an enact or deact leads to the addition or deletion of a *rea* proposition in the normative facts, such that it is remembered that the agent has or has not enacted a certain role.

4 Implementing Multi-agent Organisations

In this section we show by example how the normative multi-agent organisation programming language can be used to implement multi-agent organisations. To provide a broader view on the intended application area for our language, we do not limit ourselves to the toy example of the railway system.

In the railway simulation agents can be at the platform (being expressed as at_platform) or in the train (being expressed as in_train). If the agent is at the platform and not in the train, she can enter the train by performing an **embark** action, of which the result is that the agent is in the train and not at the platform anymore. The external actions agents can perform to change the environment are expressed by brute effects. Consider, for example, the brute effect of the **embark** action:

$$(\texttt{at\_platform}(i), -\texttt{in\_train}(i)) \ \texttt{embark} \ (-\texttt{at\_platform}(i), \texttt{in\_train}(i))$$

The railway regulations state the rules of behaviour the travellers ought to follow and are expressed by means of the normative rules. Suppose, for example, that passengers are obliged to buy a ticket before entering on the platform. Violating this norm is not considered to be a serious violation and the sanction is a fine of 10 credits. Being in the train without a ticket, however, is a more serious violation of which the sanction is a fine of 50 credits. In our approach these two rules of conduct can be expressed by the normative rules:

$$now(\texttt{at\_platform}(i) \wedge -\texttt{ticket}(i)) \Rightarrow \texttt{viol}^{tp}(i)$$
$$now(\texttt{in\_train}(i) \wedge -\texttt{ticket}(i)) \quad \Rightarrow \texttt{viol}^{tt}(i)$$

Recall that *now* is used to discern the last organisational state of a history. The above rules thus have the intuitive reading: "currently being at the platform (or in the train, respectively) without a ticket counts as a violation". Note the usage of labels *tp* (ticket platform) and *tt* (ticket train) on the violation propositions to match a violation with the norm that has been violated. They are used to discriminate from different violations in defining the sanctioning rules:

$$(\text{viol}^{tp}(i)) \;\Rightarrow\; \text{fined10}(i)$$
$$(\text{viol}^{tt}(i)) \;\Rightarrow\; \text{fined50}(i)$$

The norms defined above concern enforcement. To illustrate regimentation, suppose that the railway system allows passengers to violate the norm of travelling with a ticket only once. In other words, if a passenger has been caught travelling without a ticket in the past, then travelling without a ticket for the second time is regimented. This is expressed by means of a normative rule as:

$$F(\text{viol}^{tt}(i) \wedge XF(\text{in\_train}(i) \wedge -\text{ticket}(i))) \;\Rightarrow\; \text{viol}_{\perp}$$

Transition rule EXT_m ensures that the organisation will never end up in this situation, because all actions that will lead to $\text{viol}_{\perp}$ are blocked. Intuitively, this can be thought of as placing a gate just in front of the entrance of the train that will remain closed in case a passenger tries to embark without a ticket for the second time, making it physically impossible for the agent to enter. Note that since states that are marked by $\text{viol}_{\perp}$ will never be reached, no sanctions for $\text{viol}_{\perp}$ need to be defined.

To also show how a more complex norm of a temporal nature can be expressed in our normative language, suppose that passengers no longer need to buy a ticket before entering the train, but now should buy their ticket during their train ride. This norm can be expressed as a normative rule in the following manner:

$$F(\text{in\_train}(i) \wedge -\text{ticket}(i)U(-\text{in\_train}(i) \wedge X\perp)) \;\Rightarrow\; \text{viol}^{tt}(i)$$

intuitively meaning that agent i is committing an offence when she has not been in possession of a ticket until she got off the train. Note that due to the usage of $X\perp$ this violation is detected at the very moment the agent leaves the train.

Hitherto the focus has been on programming the normative elements of multi-agent organisations. As already mentioned, an organisation encompasses more than only normative elements. The $rea(i, \rho)$ propositions were merely used to denote the fact that agent i has enacted role ρ, and have not played a very significant part thus far. However, in combination with the normative aspects already some structural aspects of an organisation can be expressed.

As already mentioned in section 2, norms are often associated with a certain role. Consider, for example, a conference management system. Usually, for an agent playing the role of program chair other norms are in effect than for an agent playing the role of author. Then, in our approach a role somehow becomes a means of modularising the normative rules. To illustrate, consider the following normative rule:

$$now(\text{rea}(i, \text{author}) \wedge \text{registration\_closed} \wedge \text{done}(i, \text{register})) \;\Rightarrow\; \text{viol}^{reg}$$

expressing that an agent playing the role of author can still register for the conference even if the registration has already been closed. The possible sanction could then be a higher entrance fee. The antecedent of this normative rule will only be satisfied if agent i has currently enacted the role of author, and is thus only in effect for authors. Note that this normative rule refers to a concrete action instead of a declarative description of the organisation as was the case in the norms before. Of course, the inverse of this approach, stating that a certain norm is applicable for all roles except a certain role could also be taken. To express, for example, that agents not playing the role of author cannot register after the registration has been closed, is to write:

$$now(-\mathtt{rea}(i, \mathtt{author}) \wedge \mathtt{registration\_closed} \wedge \mathtt{done}(i, \mathtt{register})) \Rightarrow \mathtt{viol}_\bot$$

At the structural level of an organisation it is often specified which roles are (in)compatible with each other. If two roles are denoted as incompatible this means that these two roles cannot be played by one and the same agent. For example, in the conference management system it might not be allowed for a reviewer to be an author. In our normative multi-agent programming language this can be expressed as:

$$\mathrm{F}(\mathtt{rea}(i, \mathtt{reviewer}) \wedge \mathtt{rea}(i, \mathtt{author})) \Rightarrow \mathtt{viol}_\bot$$

5 Conclusion and Future Work

In this paper we have presented the syntax and operational semantics of a programming language for implementing norm-based multi-agent organisations. These organisations are then developed as a separate entity apart from the agents that will interact with the organisation. In particular, the presented programming language allows for the implementation of a multi-agent organisation by means of norms, being enforced by monitoring, regimenting and sanctioning mechanisms. More specifically, the programming language allows for the expression of more abstract, declarative ought-to-be norms and also allows to refer to concrete actions that have been performed by agents. Although this programming language mainly deals with the normative aspect of an organisation, already some preliminary results were shown of how to deal with the structural aspect of an organisation.

Our ultimate goal is to design a fully-fledged multi-agent programming language based on organisational concepts. The current proposal presented in this paper primarily deals with the normative aspect of multi-agent organisations. Future work aims at extending the programming language with constructs to also support the implementation of the other aspects of multi-agent organisations as mentioned in section 2. In particular, one of our short-term goals is to extend the simple view on roles presented in this paper with a view on roles that better reflects roles as used in multi-agent design methodologies. To what extend norms can be used to ensure well-formedness of the structural specification of the organisation as explored in section 4 should also be further investigated.

Another important issue is that in this paper the architecture is a centralised one. That is to say, the organisation determines the effect agent's actions have on the environment. For the sake of scalability, future research should explore possibilites of decentralising the organisation.

Further, we also aim at incorporating more complex forms of enforcement (e.g., policing agents) and norm types (norms with deadlines, for example). Also the computational cost of the constructs presented should be investigated.

Acknowledgments

This research was supported by the CoCoMAS project funded through the Dutch Organization for Scientific Research (NWO). The authors are grateful for the valuable suggestions, comments, and contributions provided by Davide Grossi.

References

1. Sierra, C., Rodríguez-Aguilar, J., Noriega, P., Esteva, M., Arcos, J.L.: Engineering multi-agent systems as electronic institutions. UPGrade 4 (2004)
2. Zambonelli, F., Jennings, N., Wooldridge, M.: Organisational rules as an abstraction for the analysis and design of multi-agent systems. IJSEKE 11(3), 303–328 (2001)
3. Zambonelli, F., Jennings, N., Wooldridge, M.: Developing multiagent systems: the GAIA methodology. Acm Tosem 12(3), 317–370 (2003)
4. Dignum, V.: A Model for Organizational Interaction: Based on Agents, Founded in Logic. SIKS Dissertation Series (2003)
5. Hübner, J., Sichman, J., Boissier, O.: Developing organised multi-agent systems using the $\mathcal{M}$oise$^+$ model: Programming issues at the system and agent levels (manuscript)
6. Esteva, M., Rodríguez-Aguilar, J., Sierra, C., Garcia, P., Arcos, J.: On the formal specifications of electronic institutions. In: Agent Mediated Electronic Commerce, The European AgentLink Perspective, pp. 126–147. Springer, London (2001)
7. Ferber, J., Gutknecht, O., Michel, F.: From agents to organizations: an organizational view of multi-agent systems. In: AOSE IV, pp. 214–230 (2004)
8. Esteva, M., Rodríguez-Aguilar, J., Rosell, B., Arcos, J.: Ameli: An agent-based middleware for electronic institutions. In: Kudenko, D., Kazakov, D., Alonso, E. (eds.) AAMAS 2004. LNCS, vol. 3394. Springer, Heidelberg (2005)
9. Watt, D.A.: Programming Language Design Concepts. John Wiley & Sons, Chichester (2004)
10. Dignum, F.: Abstract norms and electronic institutions. In: Proc. of RASTA 2002, Bologna, Italy, pp. 93–104 (2002)
11. Aldewereld, H.: Autonomy vs. Conformity - an Institutional Perspective on Norms and Protocols. PhD Thesis, Universiteit Utrecht (2007)
12. Ricci, A., Viroli, M., Omicini, A.: Give agents their artifacts: the A&A approach for engineering working environments in MAS. In: Proc. of AAMAS 2007, pp. 1–3. ACM Press, New York (2007)
13. Dastani, M., Grossi, D., Tinnemeier, N., Meyer, J.J.: A programming language for normative multi-agent systems (in submission)
14. Meyer, J.J.C., Wieringa, R.J. (eds.): Deontic logic in computer science: normative system specification. John Wiley & Sons, Inc., New York (1994)
15. Grossi, D.: Designing Invisible Handcuffs. Formal Investigations in Institutions and Organizations for MAS. PhD thesis, Utrecht University, SIKS (2007)
16. Searle, J.: The Construction of Social Reality. Free Press (1995)

17. Castelfranchi, C.: Formalizing the informal?: Dynamic social order, bottom-up social control, and spontaneous normative relations. Journal of Applied Logic 1(1-2), 47–92 (2004)
18. Coutinho, L., Sichman, J., Boissier, O.: Modeling organization in mas: A comparison of models. In: Proc. of SEAS 2005, Uberlândia, Brazil (2005)
19. Odell, J., Parunak, H.V.D., Fleischer, M.: The role of roles in designing effective agent organizations. In: Software Engineering for Large-Scale Multi-Agent Systems, Research Issues and Practical Applications, pp. 27–38 (2003)
20. Emerson, E.: Temporal and modal logic. In: Handbook of Theoretical Computer Science, Formal Models and Semantics, Volume B, pp. 995–1072. MIT Press, Cambridge (1990)
21. Plotkin, G.D.: A structural approach to operational semantics. Technical Report DAIMI FN-19, University of Aarhus (1981)

Jazzyk: A Programming Language for Hybrid Agents with Heterogeneous Knowledge Representations

Peter Novák

Department of Informatics
Clausthal University of Technology
Julius-Albert-Str. 4, D-38678 Clausthal-Zellerfeld, Germany
peter.novak@tu-clausthal.de

Abstract. Different knowledge representation tasks require different knowledge representation techniques. Agent designers should therefore be able to easily exploit benefits of various knowledge representation technologies in a single agent system.

I describe here a modular agent programming language *Jazzyk* based on the programming framework of *Behavioural State Machines* (*BSM*). *BSM* framework, and thus also *Jazzyk*, draws a strict distinction between a knowledge representational and a behavioural level of an agent program. It supports a high degree of modularity w.r.t. employed KR technologies, and at the same time provides a clear and concise semantics.

1 Motivation

No single knowledge representation (KR) technology offers a range of capabilities and features required for different application domains and environments agents operate in. For instance, purely declarative KR technologies offer a great power for reasoning about relationships between static aspects of an environment, like e.g. properties of objects. However, they are not suitable for representation of topological, arithmetical, or geographical information. Similarly, a relational database is appropriate for representation of large amounts of searchable tuples, but it does not cope well with representing exceptions and default reasoning. Hence, an important pragmatic requirement on a general purpose AOP framework is *an ability to integrate heterogeneous KR technologies* within a single agent system. An agent programming framework should not commit to a single KR technology. The choice of an appropriate KR approach should be left to an agent designer and the framework should be *modular* enough to accommodate a large range of KR techniques, while at the same time providing flexible means to encode agent's behaviours.

I recently proposed a framework of *Behavioural State Machines* (*BSM*) [13,12], a general purpose computational model based on the Gurevich's *Abstract State Machines* [4], adapted to the context of agent oriented programming. The *BSM* framework is a culmination of our previous efforts ([14] and [15]) to propose a solid

K.V. Hindriks, A. Pokahr, and S. Sardina (Eds.): ProMAS 2008, LNAI 5442, pp. 72–87, 2009.

theoretical basis for a lightweight, yet highly modular agent programming language. It treats heterogeneous knowledge bases of an agents on a par, i.e. does not prefer one over another thus allowing programmers to exploit strengths of various KR approaches in an agent system.

The main purpose of this paper is to describe *Jazzyk* (Section 3), a programming language based on the theoretical framework of *Behavioural State Machines* (Section 2), together with details of its implemented interpreter. Development of the *BSM* framework is an application driven research, therefore I furthermore provide a sketch of *Jazzbot* (Section 4), a case study demo application implemented in *Jazzyk*. The paper concludes with a discussion of *Jazzyk* (Section 5), related work and future development of this line of research (Section 6).

2   Behavioural State Machines

Before introducing the details of *Jazzyk*, first I briefly introduce its theoretical basis: the framework of *Behavioural State Machines (BSM)*. *Behavioural State Machine* computational model is heavily inspired by the Gurevich's *Abstract State Machines* [4] framework.

The underlying abstraction is that of a transition system, similar to that used in most logic based state-of-the-art BDI agent programming languages *AgentSpeak(L)/Jason*, *3APL*, or *GOAL* [2,6]. States are agent's mental states, i.e. collections of agent's partial knowledge bases, or *KR modules*. The state of the environment is treated as a KR module as well. Transitions between the agent's mental states are induced by *mental state transformers* (atomic updates of mental states). An agent system semantics is, in operational terms, a set of all enabled paths within the transition system, the agent can traverse during its lifetime. To facilitate modularity and program decomposition, *BSM* provides also a functional view on an agent program, specifying a set of enabled transitions an agent can execute in a given situation.

Behavioural State Machines draw a strict distinction between the *knowledge representational layer* of an agent and its *behavioural layer*. To exploit strengths of various KR technologies, the KR layer is kept abstract and open, so that it is possible to plug-in different heterogeneous KR modules as agent's knowledge bases. The main focus of *BSM* computational model is the highest level of control of an agent: its *behaviours*.

I introduced *BSM* framework in [12] and [13], therefore some technical details are omitted here and I mainly focus on a description of the most fundamental issues. Moreover, the Subsection 2.2 introduces a reformulated version of the original *BSM* semantics equivalent to the one originally published in [12] and [13].

2.1   Syntax

A BSM agent consists of a set of partial knowledge bases handled by so called *KR modules*. A KR module is supposed to store agent's knowledge e.g. about its environment, itself, or other agents, or to handle its internal mental attitudes relevant to keep track of its goals, intentions, obligations, etc. However, because of the openness of the BSM architecture, no specific structure of an agent is prescribed and thus the overall number and ascribed purpose of particular KR modules is kept abstract. The formal definitions capture only their fundamental characteristics.

A KR module has to provide a language of query and update formulae and two sets of interfaces: *query* operators for querying the knowledge base and *update* operators to modify it.

Definition 1. (KR module) *A knowledge representation module* $\mathcal{M} = (\mathcal{S}, \mathcal{L}, \mathcal{Q}, \mathcal{U})$ *is characterized by*

- *a set of states* $\mathcal{S}$,
- *a knowledge representation language* $\mathcal{L}$, *defined over some domains* $\mathcal{D}_1, \ldots, \mathcal{D}_n$ *(with* $n \geq 0$*) and variables over these domains.* $\underline{\mathcal{L}} \subseteq \mathcal{L}$ *denotes a fragment of* $\mathcal{L}$ *including only ground formulae, i.e. such that do not include variables,*
- *a set of query operators* $\mathcal{Q}$. *A query operator* $\models \in \mathcal{Q}$ *is a mapping* $\models: \mathcal{S} \times \underline{\mathcal{L}} \to \{\top, \bot\}$,
- *a set of update operators* $\mathcal{U}$. *An update operator* $\oplus \in \mathcal{U}$ *is a mapping* $\oplus: \mathcal{S} \times \underline{\mathcal{L}} \to \mathcal{S}$.

KR languages are compatible on a shared domain $\mathcal{D}$, *when they both include variables over* $\mathcal{D}$ *and their sets of query and update operators are mutually disjoint. KR modules with compatible KR languages are compatible as well.*

From the definition we have, that a KR language not including variables is compatible with any other KR language.

Each query and update operator has an associated identifier. For simplicity, these are not included in the definition, however I use them throughout the text. When used as an identifier in a syntactic expression, I use informal prefix notation (e.g. $\models \varphi$, or $\oplus\varphi$), while when used as a semantic operator, formally correct infix notation is used (e.g. $\sigma \models \varphi$, or $\sigma \oplus \varphi$). Additionally, when the evaluation of a query formula φ by a query operator $\models$ on a state σ results in $\top$, i.e. $(\sigma \models \varphi) = \top$, we simply write $\sigma \models \varphi$, otherwise when $(\sigma \models \varphi) = \bot$, we use notation $\sigma \not\models \varphi$.

Query formulae are the syntactical means to retrieve information from KR modules:

Definition 2. (query) *Let* $\mathcal{M}_1, \ldots, \mathcal{M}_n$ *be a set of compatible KR modules. Query formulae are inductively defined:*

- *if* $\varphi \in \mathcal{L}_i$, *and* $\models \in \mathcal{U}_i$ *corresponding to some* $\mathcal{M}_i$, *then* $\models \varphi$ *is a query formula,*
- *if* ϕ_1, ϕ_2 *are query formulae, so are* $\phi_1 \wedge \phi_2$, $\phi_1 \vee \phi_2$ *and* $\neg\phi_1$.

The informal semantics is straightforward: if a ground language expression $\varphi \in \underline{\mathcal{L}}$ is evaluated to true by a corresponding query operator $\models$ w.r.t. a state of the corresponding KR module, then $\models \varphi$ is true in the agent's mental state as well. Note, that non-ground formulae have to be first ground before their evaluation (Subsection 2.2).

Subsequently, I define *mental state transformer*, the principal syntactic construction of *BSM* framework.

Definition 3. *(mental state transformer) Let $\mathcal{M}_1, \ldots, \mathcal{M}_n$ be a set of compatible KR modules. Mental state transformer expression (mst) is inductively defined:*

1. **skip** *is a mst (primitive),*
2. *if $\oplus \in \mathcal{U}_i$ and $\psi \in \mathcal{L}_i$ corresponding to some $\mathcal{M}_i$, then $\oplus\psi$ is a mst (primitive),*
3. *if ϕ is a query expression, and τ is a mst, then $\phi \longrightarrow \tau$ is a mst as well (conditional),*
4. *if τ and τ' are mst's, then $\tau|\tau'$ and $\tau \circ \tau'$ are mst's too (choice and sequence).*

An update expression is a primitive mst. The other three (conditional, sequence and non-deterministic choice) are compound mst's. Informally, a primitive mst is encoding a transition between two mental states, i.e. a primitive behaviour. Possibly labeled compound mst's introduce modularity and code re-use to the *BSM* framework. A standalone mental state transformer is also called an *agent program* over a set of KR modules $\mathcal{M}_1, \ldots, \mathcal{M}_n$.

A mental state transformer encodes an agent behaviour. I take a radical behaviourist viewpoint, i.e. also internal transitions are considered a behaviour. As the main task of an agent is to perform a behaviour, naturally an agent program is fully characterized by a single mst (agent program) and a set of associated KR modules used in it. *Behavioural State Machine $\mathcal{A} = (\mathcal{M}_1, \ldots, \mathcal{M}_n, \mathcal{P})$*, i.e. a collection of compatible agent KR modules and an associated agent program, completely characterizes an agent system $\mathcal{A}$.

2.2   Semantics

The underlying semantics of *BSM* is that of a transition system over agent's mental states.

Definition 4. *(state) Let $\mathcal{A}$ be a BSM over KR modules $\mathcal{M}_1, \ldots, \mathcal{M}_n$. A state of $\mathcal{A}$ is a tuple $\sigma = \langle \sigma_1, \ldots, \sigma_n \rangle$ of KR module states $\sigma_i \in \mathcal{S}_i$, corresponding to $\mathcal{M}_1, \ldots, \mathcal{M}_n$ respectively. $\mathfrak{S}$ denotes the space of all states over $\mathcal{A}$.*

$\sigma_1, \ldots, \sigma_n$ are partial states of σ. A state can be modified by applying primitive updates on it and query formulae can be evaluated against it. Query formulae cannot change the actual agent's mental state.

According to the Definition 1, to evaluate a formula in a state by query and update operators, the formula must be ground. Transformation of non-ground formulae to ground ones is provided by means of *variable substitution*. A variable substitution is a mapping $\theta : \mathcal{L} \to \underline{\mathcal{L}}$ replacing every occurrence of a variable in a KR language formula by a value from the corresponding domain. Variable substitution of a compound query formula is defined by usual means of nested substitution. Note however, that a variable can be substituted in sub-formulae of a compound formula only when languages of the corresponding sub-formulae share the domain of the variable in question. A variable substitution θ is *ground* w.r.t. ϕ, when the instantiation $\phi\theta$ is a ground formula.

Informally, a primitive ground formula is said to be true in a given *BSM* state w.r.t. a query operator, iff an execution of that operator on the state and the formula yields $\top$. The evaluation of compound query formulae inductively follows usual evaluation of nested logical formulae.

Notions of an *update* and *update set* are the bearers of the semantics of mental state transformers. An update of a mental state σ is a tuple $(\oplus, \psi)$, where $\oplus$ is an update operator and ψ is a ground update formula corresponding to some KR module. The syntactical notation of a sequence of mst's ∘ corresponds to a sequence of updates, or update sets, denoted by the semantic sequence operator •. Provided ρ_1 and ρ_2 are updates, also a sequence $\rho_1 • \rho_2$ is an update. Additionally, there is a special no-operation update **skip** corresponding to the primitive mst **skip**.

A simple update corresponds to semantics of a primitive mst. Sequence of updates corresponds to a sequence of primitive mst's and is a compound update itself. An update set is a set of updates and corresponds to a mst encoding a non-deterministic choice.

Given an update, or an update set, its application on a state of a *BSM* is straightforward. Formally:

Definition 5. *(applying an update)* *The result of applying an update* $\rho = (\oplus, \psi)$ *on a state* $\sigma = \langle \sigma_1, \ldots, \sigma_n \rangle$ *of a BSM* $\mathcal{A}$ *over KR modules* $\mathcal{M}_1, \ldots, \mathcal{M}_n$ *is a new state* $\sigma' = \sigma \oplus \rho$, *such that* $\sigma' = \langle \sigma_1, \ldots, \sigma_i', \ldots, \sigma_n \rangle$, *where* $\sigma_i' = \sigma_i \oplus \psi$, *and both* $\oplus \in \mathcal{U}_i$ *and* $\psi \in \mathcal{L}_i$ *correspond to some* $\mathcal{M}_i$ *of* $\mathcal{A}$. *Applying the empty update* **skip** *on the state* σ *does not change the state, i.e.* $\sigma \oplus$ **skip** $= \sigma$.

Inductively, the result of applying a sequence of updates $\rho_1 • \rho_2$ *is a new state* $\sigma'' = \sigma' \oplus \rho_2$, *where* $\sigma' = \sigma \oplus \rho_1$.

The meaning of a mental state transformer in state σ, formally defined by the *yields* predicate below, is the update set it yields in that mental state.

Definition 6 (yields calculus). *A mental state transformer* τ *yields an update* ρ *in a state* σ *under a variable substitution* θ, *iff* $yields(\tau, \sigma, \theta, \rho)$ *is derivable in the following calculus:*

$$\frac{\top}{yields(\mathbf{skip},\sigma,\theta,\mathbf{skip})} \quad \frac{\top}{yields(\oslash\psi,\sigma,\theta,(\oslash,\psi\theta))} \ \textit{(primitive)}$$

$$\frac{yields(\tau,\sigma,\theta,\rho),\ \sigma\models\phi\theta}{yields(\phi\longrightarrow\tau,\sigma,\theta,\rho)} \quad \frac{yields(\tau,\sigma,\theta,\rho),\ \sigma\not\models\phi\theta}{yields(\phi\longrightarrow\tau,\sigma,\theta,\mathbf{skip})} \ \textit{(conditional)}$$

$$\frac{yields(\tau_1,\sigma,\theta,\rho_1),\ yields(\tau_2,\sigma,\theta,\rho_2)}{yields(\tau_1|\tau_2,\sigma,\theta,\rho_1),\ yields(\tau_1|\tau_2,\sigma,\theta,\rho_2)} \ \textit{(choice)}$$

$$\frac{yields(\tau_1,\sigma,\theta,\rho_1),\ yields(\tau_2,\sigma \oplus \rho_1,\theta,\rho_2)}{yields(\tau_1\circ\tau_2,\sigma,\theta,\rho_1\bullet\rho_2)} \ \textit{(sequence)}$$

We say that τ yields an update set ν *in a state σ under a substitution θ iff* $\nu = \{\rho | yields(\tau, \sigma, \theta, \rho)\}$.

The mst **skip** yields the update **skip**. Provided a variable substitution θ, similarly, a primitive update mst $\oslash \psi$ yields the corresponding update $(\oslash, \psi\theta)$. In the case the condition of a conditional mst $\phi \longrightarrow \tau$ is satisfied in the current mental state, the calculus yields one of the updates corresponding to the right hand side mst τ, otherwise the no-operation **skip** update is yielded. A non-deterministic choice mst yields an update corresponding to either of its members and finally a sequential mst yields a sequence of updates corresponding to the first mst of the sequence and an update yielded by the second member of the sequence in a state resulting from application of the first update to the current mental state.

In the Definition 6 we assume that the variable substitution θ is ground w.r.t. all the formulae occurring in the considered mst τ.

The calculus defining the *yields* predicate provides a *functional view* on a mst and it is the primary means of compositional modularity in *BSM*. Mental state transformers encode functions yielding update sets over states of a *BSM*. The collection of all the updates yielded w.r.t. the Definition 6 comprises an update set of an agent program τ in the current mental state σ.

Finally, the operational semantics of an agent is defined in terms of all possible computation runs induced by a corresponding *Behavioural State Machine*.

Definition 7. *(BSM semantics) A BSM $\mathcal{A} = (\mathcal{M}_1, \ldots, \mathcal{M}_n, \mathcal{P})$ can make a step from state σ to a state σ' (induces a transition $\sigma \to \sigma'$), if there exists a ground variable substitution θ, s.t. the agent program $\mathcal{P}$ yields a non-empty update set ν in σ under θ and $\sigma' = \sigma \bigoplus \rho$, where $\rho \in \nu$ is an update.*

A possibly infinite sequence of states $\sigma_1, \ldots, \sigma_i, \ldots$ is a run of BSM $\mathcal{A}$, iff for each $i \geq 1$, $\mathcal{A}$ induces a transition $\sigma_i \to \sigma_{i+1}$.

The semantics of an agent system characterized by a BSM $\mathcal{A}$, is a set of all runs of $\mathcal{A}$.

Even though the introduced semantics of *Behavioural State Machines* speaks in operational terms of sequences of mental states, an agent can reach during its lifetime, the style of programming induced by the formalism of mental state transformers is rather declarative. Primitive query and update formulae are treated as black-box expressions by the introduced *BSM* formalism. On this high level of control, they rather encode *what* and *when* should be executed, while the issue of *how* is left to the underlying KR module. I.e., *agent's deliberation abilities reside in its KR modules, while its behaviours are encoded as a BSM.*

Figure 1 lists a pseudocode of the abstract interpreter cycle straightforwardly following from the introduced BSM semantics. In a single deliberation cycle 1) the agent program interpreter computes the update set ν corresponding to the agent program $\mathcal{P}$ according to the Definition 6, 2) non-deterministically chooses an update ρ from ν, and finally 3) updates the current mental state by applying the update ρ to it. Under $\_$ in the $yield(\ldots)$, we denote a substitution of the set of all the free variables used in the encoding of the agent program $\mathcal{P}$.

Algorithm 1. Abstract *BSM* interpreter
input: agent program $\mathcal{P}$, initial mental state state σ_0

$\sigma = \sigma_0$
loop
   compute $\nu = \{\rho | yields(\mathcal{P}, \sigma, \_, \rho)\}$
   if $\nu \neq \emptyset$ **then**
      non-deterministically choose $\rho \in \nu$
      $\sigma = \sigma \oplus \rho$
   end if
end loop

Additionally, the non-deterministic choice of the abstract *BSM* interpreter fulfils the *weak fairness condition*, similar to that in [11], for all the induced runs.

Condition 1 (weak fairness condition). *A computation run is weakly fair if it is not the case that an update is always yielded from some point in time on but is never selected for execution.*

The *BSM* framework assumes that the mental state of an agent, including its environment, changes only between the single executions of the deliberation cycle. Therefore in order to implement agile agents which act in their environments reasonably quickly w.r.t. the speed of change of the environment, the query and update operators should be computable procedures invocations of which shouldn't take too long w.r.t. the application domain.

3   Jazzyk, the Language and Interpreter

In order to practically test the *BSM* approach to programming agent systems, I designed and implemented a programming language *Jazzyk* and an interpreter for it. *Jazzyk* closely follows the *BSM* framework, i.e. 1) the syntax allows for one to one encoding of mental state transformers in the language and 2) the interpreter closely follows the *BSM* semantics with only minor discrepancies aimed at making the interpreting of programs more efficient. The syntax and the precise *Jazzyk* interpreter semantics, as well as all deviations from the formal semantics are discussed in this section. Finally I also briefly sketch technical details of the *Jazzyk* interpreter implementation.

3.1   Syntax

Figure 1 lists the EBNF of *Jazzyk*, which straightforwardly follows from the syntax of *BSM* introduced in Subsection 2.

According to the BSM syntax, a *Jazzyk* program is a mental state transformer. However to allow for such programs, few technical issues have to be handled as well. The KR modules have to be declared and subsequently bound to the

```
program        ::= (statement)*
statement      ::= module_decl | module_notify | mst

module_decl    ::= 'declare' 'module' <moduleId> 'as' <KRModuleType>
module_notify  ::= 'notify' <moduleId> on
                   ('initialize' | 'finalize' | 'cycle') formula

mst            ::= 'nop' | 'exit'  | '{' mst '}' |
                   update | conditional | sequence | choice
sequence       ::= mst ',' mst
choice         ::= mst ';' mst
conditional    ::= 'when' query_expr 'then' mst ['else' mst]

query_expr     ::= query 'and' query | query 'or' query |
                   not 'query' | '(' query ')'
query          ::= 'true' | 'false' |
                   <operatorId> <moduleId> [variables] formula
update         ::= <operatorId> <moduleId> [variables] formula

formula        ::= '[{' <arbitrary string> '}]'
variables      ::= '(' (<identifier> ',')* <identifier> ')' | '(' ')'
```

Fig. 1. *Jazzyk* EBNF

corresponding plug-ins implementing their functionality in a KR language of choice. Before a first update operation is invoked on a KR module, it should be initialized by some initial state. This state is encoded as a corresponding KR language formula, i.e. code block. Similarly, when a module is being shut down, it might be necessary to perform a cleanup of the knowledge base handled by the module. In order to allow for a KR module initialization and shut-down (finalization), so called notifications KR modules are introduces. They take a form of a statement declaring a formula/code block to be executed when the KR module is loaded (i.e. before the program interpretation) and when it is being unloaded (i.e. after either a call of special purpose mst 'exit', after an error during program interpretation, or after the last deliberation cycle was performed). Additionally, as a purely technical feature, also a notification after each deliberation cycle is provided. It should serve to strictly technical purposes like e.g. possible cleaning of a query cache, in the case a KR module implements such an optimization technique.

The core of *Jazzyk* syntax are rules of conditional nested mst's of the form *query* $\longrightarrow$ *mst*. These are translated in *Jazzyk* as "when <query> then <mst>". Mst's can be joined using a sequence ',' and choice ';' operators corresponding to *BSM* operators ○ and | respectively. The operator precedence can be managed using braces '{', '}', resulting in an easily readable nested code blocks syntax. The query formulae are a straightforward translation of *BSM* query syntax.

Each KR module provides a set of named query and update operators, identifiers of which are used in primitive query and update expressions. To allow the interpreter to distinguish between arbitrary strings and variable identifiers in primitive query and update expressions, *Jazzyk* allows optional explicit declaration of a list of variables used in them.

A standalone update expression is a shortcut for a *BSM* rule of the type ⊤ → <update>. An obvious syntactic sugar of "when-then-else" conditional mst is introduced as well. Moreover, the syntax accepted by the *Jazzyk* interpreter includes a powerful macro language enabling support for higher level code structures, like e.g. named mst's with optional arguments. Such extended features will be discussed below in Subsection 3.3. Right hand side of Figure 2 provides short example of a *Jazzyk* program implementing a part of the *Jazzbot* agent described later in Section 4.

3.2   Interpreter

The semantics of the *Jazzyk* interpreter closely follows the *BSM* semantics shown in Algorithm 1 with only few deviations: 1) query expressions are evaluated sequentially from left to right, 2) the KR modules are responsible to provide a single ground variable substitution for declared free variables of a true query expression, 3) before performing an update, all the variables provided to it have to be instantiated. Additionally, query operator invocations are not supposed to change the agent's mental state, however this is not possible to ensure technically on the level of the *Jazzyk* interpreter implementation.

The above listed simplifications of the original *BSM* semantics were introduced in order to make the process of agent program interpretation more efficient and more transparent to the programmer. The most important deviation from the original *BSM* semantics is the treatment of variable substitutions. In order to make evaluation of mst queries straightforward and efficient, a KR module is required to provide only a single variable valuation for a provided primitive query formula, if such exists. In the case of more possible valuations of such a non-ground query formula, the KR module is free to pick a suitable one[1].

3.3   Extended Features and the Interpreter Implementation

Jazzyk interpreter was designed to provide a lightweight modular agent oriented programming language. Except for the *vertical* modularity, i.e. modularity in terms of possibility to use, re-use, or replace heterogeneous KR languages to handle agent's underlying knowledge bases, *Jazzyk* implementation support a *horizontal* modularity in terms of modularity of the source code. For a robust programming language it is desirable to provide syntactical means to manipulate large pieces of code easily. Composition of larger programs from smaller components is a vital means for avoiding getting lost in the so called "spaghetti code".

---

[1] As far as the precise mechanism is well documented by the KR language plug-in developer.

Agent program before preprocessing with M4 syntax:	Resulting pure Jazzyk program after macro expansion:

declare module brain **as** ASP
declare module goals **as** ASP
declare module body **as** Nexuiz
 	
notify goals **on initialize** *[{*
 stay_healthy. find_box.
}]
 	
define('perceive', '
 when sense body($3) *[{$1}]*
 then add brain($3) *[{$2}]*
')
 	
perceive('sonar wall', 'inFrontOfWall') ;
when believes goals *[{stay_healthy}]* **then** {
 ...
 perceive('body health X', 'health(X)', 'X')
}
	declare module brain **as** ASP
	declare module goals **as** ASP
	declare module body **as** Nexuiz
	
	notify goals **on initialize** *[{*
	 stay_healthy. find_box.
	}]
	
	when sense body() *[{sonar wall}]*
	then add brain() *[{inFrontOfWall}]*
	;
	when believes goals *[{stay_healthy}]*
	then {
	 ...
	 when sense body(X) *[{body health X}]*
	 then add brain(X) *[{health(X)}]*
	}

Fig. 2. Example of macro preprocessing. Program is a part of *Jazzbot* agent.

To support this horizontal modularity, *Jazzyk* interpreter integrates GNU M4[2], a powerful macro preprocessor. Before a *Jazzyk* program is fed to the interpretation cycle (Algorithm 1), its source code is fed to GNU M4 preprocessor to expand and interpret all the M4 specific syntactic constructs. This way, the language of *Jazzyk* programs is extended by the full M4 language syntax.

In terms of source code modularity, by integration of GNU M4 macro preprocessor into the *Jazzyk* interpreter, it gains several important features almost "for free": definition of macros and their expansion in the source code, possibility of a limited recursive macro expansion, conditional macro expansion, possibility to create code templates, handling file inclusion in a proper operating system path settings dependent way, limited facility for handling strings, etc.

The Figure 2 provides an example of a macro expansion mechanism. A reusable mst `perceive` is defined and subsequently used in different contexts of an agent program.

To simplify debugging of agent programs, *Jazzyk* interpreter implements a full-featured error reporting following the GNU C++ Compiler[3] error and warning reporting format, what allows an easier integration of the interpreter with IDE frameworks, or programmers' editors like e.g. Eclipse, Emacs, or Vim.

Technically, *Jazzyk* interpreter is implemented in C++ as a standalone command line tool. The KR modules are shared dynamically loaded libraries installed as standalone packages on a host operating system. When a KR module is loaded, the *Jazzyk* interpreter forks a separate process to host it. The communication between the *Jazzyk* interpreter and a set of the KR module sub-processes is facilitated by an OS specific shared memory subsystem. This allows loading

---

[2] http://www.gnu.org/software/m4/
[3] http://gcc.gnu.org/

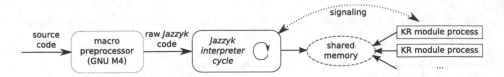

Fig. 3. *Jazzyk* interpreter scheme

multiple instances of the same KR module implemented in a portable way. The Figure 3 depicts the technical architecture of the *Jazzyk* interpreter.

The *Jazzyk* interpreter was implemented in a portable way, so it can be compiled, installed or relatively easily ported to most POSIX compliant operating systems. As of now, the interpreter was ported to Linux and Windows/Cygwin platforms. The *Jazzyk* interpreter was published under the open-source GNU GPL v2 license and is hosted at http://jazzyk.sourceforge.net/. To support implementation of 3rd party KR modules, I also published a KR module software development kit including template of a trivial KR module together with all compile/package/deploy scripts.

4   Jazzbot: Demo Application

To demonstrate the applicability of *Jazzyk* language and its interpreter and to further drive this line of research, we implemented *Jazzbot*, a virtual agent embodied in a simulated 3D environment of a first-person shooter computer game *Nexuiz*[4].

Jazzbot is a goal-driven agent. It features four KR modules representing *belief base*, *goal base*, and an interface to its *virtual body* in a *Nexuiz* environment respectively. While the goal base consists of a single KB realized as an ASP logic program, the belief base is composed of two modules: ASP logic programming one and a *Ruby* module. The interface to the environment is facilitated by a *Nexuiz* game client module.

4.1   Answer Set Programming

Answer Set Programming module [8] provides the bot with non-monotonic reasoning capabilities. It is realized by a *Jazzyk* module which integrates an ASP solver *Smodels* [20] with accompanying logic program grounding tool *lparse* [19]. Hence the syntax and the semantics of logic programs the module handles, i.e. query/update formulae, is that accepted by *lparse* and *Smodels*. Query formulae query the answer sets (stable models) of the actual logic program in the knowledge base using two query operations: skeptic and optimistic. While the skeptic query requires a query formula to be true in all the models of the knowledge base, the optimistic one requires only existence of at least one answer set satisfying the given query formula. The ASP KR module implements only a naive LP update mechanism based on updating facts.

---

[4] http://www.alientrap.org/nexuiz

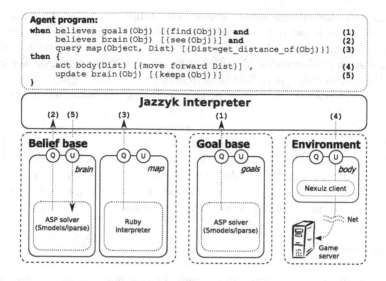

Fig. 4. Scheme of *Jazzbot*

4.2 Ruby

For representation of topological knowledge about the environment we chose an interpreted object-oriented programming language *Ruby*[5]. The *Ruby* module features a simple query/update interface allowing evaluation of arbitrary *Ruby* expressions. The functionality of the *Ruby* KR module resembles an interactive mode of the *Ruby* interpreter in which a user enters an arbitrary programming language expression on the command line and the interactive interpreter executes it and returns its value. The query/update formulae variables are bound to *Ruby* global name-space variables.

4.3 Nexuiz

The environment, *Jazzbot* operates in, is provided by a remote *Nexuiz* server. *Nexuiz* is an open-source 3D first-person shooter computer game based on the *Quake DarkPlaces*[6] engine. The *Nexuiz* KR module [10] implements a client functionality and facilitates the bot's interaction with the game server. *Jazzbot* can exploit several virtual sensors: <u>gps</u>, <u>sonar</u>, <u>eye</u>, <u>compass</u>, <u>surface sensor</u> and <u>health status sensor</u>, as well as effectors of its virtual body allowing it to <u>move</u>, <u>jump</u>, <u>turn</u>, <u>use</u> an item, <u>attack</u>, or <u>utter</u> a plain text message.

Jazzbot is a client-side bot. That means, that in order to faithfully mimic the human player style environment for the bot, the sensory interface is designed so, that it provides only a (strict) subset of the information of that a human game player can access. For instance, *Jazzbot* can only check the scene in front

---

[5] http://www.ruby-lang.org/
[6] http://icculus.org/twilight/darkplaces/

of it using the directional sonar sensor. The rendering of a whole scene also is inaccessible to it, so only a single object can be seen at a time. Similarly to a human player, *Jazzbot* can reach only to the local information about its environment and information about objects which it cannot see, or are located behind the walls of the space it stands in, are inaccessible to it.

Jazzbot's behaviours are implemented as a *Jazzyk* program. *Jazzbot* can fulfill e.g. search and deliver tasks in the simulated environment, it avoids obstacles and walls. Figure 4 depicts the architecture of *Jazzbot* and features a *Jazzyk* code chunk implementing a simple behaviour of picking up an object by mere walk through it and then keeping notice about it in its ASP belief base. Note that all the three used KR modules are compatible with each other, since they share the domain of character strings. Hence all the variables used in *Jazzbot*'s programs are meant to be character string variables.

5   Discussion

In my view, an agent programming language is a *glue* for assembling agent's behaviours. Furthermore, it should facilitate an efficient use of its knowledge bases and interface(s) to the environment.

However, a programming language is a software engineering tool, in the first place. Even though its primary utilization is to provide expressive means for behaviour encoding, at the same time it has to fulfill requirements on modern programming languages. Programs have to be easily readable and understandable and the language semantics should be transparent to a programmer, i.e. as clear and simple as possible.

The *BSM* framework, and in turn *Jazzyk*, its implementation, is an attempt to satisfy these requirements in a working system obeying design principles of *simplicity*, *modularity* and *semantic transparency*.

1. *BSM* in the core allow implementation of agent programs in a form of simple non-deterministic reactive behaviours. Their precedence and relations can be steered by nesting of behaviours (mst's) and their combinations by operators of non-deterministic choice and chaining,
2. *Jazzyk* itself is a lightweight language. To support modularity and further extensibility, it exploits a power of a macro preprocessor allowing implementation of code templates and higher level syntactic constructs like e.g. general purpose perception or goal handlers (as sketched in the Figure 2),
3. finally, the proposed simple semantics of *BSM* stems from that of Gurevich's *Abstract State Machines* (*ASM*) framework, formerly known as *Evolving Algebras*. This relationship allows further transfer of *ASM* extensions and modeling tools, like logic for *ASM* to the *BSM* framework.

It can be argued that *Jazzyk* is oversimplified and does not follow the popular tradition of *BDI* [18] architectures. We already addressed these issues in [14]. There we showed how a *BDI* agent architecture can be implemented in a modular way in a framework close to *BSM* with an advantage, that an agent system designer has a freedom to implement a model of rationality suitable for the agent application instead of fixing it in the programming framework.

The syntactical structure of *BSM* closely resembles the one we introduced in [15]. *BSM* framework is indeed an evolution of our previous work. However the semantics of the language introduced in [15] was not simple enough and did not allow a straightforward implementation of a transparent language interpreter. Moreover, the concept of *mental state transformer* was still quite complex what led to problems with implementation of source code modularity in the language.

Our research project follows the spirit of [9], where Laird and van Lent argue that approaches for programming intelligent agents should be tested in realistic and sophisticated environments of modern computer games. To provide a substance to claims about practicality and applicability of *Jazzyk*, similarly to [21], we put *Jazzyk* to a test in such a challenging environment and we developed *Jazzbot*, a functional demonstration of a non-trivial virtual agent. We report on the details of the methodology of programming the *Jazzbot*'s behaviour and our experience with it more extensively in [16]. Because of *Jazzyk*'s modularity in terms of employed KR technologies, agent applications, such as *Jazzbot*, can be used as a test-bed for investigating applications of various KR technologies in the domain of agent systems.

6   Related Work and Conclusion

The landscape of agent programming frameworks is thriving (see e.g. a survey [1], or [2]). Most of the state-of-the-art frameworks like *3APL* [5], *Jason* [3], *GOAL* [6] and other provide a clear semantics of a resulting agent system. However, for representation of agent's beliefs, they usually provide a fixed, logic based knowledge representation technique (often *Prolog*). Following the *BDI* tradition, from the relation of agent's beliefs and goals stems a subsequent need to implement also the goal base using a related logic based KR technology. Unlike the *BSM* framework, which was designed with the motivation to allow a liberal combination of heterogeneous KR technologies in a single agent system, they do not allow a straightforward employment of e.g. an object-oriented KR approach (like *Ruby* in the case of *Jazzbot*) in one of an agent's knowledge bases.

Recently in [7], we showed that *GOAL* does not strictly commit to a single logic-based KR technology, such as e.g. *Prolog*. However, a question remains how difficult would it be to use heterogeneous KR technologies with *GOAL* as it is done in the *BSM* framework. Because of the model of rationality *GOAL* uses (blind commitment), there must be a close relationship between the KR languages of belief and goal bases. *BSM* do not require such a relationship to exist, it is rather a task of a programmer to encode such a relationship whenever necessary. Macro `perceive` in the Figure 2 provides such an example: it relates a perception to its projection in the agent's belief base.

In [17], authors describe *Qsmodels* architecture based *Quake* bots implemented in plain ASP/*Smodels*. *Qsmodels* bots use planning as the primary approach to implementation of behaviours. I rather take a position that logic-based techniques are better suited for modeling static aspects of an environment, rather than for steering agents' behaviours. Unlike *Qsmodels* planning bot, *Jazzbot* is a rather reactive agent with a strong support for deliberative features.

The main contributions of this paper are a detailed description of the programming language *Jazzyk* together with its interpreter and a rough overview of the functionality of *Jazzbot*, a case study demonstrating applicability of *Jazzyk* language. The *Jazzbot* project is a driver for my future work. In this context I will focus on development of techniques for programming agents based on the template of *Jazzbot*, so that I can better understand a methodology for programming such systems. The aim is to design at least a fragmentary formal higher level specification language based on a flavor of modal logic, which would allow a straightforward translation (compilation) into raw *Jazzyk* programs. On a technical side, to complement the current family of *Jazzyk* KR modules, we plan to implement a *Prolog* module based on *SWI Prolog*[7] and a *Scheme* module based on *GNU Guile*[8]. We are also working on a module allowing inter-agent communication via an established MAS platform middleware.

Acknowledgments

I am grateful to Koen Hindriks for his support, constructive criticism and considerable contribution to simplification of the *BSM* semantics. Bernd Fuhrmann contributed to the development of the *Jazzyk* interpreter and Michael Köster with David Mainzer implemented the KR modules for the *Jazzbot* project.

References

1. Bordini, R.H., Braubach, L., Dastani, M., Seghrouchni, A.E.F., Gomez-Sanz, J.J., Leite, J., O'Hare, G., Pokahr, A., Ricci, A.: A survey of programming languages and platforms for multi-agent systems. Informatica 30, 33–44 (2006)
2. Bordini, R.H., Dastani, M., Dix, J., Seghrouchni, A.E.F.: Multi-Agent Programming Languages, Platforms and Applications. Multiagent Systems, Artificial Societies, and Simulated Organizations, vol. 15. Kluwer Academic Publishers, Dordrecht (2005)
3. Bordini, R.H., Hübner, J.F., Vieira, R.: Jason and the Golden Fleece of Agent-Oriented Programming. In: Multiagent Systems, Artificial Societies, and Simulated Organizations [2], ch. 1, vol. 15, pp. 3–37 (2005)
4. Börger, E., Stärk, R.F.: Abstract State Machines. A Method for High-Level System Design and Analysis. Springer, Heidelberg (2003)
5. Dastani, M., van Riemsdijk, M.B., Meyer, J.-J. (eds.): Programming Multi-Agent Systems in 3APL. In: Multiagent Systems, Artificial Societies, and Simulated Organizations [2], ch. 2, vol. 15, pp. 39–68 (2005)
6. de Boer, F.S., Hindriks, K.V., van der Hoek, W., Meyer, J.-J.C.: A verification framework for agent programming with declarative goals. J. Applied Logic 5(2), 277–302 (2007)

---

[7] http://www.swi-prolog.org/
[8] http://www.gnu.org/software/guile/

7. Hindriks, K., Novák, P.: Compiling GOAL Agent Programs into Jazzyk Behavioural State Machines. In: Bergmann, R., Lindemann, G., Kirn, S., Pĕchouček, M. (eds.) MATES 2008. LNCS, vol. 5244. Springer, Heidelberg (2008)
8. Köster, M.: Implementierung eines autonomen Agenten in einer simulierten 3D-Umgebung - Wissensrepräsentation. Master's thesis (2008)
9. Laird, J.E., van Lent, M.: Human-level AI's killer application: Interactive computer games. AI Magazine 22(2), 15–26 (2001)
10. Mainzer, D.: Implementierung eines autonomen Agenten in einer simulierten 3D-Umgebung - Interaktion mit der Umwelt. Master's thesis (2008)
11. Manna, Z., Pnueli, A.: The temporal logic of reactive and concurrent systems. Springer, New York (1992)
12. Novák, P.: An open agent architecture: Fundamentals. Technical Report IfI-07-10, Department of Informatics, Clausthal University of Technology (November 2007)
13. Novák, P.: Behavioural State Machines: programming modular agents. In: AAAI 2008 Spring Symposium: Architectures for Intelligent Theory-Based Agents, AITA 2008, March 26-28 (2008)
14. Novák, P., Dix, J.: Modular BDI architecture. In: Nakashima, H., Wellman, M.P., Weiss, G., Stone, P. (eds.) AAMAS, pp. 1009–1015. ACM, New York (2006)
15. Novák, P., Dix, J.: Adding structure to agent programming languages. In: Dastani, M., El Fallah Seghrouchni, A., Ricci, A., Winikoff, M. (eds.) ProMAS 2007. LNCS, vol. 4908, pp. 140–155. Springer, Heidelberg (2008)
16. Novák, P., Köster, M.: Designing goal-oriented reactive behaviours. In: Proceedings of the 6th International Cognitive Robotics Workshop, CogRob 2008, Patras, Greece, July 21-22 (2008)
17. Padovani, L., Provetti, A.: Qsmodels: ASP planning in interactive gaming environment. In: Alferes, J.J., Leite, J. (eds.) JELIA 2004. LNCS, vol. 3229, pp. 689–692. Springer, Heidelberg (2004)
18. Rao, A.S., Georgeff, M.P.: An Abstract Architecture for Rational Agents. In: KR, pp. 439–449 (1992)
19. Syrjänen, T.: Implementation of local grounding for logic programs with stable model semantics. Technical Report B18, Digital Systems Laboratory, Helsinki University of Technology (October 1998)
20. Syrjänen, T., Niemelä, I.: The Smodels System. In: Eiter, T., Faber, W., Truszczyński, M. (eds.) LPNMR 2001. LNCS, vol. 2173, pp. 434–438. Springer, Heidelberg (2001)
21. van Lent, M., Laird, J.E., Buckman, J., Hartford, J., Houchard, S., Steinkraus, K., Tedrake, R.: Intelligent agents in computer games. In: AAAI/IAAI, pp. 929–930 (1999)

PRESAGE: A Programming Environment for the Simulation of Agent Societies

Brendan Neville and Jeremy Pitt

Intelligent Systems & Networks Group
Dept. of Electrical and Electronic Engineering
Imperial College London
London, SW7 2BT, UK
brendan.neville@imperial.ac.uk, j.pitt@imperial.ac.uk

Abstract. The paradigm of agent societies has proved particularly apposite for modelling multi-agent systems for networked applications, in particular when the network is open, dynamic and decentralised. In this paper, we describe a software environment which can be used for simulation and animation of these models, allowing a system designer to investigate the complex social behaviour of components, the evolution of network structures, and the adaptation of conventional rules. Effectively, the environment serves as a rapid prototyping tool for agent societies, where the focus of interest is long-term, global system behaviour as much as the verification of specific properties.

1 Introduction

Networked computers and multi-agent systems (MAS) are commonly used as a platform for a new range of applications in for example manufacturing, health, transport, commerce, entertainment, education, and social interaction. Features of these applications include the dynamic network infrastructure, heterogeneous components, unpredicted events, sub-ideal operation (failure to comply to specifications), incomplete and inconsistent information, absence of centralised control, and so on. Techniques from autonomic computing [1] and adaptive systems [2] have proved useful in addressing some of these features; for others the idea of an agent society has been proposed (e.g. [3,4]) which has emphasised the need for conventional rules and social relationships between components.

There still remains though a requirement for system designers and software engineers to retain some understanding of the application under development, and especially of complex systems where random events, erratic behaviour, and self-modification can render the system opaque to mathematical analysis. In the past, rapid prototyping has proved to be an extremely effective tool in helping to understand large-scale MAS, for example in abstracting away from details in order to verify that certain desirable properties hold. However, in autonomic, large-scale MAS, there is an additional requirement not just to verify properties, but also to observe the global outcomes that are the consequence of social interactions and a myriad of independent, local decisions and actions.

K.V. Hindriks, A. Pokahr, and S. Sardina (Eds.): ProMAS 2008, LNAI 5442, pp. 88–103, 2009.

In this paper, we propose a rapid prototyping tool whose emphasis is on the simulation of agent societies and the social relationships between agents, allowing the designer to study social behaviour of components, the evolution of network structures, and the adaptation of conventional rules. In this sense, it occupies a space distinct from powerful application development environments, like JADE [5]; agent based modelling and simulation tools [6,7] where the primary purpose is to model and explain the behaviour of non-artificial agents; and other rapid prototyping environments for MAS (e.g. [8,9]) whose principal function is, as stated above, to verify system-wide properties. We illustrate the use of the environment in examining three systems for trust, recommendations, and resource allocation.

The rest of this paper is structured as follows, section 2 provides a set of non-functional requirements and a brief overview of how a user develops and runs a test-bed using the platform. The platform architecture including the underlying simulation model and core modules are discussed in section 3. In section 4 we describe in detail the agent model and agent communication language. Following this section 5 summarises the research which has been carried out using the platform. Finally in 6 and 7 we summarize existing work, conclude and set out our future objectives for the platform.

2   An Overview

To satisfy the functional requirement of developing a rapid prototyping and animation environment for agent societies we have paid particular attention to developing a highly customisable and extensible simulation architecture. However, in order to support the designers goals of observing social behaviour, long term global performance and adaptation we also specifically identify a set of non-functional requirements, namely:

- abstraction: the system allows the designer to tailor the degree of abstraction in their models. In particular, the primary objects of study, the agents and the network, can be as simple or complex as necessary. For example, the agents can range from reactive stubs to fully-fledged BDI agents;
- flexibility: the platform provides many options for parametrisation and re-configuration. This supports systematic experimentation as the platform can be configured to run with the independent variables set over a range of values, and the measures of interest (dependent variables) collected for each run;
- extensibility: the platform is provided with a pre-programmed set of libraries, but the designer may extend the functionality using scriptable methods and component plug-ins;
- interaction: particular emphasis is given to simplifying the front-end to 'program' an experiment, to visualise the animation as it is running, data logging, and access to external applications, such as Gnuplot, for graphical representation of data;
- scalability: the architecture of the system has been designed to support both single-processor and distributed animation, allowing simulation to feature societies comprising many hundreds of agents.

In developing a prototype the experimenter can create their agent participant types through optional use of the supplied abstract class; to ensure compatibility with the simulation calls and provide core functionality like message handling etc. They can then choose from one of the pre-defined network and physical environment modules or extend the basic Network and PhysicalWorld classes to suit their purpose. Finally they may add functionality to the platform in the form of scriptable methods and plugins.

A basic input-output overview of our simulation platform is illustrated by Fig. 1. The experimenter configures each simulation run via input-files; these files serve four main purposes, parametrising the general simulation variables, configuring the simulated agents (participants), scripting events and initialising the required plug-ins.

Once the platform has initialised as specified it enters the simulation thread and loops for the required number of iterations. During this time the user can view the progress of the simulation via visualiser plug-ins, record data using data archiver plug-ins, execute methods and launch extra plug-ins during runtime.

At the end of the simulation, the platform can be scripted to organise and archive results and input-files. It can also call external applications for example Gnuplot to create publication ready graphs.

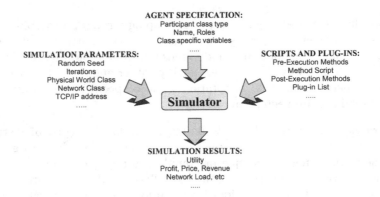

Fig. 1. Input-Output Overview of the Simulation Platform

3   Platform Architecture

The PRESAGE architecture is illustrated as a software stack (Fig. 2) depicting the base simulation module, the interfaces and abstract classes, simulation managers, and the platforms connectivity to external processes. Above this we have given some examples of how the user could utilise the classes and modules e.g. an auction scenario operating over a unstructured P2P network without a physical world. In the following sections we address each of the modules in more detail.

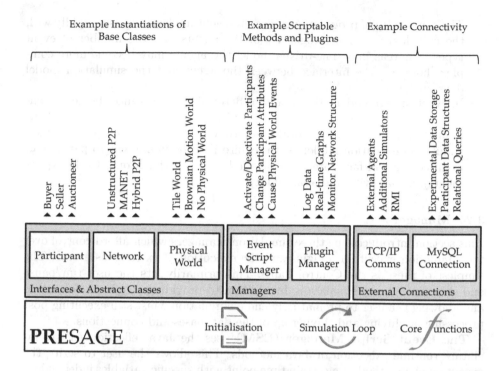

Fig. 2. Representation of the Architecture of the platform

3.1   The Base Simulation Module

The role of the base simulation module is to perform parameter initialisation, manage simulation execution, and provide generic functions to higher level modules and classes. PRESAGE takes a multi-agent discrete time-driven approach. In this simulation execution model each loop of the simulation control thread equates to a simulation time slice. For every time slice the state of the network and physical world is updated, scripted events execute, plugins perform their duties and the agent participants are given a turn to perform physical and communicative actions. By handling the agent process execution as a centralised time-driven model we ensure pseudo-concurrent execution of agent actions thus affording the advantages of Multi-agent based simulation (MABS) outlined in [10], and providing the user and agent a centralised notion of time. Concurrency is enforced by queuing actions until the end of each time slice.

We have developed a time-driven as opposed to an event-driven model of execution because:

- While event-driven models are generally seen as more computationally efficient than time-driven models due the former' ability to overlook periods of inactivity, such efficiency is absent in the case of simulating agents, since they react to changing conditions and are therefore required to constantly sense their environment.

- The complexity of programming discrete-event models increases rapidly with the complexity and heterogeneity of the agents and the number of event types. Whereas in a time-driven model the agents may become more complex, however, the interface between the agent and the simulation model does not.
- In event-driven models, the simulator determines in advance the next event based on the current state of the world and steps directly to it (without animating the states of the world in-between). This is inappropriate for our simulation execution model as we require it to be indifferent to participant architecture and facilitate probabilistic behaviour (for Monte Carlo experiments), pro-activity and adaptability.

3.2   Managers

This section introduces the three simulation managers which afford control over the simulation execution, plugins and the execution of extraneous events. The simplest of these is the Control Panel. This primarily lets the user run/pause and step through the simulation. In addition to providing progress information and allowing the user to prematurely end a simulation whist still executing post processing, archiving and tidying up of the databases and connections.

The Event Script Manager (ESM) uses the Java reflection API to facilitate runtime execution of Java methods. This allows the user to script the execution of a method at a certain time point with specific variables independent of the platforms compile time behaviour. This script initially takes the form of an input file, but events can be added through the GUI during runtime. Methods can also be scripted for execution before or after the simulation run such that the user can use them for initialisation or post processing. Given the generic nature of scripting method execution there are a vast array of possible uses, these include, triggering events in the simulated physical world, adapting the network topology, altering parameters and timing each agent's entrance or exit from the simulation.

The Plugin Manager (PM) allows the user to launch plugin modules from input files or a GUI during runtime; the key difference between plugins and methods being that plugins persist between simulation cycles meaning that they are repeatedly executed, have memory between simulation cycles and can include a user interface. As a result they form the basis of the many possible data archiving and visualisation tools. The PM, like the ESM auto-detects available plugins and allows the user to launch and remove them during runtime. A plugin can be created by simply using the plugin interface. The power of the plugin architecture is illustrated by two key plugins, the DataArchiver and the Visualiser.

DataArchiver: One key feature of any simulation platform is the ability to log experimental data. A basic DataArchiver plugin class is provided in the platform API that can create results logs in the form of spreadsheets. The specific nature of the data and its layout in the output-file is defined by the user as it is scenario dependant. This is relatively easy process of instantiating the DataArchiver's abstract method `getDataRow()` to return a row of data in the form of an array. In each simulation cycle the plugin will then get the required data and archive it in a comma separated file.

Visualisation Plugins: We provide a small group of plugins specifically designed to enable the user to create realtime visualisations of experimental data. At this time we have created three basic forms: line graphs, radial plots and network visualisation. While it is our intention to extend this library further in the future, the user can, of course, create their own as needed.

3.3 External Connections

The platform supports many types of external connection. In this section, we review three, TCP/IP connections, MySQL, and access to other external applications.

TCP/IP Communication consists of a client/server pair for communicating with external processes such as situated agents, remote servers and networking the platform to additional simulators.

The MySQL connection is managed by the platform for providing short-cut methods to perform queries and updates, in addition to managing the java-sql connection (jdbc). This enables users to store large volumes of simulation data including event logs for post-processing. The participants can also use SQL to: store beliefs, form temporary data structures from more than one table, perform mathematical functions on large datasets or quickly and efficiently search and organise a large amount of information.

External Process Invocation is handled by a number of convenience methods allowing the execution of system commands and external applications from within the platform. These can either be called by user defined code in the network, physical world, participant, or plugin classes; or by a scripted event. This is particularly useful for launching agent processes outside the simulation, calling on Gnuplot or a spreadsheet application to post-process simulation results.

3.4 Environmental Interfaces and Abstract Classes

Agent systems operate in a number of physical and network environments from fully connected static networks without the need to model a physical world to vehicular adhoc networks (VANETS). The individual properties of these environments pose unique challenges to the agent system developer, therefore it is essential that agent simulation platforms support the custom specification of these environments. In order to achieve this the PRESAGE platform contains two abstract classes namely the Network Simulation Module and a Physical World Simulation Module.

Network Simulation Module: The network module's core function is to facilitate the exchange of messages between connected peers and to simulate dynamic connectivity between the participants. Network modules are simple to create by extending the basic abstract class to determine the required behaviour. The

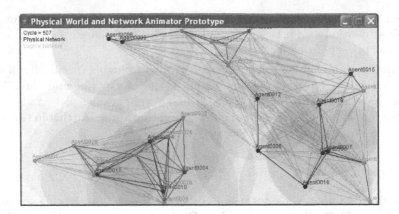

Fig. 3. Plugin creates a realtime animation of the changing positions of the agents in the simulated physical world and the effect this has on the topology of the physical and logical networks

following network types have been created: static fully/partially connected, unstructured P2P, hybrid P2P and mobile adhoc networks.

Physical World Simulation Module: The platform supports the inclusion of a simulated spatial environment for the agents. Like the simulated network, the physical world is an interface class which allows for custom specification by the experimenter. The basic interface supports the addition and removal of participants from the world and facilitates the sensing and effecting of their environment. It is up to the user to define the valid actions and their effect on the state of the world, in addition to any rules of the environment not determined by agent behaviour.

An example of using the physical world and network interfaces is an instance of a wireless mobile adhoc network (MANET) simulation. In our configuration the agents can move in a two dimensional environment and can sense the relative position of nearby peers. The world itself bounces agents when they interact with its boundaries causing the agents to move in a Brownian motion. The spatial data of the world is used by the network module to calculate the physical connections of the network based on relative distances between peers and their wireless transmission ranges. The physical network topology can then be used to infer the logical connectivity of the participants. A realtime visualisation of the physical world and the resultant network is provided by a plugin shown in Fig. 3.

4   Agents, Participants and Communication

The principal component of the platform is its collection of agents, whose interaction with one another and their environment is our primarily interest. In theory it would be ideal for the platform not to constrain the design of the agents

Table 1. Required methods and variables for a simulation participant

Variables	
public String gUID	globally unique identifier: defined from input file
public Queue inbox	to allow the network module to en-queue messages to the agent
Methods	
public boolean isRole(String role);	returns true if role is one of the par-ticipants roles.
public void execute();	called by the simulation thread upon a participants turn.
public void onActivation();	called by the platform when the agent becomes active in the simu-lation.
public void onDeActivation();	called by the platform when the agent is removed from the simula-tion.

in any way. However in order to interact with the base simulation model and ensure the interoperability of participants a degree of homogeneity is required. Table 1 lists these prerequisites. Externally the agent must have a globally unique identifier (GUID), defined roles and communicate via a common agent communication interface (as defined in the following section). However, internally the requirements simply facilitate the interaction with the simulation platform, for instance activation/deactivation of the agent and calling the agent to take it's turn via a public methods e.g. `execute()`. The user may also customise the simulation thread to allow them to interleave the execution of agents, this is achieved by replacing the `execute()` method with a series of sub-methods. This is the approach used in the example applications in section 5. Within these constraints the user is free to develop their own agent architecture be it reactive, deliberative, BDI or otherwise. As such the platform is neutral with respect to the agents' internal architectures.

4.1   The Participant Class

It is expected that the majority of users of the platform will be primarily interested in the interaction between agents and the evolution of behaviour within a simulated agent society. As such we have developed a root agent class `Participant` from which researchers can derive heterogeneous agents for participation in their simulations. Figure 4 shows how one might derive the necessary classes for an online auction scenario in a Virtual Organization and instantiate an heterogeneous population from them. Notice that the class hierarchy allows us to define more or less sophisticated agent strategies: from the simple buyer, socio-cognitive buyer, and onto machine learning or game theoretic buyers. The participant class handles as much of the agent's internal operation as possible

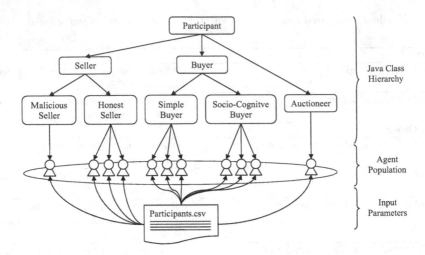

Fig. 4. Using Java OOP, Participant class and input files to define a heterogeneous agent population

(without sacrificing scenario flexibility). Its architecture is a combination of deliberative and probabilistic models, this has proved sufficiently complex for our experiments in emergent behaviour.

To create the individual participants The derived classes must then be launched and parametrised via an input-file. Each row of the file launches and specifies an individual agent's parameters. The core inputs the user must specify for each agent include, among other things, the Java class that includes the agents reasoning and communication protocols which extend our generic participant class, the agents globally unique identifier, the initial roles to be assigned to the agent. In addition the user can provide scenario specific parameters for example in our trust and e-commerce scenario the participants input file also defines what trust model each agent will adopt, its economic constraints/preferences and its character type e.g. its inclination towards and strategy for illegal, unethical and antisocial behaviour.

4.2 Agent Communication

The simulation platform aims to put minimal restriction on the internal characteristics of the participating agents. However, in order for the agents to communicate effectively some *a priori* knowledge as to the mechanisms and semantics of communication are required. Following, Pitt and Mamdani [11] who argue for the use of a protocol based semantics in the external specification of agent interaction specifically between agents with behavioural and architectural heterogeneity. Within the participant class we provide the necessary mechanisms for handling protocol based communication between the agents. In fact all the mechanisms from message sending and parsing to maintaining the state of current interactions is built in; effectively reducing the users work load to defining the protocol and the reasoning of the agents at each stage of that protocol.

In this section we discuss the defined agent communication interface which permits and facilitates the exchange of information between peers. The interface consists of a higher and lower level component pair: the agent communication language (ACL) and the mechanism for transmitting messages. Message transmission is achieved by calling the

`sendMessage(Message, InetAddress)`

method of the Network module. The Network module will either send the message via TCP/IP sockets or enqueue the message to the recipient's inbox queue; depending on whether the recipient is internal or external to the platform. We define our ACL in terms of three components: The message syntax, the mechanisms maintaining the state of a communicative context (a conversation) and the external semantics of the protocols. The following three subsections discuss the way that messages, conversations and protocols are represented, in order to give the user an understanding of how to implement a protocol and associated agent behaviour within our framework.

Message Syntax. In order for agents to parse and interpret information exchanged between them there must be an agreed upon message syntax. In our ACL a message takes the form of a seven-place term (see below) where the terms R and S denote the intended recipient and the sender respectively; these are instantiated with the agents $GUID$ values. Element C defines the type of communicative act (i.e query or purchase) being performed. P determines the protocol (i.e. CNP or Hello) under which the communicative act is being issued. CKs and CKr are the conversation keys ($ConvKey$) of the sender and recipient respectively; these are used by the agents to recognise the ongoing context in which a message should be interpreted (Pitt and Mamdani [11]). When an agent initiates a conversation they create a conversation object and a instantiate it with a locally unique conversation key. This key is then sent with all subsequent messages. When an agent receives a message without an instantiated CKr it signals that this is the first message of a new conversation; the recipient will then create a new conversation and instantiate its key before processing the message. The format of the message contents is determined by the message performative C and the protocol P being followed.

message $(R, S, C, P, CKr, CKs, Content)$;

message (Agent0056, Agent0022, introduction, hello,
$(.), (4.0)$, contents(Agent0022, $\langle$consumer, 127.0.0.1 : 9436$\rangle$));

Conversations. As an agent executes an interaction protocol with a peer it must maintain local information about the context of that interaction. The agents achieve this by creating a *conversation* object for every multi-stage interaction initiated. A conversation object has the following structure:

conversation $(CKm, CKt, tID, P, S, To, Beliefs)$;

CKm and CKt are the agents ConvKey and its peer's respectively. These ConvKeys are used to link incoming messages to an ongoing conversation and to instantiate the ConvKey fields of any replies. The fields tID and P identify whom the conversation is with and which protocol they are following. The state of the conversation S identifies at which point of the protocol (and therefore which section of the agents reasoning) the next message or timeout should refer to. To is the time at which the conversation is internally called, this can happen for a number of reasons: it could be used to end a period of open bidding in an auction protocol or simply to call a conversation to resend a message or tidy up if a peer has failed to respond. Finally the beliefs field is a set of temporary beliefs which the agent wishes to directly associate with a conversation, for instance the current highest bid in an auction.

It is necessary that the participant are able to carry out multiple conversations at any given time; the set of active conversation objects are stored in the conversations KB. Periodically the agent checks to see if any of the conversations have timed out or have completed. If the state of a conversation is completed then the conversation is removed from the KB. However if the conversation has timed out: the code associated with the protocol is passed the conversation. When we refer to the code associated with a conversation, we are referring to the user defined method that defines the agents behaviour at each stage of the protocol as describe in the next section.

Protocols and User Defined Semantics. The Participant class uses the Java reflection API in order to provide a user extensible protocol library. To add a protocol to the agent the user simply creates two methods:

```
protected    void    protocol_name(Message    msg)
```

```
protected   void   protocol_name(Message   msg, ConvKey   convkey)
```

The first method is called on receipt of any message claiming to conform to the protocol. This method performs a number of checks before calling the second method; for instance if the message is part of an ongoing conversation and if that conversation actually exists; or if the message is intended to start a new conversation in which case it will create a new conversation object. The second method is called in three situations: agent receiving a message (via the first method), a conversation timeout in which case the message is null and finally as a result of a child conversation returning. It is in the second method that the user codes the relevant agent behaviours for each stage of the protocol.

This handling of messages and conversations is added to the Participant class for the convenience of users whom do not require a specific agent architecture. With more advanced applications users can override built in conversation and messaging functions allowing messages to instead be passed over to code written in languages supported by the Java Native Interface including among others Prolog, C++ and Smalltalk.

5 Sample Applications

In this section we summarise three agent systems which we have prototyped and simulated within the PRESAGE platform.

5.1 Social Networks and Recommendation

In this scenario the prototype system under investigation is a P2P recommendation network. Whereby differing peer preferences gives rise to states of inconsistent union and the distributed architecture results in peers maintaining local, subjective and incomplete recommendation sets. The aim is for agents to base their purchase decisions on the recommendations of peers with similar preference. To do this in a traditional centralised collaborative filtering system, a server models the degree of similarity between all the peers based complete knowledge of their opinions and then uses this data to infer a desirability score for each agent to untried content pairing. Within a distributed environment this approach would cause significant computational scalability and network loading issues. We are using PRESAGE to simulate an agent society whereby peers model one another based on only the locally available recommendations. By using these peer models to self-organise their network connections the agents can exploit the localised and incomplete nature of the network to pre-filter recommendations thus increasing the utility of the incoming recommendations without being required to compute models for every peer, discovering all the available products or replicating their beliefs across the system.

5.2 Open Distributed Agent Mediated Marketplace

In this study we investigated the behaviour of an agent mediated marketplace which was intrinsically unmoderated, dynamic, and which could not guarantee that its participants would behave honestly, ethically and competently. The agents were adapted by integrating a framework for socio-cognitive reasoning (trust, recommendation and reputation) into the individual agents economic decision making. The results of our simulations show that the integration of social behaviour into the trading agent architecture can not only act as an effective mechanism for discouraging norm-violation, but also minimise the detrimental economic inefficiencies resulting from the protective measures. Details of this work can be found in [12,13].

5.3 Adaptation of Voting Rules

In previous work with agent-based mobile ad-hoc networks, vehicular networks, and virtual organizations a common scenario is for the collective use of a limited common resource. In this application of the platform, we have defined a multi-agent system which is highly volatile, in the sense that agents can be (unpredictably) 'present' or 'absent' in any time slice. The agents that are present have to vote on the distribution of resources. The problems are, firstly, to decide on an 'equitable' distribution of resources without depleting it (i.e. the 'tragedy of the commons'); and secondly, to adapt the voting rules in one time slice to (try to) ensure a 'safe' allocation in the next one. Presage is proving useful here because, given the range of different possible characteristics and complex functionality of the agents, it is straightforward to generate and configure a large and diverse population mix. The time-driven execution model supports the time slice allocation of resources, and the visualisation allows us to follow, at run-time, the key dependent variables as they change: network structure, voting rules, agent 'satisfaction', and resource allocation. Details can be found in [14].

6   Related Work

Rapid prototyping and animation of agent societies in a logical form has been effectively used in order to demonstrate and verify properties of agent societies. In [8] Vasconcelos et al present an approach to rapid prototyping multi-agent systems through the definition of a global interaction protocol. The global protocol defines the types and order of interaction between the components is used to automatically generate a set of agents which are simulated to check for desirable properties in the protocol. CaseLP [9] is a logic-based prototyping environment for specifying and verifying complex distributed applications it also provides tools for specifying certain network properties when developing prototypes of distributed systems e.g. reliability or latency of connections. We argue that these approaches provide a complimentary perspective to the one offered by PRESAGE where we are primarily interested in the global long run outcomes and dynamic behaviour of the system. PRESAGE can however produce a narrative (a sequence of actions) of its simulation of the society, this combined with a description of the social states can be used to invoke tools such as the Society Visualiser[3] to check system or protocol properties.

Muli-agent Based Simulation (MABS)[10] is a micro-level approach to simulation of complex systems. Whereby the behaviour of system components or individuals are modelled as agents. A number of MABS tools exist [15] including Swarm[1][6], Repast [2] and MASON [7] and are widely used for Agent Based Social Simulation (ABSS)[16,17,18]. In contrast to MABS the PRESAGE platform is intended as a multi-agent based simulator for agent societies; as opposed to MABS where generally the focus is upon modelling a non-agent system as a system of agents. Hence our requirement for supporting heterogeneous agent architectures and simulating properties of communication networks. ABSS uses MABS techniques to model human interactions within a multi-agent system, generally with relatively simple behaviours (on an individual agent basis) that when simulated their interactions lead to complex global behaviour. These results are subsequently used to understand and elaborate social theories. Our social agent experiments [12,13] cross-fertilise with the theories and formalisations of the ABSS field and the wider social sciences. However our interest lies

---

[1] www.swarm.org
[2] http://repast.sourceforge.net/

in using this knowledge to solve problems related to open agent societies which diverges from their use to further understand human society.

Multi-agent system development tools (for an evaluation see [19]) such as AgentBuilder[3] and JADE support analysis, design, development and deployment of multi-agent applications. More specifically, JADE[4] [5,20,21] is a robust middleware for developing FIPA[5] compliant agent applications. The JADE agent framework provides the developer with an API for message syntax and parsing and a set of standard interaction protocols thus simplifying the process of developing interoperable agents. There also exists a deployment tool [22] which supports the configuration and deployment of JADE agent based applications.

We view PRESAGE prototyping as a step before frameworks like JADE or AgentBuilder; providing a platform for investigating system wide performance, emergent behaviour, optimising interaction protocols and algorithms. We are currently working on supporting a deployment path for our test-bed participants: currently users are able to wrap the simulation participants in a class that allows them to function independently of the simulation platform.

One element of our future work is a thorough analytic comparison of PRESAGE functionality with respect to other Multi-agent programming tools such as MABS, JADE, AgentBulider, etc. Based on criteria such as, for example the type of agent, the type of society, its intended use, its intended users and so on.

7   Summary and Conclusions

Given the complex and dynamic nature of agent societies including self-governance, evolving norms and emergent behaviour, the process of developing systems which robustly exhibit desirable system wide behaviours under conditions which cannot be guaranteed; can be time-consuming and complex. In this paper we have described our approach to rapid prototyping and testing agent societies. PRESAGE affords the user centralised global monitoring and simulation control, is flexible and extensible through the use of abstract classes, event-scripting and plugins; supports heterogeneous agent architectures and the simulation of an agent system's underlying dynamic network architecture.

We have given examples of our platform being utilised to prototype and test open distributed agent systems featuring proactive behaviour, lack of centralised control, heterogeneity and adaptability. Further more our institution is currently utilising the PRESAGE platform to investigate application of game theory, alternative dispute resolution, opinion formation and norm emergence in agent societies.

Through this experience we intend to fully document and refine the framework before contributing it to the wider community. We designed and built the platforms's functional architecture to support the non-functional specification

---

[3] www.agentbuilder.com

[4] http://jade.tilab.com

[5] www.fipa.org

presented in section 2, however, as this is an ongoing development we have yet to implement these requirements in full. Future work includes tools for automated exploration of the parameter space, greater variety of predefined agent architectures and extended support for deployment on multi-core and cluster computing.

Acknowledgments

This work has been undertaken in the context of the EU-funded ALIS[6] project(IST 027968). We are also grateful for the useful comments of the anonymous referees.

References

1. Kephart, J.O., Chess, D.M.: The vision of autonomic computing. IEEE Computer 36(1), 41–50 (2003)
2. DeLoach, S., Oyenan, W., Matson, E.: A capabilities-based model for adaptive organizations. Autonomous Agents and Multi-Agent Systems 16(1), 13–56 (2008)
3. Artikis, A., Pitt, J., Sergot, M.: Animated specifications of computational societies. In: Castelfranchi, C., Johnson, L. (eds.) Proc. of the First International Conference on Autonomous Agents and Multi-Agent Systems, pp. 1053–1062. ACM Press, New York (2002)
4. Sierra, C., Rodríguez-Aguilar, J., Noriega, P., Esteva, M., Arcos, J.: Engineering multi-agent systems as electronic institutions. European Journal for the Informatics Professional V(4), 33–39 (2004)
5. Bellifemine, F., Poggi, A., Rimassa, G.: Jade - a fipa-compliant agent framework. In: Proceedings of PAAM 1999, pp. 97–108 (April 1999)
6. Minar, N., Burkhart, R., Langton, C., Askenazi, M.: The swarm simulation system, a toolkit for building multi-agent simulations (1996)
7. Luke, S., Cioffi-Revilla, C., Panait, L., Sullivan, K., Balan, G.: Mason: A multiagent simulation environment. simulation 81(7), 517–527 (2005)
8. Vasconcelos, W., Robertson, D., Sierra, C., Esteva, M., Sabater, J., Wooldridge, M.: Rapid prototyping of large multi-agent systems through logic programming. Annals of Mathematics and Artificial Intelligence 41(2-4), 135–169 (2004)
9. Martelli, M., Mascardi, V., Zini, F.: A logic programming framework for componentbased software prototyping (1999)
10. Davidsson, P.: Multi agent based simulation: Beyond social simulation. In: Moss, S., Davidsson, P. (eds.) MABS 2000. LNCS, vol. 1979, pp. 97–107. Springer, Heidelberg (2001)
11. Pitt, J., Mamdani, A.: A protocol-based semantics for an agent communication language. In: Proceedings 16th International Joint Conference on Artificial Intelligence IJCAI 1999, pp. 485–491. Morgan-Kaufmann, San Francisco (1999)
12. Neville, B., Pitt, J.: A computational framework for social agents in agent mediated e-commerce. In: Omicini, A., Petta, P., Pitt, J. (eds.) Engineering Societies in the Agents World IV. Springer, Heidelberg (2004)

---

[6] www.alisproject.eu

13. Neville, B., Pitt, J.: A simulation study of social agents in agent mediated e-commerce. In: Proceedings of the Seventh International Workshop on Trust in Agent Societies (2004)
14. Carr, H., Pitt, J.: Adaptation of voting rules in agent societies. In: Proceedings AAMAS Workshop on Organised Adaptation in Multi-Agent Systems (OAMAS) (2008)
15. Gilbert, N., Bankes, S.: Platforms and methods for agent-based modeling. Proc. of the National Academy of Sciences of the United States of America 99(10), 7197–7198 (2002)
16. Conte, R., Edmonds, B., Moss, S., Sawyer, R.K.: Sociology and social theory in agent based social simulation: A symposium. Comput. Math. Organ. Theory 7(3), 183–205 (2001)
17. Conte, R.: Agent-based modeling for understanding social intelligence. Proceedings of the National Academy of Sciences of the United States of America 99(10), 7189–7190 (2002)
18. Davidsson, P.: Agent based social simulation: A computer science view. J. Artificial Societies and Social Simulation 5(1) (2002)
19. Ricordel, P.M., Demazeau, Y.: From analysis to deployment: A multi-agent platform survey. In: Omicini, A., Tolksdorf, R., Zambonelli, F. (eds.) ESAW 2000. LNCS, vol. 1972, pp. 93–105. Springer, Heidelberg (2000)
20. Bellifemine, F., Poggi, A., Rimassa, G.: Developing multi-agent systems with jade. In: Castelfranchi, C., Lespérance, Y. (eds.) ATAL 2000. LNCS, vol. 1986, pp. 89–103. Springer, Heidelberg (2001)
21. Bellifemine, F., Rimassa, G.: Developing multi-agent systems with a fipa-compliant agent framework. Softw. Pract. Exper. 31(2), 103–128 (2001)
22. Braubach, L., Pokahr, A., Bade, D., Krempels, K.-H., Lamersdorf, W.: Deployment of distributed multi-agent systems. In: Gleizes, M.-P., Omicini, A., Zambonelli, F. (eds.) ESAW 2004. LNCS, vol. 3451, pp. 261–276. Springer, Heidelberg (2005)

An Organisational Platform for Holonic and Multiagent Systems

Nicolas Gaud, Stéphane Galland, Vincent Hilaire, and Abderrafiâa Koukam

Multiagent Systems Group,
System and Transport Laboratory
University of Technology of Belfort Montbéliard
90010 Belfort cedex, France
{nicolas.gaud,stephane.galland,
vincent.hilaire,abder.koukam}@utbm.fr
http://set.utbm.fr

Abstract. JANUS is a new multiagent platform that was specifically designed to deal with the implementation and deployment of holonic and multiagent systems. It is based on an organisational approach and its key focus is that it supports the implementation of the concepts of role and organisation as first-class entities. This consideration has a significant impact on agent implementation and allows an agent to easily and dynamically change its behaviour. The platform also natively manages the concept of holon to facilitate the deployment of holonic multiagent systems and thus contributes to fill the gap between conception and implementation phases in this domain. This article draws a complete description of JANUS and its main characteristics. A small example of a market-like community is also provided with the associated code review to illustrate the impact of a full organisational approach in terms of code modularity and reusability.

Keywords: Agent Oriented Software Engineering, Holonic Modelling, Multiagent systems implementation and deployment, Holonic multiagent systems.

1 Introduction

Dastani and Gomez-Sanz [1] consider that agent-oriented applications will only be taken up by industry if the gap between multiagent systems specification and design on the one hand and multiagent systems implementation on the other hand is bridged. Our approach consists in filling the gap between design and implementation metamodels, and thus facilitate the transformation between them. Filling that gap requires a platform, whose metamodel offers an implementation as straight as possible of the concepts used for the design of the solution.

This article deals with the last steps of the software development process, dedicated to the implementation and deployment of Multi-Agent Systems and Holonic Multi-Agent Systems applications (MAS and HMAS from now on). It introduces the JANUS platform, that is specifically designed to deal with MAS

K.V. Hindriks, A. Pokahr, and S. Sardina (Eds.): ProMAS 2008, LNAI 5442, pp. 104–119, 2009.

and HMAS. The metamodel of this platform corresponds to a fragment of the CRIO metamodel [2,3,4] that aims at providing a full set of abstractions to model MAS and HMAS under an organisational perspective. CRIO adopts the system development approach defined in the Model Driven Architecture (MDA) [5] and the elements of this metamodel are organised in three different domains. (i) The Problem domain (CIM[1]) deals with the user's problem in terms of requirements, organisations, roles and ontologies. (ii) The Agency domain (PIM[2]) addresses the holonic solution to the problem described in the previous domain. (iii) Finally, the Solution Domain (PSM[3]) describes the structure of the code solution in the chosen implementation platform. This last domain thus corresponds to the Platform Specific Model, and it is dependant of the JANUS platform presented in this paper.

Holonic multiagent systems are based on self-similar and recursive entities, called Holons. In Multiagent systems, the vision of holons is closer to the one that MAS researchers have of *Recursive* or *Composed* agents. An holon is thus a self-similar structure composed of holons as sub-structures and the hierarchical structure composed of holons is called an *holarchy*. An holon can be seen, depending on the level of observation, either as an autonomous "atomic" entity or as an organisation of holons (this is often called the *Janus effect*). Using a holonic perspective, the designer can model a system with entities of different granularities. He can recursively model sub-components of a bigger system until he achieves a stage where the requested tasks are manageable by atomic easy-to-implement entities. Implementing holonic models requires a platform able of managing the concept of nested hierarchy, but most MAS platforms consider agents as atomic entities. It is therefore difficult to implement the concept of holon, and provide an operational representation of models combining several levels of abstraction, using such platforms.

In the CRIO metamodel, organisations are considered as independent modelling units and blueprints easily reusable in various applications. The key point of this modular definition of organisations is based on the concepts of role and capacity [6]. In order to easily implement models based on CRIO requires a platform whose metamodel considers the role as a first-class entity, independent of the agent. On this aspects, the Madkit[4] platform [7] and its extension MOCA [8] have come to our attention, as they both manage the concept of role. However, Madkit does not consider the role as a first-class entity. Indeed, the behaviour associated with the role is directly implemented in the agent who plays it. Roles are strongly linked to agents architecture. This approach harms organisations reusability and modularity. MOCA considers roles as first-class entities, but sets strict constraints on their implementation. For example, an agent may not play several times the same role. These two platforms do not provide concepts to easily implement MAS designed with an organisational approach. Moreover, neither

---

[1] Computation Independent Model, first level of model in MDA.
[2] Platform Independent Model, second level of model in MDA.
[3] Platform Specific Model, third level of model in MDA.
[4] http://www.madkit.org/

of them manage the concept of holon. JANUS was specifically designed to deal with the holonic and organisational aspects. Its goal is to provide a full set of facilities for launching, displaying, developing and monitoring holons, roles and organisations. The heart of the implementation of its organisational model was inspired by the approaches adopted in the CRIO metamodel, Madkit and MOCA platforms. And it also integrates all the concepts necessary for an easy implementation of holonic multiagent systems.

This paper is organised as follows. Section 2 describes the metamodel of the JANUS platform, then its general architecture is presented in section 3. Section 4 details the key characteristics of this platform, and especially the implementation of the communication between roles modelled as first-class entities. This section also outlines the key points behind the implementation of the concept of holon. The implementation of a market-like community is described in section 5, to emphasize the advantage of considering a role as a first-class entity. Finally section 6 provides some conclusion statements.

2   Metamodel of the Janus Platform

This section is dedicated to the presentation of the metamodel of the JANUS platform. Its main concepts are described in the UML diagram, presented in figure 1.

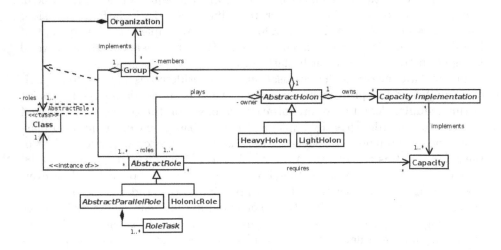

Fig. 1. UML diagram of a part of the metamodel of the JANUS platform

JANUS was designed to facilitate the transition between design and implementation phase. It thus provides a direct implementation of the five key concepts used in the design phase : organisation, group, role, holon and capacity.

The organisation is implemented as a first-class entity (a class in the object-oriented sense), which includes a set of roles classes. An organisation can be instantiated in the form of groups. Each group contains a set of instances of different classes of roles associated with the organisation which it implements. The number of authorized instances for each role is specified in the organisation. A role is local to a group, and provides holons playing the role the means to communicate with other group members. One of the most interesting aspects of JANUS covers the implementation of roles as first class entity. A role is seen as a full-fledged class, and the roles are implemented independently of the entities that play them. Such an implementation facilitates the reuse of organisations in other solutions, but also allows a wide dynamic for roles.

An agent is represented by an atomic holon (a non-composed one). Janus defines two main types of holon: *HeavyHolon* and *LightHolon*. A *HeavyHolon* has its own execution resource (one thread per holon), and can therefore operate independently. The *LightHolon* is associated with synchronous execution mechanisms and it is very useful to develop multiagent-based simulations (an approach similar to the synchronous engine of Madkit[5]). This architecture fits into a synchronization model, which defines the various execution policies of the system and holons in charge of their implementation. A holon can play simultaneously multiple roles in several groups. It can dynamically access to new roles and leave ones that are no longer in use. When an holon accesses a role, he obtains an instance of the class of this role that it stores in its roles container. Respectively, when it leaves a role, the corresponding instance is removed. The size of a holon, in terms of code, is always minimal because it only contains the instances of the roles he plays at a given moment. To access or leave a role, a holon must meet the access and liberation conditions of the role and those of the corresponding group. This mechanism provides many advantages in terms of security, since holons have access to the behaviour of a role (and thus get the corresponding executable code) only if it fulfills these conditions. Each instance of an organisation (or groups) can have specific access and liberation rights. The access and leave conditions of roles are in contrast defined at the organisation level, and cannot be changed at runtime. To model composition relationships between holons, an organisational approach is also adopted. A composed holon is called super-holon. A super-holon do not directly maintain references on its members, it is composed of a set of groups where its members play various roles and contribute to the fulfillment of the goals assigned to their super-holon(s). The approach used to model a super-holon is detailed in section 4.2.

The notion of capacity enables the representation of holon competences. Each holon has, since its creation, a set of basic skills, including the ability to play roles (and therefore communicate), to obtain information on existing organisations and groups within the platform, create other holons, and obtain new capacities. The capacity concept is an interface between the holon and the roles it plays. The role requires some capacities to define its behaviour, which can then be invoked in one of the tasks that make up the behaviour of the role. The set of capacities required by a role are specified in the role access conditions. A capacity can be implemented in various ways, and each of these implementation

---

[5] See http://www.madkit.net/site/madkit/doc/devguide/synchronous.html

is modelled by the notion of *Capacity Implementation*. This concept is the operational representation of the concept of service defined in the Agency domain. Currently JANUS does not implement a matchmaking procedure for capacities. This aspect is under development, and our approach is inspired by the works of [9,10].

In addition to these concepts, Janus provides a range of tools to facilitate the work of the developer. The various features offered by Janus will be described in the next section.

3   Kernel and General Architecture of Janus

The architecture of the JANUS platform is shown in Figure 2. Janus is developed in Java 1.5. The heart of the platform is embodied by its kernel, which provides the implementation of the organisational model and of the concept of holon. The kernel was then extended to integrate simulation module and holons in charge of the operation of the platform and its integration with the applications.

The various features provided by the JANUS kernel are described below:

- The **Organizational Management System** manages organisations and their instantiations in the form of groups. It also provides mechanisms for the

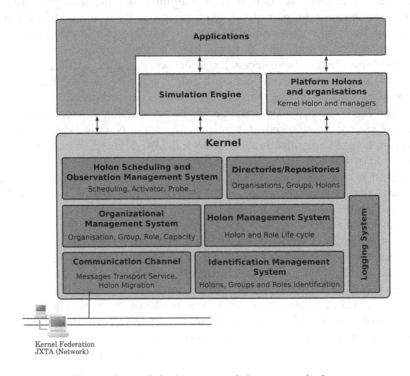

Fig. 2. General Architecture of the JANUS platform

dynamic acquisition, instantiation and liberation of roles, as well as mechanisms for the dynamic acquisition and execution of capacities. Organizational aspects are managed at the lowest level in the platform so that everything holon, including the platform ones, have access to this functionality. This module is linked to the kernel holon in charge of maintaining this information with other remote kernels (through the Communication Channel).

- **Holon Management System** : The kernel also provides all the tools necessary for the holon life cycle management: identify, launch, stop, etc. Each type of holon (*HeavyHolon* and *LightHolon*) natively provides a set of execution policies for its roles, as well as various policies for the messages management.
- The **Communication Channel** control the exchange of messages within the platform and also with remote kernels (inside the kernel federation). Considering a role as a first-class entity affects this aspect of the platform. Communication Management within JANUS will be detailed in the section 4.1.
- The **Identification Management System** provides all the necessary mechanisms for assigning a unique address (GUID) to all elements of the model which need it. Thus, the holons, groups, and roles have a unique address within a kernel federation.
- **Directories/Repositories** maintains a directory all the groups (GroupAddress ↦ Group), organisations (Class< *? extends Organization* > ↦ Organization) and holons (HolonAddress ↦ Holon) defined in the kernel. A capacity directory associating existing capacities and their available implementations is under development.
- **Holon Scheduling and Observation Management System**: JANUS provides two basic policies for holons scheduling: a concurrent execution model and a synchronous engine inspired by the Madkit one. This module also provides instrumentation based on probes allowing a role to observe another role. Unlike Madkit which manages the observation rights at the agent-level (agent who implements or not the interface *ReferencableAgent*), JANUS manages it at the role-level. It allows a more refined management of the observation rights. A holon may permit observation of one of its roles and prohibit it for the others.
- **Logging System**: All applications based on JANUS have access to a logging system integrated to the platform, which facilitates the debugging process. Logs may be directly displayed or stored in a file. This system may be changed and integrated into existing systems. The current implementation of this feature is based on log4j [6] provided by the Apache Software Foundation.

As Madkit, JANUS exploits its own model in the design of the platform, and all services are managed by holons. The kernel is thus linked to a *KernelHolon*, which contains all the local organisations responsible for managing the platform, and represents its kernel in the federation distributed over the network. A kernel federation is an organisation in charge of managing the various exchanges

---

[6] More detail at the following address: http://logging.apache.org/log4j/docs/index.html

between kernels and spreading information about the organisational model such as the creation of a new organisation or a new group, migration of a holon, etc.

The architecture of JANUS respects the overall FIPA reference architecture[7]. Only ACL[8] related features are not yet fully implemented. To compensate for this gap, it is foreseen in short term to integrate the relevant part of JADE to ensure a full compatibility of JANUS with the FIPA standard.

4   Main Characteristics of Janus

This section is devoted to the presentation of the main characteristics of the JANUS platform. Issues related to the implementation of the concept of holon and communication mechanisms between roles are specifically focused.

4.1   Communication

To communicate, holons must belong to a common group and play a role in this group. If a group is distributed among several kernels, an instance of this group exists in each kernel, and all the instances have the same name.

Communication in JANUS is based on the roles. Messages are delivered to agents according to their roles. This mode of interaction allows the implementation of communications between an emitter and several receivers (one-to-many communication [11]). The address of the receiver agents is dynamically discovered according to the roles they play. When several agents play the same role within the same group, a mode of communication based on role and agents identifier may also be used to distinguish which role player will receive the message. Although the explicit agent identifier is known, messages always require a recipient role to be handled. This kind of interaction allows the implementation of communication between two identified agents (one-to-one communication).

Each holon owns a personal mailbox for sending and receiving messages. A holon may simultaneously play multiple roles and dynamically acquire new ones. The role is the way for a holon to interact in the particular interaction context represented by the group. Roles constitute the basis of all interactions. Each role thus has its own mailbox (cf. figure 3) and the mailbox of a holon is just the arrangement of all the mailboxes of its roles. A holon can therefore receive messages only through its roles.

4.2   Implementation of the Concept of Holon

In addition to its role model, one of the main contributions of JANUS is embodied in the native management of the concept of holon. Two main aspects have to be distinguished to implement a holon with JANUS : (i) The first aspect deals with the implementation of a non-composed holons and the conception of a

---

[7] FIPA Abstract Architecture: http://fipa.org/specs/fipa00001/SC00001L.html
[8] Agent-Communication-Language.

general holon architecture able to integrate the capacities owned by the role and the roles he's currently playing. This architecture have to provide means to manage roles and capacities life cycle and dynamically acquire new ones. (ii) The second aspect concerns the manner of implementing a composed holon to ensure communication between a super-holon and its members, located at two different levels of abstraction. Both aspects will be detailed in the following subsections.

Atomic Holon Architecture. An atomic holon is primarily a roles and capacities container. The roles container provides the necessary means for the roles of a holon to interact in the internal interaction context of a holon. The local mechanism of interaction inside a holon is called influence and it is implemented using an event-based communication. Each role can register itself to inform its holon that it wishes to receive all the influences of a given type. Figure 3 describes the architecture of an atomic holon in JANUS. Section 5 will detail a concrete example of the influence mechanism.

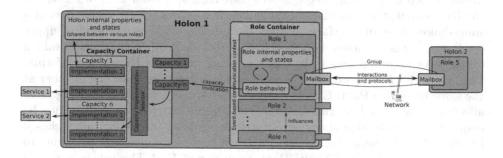

Fig. 3. Architecture of an atomic holon in JANUS

The capacity container stores all the capacities owned by the holon and all the available implementations for each of them. It also ensures their execution when a role invokes a capacity. Two main types of capacities execution are available in JANUS: synchronous or asynchronous. In the first mode, the capacity is directly executed when it is invoked by the role. The execution of the capacity temporarily interrupts the execution of the current role that is waiting for capacity termination. In the second mode, the execution of the role is not interrupted, the capacity is executed after the current role, after all the roles of holon or in parallel. The corresponding role is then informed of the outcome. This last mode is particularly interesting when the capacity is realized by a service provided by the members of a super-holon. It avoids blocking the execution of the super-holon while its members perform a given task, the holon can thus continue the execution of its other roles.

Composed Holon Implementation. Two overlapping aspects have to be distinguished in composed holons: (i) the first is directly related to the holonic nature of the entity (a holon, called super-holon, is composed of other holons, called sub-holons or members) and deals with the government and the administration of a super-holon. This aspect is common to every holon and thus called the *holonic* aspect. (ii) The second aspect is related to the problem to solve and the work to be done. It depends on the application or application domain. It is therefore called the *production* aspect. A composed holon (super-holon) thus contains at least a single instance of a *holonic organisation* to precise how members organise and manage the super-holon and a set (at least one) of *production organisations* describing how members interact and coordinate their actions to fulfill the super-holon tasks and objectives.

The *holonic organisation* is the basis of the holon government and it represents a *moderated group* (see [12]) in terms of roles (called *holonic roles*) and their interactions. In a moderated group, a subset of the members will represent all the sub-holons in the outside world. This management structure was adopted due the wide range of configurations it allows. Four *holonic roles* are defined to describe the status of a member inside a super-holon: (i) **Head**, decision maker: it represents a privileged status conferring a certain level of authority. (ii) **Representative**, interface of the holon: it is an externally visible part of a super-holon, it is an interface between the outside world (same level or upper level) and the other holon members. It may represent other members in taking decisions or accomplishing tasks (i.e. recruiting members, translating information, etc). The *Representative* role can be played by more than one member at the same time. (iii) **Part**: Classical members. Normally in charge of doing tasks affected by head, a *Part* can also have an administrative duty, and it may be employed in the decision making process. It depends on the configuration chosen for modelling the super-holon. The *Part* role represents members belonging to only one super-holon. (iv) **Multi-Part**: extension of *Part*. This role is played by sub-holons belonging to more than one super-holon.

To manage a super-holon, members have to be able to communicate with their super-holon, located at a higher level of abstraction. One of the main problems in implementing this inter-level communication comes from the fact that in JANUS and considering the role as first-class entity, two holons can communicate only if they belong to a common group. This rule implies that a super-holon must share at least one group with its members to enable the transfer of information between two adjacent levels of abstraction. Several alternatives may be considered to implement the notion of super-holon. Our study is limited to the following three alternatives:

1. The first alternative is to appoint one member to represent the rest of the community to the upper level. This approach is described in figure 4. The holon H_3 plays the *representative* role and represents the community at level $n + 1$.

   Members playing the *representative* role appear as the most suitable to perform this role of representation. But in a super-holon, several members may play this role, which means that one of the representatives in particular

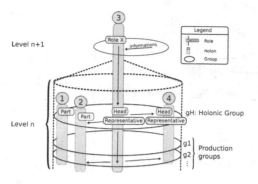

Fig. 4. One way to implement the structure of a composed holon

is identified (or elected). The community can be represented at the upper level by only one member. While this approach appears to be the simplest, it introduces a hierarchical distinction between representative members who may be elected, and therefore it is not completely consistent with the definition provided for the *representative* role in the CRIO metamodel. Moreover, this approach raises two other problems. First, from an abstract point of view, a super-holon is a separate entity distinct from its members. The fact that one of the members represent the community at the upper level means that it may play roles defined by organisations at a higher level of abstraction. Thus, the holon H_3 plays both the role X at the level $n+1$, and various roles in the production groups at level n. To be consistent, the super-holon must be clearly distinguished from its members. Playing roles at the different levels of abstraction could create interference problems or conflicts between these roles.

In addition, the *representative* role is not exclusive of other holonic roles. Thus, it can be played by a holon who also plays the *Multipart* role. Such an holon would then be shared between two holons of level n, and may represent them at the level $n+1$. The problems of confusion and conflict between levels of abstraction would be very important. This approach is the simplest, but it is not optimal.

2. To clearly distinguish the different levels of abstraction and to avoid possible interference between roles defined at different levels, another approach is possible. The latter is depicted in figure 5(a). In this approach, the super-holon is clearly distinguished from its members. A new entity is created at level $n+1$. A new group $g0$ is introduced at the level n to make the interface between the various members' representatives and the super-holon. Indeed, a super-holon must be clearly separated from its members and can only communicate with their representatives. A new role is so introduced: the role *Super*, to enable the super-holon to communicate with the representatives of its members in the group $g0$. This approach is the most consistent with

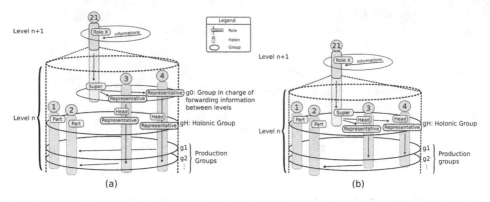

Fig. 5. Theoretical model (a) and concrete structure (b) of a composed holon in JANUS

the CRIO metamodel, but requires the creation of an additional group in all composed holons, and the implantation of a holon becomes more complex.

3. In order to keep the benefits of the previous alternative, while avoiding the additional costs due to the creation of a new group, a third approach based on a compromise between the two previous ones, has been adopted. The implementation of the holonic organisation adopted in Janus is based on this alternative and it is presented in figure 5(b). In this approach, the group $g0$, previously described, is merged with the holonic group. This group is indeed present in all composed holons. A new role is introduced in the holonic organisation, the role *Super*, to represent the upper level and thus allow the transfer of information between the super-holon and representatives of its members. This approach offers the best compromise between compatibility with the CRIO metamodel and implementation performances.

5   A Market Organisation Example

To clarify the implementation of roles as first-class entity, role dynamics and role communication, a short example of a market-like community designed using the CRIO metamodel and implemented with the JANUS platform is presented. It is a classical case study, already used to illustrate the AALAADIN metamodel and the Madkit platform [13].

All organisations, groups, roles and holons required to implement this example are shown in Figure 6. This example is applied to the domestic travel market. A customer, modelled by the *Client* role, who wishes to obtain the best available travel offer, either in terms of price or in terms of travel time, makes its proposal and sends it to the *CBroker*. This latter will forward the information to the *PBroker* role, who broadcasts it to the various available *Providers*. Depending on the criterion chosen by the customer (time or price), the *PBroker* determines the best proposal and inform the *Client*. *Client* and the best *Provider* then create an instance of the contracting organisation to finalize the order and make

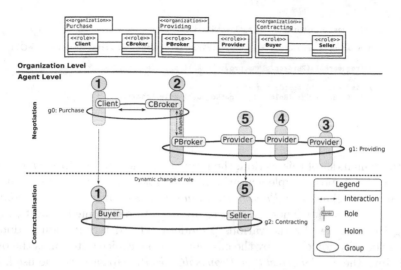

Fig. 6. The organisations and groups of a market-like community in Janus

the payment. Specifically, the proposed example may implemented using three kinds of holons : *Client* (Holon 1), *Provider* (Holons 3, 4 and 5), *Broker* (Holon 2), three organisations : *Purchase, Providing, Contracting,* and six roles. Each organisation is stored in its own java package containing its java class and those of its roles. The source code of the *Purchase* organisation is provided below:

```
1   public class PurchaseOrganization extends Organization {
2       private static Organization instance=new PurchaseOrganization();
3       //Each organisation is a singleton inheriting from Organization class.
4       protected PurchaseOrganization(){
5           super();
6           //Add classes of roles that are defined on this organisation
7           addRole(Client.class);
8           addRole(CBroker.class);
9       }
10      public static Organization getInstance() { return instance; }
11  }
```

Each kind of holon is also defined in its own class. The source code of the Holon 2 playing the *CBroker* and *PBroker* roles, is described below:

```
1   public class BrokerHolon extends HeavyHolon {
2       @Override
3       public void live() {
4           //static holon capacities initialization : adding those required by the PBroker role
5           addCapacity(FindLowestCostProposalCapacity.class, new
                   FindLowestCostProposalCapacityImpl(this));
6           addCapacity(FindShortestTimeProposalCapacity.class, new
                   FindShortestTimeProposalCapacityImpl(this));
7
8           GroupAddress clientGA = getOrCreateGroup(PurchaseOrganization.getInstance());
9           //Request the CBroker role
```

```
10      if(requestRole(CBroker.class,clientGA)){ println("role CBroker assigned"); }
11
12      GroupAddress providerGA = getOrCreateGroup(ProvidingOrganization.getInstance());
13      //Request the PBroker role
14      if(requestRole(PBroker.class,providerGA)){ println("role PBroker assigned"); }
15
16      //Simplest role scheduling
17      while(true) { for (Role role : getRoles()) role.behavior(); }
18    }
19  }
```

In the remainder of this section, the implementation of the *PBroker* role is detailed. In the proposed implementation, the *PBroker* role requires two capacities to defined its behaviour : *FindShortestTimeProposalCapacity* and *FindLowestCostProposalCapacity*. These capacities are used to determine the best proposal among those offered by the various providers. This determination is done according the criterion chosen by the customer. If the choice criterion is the overall travel time, the *FindShortestTimeProposalCapacity* capacity will be used, if the criterion is the cost, it will the *FindLowestCostProposalCapacity* capacity.

In addition, the *PBroker* role is dependent on the *CBroker* role. This latter enable the transfer of information between the *Purchase* and *Providing* organisations. To access to the *PBroker* role, a holon have to prior possess the *CBroker* role. These constraints of capacity and dependencies between roles are implemented using special types of access conditions for obtaining a role

```
1   public class PBroker extends AbstractRole {
2       // ...Attributes of the role ...
3       private int current = 1; // the current state
4       public PBroker() {
5           super();
6           //Definition of the dependencies of role
7           List<Class<? extends Role>> requiredRoles = new LinkedList<Class<? extends Role>>();
8           requiredRoles.add(CBroker.class);
9           SatisfyRoleDependenciesCondition roleCondi = new SatisfyRoleDependenciesCondition(
                requiredRoles);
10          //Definition of the capacities required by the role
11          List<Class<? extends Capacity>> requiredCapacities = new LinkedList<Class<? extends
                Capacity>>();
12          requiredCapacities.add(FindShortestTimeProposalCapacity.class);
13          requiredCapacities.add(FindLowestCostProposalCapacity.class);
14          HasAllRequiredCapacitiesCondition capCondi = new HasAllRequiredCapacitiesCondition(
                requiredCapacities);
15          //Addition of role access conditions
16          addObtainCondition(capCondi);
17          addObtainCondition(roleCondi);
18      }
19      //The core of the behavior of the role.
20      public void behavior() {
21          current = Run();
22      }
23      //This methods correspond to the translation in java code of the statechart describing
24      //the behavior of the role. This statechart was defined during the design phase
25      private int Run() {
26          switch (current) {
27      //The role register itself to signify that it want to receive a particular type of
```

```
28    //influence, in this case those from the role CBroker
29        case 1 : registerForRoleInfluence(TravelRequestInfluence.class);
30            return 2;
31    //Waiting for the arrival of the influence from the CBroker role
32        case 2 : influence = (TravelRequestInfluence)getNextInfluence();
33            if (influence != null) return 3;
34            return 2;
35        // ...
36        //Get the next message in the mailbox associated to the role
37        case 5 :m = getNextMessage();
38        //...
39            List input = new ArrayList();
40            input.add(proposalList);
41
42            if (requestType == TravelRequestType.LowestCost) {
43                selected = FindLowestCostProposalCapacity.class;
44        //Synchronous Execution of the FindLowestCostProposalCapacity capacity
45                callAndExecuteCapacity(selected, id, input);
46            } else if (requestType == TravelRequestType.ShostestTime) {
47                selected = FindShortestTimeProposalCapacity.class;
48        //Synchronous Execution of the FindShortestTimeProposalCapacity capacity
49                callAndExecuteCapacity(selected, id, input);
50            } else println("Error in Request Type");
51            return 7;
52        //Awaiting the result of the execution of the capacity
53        case 7 :if (isResultAvailable(selected, id)) {
54            output = getResult(selected, id);
55            return 8;
56            }
57        return 7;
58        //Selecting the best offer and inform the selected provider
59        case 8 :Best = (Proposal)output.get(0);
60            BestProvider = proposals.get(Best);
61            sendMessage(BestProvider, Provider.class, new StringMessage("Proposal Accepted"));
62            return 9;
63
64        case 9 :m = getNextMessage();
65            if ((m != null) && (m instanceof TransfertMessage)) {
66                return 10;
67            }
68            return 9;
69        //The role emits an influence and informs all the roles that are listening to
70        //this kind of influence (i.e. CBroker)
71        case 10 : influenceHolon(new TransfertInfluence(((TransfertMessage)m).getGroupAddress
                ()));
72            println("PBroker Finish");
73            return 2;//Return in the waiting state
74        default : return 1;
75        }
76    }
77  }
```

(*ObtainConditions*). Consider now the source code of the *PBroker* role in order to clarify these different aspects.

Figure 7 provides a part of the UML sequence diagram describing mechanisms associated to the creation of a group and the access to a role in this group. The *Broker* Holon (Holon 2) requests the address of a group implementing the *Purchase* organisation. In this example, no instance already exists, a new one is thus created, and its address is returned to the holon. Then the holon requests for access to this group and to the *PBroker* role in this group. The group and role access conditions are verified. In this case, the holon fulfills all required

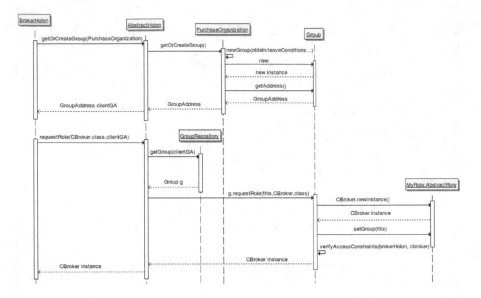

Fig. 7. UML sequence diagram of an access request to a role in a given group

conditions, it thus obtains an instance of the *PBroker* role that is added to its role container.

6   Conclusion

In this article, we have introduced the Janus platform dedicated to the implementation and deployment of MAS and HMAS. In JANUS, the notion of organisation is considered as a true Java module in its own right. The native management of the concept of capacity allows to implement a role, without making any assumption on the architecture of holons playing it, and thus promotes the reuse of organisations in various applications. However, this approach should be relativized, because it requires the definition of a significant number of classes, even for small applications (one class for each organisation, role, holon or agent architecture). So Janus aims primarily at developing large applications where modularity is essential. This aspect confirms the need to associate JANUS with a CASE tool to automatically generate significant portions of code, thus simplifying the intervention of a programmer. This CASE tool is currently under development in our Lab. In addition JANUS, providing a direct implementation of the four concepts at the base of CRIO (capacity, role, organisation and holon), contributes to reduce the gap between design and implementation phases. This platform is part of a larger effort aiming at providing a complete software tools suite for the development of complex applications in an industrial context.

References

1. Dastani, M., Gomez-Sanz, J.J.: Programming multi-agent systems (promas), a report of the technical forum meeting (April 2005),
   http://people.cs.uu.nl/mehdi/tfg/ljubljanafiles/report.pdf
2. Rodriguez, S., Hilaire, V., Koukam, A.: Fomal specification of holonic multi-agent system framework. In: Sunderam, V.S., van Albada, G.D., Sloot, P.M.A., Dongarra, J. (eds.) ICCS 2005. LNCS, vol. 3516, pp. 719–726. Springer, Heidelberg (2005)
3. Cossentino, M., Gaud, N., Hilaire, V., Galland, S., Koukam, A.: A Holonic Metamodel for Agent-Oriented Analysis and Design. In: Mařík, V., Vyatkin, V., Colombo, A.W. (eds.) HoloMAS 2007. LNCS, vol. 4659, pp. 237–246. Springer, Heidelberg (2007)
4. Cossentino, M., Gaud, N., Hilaire, V., Galland, S., Koukam, A.: A Metamodel and Implementation platform for Holonic Multi-Agent Systems. In: The fifth European Workshop on Multi-Agent Systems (EUMAS 2007), Hammamet, Tunisia (December 2007)
5. Object Management Group (OMG): MDA Guide, v1.0.1, OMG/2003-06-01 (June 2003)
6. Rodriguez, S., Gaud, N., Hilaire, V., Galland, S., Koukam, A.: An analysis and design concept for self-organization in holonic multi-agent systems. In: Brueckner, S.A., Hassas, S., Jelasity, M., Yamins, D. (eds.) ESOA 2006. LNCS, vol. 4335, pp. 15–27. Springer, Heidelberg (2007)
7. Gutknecht, O., Ferber, J.: Madkit: a generic multi-agent platform. In: The 4th International Conference on Autonomous Agents (AGENTS 2000), Barcelona, Spain, pp. 78–79. ACM Press, New York (2000)
8. Amiguet, M., Müller, J.P., Baez-Barranco, J.A., Nagy, A.: The MOCA Platform, Simulating the Dynamics of Social Networks. In: Sichman, J.S., Bousquet, F., Davidsson, P. (eds.) MABS 2002. LNCS, vol. 2581, pp. 70–88. Springer, Heidelberg (2003)
9. Sycara, K., Klusch, M., Widoff, S., Lu, J.: Dynamic service matchmaking among agents in open information environments. SIGMOD Record (ACM Special Interests Group on Management of Data) 28(1), 47–53 (1999)
10. Sycara, K., Lu, J., Klusch, M., Widoff, S.: Matchmaking among heterogeneous agents on the internet. In: Proceedings of the 1999 AAAI Spring Symposium on Intelligent Agents in Cyberspace (March 1999)
11. Gouaich, A., Michel, F., Guiraud, Y.: MIC*: a deployment environment for autonomous agents. In: Weyns, D., Van Dyke Parunak, H., Michel, F. (eds.) E4MAS 2004. LNCS (LNAI), vol. 3374, pp. 109–126. Springer, Heidelberg (2005)
12. Gerber, C., Siekmann, J.H., Vierke, G.: Holonic Multi-Agent Systems. Technical Report DFKI-RR-99-03, Deutsches Forschungszentrum für Künztliche Inteligenz - GmbH, Postfach 20 80, 67608 Kaiserslautern, FRG (May 1999)
13. Ferber, J., Gutknecht, O.: A meta-model for the analysis and design of organizations in multi-agent systems. In: Demazeau, Y., Durfee, E., Jennings, N.R. (eds.) Third International Conference on Multi-Agent Systems (ICMAS), Paris, France, july 1998, pp. 128–135 (1998)

A Complete-Computerised Delphi Process with a Multi-Agent System

Iván García-Magariño, Jorge J. Gómez-Sanz, and José R. Pérez-Agüera

D. Software Engineering and Artificial Intelligence
Facultad de Informática
Universidad Complutense de Madrid, Spain
ivan_gmg@fdi.ucm.es, jjgomez@sip.ucm.es, jose.aguera@fdi.ucm.es

Abstract. Looking for alternative ways of coordinating agents, this paper explores the adaptation of the Delphi protocol to agent systems. The Delphi protocol can be applied when a community of experts is required to deliver a consensual answer. In these cases, consensus stands for reaching an agreement among the experts about what the answer should be. This consensus reaching problem has been already considered in the literature, though its automatisation remains as a challenge. Intuitively, the experts should dialogue, interchange ideas, and change their mind as the discussion progresses. This paper presents a computerisation of discussion among expert agents and shows how they can be drawn towards a conclusion discussion by means of the Delphi process. The proof of concept is made with a document relevance evaluation problem where a community of experts decide whether a document is relevant or not. In conclusion, this paper makes an important contribution to people using Delphi processes, because the presented system is the first complete-computerised Delphi process. With respect to multi-agent systems, it has the potential to solve coordination in an original way, different from everything that has been done before.

Keywords: agent oriented software engineering, multi-agent systems, development.

1 Introduction

In multi-agent systems (MAS), the agents coordinate to achieve results. Frequently, the agents follow a rigid interaction protocol. Therefore, there are negotiations, e.g. an auction, or call for proposals, e.g. contract-net protocol, to cite two approaches. Nevertheless, the very essence of agents is missing when using these protocols. If one expected a group of humans to get organized in order to solve an issue, most probably, one would imagine them discuss among themselves first and agree in a solution. As humans, we know that discussions are not tied to a specific schema, and that despite efforts, usually they require strong moderators establishing the talk order and topics.

Towards this intuitive vision of a coordination, this paper addresses the problem with an approach of social sciences, the Delphi protocol. A Delphi survey

K.V. Hindriks, A. Pokahr, and S. Sardina (Eds.): ProMAS 2008, LNAI 5442, pp. 120–135, 2009.

is a procedure for structuring a group communication process so that the process is effective in allowing a group of individuals, as a whole, to deal with a complex problem [18]. From the uses this procedure has, this paper focuses on the consensus agreement capabilities it brings. Reaching consensus implies there are experts providing an opinion about a concrete issue and the possibility of a disagreement among those experts. Each expert is supposed to follow different criteria and use different sources of knowledge. In this context, an external client needs to obtain a consensual opinion about an issue. This implies reaching an agreement among experts.

The goal of this paper is to provide a fully computerised Delphi process. The computerisation of this Delphi process is rather challenging. Literature tells Delphi has been executed mainly by humans and sometimes with some computer assistance [34].The main obstacle is adapting the Delphi essence, which is very fuzzy, to the context of agents. Unfortunately, Delphi is very dependent on the domain and only generic guidelines about what is required can be found. Nevertheless, this paper will propose a set of elements a Delphi protocol should incorporate and what observable differences can be appreciated when using this protocol.

The Delphi integration is tested first in a document relevance evaluation domain. The problem consists in deciding if a concrete document is relevant or not in a concrete context. To answer the question, there are several expert agents designed to rate documents according to different criteria. Despite this circumstance, the paper will show how a dialogue among these agents can be established and an agreed answer obtained.

The scenario has been constructed with the INGENIAS [10] methodology. INGENIAS provides a comprehensive notation as well as a set of tools supporting modelling and implementation of specifications.

The paper is structured as follows. Firstly, Section 2 presents the Delphi method. Section 3 mentions several works related to the consensus in MAS and Section 4 briefly introduces INGENIAS and its tool support. Then, the implementation of Delphi with INGENIAS appears in Section 5. Some reflections on how questionaires are elaborated and processed appear in Section 6. The evaluation of the results obtained so far is discussed in Section 7. Finally, Section 8 mentions the conclusions.

2   Delphi Method

This method dates back to the fifties. It was created by the RAND corporation in Santa Monica, California. The method is made of structured surveys. It plans several rounds of questionaries which are sent to the different involved experts. The results collected can be included partially in a new round of questionaires, but respecting the anonymity of the participants.

This method was created initially for foresight studies, i.e., long-term decisions that guide the policy of a country or a company. Besides forecasting, there are many contexts where the Delphi Method can be applied, like reaching a consensus in a community of experts [6]. The scenario considers several experts discussing about a concrete topic. By using the Delphi method, individual experts are forced to look at the reasons of other experts. This extra information can force experts to reconsider their opinions and reach agreements.

An important part of the Delphi method consists in defining different questionaires which are to be filled in by the different experts. These questionnaires intend to re-orient the initial problem. The re-orientation can be elaborated according to the different answers supplied by experts. Therefore, each questionaire will include pieces of the answers already developed. By the intervention of the questionaire elaborator, it is assumed that the process converges in a single alternative. This mediator role is usually played by a human, though it could be replaced by a computer. This leads to the the *Delphi Conference*, i.e., a computer based Delphi method [34].

The Delphi Process in general is not rigid and its structure depends on the situation. Looking for guidelines, this paper follows the steps and guidelines stated in [5].

The Delphi approach has been applied for several areas for different uses.For instance, Roth [31] used the Delphi approach for acquiring knowledge from multiple experts. Recently; Bryant [4] applied the Delphi method for estimating the risk factors of the terrestrial chemical spill; Hayes [13] did a Delphi study of the future of marketing of the higher education; Mir'o[21] applied the delphi method to reach consensus among professionals with interest in chronic pain among children and adolescents.

The automatisation of Delphi is considered first as a set of computers and software assisting human experts in the process. In this line, literature mentions DEMOS[19], which is an on-line discussion system based on Delphi, and Turoff [34], who presents a Delphi method with computer assistance.

In 2002, Holsapple [14] provided a framework based on Delphi methodology. Within this framework the processors (human and/or computer-based) manipulates knowledge resources. This framework is descriptive, but considers and encourages the possibility of computer-based processors integrated in a delphi organisation.

3   Reaching Consensus in MAS

The problem of reaching consensus in Multi-Agent Systems is not radically new. Negotiation, for instance, can be seen as a decision-making problem where two or more parties try to find a consensus [30]. So far, approaches to this kind imply complex theories, like game theory. The solution addressed in this paper is not at the same level, since Delphi is applied mostly to humans and requires less formal methods.

The *interactive consistence*[25] property approach is similar to this paper. The *interactive consistence* ensures a faulty processor can produce a correct value based on the values supplied by other non-faulty processors. This problem is later presented as the *Byzantine Generals problem* [16]. These results are more related to the approach presented here, but not exactly the same. An expert providing a different opinion from another expert could be considered as a faulty component. Nevertheless, Delphi is not discarding opinions from *faulty* experts, because it would not be the first time a single expert is right and all the rest are wrong. Besides, all experts, potentially, can change their mind and provide different answers to the initial question, as it will be shown later on.

Another related work is from Hannebauer [12]. In this work, disagreement between different problem solving methods is solved by means of choosing the most frequent answer. In this paper, the approach is different in the sense that opinion from experts may be interpreted in different ways as their answers to the questionaires are collected. In fact, experts are allowed to change their mind when more information arrives.

The diversity of answers can be handled as well by using results from trust and reputation models [32]. The difference between these approaches can be found in the final goal of trust and reputation models: the interest in finding only one provider of the service which can be trusted enough. With Delphi, the problem is not finding one trusted service provider, but finding ways in which all service providers can be accounted.

4   INGENIAS and IDK

INGENIAS methodology for the development of multi-agent systems was presented first in Pavon [23]. Its main feature is the coverage of the whole development cycle, from analysis to implementation, and its tool support, known as the *INGENIAS Development Kit (IDK)*.

The main tool is the IDK specification editor, which allows the developer to define the MAS. This editor works as host for plugins. From those plugins, the main ones are those dedicated to code generation. Though there are several plugins for different platforms, the most relevant is the INGENIAS Agent Framework code generator. This plugin produces code for the JADE Platform [3]. This code generator has been introduced previously in the literature in [9] [8].

Therefore the IDK provides a way to develop multi-agent systems following the principles of *Model-Driven Development* [24]. The user defines the specification with the IDK Editor. This specification represents the model, on which the multi-agent system development is based. This approach provides a robust and quick technique for developing multi-agent systems.

As a matter of fact, INGENIAS methodology and IDK have been applied successfully in several areas. For instance, Gascuena [7] used INGENIAS for surveillance. Soto[33] presents how to model an knowledge management system with INGENIAS. Finally, a mobile tourist guide [22] was developed using IN-GENIAS.

All these facts makes INGENIAS and IDK suitable for the current task, i.e., model and execute a Delphi method among several agents. For the understanding of the remaining of the paper, Figure 1 contains the most relevant INGENIAS notation.

Fig. 1. The Most Relevant INGENIAS Notation

5   Representing the Delphi Method with INGENIAS Notation

According to the guidelines from [5], there should be rounds of questionnaires and a connection between them. To model them, the delphi specification starts with the definition of these two concerns. There are two main roles: *expert* role, which fills in questionaires, and *monitor* roles, responsible of elaborating questionnaires and analysing the answers. There is an additional role, the *client*, which is the one requesting the Delphi. There can be several monitors, at least 1, and several experts, at least 2, in a Delphi process.

Figure 2 captures the Delphi functionality applied to the document evaluation problem. The *evaluationUC* use case represents a client requesting a service for document evaluation by means of a Delphi survey. The service is provided by an agent playing the *monitor* role. To discover goals, the current version of the IDK permits to associate goals to identified use cases. Therfore, when the *evaluationUC* use case is performed, the *ObtainDocEvG* goal is achieved. This goal represents a future state in the system where a document has been evaluated following a Delphi process. The second use case, *delphiUC*, encapsulates the access to the questionaire filling in service offered by an agent playing the *expert* role. The *monitor* asks an *expert* to fill in a form, following the spirit of a Delphi process. The results are gathered and analysed by the *monitor* who will decide to go again into another round or finishing at the current moment. Like previous use case, this one intends to achieve a concrete goal, the *AnswerQuestG* goal. This goal represents the state of the system reached when an *expert* has filled in the supplied questionaire and a *monitor* has analysed the answer.

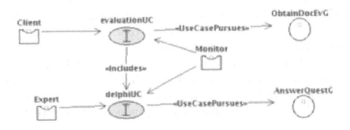

Fig. 2. Main use cases considered in the development of the Delphi process

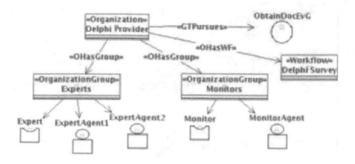

Fig. 3. MAS organisation providing the document relevance evaluation

Now, according to the methodology, the developer must define ways in which those goals are achieved. Some goals require the involvement of a group of agents, like the *ObtainDocEvG* goal, others the involvement of a few. To satisfy the first goal, *ObtainDocEvG*, an organisation is created, the *Delphi Provider* organisation. This organisation (see Figure 3) is structured into two groups, the *experts* and the *monitors*. In the *experts* group, there will be agents able to play the *expert* role. In this case, agents *ExpertAgent1* and *ExpertAgent2* are responsible of answering the different questionaires delivered by *monitors*. For the sake of initial experiments, two *expert* agents are enough, though it is scalable to many more, provided they can implement the *expert* role.

The organisation is able to provide a service by means of the *monitor* role. The service is implemented as a workflow named *Delphi Survey*. Following again Delphi instructions, the method requires at least two rounds of questionaires. The interaction among individuals in the workflow is controlled by two interactions, *AskingEval* and *DelphiCoop*, whose corresponding protocol appears in Figure 6. The first one encapsulates the interaction between the *client* and *monitor* roles to request the evaluation service. The second contains the questionaire elaboration, deliver, and answer gathering activities.

The workflow itself gathers the tasks shown in Figure 4. This workflow is relevant since no Delphi formal definition has been made, yet, according to our research. Therefore, this definition is also relevant. The workflow presented in Figure 4 starts with a client requesting the service with the task *chooseDoctT*. This task is supposed to provide the document to be evaluated by a *Delphi provider* organisation. The document is received by the *monitor* and a customised questionaire is elaborated with task *InitQuestT*. The questionaire is answered by experts by means of a task *AnsweQuestT*. The answer is processed by the *monitor* with a task *ProcessAnswerT*. As a result of this task, another round can be derived or not. If a new round occurs, the task *CreateOtherQuestT* should be executed. This would force another elaboration of questionaires and a new answer deliver by experts. If no more rounds occur, then the *monitor* delivers the result to the *client*, which processes the evaluation with task *ResultObtainedT*.

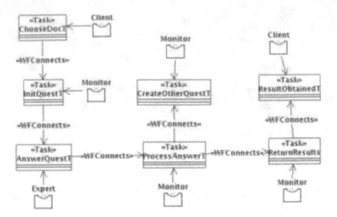

Fig. 4. Overview of the workflow used to implement the Delphi process

Some of these tasks have the responsibility of launching interactions. This is the case of *ChooseDocT*, *InitQuestT*, and *CreateOtherQuestT*. The first task creates an interaction of type *AskingEval*, while the second and third ones create an interaction of type *DelphiCoop*. As it will be seen later in Figure 6, the interaction complements the workflow definition by telling what information is passed to each agent and what tasks are expected to be triggered as a result of that information transfer.

A questionaire is represented with a *FrameFact* type, the *QuestToBeAnsweredFF* entity (see figure 5). This entity has a slot containing the questionaire in form of a string. Readers can assume the questionaire is codified as a string and passed as a slot inside of a *QuestToBeAnsweredFF*. This *QuestToBeAnsweredFF* is consumed in figure 5 by two different tasks, *AnswerQuestExpr1T* and *AnswerQuestExpr2T*, belonging to two different experts of the organisation, the *ExpertAgent1* and the *ExpertAgent2*. As a result, the tasks produce a *QuestReplyFF* entity with the answer of each expert. Similar to *QuestToBeAnsweredFF*, *QuestReplyFF* contains the questionaire in form of a string.

The specification problem requires incorporating different ways of answering questionaires depending on the experts and still keeps the protocol generic. This is achieved by redefining the content of some tasks.

To perform these tasks, it is necessary the assistance of three pieces of external software, represented in the Figure 5 with *LogGUI*, *ExpertUtils1*, and *ExpertUtils2*. The first acts as a general log to show debug information. The second provides the fill in questionnaire functionality for *ExpertAgent1*. The third does the same for *ExpertAgent2*. These tasks are not included in the workflow from Figure 4 because they are domain specific, i.e., developed ad-hoc to capture concrete means of filling in a questionaire. These tasks would take as input the output of task *AnswerQuestT*, which does belong to the workflow, and would provide outputs for the next tasks in the workflow.

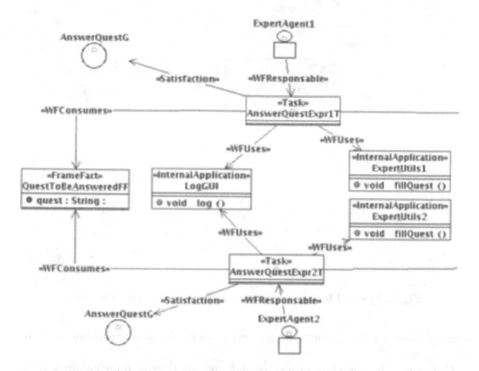

Fig. 5. Tasks representing the answering procedures of individual experts

The protocol for sending questionnaires and receiving answers is presented in Figure 6. The protocol interleaves entities of type *InteractionUnit* with task entities. Each *interaction unit* type entity represents a communication between a *Monitor* and an *Expert* role. It has associated an speech act and the information to be transmitted. For instance, the *DistQuest* interaction unit transmits the questionnaire. When the entity is transferred, the *expert* role is expected to execute several task until the expert creates a reply for the questionnaire.

In this paper, it is assumed this extra processing is provided by tasks associated to external software components, which implement the expert criteria. Once received the answer from the expert, the agent playing the *monitor* role either finds a consensus or decides to initiate another round of questionnaires. The first case implies engaging into a *Agree* interaction unit and sending the result of the consensus. In the second case, the *CreateOtherQuestT* task creates another instance of the interaction following the protocol from Figure 6. Also, it informs the expert that there was not an agreement by a *NotAgree* interaction unit.

Therefore, there can be several rounds of queries to the different experts. The dialogue among experts is not a direct one, since it happens as a result of the elaboration of the second round of questionaires. According to the Delphi method, the dialogue happens because each new round of questionaires incorporates results from the answers of all experts in the last round. Therefore,

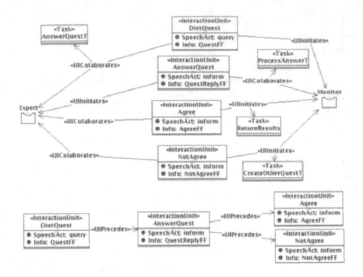

Fig. 6. Protocol for passing a questionaire and receiving the answer

a each expert has the opportunity to reconsider its decision according to the new information.

Unfortunately, the elaboration, replies and analysis of questionaires are domain specific. The adaptation of this part to other domains is left for future work. Except this part, this description is generic enough to fit into most applications of Delphi. The problem specific part is considered in more detail into the following section.

6 Domain Specific Delphi Aspects

In the Delphi processes, some domain specific aspects are necessary. For this reason, the presented research needs to select, at the beginning, a specific domain for the experimentations. The presented work selects the domain of document relevance. The computerisation of Delphi processes with other specific domains is left for future work

The customisation of the Delphi process requires determining what the questionaires are, how they are constructed, and how they are answered. Due to the document relevance evaluation nature, the customisation requires some insight into information extraction and information retrieval. This section explains how this customisation takes place, explaining how questionaires are built for the first round and subsequent ones.

The questionaires questions considers the most important sentences contained in the document to be evaluated. Experts answers to each question are created with the relevance of the sentence in the opinion of the expert. The opinion of the expert is modelled with a set of documents. This knowledge of each expert is denoted as expert profile

To simulate the human information exchange between experts, i.e. the dialog among individuals, defined in Delphi process, like expert's comments, we propose a pseudo-relevance feedback method where each expert agent try to append comments, modeled like query expansion terms, extracted from his profile to each entry of the questionaire to show the knowledge of the domain contained is his domain profile.

The delphi process is used before for the document relevance domain. For instance, Green[11] uses the Delphi method to evaluate web sites. However, that work needs human beings for the evaluation of documents. The best contribution of this paper is the following. The presented system is the first complete-computerised delphi process.

6.1   First Questionaire Generation

To generate the first questionaire, it is necessary to transform the input document in a list of queries corresponding to the questions of the questionaire.

For the elaboration of questionnaires, firstly the sentences are extracted from from the original documents. Then, the TF-ISF (Term Frequency - Inverse Sentence Frequency) [17] algorithm is applied. This algorithm selects the most informative phrases from the document. TF-ISF is defined by the following equations.

$$ISF(t) = \frac{1}{s \in t} \qquad (1)$$

where $s \in t$ is the number of sentences containing the term t.

$$TF - ISF(s) = \sum_{t \in s} tf * \log ISF_t \qquad (2)$$

where tf is the frequency of the term t in the document.

The TF-ISF method gives a higher score to keywords appearing in fewer sentences. Therefore, the most important sentences will be the ones which contain more quantity of higher scored keywords.

6.2   Relevance Assessments

To compute the relevance for each question of the questionaire, the presented system uses a similarity function that is able to compare these questions with the documents retrieved from the expert profile.

A relevance value is assigned to each question of the questionaire and a global relevance value is computed for the whole questionaire. This global relevance is computed using the mean average value of our similarity function for the questions contained in the questionaire. The referee use this global value in each round to know if the consensus has been reached.

For this task, the presented system uses the default similarity measure implemented in Lucene[1] that is co-related with the cosine in the Vector Space Model [2], i.e., for a collection D, document d and query q containing terms t_i :

$$sim(q, d) = \sum_{t \in q} \frac{tf_{t,q} * idf_t}{norm_q} * \frac{tf_{t,d} * idf_t}{norm_d} * coord_{q,d} * weight_t \tag{3}$$

where

$$tf_{t,x} = \sqrt{freq(t, X)} \tag{4}$$

$$idf_t = 1 + log \frac{|D|}{freq(t, D)} \tag{5}$$

$$norm_d = \sqrt{|d|} \tag{6}$$

$$coord_{q,d} = \frac{|q \cap d|}{|q|} \tag{7}$$

$$norm_q = \sqrt{\sum_{t \in q} tf_{t,q} * idf_t{}^2} \tag{8}$$

$tf_{t,x}$ represent the non-linear frequency of the terms in the query or in the documents; idf is the Inverse Document Frequency of the terms in the collection; $norm_d$ and $norm_q$ are measures to normalise the document and query length. Finally, $coord_{q,d}$ is a score factor based on how many of the query terms are found in the specified document. Typically, a document that contains most of the query's terms will receive a higher score than another document with fewer query terms.

6.3 Next Questionaires Generation

Building the questionaires for the next rounds is necessary to take in account the comments generated by the experts in the first round. For this task, the questions with highest relevance are increased with the words/comments proposed by each expert agent. This method is very similar to query expansion process using pseudo-relevance feedback [2] to extract the terms candidates to become comments.

One of the main approaches to query expansion is based on studying the difference of term distribution between the whole collection and the subsets of documents that can be relevant for the query or, in our case, for the question of the questionaire. It is expected that terms with little informative content have a similar distribution in any document of the collection corresponding in this work to the expert agent profile. On the contrary, terms closely related to those of the question of the questionaire are expected to be more frequent in the

---

[1] http://lucene.apache.org/

top ranked set of documents than in other subsets of documents existing in the expert profile. All the documents are retrieved from the expert profile with the original question.

The query expansion method used for comments generation is defined by two steps. The first step is devoted to extract a candidate terms list to expand the questions contained in the questionaire received by the expert agent from the referee. These candidate terms are extracted from the top ranked documents returned by the first-pass retrieval on the expert profile, which are represented by a inverted index of relevant documents.

After extracting the terms from the n first documents returned, Divergence From Randomness (DFR)[1] can be used to rank the candidates. The DFR term weighting model infers the informativeness of a term by the divergence between its distribution in the top-ranked documents and a random distribution. The most effective DFR term weighting model is the *Bo1 model* that uses the Bose-Einstein statistics[27,20]:

$$w(t) = tf_x * log_2 \frac{1 + P_n}{P_n} + log_2(1 + P_n) \tag{9}$$

where P_n is given by $\frac{F}{N}$; F is the frequency of the term in the expert profile, and N is the number of documents in the expert profile; tf_x is the frequency of the query term in the n top-ranked documents retrieved from the expert profile.

In the second step we need to re-weight the candidate terms to append them to questions. To carry out this task we have used the well-know Rocchio algorithm[29]:

$$qtw = \frac{qtf}{qtf_{max}} + \beta * \frac{w(t)}{w_{max}(t)} \tag{10}$$

where qtw is the weight of the candidate term in the question; qtf is the frequency of term in the question; qtf_{max} is the term with highest frequency in the question; β is a parameter; $w(t)$ is the value assigned by Bose-Einstein statistics; $w_{max}(t)$ is the highest value assigned by Bose-Einstein statistics.

For each round the system carries out a new expansion on the questions contained in the questionaires.

7   Evaluation of the Delphi Method

The evaluation of the system implementing Delphi follows the guidelines established for the evaluation of an information retrieval system. This evaluation requires, first, determining a test document collection. These collections are usually processed by humans before hand determining, for concrete queries, which documents should be retrieved from the collection.

Once prepared the collection of documents, the system is tested by asking if a document is relevant or not. The relevance is measured with the Delphi method, i.e., asking the system, and without the method, i.e., applying a TF-IDF technique directly to the document. This way, it is checked whether the Delphi method implemented with agents really improves a stand alone technique.

7.1 Preparing the Experiment

Document collections from information retrieval discipline establish, for a given document, which other documents are really related to and which are not. This paper uses the collection provided by CLEF (Cross-Language Evaluation Forum) [26] for the Spanish language. The name of the collection used in this paper is EFE94. It was constructed by the international news agency EFE from all the news received during 1994. The size of the collection is 215.738 documents. The collection includes a set of topics and relevance assessments produced by humans.

Each expert profile is made of 5452 relevant documents extracted from the relevance assessments of the collection. The *train set* is divided between the different experts also without overlapping between them. The document test set is made of 104 documents from the relevance assessments of the test collection, 54 relevant and 50 non-relevant. There is no overlapping among the documents of the training set and the documents used for the expert profiles. In our experiments the documents contained in the test set must be judged by Delphi agent system to know their relevance using the consensus among expert agents.

7.2 Evaluation Results

The system constructed so far determines if a document is relevant, which is an aspect studied by information retrieval discipline. Therefore, it makes sense to measure its efficacy with information retrieval techniques. Commonly, the evaluation of an information retrieval technique requires talking about Precision, Recall and F1[28]. Precision is defined as the ratio of good assessments (relevant and non-relevant) selected to total number of assessments. Recall is defined as the ratio of relevant documents selected to total number of relevant documents available. F1 combines precision and recall into a single number. Increasing both precision and recall is the best result. However, only increasing one of them is the most common. In this evaluation, both precission and recall increase.

The results from our experiments are presented in the following table

	Only TF-IDF	TF-IDF with DELPHI
Precision	0.86	0.92(+6.5%)
Recall	0.84	0.96(+12.5%)
F1	0.84	0.93(+9.6%)

The improvement is significant in every concern. Nevertheless, alternative measurements were applied to verify the result, concretely with the ROC [15] method:

$$HitRate = \frac{tp}{tp + fn} \qquad (11)$$

$$FalseAlarmRate = \frac{fp}{fp + tn} \qquad (12)$$

where the number of true positives, denoted tp, are the number of positive examples correctly identified as such. The number of false positives, denoted fp, are the number of negatives that are miss-classified as positive. The definitions for true negatives tn and false negatives fn are analogous. According to this, our experiment results are presented in the following table.

	Without DELPHI	DELPHI
Hit Rate	0.84	0.96(+12.5%)
False Alarm Rate	0.12	0.12(=)

Again, it can be observed the use of Delphi method achieved an improvement of the performance, greater than the one achieved without cooperation among agents. On the other hand, a very good general performance is obtained, because our system is capable to detect on average, 9 out of every 10 relevant documents.

8   Conclusions and Future Work

This paper presents a Multi-agent based Delphi process for the document relevance domain. This system is the first complete-computerised process of the Delphi method.

Furthermore, the Delphi Method is a technique that promises a new way of dealing with the coordination of agents.

A complicate part of this method consists in determining which questions should appear in the questionaire and a proper method of elaborating, as well as analysing, answers. This part is domain specific. For the presented experimentations, the document relevance domain is selected. Nevertheless, there are already some reusable content, like the MAS specification and a part of the MAS implementation. The domain-specific part is encapsulated in certain *Task* entities and certain external components.

The presented system can be adapted to other specific domains. This adaptation is left for future work.

Acknowledgements

This work has been supported by the project Methods and tools for agent-based modelling supported by Spanish Council for Science and Technology with grant TIN2005-08501-C03-01, and by the grant for Research Group 910494 by the Region of Madrid (Comunidad de Madrid) and the Universidad Complutense Madrid.

References

1. Amati, G., Rijsbergen, C.J.V.: Probabilistic models of information retrieval based on measuring the divergence from randomness. ACM Trans. Inf. Syst. 20(4), 357–389 (2002)
2. Baeza-Yates, R.A., Ribeiro-Neto, B.A.: Modern Information Retrieval. ACM Press / Addison-Wesley (1999)

3. Bellifemine, F., Poggi, A., Rimassa, G.: Developing multi-agent systems with a FIPA-compliant agent framework. Software-Practice and Experience 31(2), 103–128 (2001)

4. Bryant, D.L., Abkowitz, M.D.: Estimation of terrestrial chemical spill risk factors using a modified delphi approach. Journal of Environmental Management 85, 112–120 (2007)

5. Cuhls, K.: Delphi method. Technical report, Fraunhofer Institute for Systems and Innovation Research (2003)

6. Dalkey, N., Helmer, O.: An Experimental Application of the Delphi Method to the Use of Experts. Management Science 9(3), 458–467 (1963)

7. Gascuena, J., Fernandez-Caballero, A.: The INGENIAS Methodology for Advanced Surveillance Systems Modelling. In: Mira, J., Álvarez, J.R. (eds.) IWINAC 2007. LNCS, vol. 4528, pp. 541–550. Springer, Heidelberg (2007)

8. Gómez-Sanz, J., Fuentes, R., Pavón, J.: Enabling Rapid Prototyping using Decoupling of Code Skeletons and Code generation Process. Infocomp. Journal of Computer Science, 26–34 (2006)

9. Gómez-Sanz, J., Pavón, J.: Defining coordination in multi-agent systems within an agent oriented software engineering methodology. In: Proceedings of the 2006 ACM symposium on Applied computing, pp. 424–428 (2006)

10. Gomez-Sanz, J.J., Fuentes, R., Pavon, J.: The INGENIAS Methodology and Tools. In: Agent-oriented Methodologies, pp. 236–276. Idea Group Publishing (2005)

11. Green, J.W.: Delphi method in web site selection: Using the experts. The Reference Librarian 33(69-70), 299–310 (2001)

12. Hannebauer, M.: Multi-phase consensus communication in collaborative problem solving. In: Proceedings of the Third Workshop on Communication-based Systems, pp. 131–146. Kluwer, Dordrecht (2000)

13. Hayes, T.: Delphi study of the future of marketing of higher education. Journal of Business Research 60, 927–931 (2007)

14. Holsapple, C., Joshi, K.: Knowledge manipulation activities: results of a delphi study. Information and Management 39, 477–490 (2002)

15. Konstan, J.: Introduction to recommender systems: Algorithms and Evaluation. ACM Transactions on Information Systems (TOIS) 22(1), 1–4 (2004)

16. Lamport, L., Shostak, R., Pease, M.: The byzantine generals problem. ACM Trans. Program. Lang. Syst. 4(3), 382–401 (1982)

17. Larocca Neto, J., Santos, A.D., Kaestner, C.A.A., Freitas, A.A.: Document clustering and text summarization. In: Proceedings of the 4th International Conference on Practical Applications of Knowledge Discovery and Data Mining, London, pp. 41–55 (2000)

18. Linstone, H., Turoff, M.: The Delphi Method: Techniques and Applications. Addison-Wesley Pub. Co., Advanced Book Program (1975)

19. Luehrs, R., Pavón, J., Schneider, M.: DEMOS Tools for Online Discussion and Decision Making. In: Cueva Lovelle, J.M., Rodríguez, B.M.G., Gayo, J.E.L., del Pueto Paule Ruiz, M., Aguilar, L.J. (eds.) ICWE 2003. LNCS, vol. 2722, pp. 525–528. Springer, Heidelberg (2003)

20. Macdonald, C., He, B., Plachouras, V., Ounis, I.: University of Glasgow at TREC 2005: Experiments in Terabyte and Enterprise Tracks with Terrier. In: Proceeddings of the 14th Text REtrieval Conference (TREC 2005) (2005)

21. Mir, J., Huguet, A., Nieto, R.: Predictive factors of chronic pediatric pain and disability: A delphi poll. The Journal of Pain 8(10), 774–792 (2007)

22. Pavón, J., Corchado, J., Gómez-Sanz, J., Ossa, L.: Mobile Tourist Guide Services with Software Agents. In: Karmouch, A., Korba, L., Madeira, E.R.M. (eds.) MATA 2004. LNCS, vol. 3284, pp. 322–330. Springer, Heidelberg (2004)
23. Pavón, J., Gómez-Sanz, J.: Agent Oriented Software Engineering with INGENIAS. Multi-Agent Systems and Applications III 2691, 394–403 (2003)
24. Pavón, J., Gómez-Sanz, J., Fuentes, R.: Model Driven Development of Multi-Agent Systems. In: Rensink, A., Warmer, J. (eds.) ECMDA-FA 2006. LNCS, vol. 4066, pp. 284–298. Springer, Heidelberg (2006)
25. Pease, M., Shostak, R., Lamport, L.: Reaching Agreement in the Presence of Faults. Journal of the ACM (JACM) 27(2), 228–234 (1980)
26. Peters, C., Braschler, M.: European research letter: Cross-language system evaluation: The clef campaigns. JASIST 52(12), 1067–1072 (2001)
27. Plachouras, V., He, B., Ounis, I.: University of Glasgow at TREC2004: Experiments in Web, Robust and Terabyte tracks with Terrier. In: Proceeddings of the 13th Text REtrieval Conference (TREC 2004) (2004)
28. Rennie, J.: Derivation of the F-Measure. In other words 1, 4
29. Rocchio, J.J.: Relevance feedback in information retrieval. In: Salton, G. (ed.) The SMART retrieval system, pp. 313–323. Prentice Hall, Englewood Cliffs (1971)
30. Rosenschein, J., Zlotkin, G.: Rules of Encounter: Designing Conventions for Automated Negotiation Among Computers. MIT Press, Cambridge (1994)
31. Roth, R.: A Delphi approach to acquiring knowledge from single and multiple experts. In: Proceedings of the 1990 ACM SIGBDP conference on Trends and directions in expert systems, pp. 301–324 (1990)
32. Sabater, J., Sierra, C.: Reputation and social network analysis in multi-agent systems. In: Proceedings of the first international joint conference on Autonomous agents and multiagent systems: part 1, pp. 475–482 (2002)
33. Soto, J.P., Vizcano, A., Portillo, J., Piattini, M.: Modelling a Knowledge Management System Architecture with INGENIAS Methodology. In: Proceedings of the 15th International Conference on Computing (2006)
34. Turoff, M., Hiltz, S.: Computer Based Delphi Processes. In: Gazing into the Oracle. The Delphi Method and its Application to Social Policy and Public Health, pp. 56–85. Jessica Kingsley Publishers, London (1996)

How Situated Is Your Agent?
A Cognitive Perspective

Daghan L. Acay[1], Liz Sonenberg[1], Alessandro Ricci[2], and Philippe Pasquier[3]

[1] DIS, The University of Melbourne 111 Barry Street Victoria 3010, Australia
lacay@pgrad.unimelb.edu.au,
l.sonenberg@unimelb.edu.au
[2] DEIS, U. Bologna in Cesena Via Venezia, 52 Cesena (FC), Italy
a.ricci@unibo.it
[3] SIAT, Simon Fraser University, 102 Ave. Surrey, British Columbia, Canada
pasquier@sfu.ca

Abstract. Software agents are situated in an environment with which they interact reactively or in a goal-directed fashion. Generally, such environments do not assume a structure, hence are deemed to be unpredictable. Recent approaches adopt an environment model where artifacts form the building blocks. Artifacts represent functional components that an agent can exploit for reaching its goals. It has been argued that software agents can improve/amend their capabilities at run time through the use of (new) artifacts as possible means. We argue that such a run time adaptation by the agents can be realized by creating an appropriate relationship between agent reasoning and the functionality of the artifacts. We have coined the term *extrospection* to refer to the act of an agent *reasoning about the tools*. In this paper, we first identify the features of extrospection, then, we extend the belief, desire, intention (BDI) agent deliberation cycle to encompass extrospection.

1 Introduction

Although, there is a growing body of work in the agent literature that highlights the importance of the environment for agent systems [1], the relation between the agent and the environment at the cognitive level has not been well established. For example, an agent designer, in general, is responsible for constructing an internal environment model that may be consulted during deliberation. Such an internal model reflects an agent designer's anticipation about objects and available actions in the environment, in contrast to the actual environment as the agent experiences at run time. Thus, the cognitive awareness of the agent about the environment does not drive from the actual interaction but is limited to the agent designer's intuition at design time.

As the scale of Multi-Agent Systems (MASs) increases, the above approach to agent design leads to two problems. First, when the agent and the environment it acts in are developed by different designers, e.g. in the context of web services,

K.V. Hindriks, A. Pokahr, and S. Sardina (Eds.): ProMAS 2008, LNAI 5442, pp. 136–151, 2009.

the designer of an agent can not capture all the possible service combinations (i.e. environment). Second, even if the agent designer presumes a subset of services and constructs an internal model accordingly, the overall agent environment interaction is still prone to failures. The reason is that inconsistency between the internal model and the actual environment may arise over time. For example, some services included in the agent's internal model may become unavailable (off-line) or be inconsistent (due to the service (up/down)grade).

So agents should learn, understand and adapt to, their environments at run time. In this paper, we argue that the adaptation could be more tractable if agent environments are engineered in some manner. Ricci et. al. [2], in their agent and artifact framework (A&A), suggested 'artifact' as a possible abstraction to model non-agent entities in the environment. Although they suggested an 'artifact manual' for autonomous discovery and use of artifacts at run-time, they considered it as future work.

Previously, a possible way of representing artifact manuals using description logic has been exploredand a formal language for writing artifact manuals, called OWL-T [3] was introduced. In the context of this paper, we will call the combination of an artifact and the associated manual a 'tool[1].' The aim in this paper is to explore the relation between agent reasoning and tool specification so that agents can modify their behavior at run time, based on tool availability. In our case, the behavior modification is realized by agents flexibly substituting tools as means for their goals.

The 'cognitive situatedness' mentioned in the title reflects our idea that agents should adapt to the environment by discovering and using tools as alternative means at run-time. Real-time discovery, selection, and use of tools is referred to as *extrospection*, a term that we have coined to emphasize the externally influenced nature of reasoning. The term *extrospective agent* refers to agents endowed with this capability.

It is fair to interpret extrospection as another way to capture adaptation (i.e. learning and planning) and introducing a new term may seem hardly justifiable. On the other hand, the reader should bear in mind that extrospection approaches the adaptation problem from an environment design perspective instead of an agent design perspective. That is, our use of the term has implications for engineering an agent environment such that the adaptation is tractable. Thus, the fundamental questions for extrospection are: how can we engineer the agent environment? what are the implications of environment engineering to the reasoning cycle (i.e. query, learn, deliberate, plan, execute)? etc. For that, we believe a new term is helpful.

Expected benefits of using tools for MAS development include: (i) agents can complete the design by discovering and opportunistically using tools at run time (in Sec. 5), (ii) the reuse of components will be enhanced (implicitly argued throughout the paper), and (iii) domain independent meta-level reasoning can be built into the agents (in Sec. 6).

---

[1] One reason is that the term *artifact* has a computational emphasis whereas, *tool* has emphasize on reasoning.

2   Background: Philosophical Underpinnings

The A&A framework introduces artifacts as first class entities along with agents for developing a MAS. Similar to the A&A framework, our work on extrospective agents is inspired by the psychological theory called Activity Theory (AT) [4]. It is emphasized in AT that humans have the potential to change their environments. In other words, humans no longer live in natural habitats but populate them with tools to make the environment more suitable for their practices. Thus, their speed, power, and intelligence are enhanced beyond their innate nature through the proper use of tools.

Another important claim of AT is that tools represent the scrutinization of the experiences of those who have encountered and solved a particular problem in the past [4]. The solutions manifest themselves in (i) the physical properties of the tool (e.g. shape, size, etc.) and (ii) the knowledge of the functionality and the use of tools. The availability of tools influences the agent's behavior through its physical characteristics, e.g. body posture, approaching angle. Moreover, tool availability can modify the choice of action after the knowledge of the tool use is acquired, e.g. in the existence of a table, putting a hot cup on the table instead of dropping the cup.

In that sense, our work is complementary to the A&A framework where a computational model for artifacts has been introduced, as we introduce a computational model for the cognition of tool use. The A&A framework and the extrospective agent together aim to benefit from the claims of the AT in the context of the MAS development and execution.

3   An Example: Production Cell

The problem we are addressing is the run time adaptation of agents to different environments. Firstly, the agent designer does not need anticipate possible actions in the environment. Thus, the agent needs to discover what it can do in the environment. Secondly, actions in the environment may not be fixed due to changes (e.g. some services may go off line, new services can be introduced, or present services may be updated). Thus, we have chosen an example that reflects these points and rather simple in nature.

The example of production cell is taken from Meneguzzi et. al. [5] where a variety of component types with different production demands are produced. An agent *with the knowledge of the production demands of the components* is designed to work in different production cells. That is, the agent should discover and use production units (i.e. adapt) in the production cell it is situated. Moreover, the agent should be responsive to the changes such as failure, removal, addition, or upgrade. The task of the agent is to schedule components to the existing units.

An instance of the production cell with six devices (a Feed Belt, a Deposit Belt, four Processing Units) and a Crane that can freely move the components over the devices in the cell is considered here. Components that need to be processed enter the production cell through the Feed Belt. After a component is processed, it is removed from the cell through the Deposit Belt. Each Processing Unit can perform a set of operations and can accommodate a single component at a time. The type of a component determines the necessary operations that should be executed on the component.

Meneguzzi et. al. [5] have modeled the overall production unit as a single agent with propositional planning capability. Besides, we assume two distinctive entities, e.g. tools, and an agent. The tools such as the Feed Belt, the Deposit Belt, and Processing Units form the environment for the agent. Yet, the Crane is conceived as an agent with the capability of moving the components over the tools.

For future reference we give following details. The Process Unit 1 `procUnit1` can drill a component whereas the `procUnit2` can both drill and paint. Similarly, the `procUnit3` can cut and the `procUnit4` can polish a component. Moreover, there are three types of components that may come to the production cell. The first type `type1` requires drilling and the `type2` requires painting and drilling. The third type `type3` requires both cutting and polishing.

4 Extrospection Framework

The two important aspects of the extrospection framework are the agents and the tools in the environment. In addition, we introduce a third layer where the functionality of tools is symbolically represented as 'artifact manuals' [2]. Next we will detail each layer.

4.1 The Artifact Layer

We adopt the A&A meta-model [2], where the notion of artifact is used to model non-autonomous state-ful entities, specifically designed by MAS environment engineers to encapsulate some kind of function[2], and to be instantiated and used dynamically by agents to support their activities.

The functionality of an artifact is structured in terms of *operations*, whose execution can be triggered by agents through the artifact's *usage interface* which in turn is composed of *controls*. Agents can trigger and control the operation execution through controls with the necessary input parameters. Besides the controls, the usage interface might also contain a set of *observable properties*; the properties whose dynamic values can be observed by agents without necessarily interacting with (or operating upon) the artifact.

The execution of an operation may result in changing the artifact's inner (i.e., non-observable) state. The operation execution can be conceived as a process, combining the execution of possibly multiple atomic guarded operation steps. Operation steps are guarded by asserting *preconditions* for execution. In order to avoid interferences, the usage interface is disabled during the (atomic) execution

---

[2] The term *function* is used here as in the design theory, a synonym of functionality.

of a single operation step. The operations execute asynchronously to the activity of the agent. The information flow from artifacts to agents is modeled in the form of observable signals that are perceived by agents.

As a principle of composition, artifacts can be linked to enable the artifact–artifact interaction. This is realized through the *link interfaces*, e.g. using a remote control with a TV. The artifact topology is handled by the notion of *workspace*. Agents can use and observe only the artifacts belonging to their workspace. Workspaces provide basic default tools (artifacts) that agents can use to dynamically discover the artifacts currently available in the workspace (registry tools), to instantiate dynamically new artifacts (factory tools), to manage organization and security issues (organization tools), and so on." The artifacts of different workspaces – possibly on different network nodes– can be linked through the link interfaces discussed above. Agents can join and work simultaneously on multiple workspaces.

Analogously to the artifacts in the human case, in A&A each artifact is equipped with a "manual" describing: the artifact's function (i.e., its intended purpose), the artifact's usage interface (i.e., the observable "shape" of the artifact), and artifact's *operating instructions* (i.e., the correct use of the artifact). The manual is meant to be inspected and used at run time by agents, for reasoning about how to select and use artifacts. In this paper, the manual is described using the concept layer and discussed in Sec. 4.2.

Considering the A&A framework, we introduce some assumptions that are necessary to limit the reasoning about tools.

Assumption 1 (A1). *All operations supported by a tool are atomic and do not support concurrency.*

A1 simplifies the tool use for metalevel reasoning, as does A2.

Assumption 2 (A2). *Operation generates a* finished *event when execution completes.*

A3 emphasizes the asynchronous execution of tools and adds a temporal constraint.

Assumption 3 (A3). *Operations takes certain amount of time independent of agent activities.*

Finally, we assume that each tool may have more than one functionality. For each functionality there is one and only one operating instruction.

Assumption 4 (A4). *A tool may have multiple functionality. Each functionality is realized through a single operating instruction.*

We may apply these assumptions to the production cell example. The `procUnit2` conforms A4 by having two functionalities. A functionality can be realized by following the respective operating instruction. When the `procUnit2` is drilling a component, it is assumed to be busy (A1, A3). Yet, the agent may concentrate on other activities during drilling (A3). The agent will be informed – regardless of working on another activity– when drilling completes (A2).

In addition to the above assumptions, the production demand of a component may incorporate multiple tools. For example, a component of `type3` may requires both the `procUnit3` and the `procUnit4`. Thus, the use of tools requires two sorts of scheduling/planning tasks.

The first type of planning is employed for realizing the precondition/guards of the operations of a single tool. For example, the extrospective agent (Crane for this example) needs to plan to acquire the knowledge regarding the preconditions for drilling, e.g. `holeCoord(X,Y)`. Only after this information is available to the agent, the `startDrill` operation can be invoked over the tool. The second is necessary for orchestrating the use of multiple tools within a single intention. For example, the crane agent is responsible for planning to move components from one machine to another using its *moving* capability.

4.2   The Concept Layer

The concept layer symbolically describes the functionality and the operating instructions of the artifact (i.e. artifact manual). Through the concept layer, agents can incorporate tools' use knowledge into their deliberation cycle. The language OWL-T [3] is used for this purpose. T stands for (T)ool and OWL for the variant of description logic, Web Ontology Language (OWL) [6].

Artifact manual written by OWL-T can be compared – but can not be reduced– to API documentation for software objects. An *API documentation* conveys the functionality of the implemented objects to a human programmer. However, such documents are not useful for the software agents since they are written in natural language. Besides, the OWL-T is a formal language targeting the software agents. Analogous to an API documentation, if the concept layer is not supplied by the environment designer, it does not hamper the artifact operation given that the agent knows the existence of the tool and the corresponding operating instructions (i.e. internal model supplied by the agent designer). The OWL-T is merely useful for run time discovery. That is why we introduce the concept layer as a separate layer.

Here, we will concentrate on the three most relevant aspects that are captured by the OWL-T. The detailed account for the OWL-T has been given by Acay et. al. [3]. Firstly, the OWL-T aims to relate the *goals* of an agent and the *functionality* of a tool. For example, the functionality of the `procesUnit1` can be defined as `drill(C)`[3]. Then, an agent, which has a component of `type1`, can associate `procesUnit1` as a possible means to process the component.

Secondly, the OWL-T captures the *operations* and the associated *preconditions*. For example, an operation of `procesUnit1`, e.g. `startDrill` with the associated precondition `drillSize(X)` is captured using OWL-T. OWL-T also identifies the link between the precondition of an operation and the beliefs of the agent. That is, the OWL-T enforces the agent to have a belief of the form `drillSize(X)` before executing an operation.

---

[3] As convention we use upper case letters for the variables in terms and lower case letters for the constants.

Finally, the OWL-T captures the *operating instructions* of tool for a particular functionality (see A4). We define an operating instruction as a sequence of operations that should be followed to realize the tool functionality. For example, `procesUnit1` may require the agent to enter the coordinates of the hole via the operation `enterCoor(X,Y)` by a number pad. In this respect, `enterCoor(X,Y)` should precede `startDrill`.

The concept layer is updated when there is a change in the artifact layer e.g., new artifact is included, existing artifact is updated, etc. However, concept layer update will not be covered here due to space limitations. The following sections elaborate on the extrospective agent under the assumption that the artifact layer and the concept layer are synchronous.

5   The Extrospective Agent Mind

The extrospective agent architecture depicted in Fig. 1 is based on the Jason BDI agent architecture by Bordini and Hübner [7]. Similar to the BDI agent, the extrospective agent has beliefs about the state of the environment. The beliefs are updated through sensing. The extrospective agent also has a set of goals. Each goal defines a desired state of the environment that the agent wants to reach. Finally, the agent acts in the environment through its effectors. Generally, in BDI agent literature, agents are employed with a library of plans. The plans are partial recipes that guide the agent through means-ends analysis [8].

The architectural additions leading to the extrospective agent aim to support: (i) querying the concept layer to discover tools, (ii) selecting which tool to use, (iii) planning for orchestration and operation enabling, and (iv) focus management during the tool use. For the details of data repositories in Fig. 1 such as the belief base, the events, the plan library, and the intention we refer the reader to [7]. Here, we will concentrate on the extensions.

When an agent enters an environment, it should discover the tools. Run time discovery is done via a query mechanism. Query mechanism can be thought as

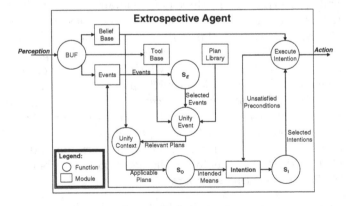

Fig. 1. The extrospective agent architecture

a goal directed perception since, the agent queries the environment based on its goals. If there is a match between agent's goal and the tool in the environment, *special percepts*[4] are sent to the agent. Different query strategies are discussed in Sec. 5.1.

The first addition is the data repository called the *tool base* (TB). Logically, the concept layer resides in the environment and TB resides in the agent. The TB stores the knowledge about a particular tool that the agent has discovered before. The TB is also different form plan library (PL). TB is populated proactively at the run time by special percepts whereas PL is developed by the agent designer at the design time and static. The existence of the TB increases the potential success of the agent in novel and dynamic environments.

The TB is also distinguished from the PL for its support for planning. Planning for realizing the context condition [7] of a plan originating from the PL may seem similar to the planning for realizing the preconditions of each operation of the plan originating from the TB. Yet, planning for the context condition requires even more anticipation (extended internal model) by the agent designer, e.g. cost of an action, time taken, etc. Planning for the context also has a larger search space [5], hence may not be viable for resource bounded agents. The TB overcomes the first difficulty by mirroring the concept layer that is supplied by the environment designer. Such information is also valuable for pruning the search space for planning using the operating instructions. The related work incorporating planning to the BDI agents is considered in Sec. 7.

The other two extensions to the Jason model are the arrows between (i) the belief update function (BUF) and the TB and (ii) the intention execution function and the intention module. The former arrow represents the process that parses the special percepts into the TB. The latter arrow corresponds to the planning for precondition satisfaction.

5.1   Abstract Interpreter

The overall abstract interpreter[5] of the extrospection agent is given in Table 1. The basic structure for decision making is a loop, in which the agent continuously:

- observes the world and updates its beliefs,
- deliberates on which ends to achieve,
- uses means-ends reasoning to find the applicable plans from the tool base or internal plan library, queries the concept layer if necessary,
- acts until the entire plan is consumed

The extrospective agent program starts with the initialization of the the agent's goals and beliefs. Beginning of every reasoning cycle starts updating the belief set, $buf(B,\rho)$, the event set, $buf(\rho)$, similar to AgentSpeak agents [7]. In addition,

---

[4] Percepts that are related to tool information are distinguished from other percepts.
[5] This section relies on the AgentSpeak(L) terminology given in Rao [9].

the tool base is the update by processing the set of special percepts[6] received from the environment, buf(TB,ρ).

After the BUF is done, the options function $options$(G,E) will generate new goals by taking the unsatisfied goals left from the previous execution cycle and the new events generated either by percepts (external goals) or by the intention stack (internal goals). The resulting goal set G^7 represents the ends that the agent wants to achieve.

Unify event function (UEF) $unifyEvent(S_e$(G),PL,TB) takes the current goal set, the TB, and the PL and matches the available means with the goals (i.e. ends) of the agent. The UEF returns the selected goal-means pairs as *relevant plans* P_r. If P_r is empty then the agent automatically *queries* the environment to discover tools. To avoid infinite loop, the agent should not already *believe* that there is no tool available ($\neg$**Bel**(noTool(G))). In the latter case, the goal and the related intention is dropped. Because the agent is sure that, neither the available tools in the environment nor the plans in the agent's PL can accomplish the goal.

It is important to note that, querying the concept layer only if the agent could not find any means in its TB or PL corresponds to just one strategy. We employed this strategy in Table 1. A more general approach may include different query strategies. For example, the agent may (i) query before every means-ends reasoning or (ii) query at every percept update. Although, the time required for processing the percepts increases, the former strategy is beneficial for finding the most effective tool as means and the latter is beneficial for synchronizing the TB with the concept layer to decrease the chance of misinformed means-ends reasoning due to out of date TB.

The query strategy becomes important in the context of dynamic environments. As it has been mentioned in Sec. 3, the agent may need to adapt to the changes such as Process Unit upgrades and failures. In such situations, the concept layer is updated accordingly to reflect such changes. The synchronization of the TB with the concept layer is then a question of selecting the appropriate query strategy based on the characteristics of the environment, e.g. the rate of change in the tool composition. At this stage, we will not consider those situations and stay faithful to the query after failure strategy.

If the agent can find a relevant plan – either from the TB or from the PL– it tries to find an *applicable plan* through unify context function (UCF) $unifyContext(P_r,B)$. The UCF filters the relevant plans by finding those whose context is satisfied by the beliefs of the agent. Again, if the applicable plan set π is empty then the agent drops the goal as mentioned above.

The option selection function $S_O(\pi)$ selects the plan to be executed π_{im}. The selected plan is pushed to the intention set by $pushIntention$(G,π_{im}) function.

---

[6] At the initial state there are no percepts regarding the tools since, they are only available after a query.

[7] Strictly speaking, both the achieve goals and the test goal are events [7]. Here, we are interested in the achieve goals.

Table 1. The abstract interpreter for the extrospective agent

```
B ← B₀
G ← G₀
WHILE true
    WHILE not empty(ρset)%get percepts ρset from the environment
            %get next percept ρ from ρset
            B ← buf(B,ρ)
            E ← buf(ρ)
            T ← buf(TB,ρ)
    END WHILE
    G ← options(G,E)
    Pr ← unifyEvent(SE(G),PL,TB) %unifies plan,goal,tool
    IF Pr = Ø THEN
        IF not ¬Bel(noTool(G))
            query(G)
        ELSE
            dropGoal(G)
        END IF
        CONTINUE
    END IF
%At this point we have relevant plan(s)
    π ← unifyContext(Pr,B) %unifies plan, belief
    IF empty(π)
        dropGoal(G)
        CONTINUE
    ELSE
%At this point we have applicable plan(s)
        πim = SO(π)
    END IF
    I = pushIntention(G,πim)
    πi = SI(I)
    WHILE ¬ endOfPlan(πi)
        IF πi ∈ PL
            α = head(πi)
            IF action(α)
                execute(α)
            ELSE IF goal(α)
                updateEvents(α)
            END IF
        ELSE IF πi ∈ TB
            α = head(πi)
            WHILE not empty(preList(α))
                p = next(preList(α))
                IF checkPre(p,B)
                    unify(p,B,πi)
                ELSE
                    πi = [p|πi] % update intention
                END IF
            END WHILE
            α = head(πi)
            IF action(α) % check the updated intention
                execute(α)
            ELSE IF goal(α)
                updateEvents(α)
            END IF
        END IF
        πi ←tail(πi)
        πi = SI(I)
    END WHILE
END WHILE
```

Since the execution of agent and the artifact is asynchronous, the intention selection function $S_I(\text{I})$ is responsible for suspending and resume the currently active intention. The details of the option selection function and the intention selection functions are given in Sec. 6.

The only branching after the intention selection is based on the origin of the plan. If the plan came from the PL then the standard execution of the Jason agent continues until all the steps of the plan are executed. The plans from the TB can be executed, if the preconditions for each operation unify with the agents beliefs. Otherwise, the agent should plan to satisfy before executing it (see Sec. 4.2). The difference between the precondition and the context condition is that the first one applies to each operation in an operating instruction, but the later applies to the whole plan and is checked once during *unifyContext*. Thus, agent consumes internal plans blindly whereas executes the operations of tool cautiously [10].

The planning for precondition is achieved by updating the intention stack by pushing the preconditions as goals before the invocation of the operation $\pi_i = [p|\pi_i]$. The goals force the agent to restart the overall deliberation cycle. So, the agent finds new plans and generates new intentions to act until the preconditions of the operation are believed (the preconditions hold in the agent's belief set).

6   Metalevel Reasoning

Metalevel reasoning is concerned with the event focus S_E, the plan preference S_O, and the intention prioritization S_I. Constructing those functions, hence metalevel reasoning, is domain dependent and heavily relies on the knowledge of the domain expert [7]. In this section, we propose a domain independent metalevel reasoning rules based on the assumptions introduced in Sec. 4.1.

6.1   Option Selection

The first rule handles the situations where the agent has relevant plans available both from the PL and the TB. A strategy for S_O is to select the plan originating from the PL. The reason is that plans originating from the PL are assumed to be applicable without further deliberation in the environment since they are anticipated by the agent designer. For the rest, the agent should do the discovery and planing at run time which is more time consuming. The syntax for the rule uses $\bowtie$ to indicate that the plan is supported by the tool, $\supset$ is used as implication, and *appPlan(Goal)* returns applicable plans.

Rule 1 (OS1). $\pi_1 = appPlan(\varphi) \wedge \pi_2 = appPlan(\varphi) \wedge \pi_1 \in PL \wedge \pi_2 \bowtie T \wedge T \in TB \supset INT(\pi_1)$

The Rule 1 states that if there are two *applicable plans* for goal φ then the agent intends the one which originates from the PL.

The second rule is suggested to capture the preferences of environment designer for the tool use. For example, the environment designer may want agents to use the `procUnit2` for drilling. Such preference is conveyed by the utility function given by agent designer and used by the agents will while choosing between functionally equivalent tools.

Rule 2 (OS2). if $\pi_1 = appPlan(\varphi) \wedge \pi_2 = appPlan(\varphi) \wedge \pi_1 \bowtie T_1 \wedge \pi_2 \bowtie T_2$ and $T_1 \succ T_2 \supset INT(\pi_1)$

where $\succ$ is an ordering relation of the form $T_1 \succ T_2 := f(T_1, \varphi) > f(T_2, \varphi)$ and $f : T \times G \to \mathbb{R}$

Rule 2 states that if there is a utility function f that orders the tool preference for a goal then the agent will use higher rated tool.

Finally, the third rule is a heuristic form of Rule 2 and handles the situations where there are two functionally equivalent tools and no selection function. In those situations, S_O selects more specific tool. By the more specific tool, we mean a tool with less functionality. For example, if the agent needs to drill a hole, it prefers the `procUnit1` over the `procUnit2`. If one compares Rule 2 to Rule 3, he/she observes that the behavior of the agent differs, though, the behavior due to Rule 3 may be sub optimal.

Rule 3 (OS3). $\pi_1 = appPlan(\varphi) \wedge \pi_2 = appPlan(\varphi) \wedge \pi_3 = appPlan(\psi) \wedge \pi_1 \bowtie T_1 \wedge \pi_2 \bowtie T_2 \wedge \pi_3 \bowtie T_2 \supset INT(\pi_1)$

The Rule 3 states that if tool T_1 is a more specific tool than T_2 then the agent intends to use the tool T_1.

In future, we intend to incorporate a computational notion for affordance [11] by extending the Rule 2. For example, a tool such as a *chair* can afford for *sitting* to *get rest, stepping on* for *elevation,* or to *stack things* for *organization.* The evaluation function may rank various affordances to guide the agent actions, e.g. suggesting sitting.

6.2 Intention Handling

Intentions are used for balancing deliberation and action in resource bounded agents. The intention commitment strategies have been focus of attention [10,12]. However, previous strategies consider only dropping the intention when some conditions hold [10]. In many situations, such a strategy may not be feasible because it wastes the time used for deliberation. In the worst case, some actions cannot be reversed. Thus dropping an intention has adverse side effects. In some cases, suspending an intention is a better strategy. By suspending an intention, the agent also saves time from future deliberation. This section explores conditions for suspending and resuming intentions based on the assumptions introduced in Sec. 4.1.

The three rules with the increasing level of reactiveness to the events are named as (i) blind use, (ii) dedicated use, and (iii) lazy use. An agent that adopts the blind use strategy would not pay attention to new events until it reaches its current goal. That is, if two goals need to use the same tool, e.g. drill, then the agent suspends one of the goals until it believes that it reaches the first goal.

The logic language we have used to formalize the intention handling is first order multi-modal logic with modalities $\Diamond$ (eventually), $\square$ (always), $\bigcirc$ (next), $\bigcup$ (until) defined in Rao and Georgeff [10]. The notation INT_T is used to denote the intention to use a tool with the superscript INT_T^S denotes the suspended intention and the operator $\|$ denotes concurrent intentions. An intention is said to be suspended if it is in the intention set but not pursued and two intentions are said to be concurrent if both appear in the intention set. So the blind use can be given as follows;

Rule 4 (IS1). $(INT_T(\varphi) \| INT_T(\psi)) \supset (INT_T(\varphi) \| \bigcirc INT_T^S(\psi) \bigcup Bel(\varphi) \wedge \bigcirc INT_T(\psi))$

The Rule 4 states that if the agent intends to use a tool T for goal φ and for goal ψ then it suspends the second intention (due to A1) in the next step *until* it believes that the goal φ is reached and resumes the intention for goal ψ as soon as φ. For example, an agent in the production cell would ignore all the incoming components until it finishes the current component. The Rule 4 can be used for the situations where the component arrival is scarce and finishing a component is more important than processing more components.

The second rule is called *dedicated use* and allows the agent to suspend its current intention until the tool completes the operation (due to A3). That is, the agent starts the operation and suspends the intention that the operation belongs and handles other events. Meanwhile, the agent is still focused on the state of the tool. When the agent receives the notification from the environment regarding the operation completion (due to A2), the agent resumes its previous intention. The next rule identifies the behavior for dedicated use.

Rule 5 (IS2). $INT_T(\varphi) \supset (\bigcirc INT_T^S(\varphi) \bigcup Bel(\varphi) \wedge Bel(done(o)) \wedge INT_T(\varphi))$

The rule 5 states that the agent suspends the intention to reach φ in the next step until it believes φ is reached and operation o is finished $done(o)$ when it resumes the intention $INT_T(\varphi)$. For example, an agent in the production cell may set one of the Processing Units for drilling a component. The difference between the Rule 4 and the Rule 5 is that the agent is not idle during the operation execution. It will suspend the intention for the component and waits for other components to arrive. The dedicated use rule balances the deliberation and action but may lead to delays in processing times. For example, assume a component of `type2` comes while a component of `type1` was being painted then the agent will dedicate the `procUnit1` to the second component. Thus, drilling the first component will be delayed. The dedicated use rule is suitable for situations where intentions are not time critical and can be suspended indefinitely.

Finally the third rule, called the *lazy use*, favors the event handling to the intention completion. In fact, the agent will not resume an intention until another goal needs one of the tools that the suspended intention is holding. The formalization of the lazy use is composed of two rules for suspending and resuming the intentions.

Rule 6 (IS3). *(i)* $INT_T(\varphi) \supset (\bigcirc INT_T^S(\varphi) \bigcup Bel(\varphi))$
    (ii) $(INT_T^S(\varphi) \parallel \Diamond INT_T(\psi)) \supset (\bigcirc INT_T(\varphi) \parallel INT_T^S(\psi) \bigcup Bel(\varphi) \wedge INT_T^S(\varphi))$

The Rule 6(i) states that the agent suspends the intention to reach φ as soon as it starts it. The Rule 6(ii) tells how this intention is resumed when eventually another goal ψ appears in the intention set that requires the use of the tool that the suspended intention holds. For example, the agent in the production cell may leave a component over the drilling unit until another component needs to be drilled. Thus, the agent ignores the unfinished component until it needs the tool for another component. Doing so, the agent will have more time for deliberation and event handling. The lazy use rule is suitable for the situations where the intentions are less important then the events.

7   Related Work

Planning for BDI agents has recently been considered by several researchers. Walczak et. al. [13] have described a planning approach using utility functions. They have introduced the formal planning problem based on domain object models. Meneguzzi et. al. [5] concentrate on the deliberation cycle for agents and include a planning component, Graphplan, before intention selection. Sardina et. al. [14] concentrate on the similarities between hierarchical task network (HTN) planning [15] and the BDI approach, and also identify a formal operational semantics for their work.

All the planning problem formalizations above – including our formalization of operations – are similar to the STRIPS [16] notation. Further similarities with Walczak et. al. [13] are the use of a utility function and partial plans as heuristics for planning. Their utility function corresponds to our option selection Rule 2. Their partial plan heuristic corresponds to our operating instructions of tools.

The two major differences between our work and the previous planning research are the source of the information necessary for planning and the type of planning. First, in our case, the information regarding the planning problem, e.g. operations, is retrieved from the environment, whereas before it was considered within the agent model. In previous approaches, the agent's internal world model needs to be modified every time the environment changes, whereas in our approach the concept layer that belongs to the environment allows the extrospective agent to adopt its behavior at run time.

Second, planners such as HTN planners return a complete plan from the initial state to the goal state. Thus, the agent is *conservative* and does not initiate any action unless the planning problem is fully solved. Such look-a-head planning is useful when the success of the plan should be guaranteed before action commences. On the other hand, BDI planners adopt a plan-when-needed approach where planning is only triggered when a sub-goal is encountered in the plan description. Such planning does not return complete plans, hence cannot estimate the future success. Thus, the agent is *opportunistic* and acts even though it can not predict possible future failures. If the agent environment is changing faster than the planning time then plan-when-needed will perform better than look-a-head planning [14]. Our planning approach is more conservative than plan-when-needed since it checks the preconditions of an operation before attempting it. Yet, our work is more optimistic then HTN planners, since it does not wait until a full plan is found but only assures that the current step can be executed.

In the planning sense, the work by Hübner et. al. [17] is more similar to our approach. Instead of augmenting the BDI cycle with a look-a-head planner, they use BDI programming patterns to turn the BDI planner into a declarative plan engine similar to the approach explained in Sec. 5.1. They define programming patterns for error recovery and retry condition purely based on the Jason programming language.

Apart from planning, we also like to remind the reader of the intention handling mechanism in Rao and Georgeff [10] and Cohen and Levesque [12]. As mentioned above, both works consider conditions for dropping an intention. In our case, we have introduced an intention suspension mechanism, as we rely on the tool assumption that guarantees the operation completion event.

8   Conclusion

In this paper, we have argued that agent adaptation can benefit from (i) engineering the agent environment, and (ii) designing agents with the capability to reason about the functionality of artifacts as alternate means for achieving their goals.

Drawing from Activity Theory [4], we have identified tools as the basic building blocks of such a design perspective. We have concentrated on the BDI agent framework as a particular agent architecture and elaborated some extensions suited to developing extrospective agents. The extensions concentrate on: (i) querying the environment to discover tools; (ii) selecting which tool to use; (iii) planning for orchestration and operation enabling; and (iv) intention management during tool use.

Possible future work includes: a formal theory for tool use; the formalization of the tool concept; and how agents can reason about tools. Selecting a tool is one aspect that we have considered in this paper. A question we have not yet addressed is whether an agent can use one tool as a substitute for another. We believe that consulting situated theories of mind in psychology such as ecological psychology, distributed cognition, and activity theory will be useful in developing our ideas further.

Other future work is to consider practical extensions. It will be useful to combine the A&A platform with an extrospective agent architecture to provide a full MAS development environment. The new framework should then be evaluated in more complex domains, such as web service management.

References

1. Weyns, D., Omicini, A., Odell, J.: Environment as a first-class abstraction in multi-agent systems. Autonomous Agents and Multi-Agent Systems 14(1), 5–30 (2007)
2. Ricci, A., Viroli, M., Omicini, A.: CArtAgO: An infrastructure for engineering computational environments in MAS. In: Weyns, D., Parunak, H.V.D., Michel, F. (eds.) 3rd International Workshop Environments for Multi-Agent Systems, Hakodate, Japan, pp. 102–119 (2006)
3. Acay, D.L., Pasquier, P., Sonenberg, L.: Extrospection: Agents reasoning about the environment. In: 3rd International Conference Intelligent Environments (2007)
4. Leont'ev, A.N.: Activity, consciousness and personality. Prentice-Hall, Englewood Cliffs (1978)
5. Meneguzzi, F.R., Zorzo, A.F., Mòra, M.D.C., Luck, M.: Incorporating planning into BDI agents. Scalable computing: Practice andexperience 8 (2007)
6. Knublauch, H., Horridge, M., Musen, M., Rector, A., Stevens, R., Drummond, N., Lord, P., Noy, N.F., Seidenberg, J., Wang, H.: The Protégé OWL experience. In: 4th International Conference Semantic Web, Galway, Ireland (2005)
7. Bordini, R.H., Hübner, J.F.: BDI agent programming in AgentSpeak using Jason. In: Toni, F., Torroni, P. (eds.) CLIMA 2005. LNCS, vol. 3900, pp. 143–164. Springer, Heidelberg (2006)
8. Wooldridge, M.: An Introduction to Multiagent Systems. John Wiley & Sons, Chichester (2002)
9. Rao, A.S.: AgentSpeak(L): BDI agents speak out in a logical computable language. In: van Hoe, R. (ed.) 7th European Workshop Modelling Autonomous Agents in a Multi-Agent World, Eindhoven, The Netherlands (1996)
10. Rao, A.S., Georgeff, M.P.: Modeling rational agents within a BDI-architecture. In: 2nd International Conference Principles of Knowledge Representation and Reasoning (1991)
11. Gibson, J.J.: The ecological approach to visual perception. Houghton Mifflin (1979)
12. Cohen, P.R., Levesque, H.J.: Intention is choice with commitment. Artificial Intelligence 42(2-3), 213–261 (1990)
13. Walczak, A., Braubach, L., Pokahr, A., Lamersdorf, W.: Augmenting BDI agents with deliberative planning techniques. In: Bordini, R.H., Dastani, M., Dix, J., El Fallah Seghrouchni, A. (eds.) ProMAS 2006. LNCS, vol. 4411, pp. 113–127. Springer, Heidelberg (2007)
14. Sardina, S., de Silva, L., Padgham, L.: Hierarchical planning in BDI agent programming languages: A formal approach. In: 5th International Joint Conference Autonomous Agents and Multiagent Systems, New York, NY, USA, pp. 1001–1008 (2006)
15. Erol, K., Hendler, J., Nau, D.S.: Semantics for hierarchical task-network planning. Technical report, Univ. of Maryland Institute for Advanced Computer Studies Report No. UMIACS-TR-94-31, College Park, MD, USA (1994)
16. Nilsson, N.J., Fikes, R.E.: STRIPS: A new approach to the application of theorem proving to problem solving. Artificial Intelligence 2(3-4), 189–208 (1971)
17. Hübner, J.F., Bordini, R.H., Wooldridge, M.: Programming declarative goals using plan patterns. In: Declarative Agent Languages and Technologies IV, pp. 123–140. Springer, Heidelberg (2006)

An Awareness Model for Agents
in Heterogeneous Environments

Dirk Bade, Lars Braubach, Alexander Pokahr, and Winfried Lamersdorf

University of Hamburg, Department of Informatics
Distributed Systems and Information Systems Group
{bade,braubach,pokahr,lamersd}@informatik.uni-hamburg.de

Abstract. One of the constituting characteristics of software agents is their ability to sense the environment. The reception and processing of percepts is a key element for the agent's internal reasoning process and essential for interacting with other entities in the environment. But sensing the environment is often seen as an abstract concept which is practically more or less reduced to the simple processing of some domain-specific message content. In order to be generally applicable among different multi-agent applications a common model of an environment incorporating an extensible set of entities, distribution protocols, and representation- as well as query languages needs to be established. Therefore, we propose a generic, extensible and adaptable model for resource-aware agents. It is organized into different information channels to help directing the focus of interest to specific aspects of the environment. Several discovery- and distribution protocols as well as different representation- and query languages may be used to satisfy the requirements of dynamic environments. The whole model is realized with a dedicated service agent on each platform, which local as well as remote agents can query for environmental information. This way, repeatedly and redundantly integrating these features into every agent application can be avoided and agent developers only have to deal with a simple protocol-API to access the information. Due to our highly flexible and adaptable model, we can face the heterogeneity of multi-agent applications operating in infrastructure- as well as mobile ad-hoc networks.

1 Introduction

Agent definitions often cover the notion of an agent's environment defining an agent as an entity, which is capable of perceiving its environment through sensors and acting upon this environment through effectors [24,14,10]. In order to be of any use for an agent or agent application, there has to be a common understanding of what constitutes an environment, how the entities are represented and how the agents can share their knowledge of the environment with each other. Although these aspects may seem natural and trivial for a model, in most of todays agent platforms the environment is only modeled implicitly or even not at all [31].

In order to access some resource, an agent needs to know about its existence, its address and the interaction protocol to use. These details are often hardwired

K.V. Hindriks, A. Pokahr, and S. Sardina (Eds.): ProMAS 2008, LNAI 5442, pp. 152–167, 2009.
© Springer-Verlag Berlin Heidelberg 2009

into the agent's code and hence not adaptable to changes in the environment. In order to deal with dynamic environments, most agent platforms (e.g. FIPA compliant platforms) thus offer yellow-page services (e.g. a directory facilitator, DF [9]), so an agent can lookup appropriate resources at runtime. Drawbacks of this solution are: 1) resources like databases, documents or hardware components cannot be directly registered with existing DFs. They need some kind of service wrapper offered by an agent and 2) in case a required resource cannot be found, an agent has to search for other yellow-page services by itself.

Therefore, this paper proposes a generic, adaptable and flexible model of the environment with extensible knowledge distribution protocols and representations. This model aims to be used in heterogeneous systems, where on the one hand different kinds of entities need to be considered and on the other hand the usage of computational resources (e.g. computing power, network bandwidth, reliability) needs to be adapted to the current execution environment and context. For this reason the presented model may be used in real world agent applications and is appropriate for agents residing on powerful computers in infrastructure networks as well as agents executed on mobile devices in ad-hoc networks.

The rest of the paper is structured as follows: Section 2 introduces the notion of environment and our presented environment model. In sections 3 and 4 different ways of representing and distributing information are addressed. Section 5 introduces our prototypical implementation. The related work part in section 6 highlights other environmental models as well as research efforts in the field of perception, adaptation and ad-hoc networks. Finally, the paper concludes with a subsumption of our proposed solution and our prospect of future work.

2   Environment Model

The environment of an entity is its surrounding, which has an implicit or explicit influence on the entity. It defines the properties and conditions under which an entity exists and provides the processes and principals that govern and support the exchange of information [21]. On the one hand, the environment can be seen as the *execution environment* of an agent, consisting of the execution engine, the agent platform, the message transport system, etc. On the other hand the environment relates to all entities external to the agent platform like the agent's communication partners, a database to work with, a sensor (e.g. measuring the temperature) or documents that are processed by the agent. In contrast to the execution environment, this external view is called the *logical* or *application environment* of an agent [17,18]. There are also a number of other environmental models that are directed at different aspects of an environment like real world entities or the social links between agents for example [21], but these are not further discussed in this paper.

2.1   Entities and Events

The basis of an environmental model are entities and events. An entity is an abstraction of either an agent, an object or in general a (social) communication partner [21] and may have several descriptive attributes and a unique identifier to refer to. In [23] a further distinction between goal-oriented (agents) and function-oriented entities (boundary-, resource- and coordination artifacts) is made. While agents are autonomous and social acting entities running on a single node within a distributed system, artifacts offer some kind of function or service, may span over multiple nodes and can be combined to complex artifacts.

Besides the entities we also have to specify, which kind of environmental events may be of interest to an agent. Because a model normally does not represent a static but a dynamic (or in case of e.g. mobile devices and ad-hoc networks highly dynamic) environment, it is not sufficient to know which entities are present, but additionally to be informed once their state changes and whether new entities are available or existing ones disappeared. Such events can be categorized according to their originator into three different classes [18]:

Environment-originating. This type of event is caused by the *autonomous process* [21] of the environment, which reflects some kind of external intervention, e.g. the user shutting down an agent platform.

Entity-originating. If an entity carries out some action, that leads to an internal state change in some other entity, this state change is said to be entity-originating. E.g. the sending and receiving of a message may set an agent into a busy-state, which possibly needs to be announced to other agents.

Self-originating. To this class belongs every event that is not externally caused, e.g. an agent finishing some calculations or the awakening after a timeout.

We are not only concerned about entities but as well about events, because information in a logical environment - in contrast to a natural environment - does not spread automatically throughout the environment. The information that a light switch is turned on for example, is automatically sensed by every real-world entity nearby that is equipped with appropriate sensors (similar to a broadcast). In a logical environment this information has to be explicitly exchanged (unicasted) between the entities by distributing messages containing the new state of the switch artifact. Broadcasts are often not applicable in such an environment, since its scope is restricted to administratively bounded subnets.

In order to model entities as well as entity-related events, we specified a set of requirements that have to be met by an environment model in order to achieve the ability of environmental awareness. These requirements will be introduced in the following.

2.2   Model Requirements

One of the key characteristics of agents is their ability to react to changes in their environment and thereby adapt themselves to the current context. For this reason, agents are often deployed in dynamic environments. In order to provide an appropriate model of the agent's surrounding we derived a set of requirements on the basis of such environments' characteristics. These requirements are as follows:

Awareness. Sensing the environment is a continuous process. But as stated above, changes in a logical environment are effectuated by certain events. Our proposed model should therefore be able to detect as well as to proclaim such events.

Heterogeneity. The need to deal with heterogeneity relates to two different aspects. On the one hand, we face a multitude of different entities in the environment that somehow have to be represented in the model. On the other hand the model should be used in different infrastructure settings and hence be applicable to servers and mobile devices as well as to infrastructure- and ad-hoc networks.

Adaptivity. Supporting the deployment of the model in different infrastructures and dynamic environments also requires to adapt the model to specific conditions. These conditions may affect the way events are processed and proclaimed in the environment. This requirement depends on the ability to be extensible.

Extensibility. It should be possible to extend the model in multiple ways. Firstly, the types of entities represented in the model are to be left open, because the model should be usable in a wide range of applications. Secondly, different ways of how to represent an entity should be supported in order to meet the needs of different applications. And thirdly, the way events are proclaimed by the model should be extensible as the infrastructure may require specific forms of information distribution.

Standards. The model should adhere to existing standards for representing and distributing knowledge in order to seamlessly integrate information coming from different sources.

Usability. Having a model which meets all the above stated requirements, but which can be used neither by a developer nor by any user due to its complexity is inappropriate for open systems. Therefore, the interfaces of the model should be kept simple to allow for easy querying and extending.

In order to meet these requirements, we propose a layered architecture for the environment model, which is presented in the following.

2.3   Architecture

We identified three layers, that focus different aspects of the model: 1) information, 2) representation and 3) distribution. The architecture is depicted in figure 1. First of all, one needs to reason about the types of entities (e.g. remote agent platforms, agents, services or some specific hardware possibly needed for execution), that may be of interest for an agent as well as events, that may occur in an environment, such as (dis)appearing of entities or changes in the state of an entity. Sensors are responsible for gathering information about such events. These aspects are addressed on the upper layer of the architecture. To allow directing the focus of interest to specific kinds of entities, this layer should be organized in a way that combines similar types of entities and events (cf. section 2.4).

The middle layer provides different possibilities to represent an entity. Normally, information about entities is internally stored in a programming language-specific unit (e.g. an object or a structure). In order to distribute this information within a network, these units have to be serializable. But additionally, one might want to query specific fragments of information or use some kind of logic to derive implicit knowledge from explicit information. Therefore, these units have to be transformed into some other representation. For this purpose, different representation and query languages, transformation services as well as the support for ontologies are situated in this layer (cf. section 3).

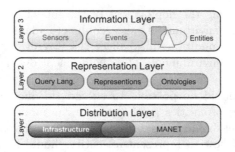

Fig. 1. Architecture of the environment model

The lower layer provides support for different distribution mechanisms. Exchanging knowledge among the agents in the environment is done by using adequate protocols that actively distribute the information. To allow for heterogeneity and the adaptation of the distribution mechanisms to the current context, multiple protocols as well as a generic interface to integrate new protocols are to be provided (cf. section 4). We distinguish protocols for the use in infrastructure networks on the one hand, and protocols especially designed for mobile ad-hoc networks on the other hand.

Before the distribution and representation of information are subsequently addressed, the organization of the upper layer shall be presented in the following. According to the requirements, this layer should manage the entity information in a way that is intuitive to understand for users, easy to extend for developers and simple to query for other agents.

2.4   Information Organization

In order to direct the perception on particular aspects, the information contained in the model is structured in a way, that an agent can choose among different topics. As a metaphor for structuring these kinds of information we used the notion of *channels*. The concept of channels (cf. Microsoft's *Active Channel* [19]) is intuitive for users and suits the needs of our environment model. A channel can be thought of as a FIFO-pipe. Channel news are fed into the pipe at one end, interested entities receive the updates in chronological order at the other end and may further distribute the news on their behalf. An entity claims its interest by subscribing for a specific channel and hence only receives the desired kind of information, possibly further restricted by using a language-dependent query and a set of constraints.

In order to integrate more topics (e.g. types of entities) into this model, a developer simply has to provide some channel-specific classes and register them with the environment agent. Other agents get to know about these channels when introducing themselves to the environment agent for the first time or by subsequent updates of channels the agent already subscribed for.

2.5 Example

To illustrate the usage of the environmental model and the proposed mechanisms to integrate different distribution and representation methods, an example is presented in the following.

Image Search. Imagine an agent, whose task is to search for images given some keywords and constraints. For this task prior knowledge (provided by the user or developer) of one or more image databases is normally required. This may be acceptable for static environments, where the agent has permanent access to a database in its local network or the Internet. But in a dynamic environment the addresses have to be acquired during runtime using some discovery mechanism. But this requires additional effort by the developer, as she has to write the code for accessing different discovery services on her own. Using an environmental model provided by the local agent platform, the agent only has to query the model. It is the task of the model to gather environment information from different sources and present it to the agent on request. If the agent is executed on a mobile device, the model may restrict the ways of gathering information to save transmission costs or even delay the request until an appropriate and low priced Internet access is available.

3 Representing Information

In order to distribute information about the state of the environment and its entities, the agents have to use specific protocols to spread the information. This implies, that the information is represented in a format, which can be serialized and understood by the communicating parties. Most exchange protocols use very simple and proprietary languages to describe entities and their state. Others in contrast apply expressive and standardized languages. But not only the representation is important, but also the ability to query and filter specific information. For example, an agent could only be interested in document artifacts, the existence of other artifacts does not concern the agent and should not be revealed to it. In [7] general insufficiencies and problems of commonly used exchange protocols are described:

Lack of Rich Representations. Commonly used languages lack rich representations in order to describe a multitude of different entities and to be able to derive implicit knowledge from the explicit descriptions.

Insufficient Constraint Support. In order to reduce the results of a query in some way, the usage of constraints should be supported. Often this feature is not part of a protocol's language.

Vague Matching. Most protocols try to match a query against the knowledge base only on a syntactical level, e.g. using string equality. Fuzzy matching or including semantical information would often lead to better results.

Scarce Ontology Support. Ontologies could be used to get to a common agreement on terms and statements. When using different exchange protocols in an interaction the usage of ontologies is all the more important as they can help to transform one representation into another.

A simple string-based approach is easy to implement and not very resource demanding, but it suffers from the above mentioned insufficiencies and problems. But since we do not want to restrict the usage of any representation language, our model is generic in a way, that commonly used languages are directly supported and new languages can easily be integrated. To make sure, that two communicating parties understand each other, even if they share no common language, we nevertheless propose a simple, proprietary string-based language as the least common denominator.

In order to support different content languages independent of the used distribution protocol, some kind of content transformation from one language into another has to be done. For example, an agent may request information about some service using an RDF query language (e.g. RDQL [26]), but the results should be returned as a list of simple strings, so that they can be further processed easily. The environment agent therefore has to convert the model into an RDF representation, execute the query and flatten the results to simple strings in order to wrap them in a response message. Such transformation services are an optional part of our model, since this can be a complex task. The usage of ontologies may ease this transformation, but additionally also supports the understanding and interpretation of exchanged knowledge.

4   Distributing Information

A lot of research has been carried out in the field of information distribution and a broad variety of protocols have been specified for this purpose (e.g. Jini [27], UPnP [29], JXTA [28]). These protocols more or less try to find answers to the following questions: 1) how does a newly available entity announces its presence in case it does not know about any other entities? 2) What happens if an entity disappears without explicitly announcing its withdrawal? and 3) How to efficiently distribute information between peers in a way that is scalable, adaptable, reliable and secure? Because our requirements also take the heterogeneity of the infrastructure into account, we raise one more question: How to deal with all the existing protocols and standards for infrastructure and mobile ad-hoc networks (MANETs) ?

Instead of inventing one more proprietary protocol that suits our needs, the proposed solution adopts existing protocols, that are already in use. Depending

on the context the protocol that best fits the current requirements is chosen.
In case the agent platform is running on a resource constrained device (e.g. a
smartphone) the model additionally has to take care which protocol to choose in
order to reduce the amount of used resources (e.g. network throughput, processor
cycles, memory) to a minimum.

A protocol serves two different purposes: 1) a protocol may be used to initially
find remote entities, e.g. other environment agents to share knowledge with and
2) to distribute knowledge. For example, when an agent is newly created and has
the task to find a specific service (e.g. an image database) the developer normally
has to tell the agent beforehand how to find such an artifact. In our approach the
agent delegates this task to the environment model which in turn may choose
among several different protocols in order to find the resource by itself. E.g. it
may try to find the artifact directly by sending a multicast, it may use specific
protocols to query a registry about an available service or it may contact other
agents in order to get some help. Precondition for the latter choice is some
kind of address book containing other contacts. When a platform is started, the
agent first tries to find a set of initial contacts, i.e. environment agents running
on remote platforms, with which it henceforth exchanges information about the
environment and any new events. This way, the agent successively also learns
about other available contacts and a network of information providers is spanned.

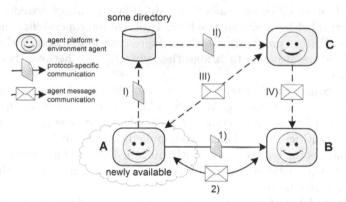

Fig. 2. Contacting remote environment agents

Figure 2 illustrates the architecture and the process of finding contacts in a
simplified manner. In a first step a newly available agent platform respectively
the newly created environment agent A initially tries to find other contacts (interaction 1). Once a contact has been found the agents may mutually subscribe
to information channels and exchange information (interaction 2). From now on-
wards these two agents inform each other once an event occurs, which impacts
one of the channels the agents subscribed for. In parallel, the newly created
environment agent may register itself with some kind of directory (e.g. a Jini
lookup service, a JXTA peergroup, a directory facilitator, etc.), so that other
agents registered with or querying the directory become aware of the new agent

(interaction I). This way, agent C receives the contact details of agent A by the directory service (interaction II), contacts the agent and exchanges environment information (interaction III). As part of the environment information, address details of agent C are forwarded to agent B, which in turn sends a message to agent C to introduce itself. This way, a virtual network is spanned.

4.1   Protocol Requirements

We specified a set of requirements with which we compared different protocols and created some metric in order to infer a proposal for a best-suit protocol in a given context. These requirements were derived from our environment model requirements and aim at the general characteristics of discovery protocols:

Decentralized Operability. This requirement focuses on the overall architecture of a protocol. In general we distinguish between client/server- and peer-to-peer protocols. Especially for unreliable MANETs a peer-to-peer approach is vitally important, because of the absence of a single-point-of-failure. But also scalability and the locality of information have to be taken into account.

Interoperability. This point comprises two different aspects. Due to heterogeneity, protocols and their implementation respectively should be inter-platform as well as inter-protocol operable. Platform-interoperability is achieved either by being available for different operating systems or by being interpreted by a virtual machine. Protocol-interoperability means that a protocol either uses a standardized representation format or that proxies or bridges are available to bridge the syntactic gap between two or more protocols.

Awareness Support. The term *awareness* needs to be distinguished from the terms *lookup* and *discovery*. While the latter ones describe a single action, awareness refers to a continuous process, where state changes are pushed to interested entities rather than actively pulled periodically [16]. When pushing state changes the receiver is instantly informed about the new state and any inconsistencies between the actual state of the environment and the state of the model may be corrected early.

Lease Mechanisms. Such mechanisms are used in order to prevent a system from finally being blocked by outdated information. Without employing lease mechanisms withdrawing entities would have to explicitly deregister upon leaving the system. Since a withdrawal might not necessarily be intended (e.g. unexpected connection aborts) one cannot rely on proper deregistrations and hence some kind of lease should be supported. This feature is especially important for highly dynamic environments (e.g. MANETs).

Resource Demands. Considering a highly dynamic environment as well as resource constrained devices, protocols should only require a minimum of messages being exchanged and computational resources being used. This requirement also comprises the need for being scalable.

Scope. Some protocols rely on multicast-messaging, specific routing-protocols or e.g. DHCP-server for configuration settings, and are therefore restricted to being used within local subnets. Other protocols are technology-dependent in a way, that also restricts their application to locally or administratively bounded networks (e.g. Bluetooth SDP). In order to be used in an Internet-scale distributed system, a protocol should therefore support standard Internet-protocols. Optionally limiting the scope may be desired in order to restrict traffic to a reasonable amount.

Representation/Filtering. Information about entities must be represented in a serializable format in order to be distributed in a network. Several standards exist for this purpose, starting from flattened string representations to expressive logical descriptions. But information must not only be represented, but a protocol must also be able to filter information beforehand in order not to cause too much unnecessary traffic and resource exhaustion.

With these requirements we evaluated some of the most promising protocols for infrastructure as well as mobile ad-hoc networks [1]. Table 1 gives an overview of our results (restricted to infrastructure protocols). A similar evaluation of protocols to be used in MANETs (e.g. *Bluetooth SDP* [4], *Konark* [11], *DEAPspace* [20], *Card* [12], *Scalable Service Discovery for MANET* [25], etc.) has also been done. But most protocols are specifically designed to be used in MANETs with certain characteristics and it is therefore difficult to compare these protocols with each other. The results of our evaluation show that all of the protocols have their advantages and disadvantages in certain areas, which corroborates our approach of adaptively choosing an appropriate protocol at runtime depending on the context.

Table 1. Evaluation of distribution protocols for infrastructure networks[1]

	Decentralized Operability	Inter-operability	Awareness Support	Lease-Mechanism	Resource-demands	Scope	Represent./Filtering
Jini	O	O	+	++	-	O	O
SLP	O	+	- -	+	O	-	+
UPnP	+	+	+	- -	-	-	+
Salutation	++	O	O	- -	O	O	+
JXTA	++	++	- -	+	O	++	+
	- - very bad, - bad, O sufficient, + good, ++ very good						

5   Prototypical Implementation

In order to prove that our approach is realizable, we implemented a prototypical component for the *Jadex BDI Agent System* [5]. The component is responsible for creating and updating the model of the environment as well as to make the information available to any local or remote agents. The component itself (called *resource facilitator*, RF) is realized on the application level as a service agent, running on the agent platform[1] (comparable to the FIPA directory facilitator

---

[1] Currently only the Jadex standalone platform as well as Jadex' adapters for JADE [2] and DIET [15] are supported.

for example). This way, only one instance of the environment model needs to be managed on every platform.

In a first step we chose the objects, contained in the model, to be the set of possibly interesting entities, that an agent might want to be aware of. These are specific for every device and are categorized as follows:

Hardware. The hardware resources of the device, like e.g. processor, memory, network interfaces, screen, storage and their corresponding attributes like capacity or current workload.

Software. Besides the hardware, the software infrastructure of a device may also be of interest. Therefore, the model contains a set of properties of the agent platform, the virtual machine and the operating system.

Location. If possible, a device also offers some location information. This may be in the form of a descriptive statement (for the user), a network address, GPS coordinates, etc. and may be used for example, to choose a nearby resource among a multitude of offered resources.

Services. If an agent offers a service, this is normally registered with a local or remote directory facilitator (DF). Other agents looking for this service have to know the address of the DF in order to get the contact details of the provider. Information about services as part of the environmental model is automatically distributed within the environment and is available for every interested party without the need to know the directory where the service has initially been registered.

Agents. As agents often want to communicate with other agents in order to cooperate, they would benefit of information about possible communication partners. This way an agent could dynamically find counterparts without the need for the user providing contact details.

Heartbeat. A heartbeat can be thought of as an abstract entity and is therefore included in the environment model as an alternative to lease mechanisms (further described below).

As stated earlier we use a channel abstraction to query and distribute the information. The left-hand side of figure 3 depicts the organization of the model. Information coming from several local information providers is fed into the appropriate channels. Each channel internally processes the information independently for every subscriber. Processing incorporates the execution of queries, the application of constraints (e.g. limiting the result set) and the transformation into a desired representation language.

Noteworthy is the above mentioned heartbeat channel offered by every RF. Using this channel one can force a remote RF to periodically sent a heartbeat (as long as no other message is sent). This way, one can make sure that the whole agent platform is still running. Combined with other channel subscriptions the integrity of nearly every entity residing on a remote platform can be monitored. For example, to make sure a remotely offered service is available, one can subscribe to the heartbeat channel and the service channel. When no heartbeat is received, the platform is supposed to be unreachable and hence the service. In case the platform is still running, but not the service, the RF would have posted

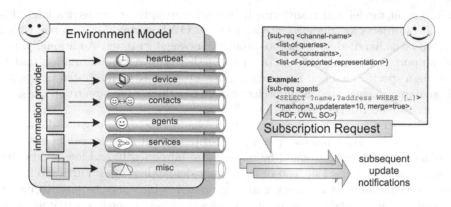

Fig. 3. Organization of the model into channels

the information through the services channel. As a consequence the heartbeat circumvents the need for lease-times for entity information. Information about unreachable devices and their resources respectively is subject for the model's internal garbage collection.

In the given example (figure 3) an agent subscribed for the *agents*-channel in order to get to know about any other agents in the environment. The subscription request contains an *RDQL*-query focusing only on the name and address of other agents as well as a set of constraints to further straighten the results and finally an ordered list of supported representation languages in one of which the result shall be transformed.

When a platform is started, the RF initially collects information about the local resources by evaluating attributes provided by the user or the virtual machine and by asking the local directory facilitator and the local agent management system. In order to gather information about the external environment and its entities the RF has to query remote RFs and subscribe to specific channels. For this purpose, we designed a simple subscription protocol and multiple methods for initially finding remote RFs (e.g. by multicast, by other contacts and by protocol specific first-contact mechanisms, e.g. by joining dedicated JXTA peergroups or by requesting a Jini lookup service). Additionally, each RF maintains a list of formerly known contacts which also might be contacted. The subscription protocol is a two-way protocol, allowing RFs to introduce each other. During the initiation phase the RFs exchange device information as well as information about offered channels, distribution protocols and supported content languages.

Additionally, we designed a generic interface for distribution protocols. In order to exchange and query channel information an adapter needs to be written for every supported protocol. Such an adapter takes the information to be distributed as well as several attributes like update events, update intervals and addressees as input and sends the information on demand or at specific points in time to each subscriber.

In order to deal with the different content languages additional subcomponents are needed. Such a component takes the information stored in the environment model and transforms it into an appropriate representation. This way, Java objects are mapped into an RDF or OWL syntax, for example, which is afterwards handled by a protocol specific message wrapper. Additionally, the RF supports query languages in order to further reduce the information that is sent via a specific channel. For example, one might only be interested in agents, whose names have a predefined prefix or devices, which have powerful processors or a broadband Internet connection.

In a last step, we parameterized all the mechanisms in order to gain adaptation during runtime. For example, when the throughput of the network connection decreases, model updates could be made more infrequently and low-bandwidth protocols could be used instead of the highly demanding ones. Further on, language specific information merger are supported, which may be used to merge delayed channel updates (e.g. no update is sent when a newly created agent is immediately terminated). In addition we implemented a message pool, storing channel updates for each addressee so that these can be merged before they are finally sent as a single message.

The RF-component as well as several subcomponents have already been implemented. The implementation is compatible with the *J2SE v1.3* and the *J2ME Personal Profile v1.0* and may therefore also be executed on mobile devices.

6 Related Work

A lot of research has already been carried out in the areas affecting this work. Agents and their environment for example have been investigated by numerous researchers. Russel and Norvig [24] as well as Ferber [8] discuss a number of key properties for classifying environments. Furthermore, Odell [21] distinguishes between the physical- and the communication environment, lists required principles and processes and also considers spatial and temporal aspects. A survey of the state-of-the-art environment models can be found in [30], where additionally the aspect of mobility and associated *place* and *region* abstractions are taken into account. Unfortunately, none of these authors aim at a practical design of their proposals and concentrate on the conceptual level. Another prominent model are the artifact and coordination context abstractions by Ricci and Omicini [22]. Their approach has some similarities with ours, but concentrates on the exploitation of artifacts supporting the coordination of agents, while we focus on the infrastructural support for exchanging artifact representations in general.

Mertens et al. [17] address the adaptation in a multi agent system for example, but in contrast to our approach the environment adapts itself to the applications' needs, which is practically impossible in the open distributed systems we address. A need for adaptation in dynamic environments is also backed by Chen and Kotz [6], who state that context-aware applications will be more effective and adaptive to users' needs. For the application of agents in mobile ad-hoc networks standardization proposals have been published by FIPA [3] and Lawrence [13] in 2002. Unfortunately, work on this topic seems to have been discontinued by FIPA.

The reason for designing a new model instead of adapting one of the existing approaches is twofold. Firstly, most of the research has been done at a conceptual level and is not suitable for a concrete design or implementation. Secondly, the few existing environment models that agent platforms offer, are targeted either at specific application domains or infrastructures and are therefore not applicable in heterogeneous environments. Additionally none of the models found in literature addresses the organization of the model and the distribution of the knowledge among the agents as well as representation and query languages for information.

7 Conclusion and Future Work

This paper introduced an environment model for multi-agent systems, which provides agents with an impression of accessible entities in their logical surrounding. The entities may be other agents or some kind of functional artifact. We opposed no restrictions on the types of entities, whose representations are contained in the model. Although we suggested a common basis of entities (hardware, software, agents and services) to be included, the model is easily extensible to integrate other types of entities (e.g. documents, real-world entities, etc.) as well. In order to focus specific aspects when sensing the environment, the model is organized in different information channels, which an agent can subscribe to. The information is then distributed actively between the agents in the environment by adaptively choosing one or more distribution protocols. The choice is up to the environment agent, responsible for managing the model, and depends on the context, which is made up by the user's preferences and the supporting hardware infrastructure. Freedom of choice also holds for the kind of representation used for describing entities. A generic interface allows for using description languages ranging from simple string-based languages to complex logics.

Due to the flexibility of the proposed model it is suited to be used in heterogeneous environments, where on the one hand different types of entities need to be represented and on the other hand various execution platforms, ranging from resource constrained mobile devices to fully equipped servers need to be considered. Because the model relies on different distribution protocols and representation languages to choose from, it can adapt itself to changing environmental conditions and thus deal with the dynamics of an environment at runtime.

Our prospect of future work is directed at multiple improvements. One aspect is the integration of privacy policies making it possible to restrict the access to certain information. Another aspect aims at different roles for environmental agents. Most existing peer-to-peer networks are backed by some kind of *supernodes*, which process more traffic than others in order to unburden resource constraint nodes in the periphery. We are adopting this approach to enhance scalability by introducing a contact-based overlay network in which some agents have a more global view on the environment than others.

Our current research efforts point at the question, of what to do with an environment model. One very promising research field are mobile agents, since these depend on sensing the environment and choosing appropriate execution platforms. An environment model could provide better arguments for migrating on some device than a user may possibly do, especially in dynamic environments. In the prospect of mobile computing, ubiquitous computing and ambient intelligence, this could be a very promising field of research.

References

1. Bade, D.: Kontextabhaengige und eigenverantwortliche migration von software-agenten in heterogenen umgebungen. Master's thesis, Uni Hamburg (2007)
2. Bellifemine, F.L., Caire, G., Greenwood, D.: Developing Multi-Agent Systems with JADE. John Wiley & Sons, Chichester (2007)
3. Berger, M., Watzke, M.: Agents in ad hoc environments. Technical report, FIPA, FIPA00068 (December 2002)
4. Bluetooth. Bluetooth specification v.1.1. (February 2001), www.bluetooth.com
5. Braubach, L., Pokahr, A., Lamersdorf, W.: Jadex: A BDI-Agent System Combining Middleware and Reasoning. Whitestein Series in Software Agent Technologies, pp. 143–167. Birkhäuser Verlag (2005)
6. Chen, G., Kotz, D.: A survey of context-aware mobile computing research. Technical Report TR2000-381, Dartmouth College, Hanover, NH, USA (2000)
7. Chen, H., Joshi, A., Finin, T.: Intelligent agents meet jini in the aether. Cluster Computing 4(4), 343–354 (2001)
8. Ferber, J.: Multiagentensysteme - Eine Einführung in die Verteilte Künstliche Intelligenz. Addison-Wesley, Reading (2001)
9. FIPA. Fipa abstract architecture specification (December 2002)
10. Hayes-Roth, B.: An architecture for adaptive intelligent systems. Artificial Intelligence 72(1-2), 329–365 (1995)
11. Helal, S., Desai, N., Verma, V., Lee, C.: Konark - a service discovery and delivery protocol for ad-hoc networks. In: WCNC 2003, vol. 3, pp. 2107–2113. IEEE, Los Alamitos (2003)
12. Helmy, A., Garg, S., Nahata, N., Pamu, P.: Card:a contact-based architecture for resource discovery in wireless ad hoc networks. Mob. Netw. Appl. (1-2) (2005)
13. Lawrence, J.: Leap into ad-hoc networks. In: Proc. of the Ubiquitous Computing Workshop, Bologna, Italy, Media Lab Europe (2002)
14. Maes, P.: Artificial life meets entertainment. Commun. ACM 38(11), 108–114 (1995)
15. Marrow, P., Koubarakis, M., van Lengen, R.: Agents in decentralised information ecosystems: The diet approach. In: Proccedings of the Symposium on Information Agents for E-Commerce, AISB Convention, York, UK (March 2001)
16. McGrath, R.E.: Discovery and its discontents: Discovery protocols for ubiquitous computing. Technical report, University of Illinois, Department of Computer Science, Champaign, IL, USA (2000)
17. Mertens, K., Holvoet, T., Berbers, Y.: Adaptation in a distributed environment. Environments for Multiagent Systems, 49–59 (2004)
18. Mertens, K., Holvoet, T., Berbers, Y.: A case for adaptation of the distributed environment layout in multiagent applications. In: SELMAS 2005, pp. 1–8. ACM Press, New York (2005)
19. Microsoft. Introduction to active channel technology, http://msdn.microsoft.com
20. Nidd, M.: Service discovery in deapspace. IEEE Pers. Comm. 8(4), 39–45 (2001)
21. Odell, J., Parunak, H.V.D., Fleischer, M., Brueckner, S.: Modeling agents and their environment. In: Giunchiglia, F., Odell, J.J., Weiss, G. (eds.) AOSE 2002. LNCS, vol. 2585, pp. 16–31. Springer, Heidelberg (2003)

22. Omicini, A., Ricci, A., Viroli, M.: Coordination artifacts as first-class abstractions for mas engineering: State of the research. In: Software Engineering for Multi-Agent Systems IV, pp. 71–90 (2005)
23. Ricci, A., Viroli, M., Omicini, A.: Programming mas with artifacts. In: Bordini, R.H., Dastani, M., Dix, J., El Fallah Seghrouchni, A. (eds.) PROMAS 2005. LNCS, vol. 3862, pp. 206–221. Springer, Heidelberg (2006)
24. Russell, S., Norvig, P.: Artificial Intelligence: A Modern Approach, 2nd edn. Prentice-Hall, Englewood Cliffs (2003)
25. Sailhan, F., Issarny, V.: Scalable service discovery for manet. In: PERCOM 2005: Proc. of the 3.IEEE Int. Conf. on Perv. Comp. and Comm., pp. 235–244. IEEE Computer Society, Washington (2005)
26. Seaborne, A.: Rdql - a query language for rdf. (January 2004), http://www.w3.org/Submission/RDQL/
27. Sun. Jini architecture spec. v. 2.1. Technical report, Sun Micro., Inc. (December 2001)
28. Sun. Jxta v2.0 protocols specification (2007), https://jxta-spec.dev.java.net/
29. UPnP. Universal plug and play device architecture version 1.0.1. (December 2003), http://www.upnp.org
30. Weyns, D., Parunak, H.V.D., Michel, F., Holvoet, T., Ferber, J.: Environments for multiagent systems. In: E4MsAS (2004)
31. Weyns, D., Vizzari, G., Holvoet, T.: Environments for situated multi-agent systems: Beyond infrastructure. In: Weyns, D., Van Dyke Parunak, H., Michel, F. (eds.) E4MAS 2005. LNCS, vol. 3830, pp. 1–17. Springer, Heidelberg (2006)

Infrastructure for Forensic Analysis of Multi-Agent Systems*

Emilio Serrano and Juan A. Botia

Universidad de Murcia, Murcia, Spain
emilioserra@um.es, juanbot@um.es

Abstract. The contribution of this paper is an intent to state the basis for forensic analysis of multi-agent system (MAS) runs. It proposes a general approach for open source agents platforms. It consists on techniques to store, order and represent messages based on conventional observation of the events in a distributed system, particularized for the case of MAS in which agents can be distributed across a number of machines or even be mobile.

Keywords: Forensic analysis, debugging multi-agent systems.

1 Introduction

The effort made in the context of this work is focused on preparing the necessary infrastructure to perform testing activities within the process of multi-agent system (MAS) software development. Software testing [19] is in charge of assessing the validation of a software. Testing is about detecting errors in code and debugging is in charge of locating and fixing the errors. Hence, testing MAS software is about performing tests in agents, groups of agents or involving the whole MAS with the purpose of finding anomalies in the behavior of agents.

In this paper, we define a general approach to provide forensic analysis of runs in MAS developments. Forensic or post mortem analysis is usually found as a term, in the context of software projects management [2,21] but also on distributed systems analysis [8] and security [22]. We reuse it here to study the correctness of a MAS software. Thus, post mortem analysis of a MAS software is the task in charge of studying the results of a software test with the purpose of finding anomalies or undesired behavior which appeared in the execution. Notice that it is possible that, for complex systems as a MAS, wrong behavior is not detected if the software analyzed has enough complexity or the analysis is not powerful enough to do it.

---

* This research work is supported by the Spanish Ministry of Education and Science in the scope of the Research Project TIN-2005-08501-C03-02 and by the Project "Análisis, Estudio y Desarrollo de Sistemas Inteligentes y Servicios Telemáticos" through the Fundación Séneca within the Program "Generación del Conocimiento Científico de Excelencia".

K.V. Hindriks, A. Pokahr, and S. Sardina (Eds.): ProMAS 2008, LNAI 5442, pp. 168–183, 2009.

We will address here how to built a framework for any agent based platform which possibilities forensic analysis related tasks. This is the first step to provide a general framework for MAS testing and validation. However, this paper will not cover aspects related with testing or validation. It will cover only details related to providing the necessary infrastructure for forensic analysis. In order to do that, we need the necessary means to capture and represent what happened in MAS runs generated by software tests. Like in any other conventional distributed system, observable events are the only source of information we have to compound the global picture (i.e. a snapshot from now on) for MAS too. Here, we have messages among the most important events we can perceive and use to create snapshots. Moreover, like in other distributed systems, we will arrange them by using logical clocks [13]. The phases of this task are (1) including logical clocks inside messages, (2) to capture messages and log them for a posteriori analysis, (3) select an interesting set of messages from the whole set, (4) order them and (5) analyze them. The design of these phases for MAS is a delicate task. This is due to the fact that agent based software is continuously evolving. Thus, to achieve genericity (i.e. methods or techniques which are valid for a number of different agent platforms) is not trivial and needs specific technologies. Besides, ordering messages in any agents platform, considering that we could even have mobile agents is a complex issue.

In this paper, we introduce a generic approach for capturing, ordering and representing messages exchanged among agents in a run, i.e. the necessary elements to do a post mortem analysis. This approach does not depend on a specific agent platform. The main requirement we have is that source code must be available for slight modifications. This modifications are a consequence of the method we use: aspect oriented programming. Of course, the proposal also has some limitations that will be showed.

The rest of the paper is organized as follows. We will put this research in its context in section 2. Section 3 includes the techniques proposed. This techniques are illustrated with the example in section 4. To finish the paper, we offer the conclusions and the works we are developing now in section 5.

2 Related Work

There is little work on postmortem analysis on distributed systems (or multi-agent systems) when it is applied to system development [10]. However, we can find a number of works on trace based analysis applied in the field of intrusion detection. For example, the work in [12] shows an approach that targets intrusion detection in computer networks and models intrusion patterns using Colored Petri-Nets. The approach is very interesting, but it still lacks an implementation that shows its efficiency. Another work is that which appears in [7]. In this, flow graphs are used to represent potential communication activity among the processes of a distributed system. Properties, meanwhile, are represented using quantified regular expressions (QRE). This approach requires deep knowledge of tiny details in the processes of the tested system. Finally, a similar approach is that used in the GrIDS tool [22]. This system is capable of detecting large scale intrusion attacks on network systems. The most interesting part is that it builds activity graphs of the executions of the various processes in the system by monitoring them individually. After this, graphs are analyzed using some reference rules to diagnose an intrusion. We follow the same approach: capturing, ordering, representing events and detecting wrong behavior. We focus on MAS software instead.

Papers [3] and [25] present different approaches to visualize the collected traces from the activity of a distributed system. The works [9] and [11] describe an approach, centered on the concept of lattice, to perform trace checking in distributed systems. Following this approach, a lattice is built, based on the monitored events and the relations between them, to represent the system under test. The lattice is then used in a model-checker to verify the behavior of the system against a desired property. In [15], a method of specifying abstraction hierarchies to define level-wise views of a distributed message-based system is outlined. This method utilizes event-pattern mappings and complex events to represent a system's behavior.

We have detected some shortcomings in the visual representation of events captured in conventional distributed systems that we will try to solve here. For example, the software of [14] uses sequence diagrams to represent messages. We will argue in this paper that these diagrams are inadequate in some cases and offer an alternative. Another example software [6] uses space time diagrams which need totally ordered events. In MAS, we have no global time reference, thus we can not order messages by using a total order. We propose here how to deal with this limitation.

With respect to methods available for representing partial orders, discrete mathematics provides mechanisms for obtaining simplified visions of a relationship of order, i.e. the so called Hasse diagrams [20]. The algorithm to generate a Hasse diagram is not affordable when the number of events is high. In our case, we might generate a high number of messages. We will try to alleviate this with our proposal.

There is some previous work on capturing, ordering and representing messages exchanged in MAS software [24]. This work covers aspects related with capturing, ordering and representing messages exchanged in a MAS. However, when capturing and ordering, the approach does not offer any generic approach. Mobile agents are not considered there as we do in this approach. With respect to visual representation of messages, they define and use causality diagrams. But they rely on the existence of previously defined interaction protocols as it is assumed that the platform is FIPA compliant. We offer an approach for any agent platform (with some requirements), i.e. any agent communication language.

3   Global Snapshots Generation of MAS Tests

In this section we introduce how Aspect Oriented Programming can be used to capture message sending and receiving events in MAS software tests. Once this is explained, we present how logical clocks can be used to obtain a partial order of messages collected from MAS tests.

3.1 Generic Collection of Messages in an Agents Platform

Aspect oriented programming (AOP) is intend on isolating different aspects of applications in order to treat them separately and in a modular manner. Thanks to this approach, we get more adaptive, understandable and reusable developments. Though AspectJ is the most popular framework for programming with aspects in the Java programming language, we also have available others like AspectC, AspectC++, AspectC#, etc) for C, C++ and C# respectively. Hence, the following discussion, although it is done with the Java language, it is also applicable to the other languages mentioned. Hence, we can apply the approach to virtually any agent platform with modifiable and compilable source code.

Let us suppose that, without loss of generality, in the source code of the platform we have a class called **Agent**. Let us suppose also that there is a class which represents ACL messages, **ACLMessage** and that the agent sends and receives messages through **send()** and **receive()** methods (i.e. just like Jade does). Notice that this is only a convention used to properly explain the approach. Analogous structures can be found in many platforms. We see *messages collection* as an aspect. Hence, locating the parts of the code where messages are sent and received is critical. Both locations of source code are called *Jointpoints* in the AOP terminology. A jointpoint is a location of source code in which we need to connect an aspect (e.g. a method call, an exception or modifying the value of a variable). Once we have this, we need to define *Pointcuts*. A pointcut in AOP terminology defines which aspects will be applied to each jointpoint. Let us go directly to the following example:

```
pointcut callSend(Agent ag,ACLMessage msg):
   this(ag) && execution(* send(..)) && args(msg);
pointcut callReceive(Agent ag):
   this(ag) && execution(ACLMessage receive(..));
```

whose first line states that whenever an Agent calls **send()** method with an **ACLMessage** object as argument, the method **callSend()** will be called. At the second line, the explanation is analogous. Notice that, due to the use of powerful regular expressions, we can define pointcuts for any situation and platform. Once pointcuts are defined, we need now to specify the functionality for each, this is what is called an **advice**. Its structure would be like this

```
before (Agent ag,ACLMessage msg): callSend(ag,msg){
   mySniffingCode...}
after (Agent ag) returning (ACLMessage msg): callReceive(ag){
   mySniffingCode...}
```

in which we define an advice just before sending and just after receiving a message. Before sending the message we can define all which is related to processing logical clocks of sending and receiving events. After receiving a message we post-process clocks and store the message.

Of course, the proposal exposed has weaknesses. For example it is necessary to have an aspect oriented language associated with the language of the platform. Therefore the proposal depends on the developers of that aspect oriented language and it depends on the success of this paradigm. Another inconvenience is that the proposal need the source code of the platform. And therefore, the proposal depends on the developers of that platform.

Disadvantages included, the proposal outlined here gives us a significant degree of genericy (it isn't a total genericy, obviously) to make a forensic analysis for the debugging of a MAS.

3.2   Message Storing and Ordering

In this section, we will explain the `advices` we have just mentioned above. The first thing we need to start working on is a centralized storage mechanism that all agents can access. For this, we propose the use of a relational data base (RDB) server (e.g. we have used mySql and Hypersonic) as a central storage mechanism. There are at least two reasons which support this recommendation. In the one hand, a MAS might be actually distributed (i.e. it could be executed through a number of machines). JDBC is actually an option for distributed access to almost any RDB available. In the other hand, a RDB is a powerful tool for querying data. This functionality is very convenient, as the reader will understand soon (please see section 3.3).

It is important, at this point, to consider what to store in the RDB. It must be noticed that in the process of capturing and ordering messages, there is no possibility of having global variables (e.g. to provide global identifiers for agents of messages) if they are not stored in the DB. Notice that no state information can be included inside an `advice`. Hence, if an agent moves from a machine to another, no global variable can be manipulated with success inside the `advice`. For example, we can not use logical clocks with success if they are not stored in a central server before the agent moves.

Now, we need to order messages as they are collected from the MAS run. As it is explained in [13] by Lamport, we can use logical clocks to order events in a distributed system. When we have a number of processes in a distributed system (i.e. agents in this case), we can use a counter of events for each process and event (i.e. message).

We will assign a logical clock for each captured message. In fact the original logical clocks [13] aren't going to be used, an extension of them is used: the vector clocks [16]. These vectors are an array of integers (each integer in the array refers to an agent in the MAS). For a pair of such arrays, we can define order operations. More formally, for each pair of vector clocks V_1 and V_2, we define two simple operations, partial order

$$V_1 \leq V_2 \; iff \; \forall i : \; V_1[i] \leq V_2[i] \; with \; 1 \leq i \leq n,$$

and strict order

$$V_1 < V_2 \ iff \ V_1 \le V_2 \ \wedge \ \exists i : \ V_1[i] < V_2[i] \ with \ 1 \le i \le n$$

Given two events e_1 and e_2, whose logical clocks are V_{e_1} and V_{e_2} respectively, then we say that e_1 occurs before e_2 iff $V_{e_1} < V_{e_2}$.

And now we introduce the preprocessing that must be executed by agents before sending messages. Anytime an agent a_i sends a message m, it will execute the following actions:

1. It will increment i-th position of its logical clock lc_{a_i} by one, obtaining lc'_{a_i}.
2. Assign lc'_{a_i} to m.
3. Store lc'_{a_i} as the last logical clock stored for a_i.

Let us denote this procedure with `addClock`.

And now a postprocessing that must be executed by agents anytime they receive a message. When a_i receives a message m from agent a_j, it will perform this actions:

1. It will obtain obtain lc_{a_j} from m
2. It will increment i-th position of its logical clock lc_{a_i} by one, obtaining lc'_{a_i}.
3. Then $lc''_{a_i} \leftarrow \max(lc'_{a_i}, lc_{a_j}) \forall j \ with \ 1 \le j \le n$, being n the number of agents in the system
4. Store lc''_{a_i}.

Let us denote this procedure with `updateClock`.

After all messages are stored, they have to be ordered by using the clocks and the appropriated algorithm (please see section 3.4). Thus, we need to assign global identifiers to messages. In this work, we rely on the DB to generate them when they are stored. An illustrative example of how to store messages into a relation can be found in table 1. It corresponds to a contract net conversation.

Now, we can complete advices defined above with `addClock`, `updateClock` and `storeMessage`.

```
before (Agent ag,ACLMessage msg): callSend(ag,msg){
   addClock(ag,msg)
```

Table 1. Stored messages example

Message Id	Clock	Sender	Receiver	Performative
84	85,29,23,30	cliente	pValenttino	cfp
85	86,29,23,30	cliente	pDavinci	cfp
86	87,29,23,30	cliente	pAntonio	cfp
87	87,31,23,30	pAntonio	cliente	propose
88	85,29,26,30	pValenttino	cliente	propose
89	86,29,23,33	pDavinci	cliente	propose
90	91,31,26,33	cliente	pAntonio	reject
91	92,31,26,33	cliente	pValenttino	accept
92	93,31,26,33	cliente	pDavinci	reject
93	92,31,28,33	pValenttino	cliente	inform

```
}
after (Agent ag) returning (ACLMessage msg): callReceive(ag){
  updateClock(ag,msg)
}
```

To include logical clocks in messages implies a reduction of performance of the MAS (especially when there are many agents and the clocks are very large). Likewise, the agents must send a copy of the messages received to the database. However, the reduction isn't dramatic because the agent does not have to wait for data from the server (except the first moment of its execution in a container). Moreover, in pathological large systems, database could be a bottleneck. Then, there won't be problem in distributing the database on multiple servers because the order of the messages is not the order for insertion (logical clocks give the order). In this case, when an agent begins its implementation in a container, it must ask all servers which is its maximum clock stored.

Other disadvantage of the proposal is that it is necessary to specify the maximum number of agents in the system (to set a logical clock size). In principle this should not be too restrictive because this proposal consider making a forensic analysis of a MAS that we would have developed (and we would want to debug), and the developer should know this number approximately.

In principle, this is all that we need, roughly speaking, to introduce logical clock management on a Java based agent platform, by using aspects and a RDB. We will illustrate how this works with an example. Let us suppose that we have two agents a_1 and a_2. Agent a_1 stays in a container (or the corresponding execution environment of the agent platform) and a_2, after a while, moves from one container to another. Events and messages exchanged appear in figure 1. Initially, a_1 is located at container 1 and a_2 at container 2. First events which come out from the RDB are labeled with 1 and 2. They correspond to the generation of logical clocks for two agents which start running (i.e. a_1 and a_2). At point three, a_1 sends a **request** message, let it be denoted with m, to a_2. Hence, the logical clock of m is $(1,0)$, the same for the internal logical clock of a_1. The same goes for point 4 when a_2 sends a **request** to a_1. At point 5, a_2 receives the first message from a_1. Now, the new logical clock is $(1,2)$ and a copy of it is sent to the RDB. At point 6, a_1 receives the first message sent from a_2 with clock $(0,1)$. The new clock is $(2,1)$. Again, a copy is sent to the RDB. At points 7 and 8, agent a_2 moves to container 3. Before moving, it sends its clock $(1,2)$ to the RDB. Once it arrives to the new environment, asks the RDB for its clock and position within it and recovers both. The rest of the figure can be analysed analogously.

3.3   Selection of Subsets of Messages

We have to be prepared for working with a large-scale MAS, in which there it can be an enormous amount of messages to be exchanged, thus stored. For this, we need selection mechanisms to select the appropriate subset of messages. Think, for example, in the MAS we use in section 4, there is an agent which is in charge

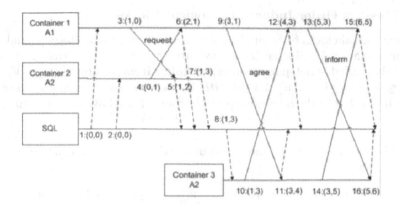

Fig. 1. MAS test with 2 agents

of presenting a graphical view of the rest of the MAS. Hence, its communication activity with the rest might be irrelevant in some post mortem analysis.

We will introduce here two simple filters we apply and that can easily be implemented in a RDB with SQL. Let A be the set of all agents in a run and M the set of messages exchanged. We will define $sender(m)$ as a function which obtains the sender of $m \in M$, and $receiver(m)$ for the receiver.

The first filter we use, considers only a subset of messages $A_c \subseteq A$ as an argument. We represent it as

$$M_c \leftarrow \{m \in M : sender(m) \in A_c \vee (\exists a \in A_c : a \in receivers(m))\},$$

i.e., we consider only messages sent and/or received by agents in A_c.

In other cases, the developer will need to do a progressive analysis, i.e. an analysis which starts focusing in one or a couple of agents and then, gradually, more agents are incorporated. Incorporation criteria can be adding those agents which are reachable through others in the agents hierarchy induced by communication links. For example, let a_1, a_2, and a_3 be agents. There are acquitances defined, such that a_1 only interacts with a_2, and a_2 only interacts with a_3. Therefore, if there is interest in studying the behavior of a_1, a progressive analysis would begin by firstly studying messages exchanged between a_1 and a_2. Then, it would expand to study those exchanged by a_1 and a_2 together with those exchanged by a_2 and a_3. The second filter performs this task.

The second filter works by considering a number of agents, let us denote it with $A_c \subseteq A$ again, and a depth, $d \in \{1, 2, \ldots\}$. For this, we recursiverly define the procedure

$$grow(A_c, 0) = A_c$$
$$grow(A_c, n) = grow(A_c, n - 1) \cup A_s \cup A_r,$$

where $A_s \subseteq A$ is the set of agents which send messages to agents in A_c, and $A_r \subseteq A$ is the set of agents which receive messages from agents in A_c. After we grow A_c, we have

$$M_c \leftarrow \{m \in M : sender(m) \in A_c \wedge (\exists a \in A_c : a \in receivers(m))\}$$

3.4   Message Order Induced by Logical Clocks

By using logical clocks to order elements in M, we induce a binary partial order relation in $(M \times M)$. In particular, we are interested in an irreflexive partial order (also called strict partial order). Remind from section 3.2 that $V_1 \leq V_2$ iif $V_1 \leq V_2$ iff $\forall i : V_1[i] \leq V_2[i]$ $with$ $1 \leq i \leq n$. As an explanation of why we are interested in the irreflexive partial order, please have a look at the graph represented on the left in figure 2. We see that $V_1 \leq V_2$. In the other hand, V_2 and V_3 are not related by $\leq$. Notice that this graph is cyclic as the relation $\leq$ is reflexive. Actually, we are interested in a strict partial order, i.e. for a pair of clocks V_1 and V_2,

$$V_1 < V_2 \; iff \; V_1 \leq V_2 \; \wedge \; \exists i : V_1[i] < V_2[i] \; with \; 1 \leq i \leq n \tag{1}$$

as it is more precise for our purposes.

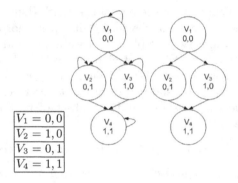

Fig. 2. Four clocks at the left, a simple partial order (centre) and irreflexive partial order (right part)

Now, we will present an algorithm to generate, from a set M of messages with their corresponding logical clocks, we denote with $lc(m)$ the logical clock of m, a graph which represents the partial order represented by the clocks. This new graph, let it be dented with $PO = (V, E)$ has a set of nodes V and edges E. Each $v \in V$ will have an identifier, id and a *content* (i.e. clocks and other needed information). We denote with $id(m)$ the identifier of message m and with *content*(m) the content of m. We will define *successors*(v), as generating the set

$$\{v_2 \in V : \exists e = (v, v_2) \in E\},$$

and we use it to obtain successors of any $v \in V$ in PO. We also use a function called $add(L, v, v')$ which adds a new edge from v to v' and introduces it into the list of edges L (if it hasn't already been inserted). Another function $update(L, L', v, v')$ invokes and $add(L, v, v')$ and adds v' to the list of nodes L' (if it hasn't already been inserted). The last one is $remove(L, v, v')$ which removes the edge from v to v' of L. We will also introduce initially a node r whose logical clock is such that $lc(r) \leq lc(m)$ $\forall m \in M$.

The algorithm appears in figure 3. It takes as an input a list of nodes in V and a partial order for the set. It generates the set of edges, E so we have $PO = (V, E)$ at the end. With this algorithm we can create acyclic graphs representing any strict partial order. Different strict partial orders available will vary on the definition and initialization of V.

Of course, the sort messages by logical time is going to have a cost on computation time bigger than if a lineal order is considered. However, we must keep in mind that a forensic analysis needs to sort messages only once. In addition,

```
1   edges ← ∅ //list of edges
2   nodes ← r //list of added nodes
3   for each v ∈ V { //for each vertex to insert
4       for each v_a ∈ nodes such that v < v_a {
5           /*for each vertex v_a already inserted, with v < v_a
                */
6           succ ← sucessors(v_a)
7           if succ = ∅
8               update(edges, nodes, v_a, v) //there aren't successors
                    , edge v_a−>v
9           else{//there are successors
10              insertedOrWait ← false
11              /*insertedOrWait true is that v has been
                    inserted or we have to wait for the next
                    value of v_a*/
12              for each v_s ∈ succ {
13                  if v_s < v { //then v_s < v < v_a, edges
                        v_a− > v− > v_s
14                      update(edges, nodes, v_a, v)
15                      insertedOrWait ← true //v has been
                            inserted
16                      remove(edges, v_a, v_s)
17                      add(edges, v, v_s)
18                  }//endif
19                  else if v < v_s insertedOrWait ← true
20                  /*v will be inserted when v_a=v_s or later,
                        wait*/
21              }//end foreach
22              /*if insertedOrWait is false, then every
                    successor isn't comparable with v, edge
                    v_a− > v*/
23              if (not insertedOrWait) update(edges, nodes, v_a, v)
24          }//end else
25      }//end foreach
26  }//end foreach
27  E← edges
```

Fig. 3. Algorithm to create a partial order graph

the algorithm is also valid to sort the messages when they occur on the fly. For this task, machines can work asides.

As an example, please remind conversation represented in table 1, and consider now the order obtained by using clocks in figure 4. In this graph, we can see how the client generates three cfp labeled messages. They are actually ordered (i.e. messages 84, 85 y 86). Notice that propose messages are not sortable (i.e. messages 87, 88 y 89), although they are effectively later to the cfp messages. In the other hand, propose messages are sent before first reject-proposal (i.e. message 90)

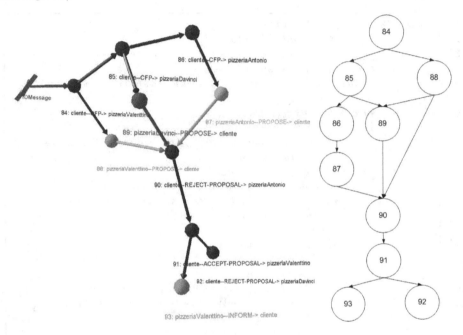

Fig. 4. A fipa-contract-net conversation graph with an irreflexive partial order between sent and received events (3D view on left, 2D view on right)

3.5   Valid Orders for Classic Representations

The usual way to represent a conversation is by using a sequence diagram although there are other representations like these proposed by El Fallah et al. [17] and Dooley graphs [23], to put some examples. We would like to emphasize that sequence diagrams are not valid for descriptive representations because they assume that all messages are comparable (i.e. there exists a total order relationship between the set of messages in a run). As we know, this is not possible in a distributed system. And a MAS is a distributed system.

Anyhow, if we still need to represent sequence diagrams by using the framework we are proposing, we should be able to create a totally ordered set of messages from a strict partial ordered graph, $MPO = (V, E)$. This total order is classically called *topological sorting*. With the M of MPO we mean that V

is compound by messages. Until now, it was compound by sent and received events. This is tricky as for any partial order, there are a number of total orders we might create, and we have to take into account that only one of them corresponds to what actually happened. Moreover, we do not know (actually we can not know) which one is that one that actually happened.

More formally, if we have a $MPO = (V, E)$, then we pursue to have a $VMPO = v_1, v_2..., v_n$, such that $V = \{v_1, v_2...v_n\}$ and $v_1 < v_2... < v_n$. To obtain that, the only thing that can not happen is that for any $v_1, v_2 \in V$, if by following the MPO we have that $v_1 < v_2$, them we have that in the $VMPO$ we have $v_2 < v_1$. In order to achieve that, for each $v \in V$ appearing at the $VMPO$, all its predecessors appear before. Simply, we create a list of nodes in which, for each v in that list, all $v' < v$ appears before in the list. It must be pointed out that (1) there is a loss of information as we generate a total order which could not correspond to what exactly happened but still be useful for post mortem analysis, and (2) there are a number of valid total orders. For example, remind figure 4 (right part) where we have message identifiers appearing in the strict partial order. From this graph, we can obtain the following valid total orders

- 84, 85, 88, 86, 89, 87, 90... (making a breadth-first search and taking into account the restriction).
- 84, 85, 86, 87, 89, 88, 90...(making a depth-first search and taking into account the restriction).
- 84, 85, 88, 86, 87, 89, 90...(other)

which would correspond to three different sequence diagrams.

4   Fire Example

In this section, we will see an example of use for the framework we propose. In this system, we represent a three floors lab in which workers (possibly hundreds of them) can freely move. The implementation is done for the Jade platform and each floor is represented by a Jade container. Hence, when a worker moves from floor to floor, it actually moves from a container to another. Each container is simulated by a different java virtual machine. Notice also that all the forensic analysis used in this example is available in ACLAnalyser.

Besides agents representing workers (i.e. user agents executed in PDAs), there are two special agents which communicate with user agents. The first one is the monitor, in charge of maintaining an approximate view of the system by receiving notifications of changes in location, from user agents. The second one is the coordinator. In case of fire, it will coordinate the evacuation process. It will choose a concrete worker as a hero in charge of picking up the fire extinguisher and use it. After finishing extinguishing the fire, it will notify the coordinator. During this process, the coordination will order agents located in floors above the fire to wait. For others located in floors above the fire, they will receive the order to get out.

The fipa-request protocol is used to notify location by user agents as initiators and monitor as participant. We have three user agents worker1 (at the

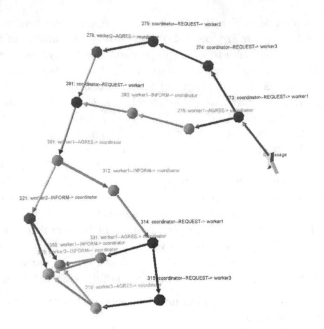

Fig. 5. Order Messages Graph

second floor), `worker2` (at the first floor) and `worker3` (at the third floor). Fire
is produced in the second floor. Hence, `worker2` must get out and `worker1` will
be the hero.

In figure 5 we see the order graph for messages exchanged among workers and
the coordination. Communication with the monitor is not considered. We have
filter the set of all messages M by using the second method of filtering where
$d = 0$ and $A_c = \{worker1, worker2, worker3, coordinator\}$.

4.1   A Post Mortem Analysis

Capturing messages from the MAS allows a post mortem study of the system.
In fact, in this example, there is apparently nothing wrong. We will see that by
looking at messages ordering we will detect some mistakes in the design.

In the graph presented above, we see how the coordinator sends successive
messages to `worker1`, `worker3` y `worker2` (with ids 273, 274, and 275 respectively). They are for ordering to get out, to wait and to pick up the fire extinguisher respectively.

Thus, we see that the coordinator is asking a worker to get out before receiving
the notification of fire extinguished. It could be possible that the designated hero
does not respond. In this case, other possibilities should be considered (e.g. other
agents should be aware of this). Thanks to this graph, we discover this subtle
mistake.

But, if we do not take into account concrete message semantics, is it still the
graph useful and informative? The answer is yes. If it occurs that a node v is not

reachable from other node v', this means that they are not related. For example, as we do not have a path between nodes 312 and 321 and vice versa, there is no relation between them. We can confirm this by looking at the meaning of messages

- 312: fire is already extinguished
- 321: worker2 (located in a floor below the fire) is already gone.

Effectively, by looking at the corresponding logical clocks,

- 312, r1=69,58,75,294,10
- 321, r2=66,58,81,297,10

we can neither say that $r1 < r2$, nor $r2 < r1$. By using a sequence diagram to represent the example, we should represent one before the other. In this case, it is very different to notice that the worker is gone before or after the fire is extinguished when we study the system behavior.

5 Conclusions and Future Work

We have shown a solid framework to capture, order and represent messages exchanged in a run of a MAS software. This is the first phase to debugging, validation and verification of MAS software: a post mortem analysis. More specifically, we have shown a combination of logical clocks theory with aspect oriented programming for the capture and the order, which is accomplished by an algorithm proposed in the paper. All these features are implemented in ACLAnalyser[1].

One of our future work is implement this framework in multiple platforms as Jadex, 2APL and Jason. We also intend to enhance the elements that are caught and their use to exploit the particularities of MAS compared to distributed systems.

We pursue to improve the expressibility of the order graph. At the end, any debugging tool used in the context of testing will be based in ordered messages represented by an order graph. Thus, such a graph own all information we need. However, we need to work in the usability of the graph to detect patterns of agents and group of agents in it.

One of the ways to improve expressibility would be to group nodes belonging to the same conversation into other kind of nodes and, again, order such new nodes. In this manner, we would have a graph of conversations, a more abstract view.

Another necessary future work is the design of a mechanism to generate causality diagrams starting from the order graph. They are a powerful tool for error diagnosis. We have already work in this topic [24]. However, in these previous works we rely on the existence of patterns for conversations (i.e. formal descriptions of conversations). In this case, we assume that there is no such concept of predefined conversations. We gain here in applicability.

---

[1] You can download it at aclanalyser.sourceforge.net.

The most important future work we are heading to is advancing towards automatic methods for debugging, validation and verification of MAS software. Currently, we are working on extending the INGENIAS metamodels to allow specifying tests. Post mortem analysis will be a powerful mechanism to inspect and inform about what happened in tests.

References

1. Iglesias, C.A., Garijo, M., Centeno-González, J.: A Survey of Agent-Oriented Methodologies. In: Proceedings of the 5th International Workshop on Intelligent Agents V, Agent Theories, Architectures, and Languages, July 04-07, pp. 317–330 (1998)
2. Birk, A., Dingsøyr, T., Stlhane, T.: Postmortem: Never leave a project without it. IEEE Software, special issue on knowledge management in software engineering 19(3), 43–45 (2002)
3. Black, J.P., Coffin, M.H., Taylor, D.J., Kunz, T., Basten, A.A.: Linking Specifications, Abstraction, and Debugging., CCNG Technical Report E-232, Computer Communications and Network Group, University of Waterloo (November 1993)
4. Bordini, R.H., Dastani, M., Dix, J., Fallah-Seghrouchni, A.E.: Multi-Agent Programming: Languages, Platforms and Applications. Multiagent Systems, Artificial Societies, and Simulated Organizations, vol. 15. Springer, Heidelberg (2005)
5. Botía, J.A., González, J.C., Gómez-Sanz, J., Pavón, J.: The INGENIAS Project. In: 6th International Workshop on Practical Applications on Agents and MultiAgent Systems. IWPAAMS 2007, Salamanca, Spain (2007)
6. Carr, S., Fang, C., Jozwowski, T.R., Mayo, J., Shene, C.-K.: ConcurrentMentor: A Visualization System for Distributed Programming Education. In: The 2003 International Conference on Parallel and Distributed Processing Techniques and Applications, June 23-26, pp. 1676–1682. Las Vegas, Nevada (2003)
7. Dwyer, M., Clarke, L.: Data Flow Analysis for Verifying Properties of Concurrent Programs. In: Proc. of ACM SIGSOFT 1994, New Orleans, LA, USA (1994)
8. Fang, W., Wang, C.-L., Zhu, W., Lau, F.C.M.: PAT: a postmortem object access pattern analysis and visualization tool. In: IEEE International Symposium on Cluster Computing and the Grid, CCGrid 2004 (2004)
9. Fromentin, E., Raynal, M., Garg, V., Tomlinson, A.: On the Fly Testing of Regular Patterns in Distributed Computations. Internal Publication # 817, IRISA, Rennes, France (1994)
10. Hallal, H., Petrenko, A., Ulrich, A., Boroday, S.: Using SDL Tools to Test Properties of Distributed Systems. In: Formal Approches to Testing of Software (FATES 2001), Workshop of the International Conference on Concurrency Theory (CONCUR 2001), Aalborg, Denmark, August 21-24 (2001)
11. Jard, C., Jeron, T., Jourdan, G.V., Rampon, J.X.: A General Approach to Trace-checking in Distributed Computing Systems. In: Proc. IEEE Int. Conf. on Distributed Computing Systems, Poznan, Poland (June 1994)
12. Kumar, S., Spafford, E.: An Application of Pattern Matching in Intrusion Detection. Technical Report 94-013, Purdue University, Department of Computer Sciences (March 1994)
13. Lamport, L.: Time, clocks, and the ordering of events in a distributed system. Commun. ACM 21(7), 558–565 (1978)

14. Lee, D.W., Ramakrishna, R.S.: Visok: A Flexible Visualization System for Distributed Java Object Application. In: Proceedings of 14th International Parallel and Distributed Processing Synposium IPDPS 2000, Cancun, Mexico, May 1-5, pp. 393–398 (2000)
15. Luckham, D.C., Frasca, B.: Complex Event Processing in Distributed Systems. Stanford University Technical Report CSL-TR-98-754, 28 pages (March 1998)
16. Mattern, F.: Virtual time and global states of distributed systems. In: Proceedings of the International Workshop on Parallel and Distributed Algorithms. LNCS, pp. 215–226. North-Holland, Amsterdam (1989)
17. Mazouzi, H., Seghrouchni, A.E.F., Haddad, S.: Open protocol design for complex interactions in multi-agent systems. In: AAMAS 2002: Proceedings of the first international joint conference on Autonomous agents and multiagent systems, pp. 517–526. ACM Press, New York (2002)
18. Miles, R.: AspectJ Cookbook, 1st edn., December 2004. Cookbooks, p. 354 (2004) ISBN 10: 0-596-00654-3
19. Myers, G.J.: The Art fo Software Testing. Wiley-Interscience, Hoboken (1979)
20. Rossen, K.H.: Discrete Mathematics and Its Applications, 5th edn. McGraw-Hill, cop., Boston (2003)
21. Stalhane, T., Dingsayr, T., Moe, N.B., Hanssen, G.K.: Post Mortem - An Assessment of Two Approaches, EuroSPI, Limrerick, Ireland (2001)
22. Staniford-Chen, S., Cheung, S., Crawford, R., Dilger, M., Frank, J., Hoaglan, J., Levitt, K., Wee, C., Yip, R., Zerkle, D.: The Design of GrIDS: A Graph-Based Intrusion Detection System. Technical Report, Department of Computer Science, University of California at Davis (January 1999)
23. Van Dyke Parunak, H.: Visualizing Agent Conversations: Using Enhanced Dooley Graphs for Agent Design and Analysis. In: Proceedings of the First International Conference on Multi-Agent Systems
24. Vigueras, G., Botia, J.A.: Tracking causality by visualization of multi-agent interactions using causality graphs. In: Dastani, M., El Fallah Seghrouchni, A., Ricci, A., Winikoff, M. (eds.) ProMAS 2007. LNCS (LNAI), vol. 4908, pp. 190–204. Springer, Heidelberg (2008)
25. Ward, P.A.S.: A Framework Algorithm for Dynamic Centralized Dimension-Bounded Timestamps. In: Proc. of CASCON 2000, Mississauga (2000)

Toolipse: An IDE for Development of JIAC Applications

Erdene-Ochir Tuguldur, Axel Hessler, Benjamin Hirsch, and Sahin Albayrak

DAI-Labor, Technische Universität Berlin
tuguldur.erdene-ochir@dai-labor.de,
axel.hessler@dai-labor.de,
benjamin.hirsch@dai-labor.de,
sahin.albayrak@dai-labor.de

Abstract. Developing agent-based applications without an integrated development environment (IDE) is difficult and error-prone. Providing good IDEs to the developers eases agent programming and enhances the quality of the output, which perhaps helps the agent-oriented paradigm to become more widely accepted. To achieve this important objective, we have developed Toolipse, a fully featured IDE prototype, based on the Eclipse platform, for the development of JIAC applications. Toolipse has been used and evaluated in teaching and a number of projects in different domains and helped their users creating pinpoint solutions.

1 Introduction

When Shoham wrote his paper on agent-oriented programming [1], he coined the phrase: "Agenthood is in the mind of the programmer". This is still the case, but nowadays application developers can choose between numerous agent frameworks, methodologies and toolkits [2,3,4]. The AgentLink Roadmap [5] still specifically notes that Tools are an important element if agent technology is ever to take hold in the real world.

Since the inception of our agent framework JIAC (Java-based Intelligent Agent Componentware), we provided tools which

- allow fast and efficient development of JIAC-based applications,
- narrow the gap between design and implementation,
- support beginners, advanced learners and experts at the same time,
- are based on standards and best practices in software engineering and tools programming.

This paper presents the third major release of the tools. The first two were stand-alone implementations [6,7]. The current one is a set of tools which has been integrated in the Eclipse[1] platform, called Toolipse. It provides visual and source code editors, extensive help components and project resource management. Toolipse is available together with JIAC on http://www.jiac.de.

---

[1] http://www.eclipse.org/

K.V. Hindriks, A. Pokahr, and S. Sardina (Eds.): ProMAS 2008, LNAI 5442, pp. 184–196, 2009.

1.1 JIAC Agent Framework

The JIAC agent framework supports the development of multi-agent systems (MAS) using BDI agents and FIPA compliant platforms. The framework has been implemented using the Java programming language. Two building blocks constitute the basic agent architecture: the component system [8] and the JIAC Agent Description Language (JADL) [9]. The basic architecture of a JIAC-based application is summarised in the MAS meta-model, which is shown in Figure 1.

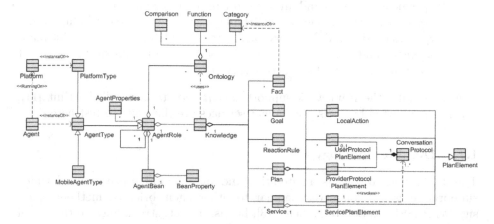

Fig. 1. JIAC MAS meta-model

In the framework, the following concepts are defined and must be supported by tools:

- Domain Vocabulary:
  - *Ontologies* define *categories*, which are used to create the beliefs and the interaction vocabulary of the agents.
  - In addition to categories, ontologies provide *functions* and *comparisons*, which can access and manipulate category instances. They are implemented in Java.
- Knowledge:
  - Initial beliefs (*facts*) using these categories are created before the agent is started.
  - *Reaction rules* constitute the reactive behaviour of an agent.
  - *Plan elements* define the behaviour of the agents. They can be deliberatively selected and then become intentions. Plan elements can be used to aggregate more complex plans by either the developer or a planning component as part of an agent.
  - *Protocol plan elements* define steps in an agent interaction for each participating agent.
  - *Service plan elements* are used to expose plan elements of an agent to other agents and are used to find services and their providers.

- Component:
  - *Agent beans* are core components and also used to wrap or connect the non-agent environment via Java APIs or user interfaces. They implement *bean roles* (to allow dynamic bean exchange at runtime) and can communicate with each other using *bean messages*.
- Deployment:
  - *Agent roles* are composites of agent functionalities and interaction capabilities (services) from the above concepts.
  - *Agents* are agent roles that have standard components as well as domain specific agent roles and are able to run on an agent platforms.
  - *Agent platforms* are agents, which play the role of an Agent Management System (AMS) and Directory Facilitator (DF) [10], i.e. they provide management and white and yellow page services, and constitute the agent environment and infrastructure services.

Additionally, the framework supports *agent unit testing* called AUnit [11], which is supported by tools, too. Agent services are the units to test here.

1.2   JIAC Methodology

The JIAC methodology is an iterative and incremental process model which supports re-use. It looks very similar to other agent-oriented methodologies, such as PASSI [12] or Prometheus [13], but is, in fact, streamlined to the use of our framework.

As shown in Figure 2, the development process starts with collecting domain vocabulary and requirements, which then are structured and prioritised. In this step, we also look for ontologies and other artifacts that can be re-used, saving time and effort. Second, we take the requirements with the highest priority and

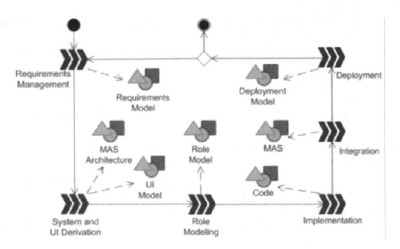

Fig. 2. JIAC methodology - iterative and incremental process model in SPEM [14] notation

derive a MAS architecture by identifying agents and the platforms where the agents reside on, and create a user interface prototype. The MAS architecture then is detailed by deriving a role model, showing the design concerning functionalities and interactions. Agents and agent roles available can be retrieved from a repository consisting of standard and domain specific configurations. We then implement the agents' behaviour by coding or adapting plans, services and protocols, which are plugged into agents during integration. This phase is accompanied with extensive unit testing. The agents are deployed to one or more agent platforms and the application is ready to be evaluated. Depending on the evaluation, we align and amend requirements and start the cycle again with eliminating bugs and enhancing and adding features until we reach the desired quality of the agent-based application.

2   Case Study

To illustrate parts of Toolipse's functionality in this paper, we have chosen the "Service Centric Bank" (SCB) scenario, a complex scenario in the bankers' world. The banking domain is currently undergoing changes towards new business models, increased customer orientation, breaking traditional value chains and integrating new areas of activities. The Service Centric Bank is an active bank, which supports multi-channel, ubiquitous customer interaction, implementing the idea of one-stop finance with many connections to finance and non-finance scenarios.

The approach [15] breaks down the complex domain into five sub-themes:

- Basic services, which mainly consist of classical banking services such as money transfers or credits.
- Information and monitoring services, i.e. a number of notifiers which observe bank accounts and transactions, and also Selective Dissemination of Information (SDI) services.
- Asset management with inclusion of customer needs and wishes and cooperation with other financial service providers.
- Customer support when dealing with authorities such as taxes, customs payments, legal regulations or invoice issuing.
- Bank as integrator, which means co-operation with non-financial service providers, e.g. in the case of customers moving.

There exist approaches or solutions for each of the sub-themes. The real challenge though is to take the independent services and interconnect them in a dynamic, customer-oriented and short-term manner. We have implemented a demonstrator of a subset of possible services using Toolipse and the JIAC agent framework, which shows agent-based planning and adaptive behaviour without hard-wiring financial workflows or supply chains. This case study has also been one of the more complex scenarios, where we have tested Toolipse's features and usability.

3   Toolipse

We have implemented Toolipse, a fully functional prototype of an IDE based on the Eclipse platform, which facilitates the development of agent applications with the JIAC agent framework, increases their quality and shortens the development time. The aim was to hide the language syntax from the developers as much as possible, to allow them to develop an agent application visually and to assist them where possible. To achieve that, it provides the following main functionalities:

- creating and building projects, managing their resources and providing an internal resource model;
- creating JADL ontologies, manipulating them visually and importing ontologies from other ontology languages;
- developing agent knowledge in a visual environment;
- testing agent behaviours with agent unit tests;
- implementing agent beans in Java;
- configuring and deploying agent roles, agents and platforms visually;
- helping and guiding the developers through the entire development process with documentations, interactive how-to's and interactive tutorials.

Each functionality is realised as an Eclipse feature consisting of one or more plugins and typically comprises wizards, editors and views, which are arranged in an own perspective.

In Toolipse, wizards are used for creating projects and skeletal structures of JIAC files; each file type has its own wizard. After creating a file, the agent developers can edit the file with the associated editor, which is in the majority of cases a multi-page editor consisting of a source code editor and of a visual editor. The source code editors support syntax highlighting, warning and error marking, folding, code formatting and code completion which suggests possible completions to incomplete language expressions. In contrast to the source code editors, which require from the developers good knowledge of the language, the visual editors of Toolipse allow to work with abstract models, to create and modify instances of the meta-model graphically. This facilitates the agent development and minimises errors. In order to achieve this, the visual editors model the JIAC concepts with the Eclipse Modeling Framework (EMF), visualise them graphically with the Graphical Editing Framework (GEF) and provide simple graphical layouts such as radial layout, zooming and modifying properties of the visualised elements with the associated dialog windows as well as with the Properties view of Eclipse.

This Properties view belongs to one of the so-called workbench part concepts: views. They are typically used to navigate through resources or to assist the editors with extra functionalities. For example, all our editors support the Outline view where the outline of the file which is currently open is displayed. In addition to the Properties and Outline view, which are general views of Eclipse, Toolipse provides its own views that navigate the developers through the JIAC

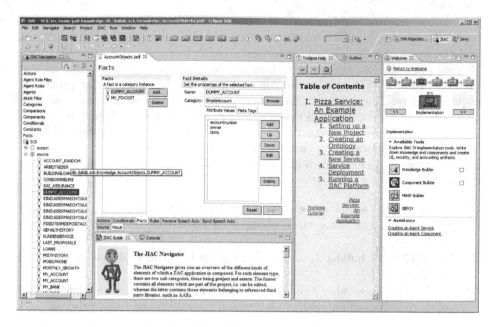

Fig. 3. Toolipse with the following components (from left to right): JIAC navigator, knowledge editor (center), JIAC guide (bottom), interactive tutorial and user guide

resources, present results of agent unit tests, to help or to guide them through the development process. Figure 3 shows the JIAC perspective with an editor and some of these views.

In the following subsections, we go into detail on the above-mentioned main features of Toolipse.

3.1   Resource and Project Management

The primary feature of an integrated development environment is a resource and project management. It supports organising project structures, navigating through resources, parsing files, caching and providing abstract resource model elements and building projects. For these purposes, Toolipse provides a resource manager, two incremental builders, a project wizard and a navigator view.

The resource manager maintains files, agent configurations and JADL language concepts in an internal model for all open JIAC projects. It is used by other components such as builders or editors. The internal model extends the Java model of the Eclipse Java Development Tools (JDT) with the JIAC meta-model. The model is always kept synchronous with the file system through a resource listener, which listens for changes on the file system and updates the model if required. Moreover, the manager uses caching methods to keep the size of the model reasonably small. For example, it creates instances of JIAC resources only once and sets the reference counter accordingly if the resource is referenced in many projects.

Two incremental builders are part of the resource and project management tools: the ontology builder which translates JADL ontologies into Java classes and the knowledge builder which converts JADL facts, reaction rules and plan elements into an executable form. Like the resource manager, the incremental builders listen for changes in the file system and trigger the build process if required. Here, "incremental" means that the builders compute all resources which depend on the changed resource and build only these relevant resources. In case of errors and warnings, the builders mark the affected resources with the corresponding annotations which are displayed in the Problems view of Eclipse, amongst others. An example build process looks as follows if an ontology file has changed or has been deleted:

1. The ontology builder calculates all ontology dependencies on the changed ontology and translates them along with the changed ontology into Java source files.
2. The JDT Java builder is activated afterwards because of new or modified Java files.
3. Finally, the knowledge builder computes the knowledge dependencies and builds the affected knowledge files, which completes the build process.

The projects created by Toolipse are also compatible to Maven[2], so that they can be build without the IDE. This feature is used, e.g. when different developers frequently integrate their work [16].

In contrast to the resource manager and the incremental builders, which are invisible to the users, the project wizard and the navigator view have UIs and are used by the developers directly. The project wizard creates a project and registers the ontology builder, the Java builder and the knowledge builder on the project as project builders. Additionally, it adds so-called project natures to the project. One of them, the JIAC project nature, indicates that the resource manager should scan the project for resources, create the corresponding model elements and update the resource model.

The last tool is the navigator which displays the resource model to support the developers with a resource view that shows only JIAC files and their contents. Moreover, the navigator also filters editor type specific resources. For example, it shows only ontologies and categories if an ontology has been opened by an ontology editor.

3.2   Domain Vocabulary

The development of an agent application typically starts with collecting the domain vocabulary, which is used to create the beliefs and the interaction vocabulary of the agents. In Toolipse, this development step is assisted by a wizard for creating JADL ontology files and a multi-page editor, which consists of a source code editor and a visual editor. While the source code editor supports syntax

---

[2] http://maven.apache.org/

highlighting and code completion, the visual editor allows the developers to create and manipulate ontologies graphically by visualising ontologies in UML[3]-like class diagrams (see Figure 4).

The visual ontology editor models an ontology as a UML class, which contains only methods (functions and comparisons), and does not contain any attribute. The categories of an ontology are represented as UML classes, which are connected with the parent ontology by UML compositions and contain only attributes. Inheritance relationships between categories are modelled as UML generalisations. In addition to the visualisation, the visual editor provides ontology editing functionalities which include importing other ontologies, creating and modifying categories graphically, implementing ontology functions and comparisons and editing attributes of a category.

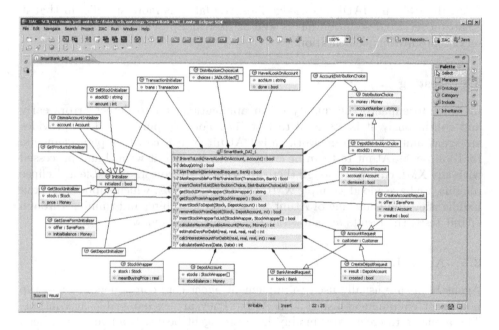

Fig. 4. The visual ontology editor modelling the SmartBank ontology of the SCB scenario

As opposed to other ontology languages such as OWL[4], it is not possible in JADL to define categories and their instances in the same file. Thus, the visual ontology editor does not support facts; however, facts can be modelled using the knowledge editor.

Furthermore, in order to support interoperability, Toolipse facilitates the development of ontologies with an import wizard, which currently translates OWL Lite ontologies into JADL.

---

[3] http://www.uml.org

[4] http://www.w3.org/2004/OWL/

3.3 Knowledge

Agent knowledge is described by JADL facts, reaction rules and plan elements. To support the agent developers in creation and maintenance of agent knowledge, Toolipse includes a knowledge editor, which comprises a source code editor and a visual editor. The visual editor is a multi-page editor, which contains a page for each knowledge type. Most of these pages are only form pages which create, edit and delete agent knowledge elements; however, the page for plan elements visualises JADL services, protocols and scripts as a flow chart and provides graphical editing functionality. Figure 3 shows the knowledge editor together with the fact form page, editing two facts of the SCB scenario.

Moreover, the IDE provides two wizards for the creation of agent knowledge files: the JADL file wizard and the service wizard. While the former is used to create arbitrary JADL knowledge files, the latter is more specific, in that it creates a service description file as well as user and provider script files for the service protocol implementation.

3.4 Testing

In order to enhance the quality of an application and to detect errors early and continuously, it is essential to test [17]. For this purpose, JIAC provides an agent unit testing framework called AUnit, which can test plan elements. In Toolipse, an AUnit test can be created with the AUnit wizard and processed with any XML editor. Although there are some XML editors available as Eclipse plugins, we have added a simple XML editor to our IDE, which supports syntax highlighting and launching of AUnit tests. After launching and running through AUnit tests, the results are shown in the AUnit results view.

3.5 Agent Beans

Agent beans are usually used to implement agent core components or to wrap non-agent environment using Java APIs. They are exchangeable at runtime. The artifacts to create and modify here are agent beans, bean roles and bean messages. The creation of these artifacts is supported in Toolipse by a number of wizards, while the implementation support of agent beans is left to JDT. For testing agent beans we rely on the JUnit[5] framework, which is also supported by JDT.

3.6 Deployment

In the last step of the agent development, the developers configure agent roles and agents, deploy them into agent platforms and launch the platforms. This development step is supported by wizards for creation of configuration files and by multi-page editors, each of them consisting of an XML editor and a visual

---

[5] http://junit.sourceforge.net/

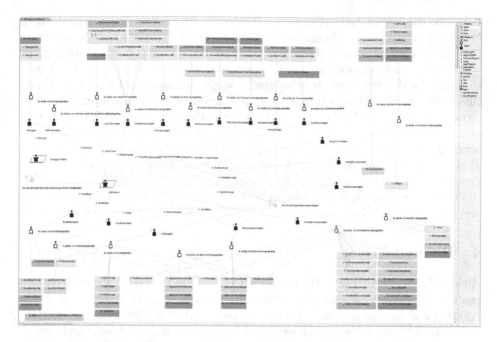

Fig. 5. The agent role editor shows agent roles, agents and agent platforms together with their relationships of the Service Centric Banking scenario

editor. While the visual editor for agents and agent roles visualises hierarchical relationships between agents and agent roles, the visual platform editor graphically represents a platform into which agents can be inserted. Both visual editors provide a set of form pages with which properties of agent roles, agents and platforms can be manipulated. Toolipse includes also a platform launcher, which can start a platform directly from the platform editor.

We have then prototyped a new agent role editor, which shows the overall structure of an agent society and allows different views on it. Figure 5 shows the new editor visualising agent roles, agents, platforms, their relationships and assembly from our SCB case study.

3.7 Helpers and Guidance

To familiarise the developers with our agent framework and its IDE, we have implemented a number of Toolipse help components, some of which extend the help system of Eclipse, while others are realised as separate components.

First of all, the IDE extends the welcome site of Eclipse with its own customised welcome site, which overviews the development steps, namely analysis, design, implementation, testing and deployment of an agent application. With each development step, a set of Toolipse and standalone tools is associated; the developers can start these tools directly from the help site.

Beside the customised welcome site, it adds so-called cheat sheets into the help system of Eclipse. These cheat sheets are interactive how-to's, which demonstrate how a JIAC concept is created with a wizard and then is manipulated with an editor.

The next help component is the user guide, which guides the developers through the development steps similarly to the Toolipse welcome site. While this welcome site is designed to be displayed in full screen mode after the installation and gives an initial overview of Toolipse, the user guide, which is realised as a view and is displayed next to the editor area, is intended for guiding the users through the entire development process. Other than the user guide, the JIAC guide gives the users only a short description of the currently selected tool, providing constant supporting information.

Furthermore, the IDE provides interactive tutorials such as a pizza delivery service, with which the developers can create a full JIAC project interactively.

4   Related Work

Although we concentrate on the needs of JIAC users in the first place, we have also evaluated a number of other agent development tools, in particular tools that help creating real-life applications. We have found the JACK Development Environment (JDE)[6] very inspiring concerning the design of an agent-based application. Based on a clear visual notation, the Design Tool and the Plan Editing Tool allow modelling an application from different views and support code generation. Together with the plan tracer and agent interaction display for runtime monitoring, the JDE is a complete toolbox for easy and fast agent-based development. We are also looking forward to test the CaFnE tool [18], which allows domain experts to develop or modify agent applications. The description and demonstrator promise a good step forward. A good standard toolkit for Jason applications has been delivered with the Jason IDE[7], which provides project management and AgentSpeak source code editing together with a number of wizards and debugging capabilities. The Cougaar IDE[8] has also been realised as a number of Eclipse plugins and provides the management and running of Cougaar projects. Whitestein created a Development Suite[9] for their Living Systems (LS) Platform. It consists of two parts: a number of Eclipse plugins for creating, re-use, debugging and monitoring of LS applications and a Modeler, realised as plugin for a UML tool, which allows the modelling of agents and their behaviour using AML [19].

5   Conclusion and Further Work

We have realised Toolipse, a fully featured IDE prototype for the fast and efficient development of JIAC agent applications, based on the Eclipse platform.

---

[6] http://www.aosgrp.com/
[7] http://jasonplugin.wikidot.com/
[8] http://cougaaride.cougaar.org/
[9] http://www.whitestein.com/autonomic-technology-platform/
   ls-ts-development-suite

We have chosen Eclipse as integration platform for our tools in compliance with best tool builder practice. The IDE supports both experts and beginners at the same time. While it provides experts with standard text editor functionalities such as syntax highlighting, warning and error marking, and code completion, beginners can create an agent application solely by using visual editor functionalities, which include visualisation, zooming, graphic layouts, creating, editing and deleting JIAC artifacts visually. Additionally, beginners and advanced learners are assisted in Toolipse with IDE and framework documentations, guides, how-to's and interactive tutorials.

Our IDE has been used and tested in teaching and by a number of projects in different domains. The feedback from the early testers was mainly positive. The main deficiency, which the testers pointed out, was lack of a code refactoring capability. They also missed a possibility to edit higher level interaction protocols, which is one of the most challenging topics. Additionally, some testers wanted a feature which supports modelling agent services with standard process modelling notations such as BPMN[10](Business Process Modeling Notation) using predefined basic services.

In the near future, we are planning a new release of our IDE, which comes with revised and enhanced text editor functionalities. We also currently rework the agent role editor, which allows to visualise all artifacts of a JIAC-based application in one diagram as well as filtering diagram information to view different aspects of the application. The next tool we are working on is a visual service design tool [20], which can model services with BPMN and transform them into executable service languages. It is not a part of Toolipse, but supports a transformer from BPMN to JADL and thus can be used as agent service modelling tool supplementary to Toolipse. Both new tools, the new agent role editor and visual service design tool, are implemented by using the Eclipse Graphical Modeling Framework (GMF), which should be used instead of the out-of-date combination of EMF and GEF. We are also planning to port all visual editors of Toolipse to GMF.

Toolipse can be downloaded at `http://www.jiac.de` and the different features can be tried directly. While we think that we have provided a fully featured and powerful toolsuite, there is always work to be done and we hope that not only will you give it a try but also let us know any further improvements that we could make.

References

1. Shoham, Y.: Agent-oriented programming. Artificial Intelligence 60(1), 51–92 (1993)
2. Henderson-Sellers, B., Giorgini, P.: Agent-Oriented Methodologies. Idea Group Publishing (2005)
3. Unland, R., Klusch, M., Calisti, M. (eds.): Software Agent-Based Applications, Platforms and Develoment Kits. Whitestein Series in Software Agent Technologies. Birkhauser Verlag, Basel (2005)

---

[10] `http://www.bpmn.org/`

4. Bordini, R.H., Dastani, M., Dix, J., Seghrouchni, A.E.F.: Multi-Agent Programming. Languages, Platforms and Applications. Multiagent Systems, Artificial Societies, and Simulated Organizations. Springer, Heidelberg (2005)
5. Luck, M., McBurney, P., Shehory, O., Willmott, S.: Agent Technology: Computing as Interaction (A Roadmap for Agent Based Computing). AgentLink (2005)
6. Fricke, S., Keiser, J., Hessler, A.: Demo-Storyboard for the JIAC IV Agent Development Environment. In: AAMAS Demonstration Session, Bologna, Italy (2002)
7. Hessler, A., Keiser, J., Feuerstack, S., Bsufka, K., Fricke, S.: Demo-Storyboard: An Agent-based Framework supporting Rapid Application Development for Telecommunication Applications. In: AAMAS Demonstration Session, New York, USA (2004)
8. Sesseler, R., Albayrak, S.: JIAC IV - an open, scalable agent architecture for telecommunications applications. In: Proceedings of the First International NAISO Congress on Autonomous Intelligent Systems (ICAIS 2002), ICSC Interdisciplinary Research (2002)
9. Konnerth, T., Hirsch, B., Albayrak, S.: JADL – an agent description language for smart agents. In: Baldoni, M., Endriss, U. (eds.) DALT 2006. LNCS, vol. 4327, pp. 141–155. Springer, Heidelberg (2006)
10. Foundation for Intelligent Physical Agents: FIPA Agent Management Specification (2004)
11. Zastrow, J.: Konzeption und realisierung eines frameworks zum testen von multiagentensystemen. Diplomarbeit, Technische Universität Berlin (2004)
12. Cossentino, M., Potts, C.: Passi: a process for specifying and implementing multiagent systems using uml (2001)
13. Padgham, L., Winikoff, M.: Prometheus: A methodology for developing intelligent agents. In: Giunchiglia, F., Odell, J.J., Weiss, G. (eds.) AOSE 2002. LNCS, vol. 2585, pp. 174–185. Springer, Heidelberg (2003)
14. Object Management Group: Software Process Engineering Metamodel (SPEM) Specification. Version 1.1. Object Management Group, Inc. (2005)
15. Mücke, A.: Service Centric Bank. PhD thesis, Technische Universität Berlin (2008)
16. Fowler, M.: Continuous integration (2000), http://www.martinfowler.com/articles/continuousIntegration.html
17. Beck, K.: Test Driven Development. By Example. Addison-Wesley/ Longman, Amsterdam (2002)
18. Jayatilleke, G., Padgham, L., Winikoff, M.: Component Agent Framework for nonExperts (CAFnE) Toolkit. In: Software Agent-Based Applications, Platforms and Development Kits. Whitestein Series in Software Agent Technology, pp. 169–195. Birkhäuser Verlag, Basel (2005)
19. Whitestein Technologies: Agent Modeling Language (AML). Language Specification. Version 0.9 (2004)
20. Küster, T.: Development of a visual service design tool providing a mapping from BPMN to JIAC. Diploma thesis, Technische Universität Berlin (2007)

Kerberos-Based Secure Multiagent Platform*

Jose M. Such**, Juan M. Alberola, Ana Garcia-Fornes,
Agustin Espinosa, and Vicent Botti

Departament de Sistemes Informàtics i Computació
Universitat Politècnica de València
Camí de Vera s/n 46022, València
Spain

Abstract. Security is becoming a major concern in Multiagent Systems (MAS), since an agent's incorrect or inappropriate behaviour may cause non-desired effects such as money and data loss. Moreover, the lack of security in some current MAS-based applications is one of the reasons why MAS technology is being slowly introduced into industry. However, adding security features such as authentication, integrity and confidentiality results in a performance penalty. In this paper, a security infrastructure for a Multiagent Platform (MAP) is presented. It is based on both the Kerberos protocol and the Linux Operating System access control. The design of this infrastructure is focused not only on security but also on efficiency so that the MAP being secured allows the development of secure and efficient Multiagent Systems.

1 Introduction

Security related studies in the Multiagent System (MAS) research field have been growing over the last few years, just like intelligent autonomous agents and MAS based applications have too. This is mainly due to the fact that the understanding of the actual risk when using these sorts of applications is needed, since an agent's incorrect or inappropriate behaviour may cause non-desired effects such as money and data loss. Therefore, security is a key issue that has to be taken into account when developing these sort of applications, and the lack of security in some current MAS-based applications is one of the reasons why MAS technology is being slowly introduced into industry.

Some Multiagent Platforms (MAPs) are now taking into account security concerns. For instance, Jade [3], SECMAP [21], Tryllian ADK [24], CAPA [14], Cougaar [1], SeMoA [5] and Voyager [6] are security-concerned MAPs. All these MAPs offer authentication, integrity and confidentiality. Moreover, some of them (as detailed in section 4) offer access control mechanisms.

* This work was supported by CONSOLIDER-INGENIO 2010 under grant CSD2007-00022 and Spanish goverment and FEDER funds under TIN2005-03395 and TIN2006-14630-C03-01 projects.
** Enjoying a grant of *Conselleria d'Empresa, Universitat i Ciència de la Generalitat Valenciana* (BFPI06/096).

K.V. Hindriks, A. Pokahr, and S. Sardina (Eds.): ProMAS 2008, LNAI 5442, pp. 197–210, 2009.

Including these security features obviously makes a MAP perform worse when comparing it to the insecure version. As stated in [20], Jade with the security add-on performs worse than normal Jade. Furthermore, this difference in performance between both versions increases when the MAS running on top of the MAP is composed of a large number of agents with a lot of interactions with each other.

This paper aims to propose a security infrastructure for Magentix, which is a high-performance MAP. Therefore, the proposal also takes into account performance concerns apart from security concerns.

A Magentix MAP can be run in different hosts that are connected by a local network or by the Internet. The Internet is an insecure place, so assuring interactions between agents located in different hosts is a necessity. Currently, network communications are secured by means of assuring authentication, confidentiality and integrity. Due to the Magentix design, all the interactions among agents are carried out via a network interface (local or remote). Therefore, if these three security features are guaranteed, interactions among Magentix agents will be assured.

On the other hand, access control is needed to ensure these three features since local attacks can be performed without the requirement of a network interface. For instance, network communications are protected, so an agent cannot sniff a communication between two other agents. However, in Magentix an agent is implemented at a lower level as a Linux process. If no access control mechanism is taken into account, all the agents can access the same local resources (for example files), so confidentiality may be compromised. These sorts of problems can be addressed if the access control mechanisms provided by Linux are used correctly. How these troubles are addressed is detailed later.

The rest of the article is organized as follows. Section 2 presents Magentix MAP and sums up its architecture. Section 3 shows different mechanisms providing authentication, integrity and confidentiality and the choice made for securing Magentix. Section 4 presents how access control can be achieved in Magentix MAP. Section 5 details the Magentix secure version integrating the concepts presented before. In Section 6, the performance of Magentix versus secure Magentix is evaluated. Finally, section 7 presents some concluding remarks.

2   Magentix Multiagent Platform

Some current MAPs are not suitable for executing complex systems because their designs are not oriented to improve efficiency and scalability issues. Previous studies ([18], [10], [22], [12], [9], [8]) have analysed some internal features of current MAPs showing that the degradation rate of both efficiency and performance is increasing according to how much the system grows.

These results have motivated the design and development of a MAP using the Operating System (OS) resources. The aim of this MAP is to offer the same services as most of the high level MAPs, but obtaining better performance using services directly from the OS. The MAP designed is called Magentix [7], and has been developed in the C language and over Linux OS.

Magentix MAP is composed of several hosts running the Linux OS (Figure 1). Each host runs a *magentix* process that manages the MAP structure, and MAP host initialization and finalization. The MAP offers some services to support agent execution and development. Services are distributed among the MAP hosts. So far, there are three services that have been developed: Agent Management System (AMS), Directory Facilitator (DF) and Message Transport Service (MTS). These three services are described by FIPA (Foundation for Intelligent Physical Agents) standards [2].

Both AMS and DF services are implemented as a Linux process. These processes are *magentix* child processes and they are replicated in each MAP host. At the same time, each Magentix agent is implemented as a Linux process and these processes are *ams* child processes. Thus, the *ams* process controls every agent through Linux OS services. The *ams* process manages agent initialisation, execution and finalisation. We can see in Figure 1 the processes tree of a Magentix host.

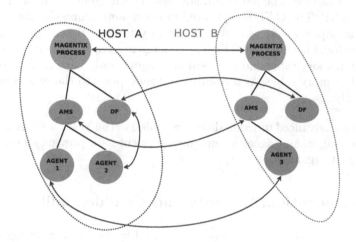

Fig. 1. Platform Structure

The MTS service has been developed as a function library. Magentix agents and services use this library to carry out their communications. The MTS service design is focused on efficiency and scalability. Its main features are:

1. Agent communication is carried out by a P2P system. It allows high scalability in agent communication. Each Magentix agent has a server socket for receiving connections from other agents by means of client sockets. To carry out a new connection an agent creates a client socket that communicates with the remote agent server socket. So, Magentix agents are client/server at the same time.
2. Each agent has a TCP connection cache that mantains the most used agent connections. This cache improves communication times since an agent does not need to create a new TCP connection each time it wants to communicate with another agent.

When a sender agent wants to send a message to a receiver agent, the MTS service checks if the sender agent has a connection associated with the receiver agent in the connection cache. If the sender agent has a connection associated with the receiver agent, the message is sent to the receiver through the connection socket. If there is no connection associated with the receiver agent, the receiver agent address is consulted, and a new TCP connection to the receiver agent is created. This TCP connection allows message sending between these two agents. The new TCP connection is inserted in the connection cache. If the connection cache is full the least used connection (LRU) is closed before creating the new one.

3. Agent addresses (host, TCP port) can be consulted directly using a shared memory table. This shared memory table returns the agent address, having been given an agent name.

This table is named the Global Agent Table (GAT) and it is managed by the AMS service. The name and address of each agent of the MAP is stored in the GAT. The GAT is replicated in every *ams* process of the MAP. The table is implemented as a shared memory table between the *ams* process and the local host agents. The *ams* process has read and write access to the shared memory table and the local host agents only have read access to the shared memory table. As a result, any agent query to the *ams* is performed efficiently.

Some other advanced functionalities are added to the MTS: a FIPA interaction protocol manager, and agent groups management as a previous mechanism to support agent organizations.

3   Authentication, Integrity and Confidentiality

Network communications are currently secured by means of assuring authentication, confidentiality and integrity. Jade, SECMAP, Cougaar, SeMoA and Voyager use Secure Sockets Layer (SSL) to provide these security features. However, other MAPs such as Tryllian ADK use ad-hoc mechanisms to offer these security features. In Tryllian ADK, authentication and integrity checks are carried out using signed files in which ADK agents are packaged.

As far as we are concerned, a mechanism providing these features is not worth designing from scratch because there are standard mechanisms such as IPSEC, SSL, TLS and Kerberos that can be adapted to agent technology. These mechanisms are discused below, and a choice is made taking into account Magentix design and performance issues.

3.1   IPSEC

IPsec (Internet Protocol Security) [16] is an IP protocol extension adding strong encryption allowing authentication services, so that, communications through this protocol are secured. IPsec is a mandatory part of IPv6, and is optional for use with IPv4. While the standard is designed to be indifferent to IP versions, current widespread deployment and experience concerns IPv4 implementations.

IPsec protocols operate at the network layer, layer 3 of the OSI model. It protects and authenticates IP datagrams among computers taking part in an IPsec community. The IP security architecture uses the concept of a security association as the basis for building security functions into IP. A security association is simply the bundle of algorithms and parameters that is being used to encrypt and authenticate a particular flow in one direction. Therefore, in normal bi-directional traffic, the flows are secured by a pair of security associations. The actual choice of encryption and authentication algorithms is left to the IPsec administrator.

3.2 SSL/TLS

Secure Sockets Layer (SSL) [15] and Transport Layer Security (TLS) [13], are cryptographic protocols that provide two end-points in Internet with authentication and information privacy. TLS is the SSL v3.1 standarization made by IETF. Only the server is usually authenticated; mutual authentication requires a Public Key Infrastructure (PKI) for the clients.

As TLS is the last version of these two protocols, it is the one compared to the other alternatives. TLS involves three basic phases: first, peer negotiation for algorithm support; second, public key exchange and certificate-based authentication; and third, symmetric cypher encryption.

3.3 Kerberos

Kerberos [19] is a network authentication protocol. It provides applications based on client/server paradigm with strong authentication using symmetric cypher encryption. Kerberos protocol uses strong cryptography allowing a client to prove its identity to a server (and vice versa) through an insecure network connection. When both the client and the server prove their identity, they can also encrypt all the communications in order to assure exchanged data confidentiality and integrity.

Kerberos makes use of a trusted third party, termed a Key Distribution Center (KDC). Kerberos works on the basis of *tickets* which serve to prove the identity of users. The KDC maintains a database of secret keys; each entity on the network shares a secret key known only to itself and to the KDC. Knowledge of this key serves to prove an entity's identity. For communication between two entities, the KDC generates a session key which they can use to secure their interactions.

3.4 Discussion

IPsec, TLS and Kerberos offer the features required: authentication, integrity and confidentiality. However, they offer these features in a different way. IPsec operates at the network layer, so it is not aware of higher level protocols included in IP datagrams. As each Magentix agent listens in a different TCP port,

IPsec is unable to distinguish between two different Magentix agents. Thus, the authentication cannot be carried out at agent level. As a result, IPsec is not suitable for our requirements in Magentix MAP.

Both TLS and Kerberos, as they operate at transport layer and application layer respectively, allow Magentix agent authentication. As TLS operates at transport layer and Kerberos does at application layer, integrating TLS in Magentix would be much easier than integrating Kerberos. The latter does not carry out data sending, this is done by the user, whereas TLS only replaces original socket functions with their secure equivalents. Moreover, encryption is user-transparent when programming using TLS, i. e., there is no explicit function to cypher data to be sent. However, in Kerberos, developers have to call API functions to encrypt and decrypt data. Therefore, Kerberos integration in Magentix seems to be harder than TLS integration.

However, there are two main reasons that make Kerberos our choice to meet Magentix communication security requirements: the Magentix messaging service design and the cryptography type.

Regarding the Magentix messaging service design, each Magentix agent has a cache that contains the most recently used connections with other agents, as detailed in section 2. This design is due to the limitation in the number of open sockets per process allowed by the Linux OS, and as MAS are systems with a high level of interactions, an agent can be conversing with much more agents than connections allowed. Hence, this design is intended to keep open the connections corresponding to the most active conversations of an agent with other agents.

Both TLS and Kerberos establish a security context between two network end-points when they authenticate to each other, and after that, the two end-points can communicate with each other in a secure way using this security context. However, Kerberos offers a key advantage when compared to TLS, i.e., Kerberos can re-use a security context in different connections. As Kerberos operates at application level, when a connection is closed the security context created can be used in a new connection with the same destination end-point. In TLS, this cannot be achieved since context negotiation is carried out each time a connection is created. Although a context re-negotiation is also allowed, this process consumes a similar amount of time to the creation of a new context. Furthermore, context negotiation is the part of TLS with the highest time consumption.

When using Kerberos to secure Magentix agent interactions, a security context established between two agents can be used in different connections between these agents, so security context negotiations are avoided as much as possible, and this would improve overall efficiency.

There is another important difference between both alternatives: the cryptography type. While TLS uses both symmetric (or secret-key) and asymmetric (or public-key) cryptography, Kerberos only uses symmetric cryptography. The same key is used by symmetric cryptography algorithms when encrypting and decrypting data, whereas asymmetric cryptography algorithms use a key to encrypt and a different key to decrypt. As a result, symmetric cryptography algorithms are usually less complex and the keys used requires less bits than asymmetric cryptography algorithms. Therefore, symmetric cryptography is more efficient than asymmetric cryptography. However, key distribution is a problem when symmetric cryptography is considered, because a pre-shared secret is needed between the encrypting entity and decrypting entity.

As the Magentix MAP is designed taking into account efficiency, it seems that Kerberos is the most suitable alternative to meet Magentix security requirements. Efficiency problems of TLS are shown in the study made by Coarfa et al. [11]. This study explains that securing a web server using TLS imposes a factor of 3.4 to 9 overhead over an insecure web server. Their measurements show that asymmetric cryptography computations are the single most expensive operation in TLS, consuming 20-58% of the time spent in the web server. There are some efforts to optimize TLS server throughput focussing on reducing the CPU costs of the TLS connection setup phase, rather than working on the TLS data exchange phase. In this way, Kuo et al. [17] present a comparative study between conventional TLS versus modified TLS that uses pre-shared keys to avoid CPU costs of the TLS connection setup phase, which implies asymmetric cryptography computations. Therefore, using pre-shared keys only symmetric cryptography is used. Results in this study show that TLS with pre-shared keys performs better than conventional TLS (as expected), but the key distribution problem arises, i. e., how two distribute a shared secret key between two entities in a secure way.

Kerberos has no key distribution problem, and it only uses symmetric cryptography, so it seems to be the most efficient alternative when securing Magentix MAP.

4   Access Control

Most of the current MAPs are developed in Java language and run on top of the Java Virtual Machine (JVM). In these sort of MAPs an agent is usually a Java thread, so that, all the agents share the memory space of the JVM process. As a result, the main problem when controlling access in these MAPs is the control of what Java objects can be accessed by each agent.

This problem is addressed in different ways by several security-concerned MAPs. For instance, agents in CAPA do not have any reference to either MAP or other agent objects. Thus, attacks based on obtaining object references are avoided. SECMAP encapsulates objects that reference agents in such a way that these objects can only be accessed by authorized agents. In SeMoA, agents cannot share classes. Other MAPs simply use existing Java technologies for object access control, e.g., Jade and Tryllian ADK. The security add-on for Jade carries out access control using Java/JAAS technology (Java Authentication and Authorization Service). The mechanism used by the Tryllian ADK is similar to the one used by a browser running a Java applet.

As in Magentix an agent is a Linux process, different agents do not share memory, so there is no requirement to introduce any additional mechanism to avoid the access of an agent to memory space of other agents. As explained in section 2, the GAT table is mapped as shared memory in all the agents and the AMS in a host, but only the AMS has write permissions, and these permissions are assured by the Linux OS.

In order to control resource access, as Magentix is built on top of the Linux OS, access control mechanisms of this OS can be used directly, i. e., users, groups and an access control list in each resource detailing the permissions for the user that owns this resource, the group that owns this resource and the rest of system users. As Magentix agents are modeled as Linux processes owned by a Linux user, access control is assured. Therefore, agents owned by the same Linux user share resources, because it does not make sense that agents with the same owner perform any kind of attack on each other.

5   Secure Magentix

This section details the security infrastructure design for the Magentix MAP. As discused in section 3, Kerberos is chosen in order to provide Magentix with authentication, integrity and confidentiality. There are some Kerberos implementations, but we use the MIT implementation [4]. There are some key concepts in Kerberos, named *principal* and *realm*. The principal is the unique name of a user or service allowed to authenticate using Kerberos. A *principal* follows the form root[/instance]@REALM. For a typical user, the root is the same as their login ID. The instance is optional. If the principal has an instance, it is separated from the root with a forward slash ("/"). All *principals* in a *realm* have their own key, which for users is derived from a password or is randomly set for services. A *realm* is a network that uses Kerberos, composed of one or more servers called *Key Distribution Centers (KDCs)* and a potentially large number of clients. Moreover, Kerberos can be configured to use slave KDC's that can be accessed if the master KDC is not available, but that is beyond of the scope of this paper.

In Secure Magentix, there is the MAP user concept. These users match a Kerberos *principal* and follow the form user@MAGENTIX. Do not confuse the MAP users with the local users of a Unix machine. Therefore, a MAP user has to login in the system in the conventional way, and then authenticate itself to Magentix (authenticating to the KDC) running the program mgx_login that is a wrapper for the kinit of the Kerberos distribution. For instance, let us have a Linux machine with a user bob. bob sits in front of the Linux machine, logs in the system an starts using it. When he needs to launch an agent in the running Magentix MAP on the local host, he has to login first executing the mgx_login program using its Kerberos *principal* (for instance, bobby@MAGENTIX).

There are two different kinds of users in secure Magentix:

- **Administrator**. The administrator of a Magentix MAP. It has the following permissions:
  - Create and delete system users *principals*.
  - Create and delete MAP services *principals*.
  - Platform launching.

- **System Users**. Users that are allowed to launch agents in a Magentix MAP. Therefore, the administrator has to create a *principal* per each user that requires launching agents. At any moment the administrator can remove an agent launching right from a user simply by removing its *principal*.

The following sections detail how Kerberos and access control mechanisms provided by the OS are integrated in Magentix.

5.1 Service Communication

Magentix services are based on information replication in each host. In order to check the integrity of this information and protect it from being accessible to non-authorized users, service communication needs to be secured. In order to do so, the administrator creates a *principal* for each service with a random key that is saved by default in /etc/krb5.keytab. That file is secured using Linux OS access control and it can only be accessed by the *root* user, so Magentix services have to run as *root* processes. Service principals follow the form service/host@MAGENTIX. For instance, if pc.example.com is going to be a part of a Magentix MAP, the administrator has to create the following *principals*: magentix/pc.example.com@MAGENTIX, ams/pc.example.com@MAGENTIX and df/pc.example.com@MAGENTIX.

When a service requires communication with another service, a security context is established as client with the *principal* of the MAP administrator and as server with the *principal* of the destination service. Using this security context the information sent is encrypted and a message integrity code is calculated. Therefore, the client is sure that the destination service is the service expected. Moreover, the destination service knows that it is being contacted by a service with the administrator identity, so the destination service will serve all the requests it receives. Thus, only MAP services can exchange information with each other. Other processes can neither send requests to the services nor observe information exchanged. Kerberos also avoid replay attacks and attacks due to the clock[1].

To carry out the implementation the GSS-API (Generic Security Service API Version 2) [23] with Kerberos as lower level security mechanism is used. The utilization of GSS-API improves portability, abstraction level and easy adaptation to newer versions of Kerberos.

5.2 Agent Launching

Agent launching process is also secured and modified to allow secure agent communications that are detailed in the next section. The aim is to assure that: first, only MAP users can launch agents, and second, resources from agents launched cannot be accessed by agents owned by a different user.

---

[1] Kerberos only allows communication among PC's taking part in a Kerberos network if they are properly synchronized, using for example NTP.

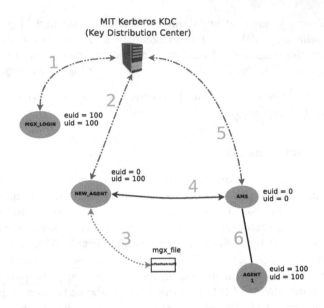

Fig. 2. Agent Launching

Figure 2 shows the process with its stages numbered. The stages are:

1. User authenticates to the KDC with the mgx_login program using its MAP identity (Kerberos *principal*).
2. User launches new_agent program that has its setuid active and runs with effective uid (euid) as root. Then, new_agent asks the KDC for a ticket to communicate with the ams service using the MAP identity of the user.
3. new_agent reads the key generated by the ams when the MAP is launched to ensure that the new_agent implementation is the one expected. The file containing this key (named mgx_file) can only be read by root, that is the reason why new_agent has its setuid active.
4. A security context is created between the ams and new_agent using the MAP identity of the ams and the MAP identity of the user that has launched the new_agent. Then, new_agent sends the request to create a new agent. Although the request is not generated by the MAP administrator, the ams accepts it in order to allow all MAP users to launch agents. The request contains: the name of the agent to be created, the Linux uid and gid of the requesting user, the key generated by the ams when the MAP is launched, the route of the agent binary and the arguments for the agent.
5. The ams asks the KDC to create an identity for the new agent by means of using the kadmin program of the Kerberos distribution. An agent MAP identity (Kerberos *principal*) follows the form agentname@MAGENTIX.
6. The ams launches the binary of the agent setting its uid and gid to the uid and gid of the Linux user that has launched the new_agent. Therefore, the agent created can only access the same Linux local resources as its owner.

Finally, when an agent dies, the ams removes its *principal*.

5.3   Agent Communication

Securing agent communication is similar to securing service communication, but agents use the indentity that the ams has created for them when creating a security context to allow a secure interaction with each other.

In order to make efficient use of security contexts, a context cache has been added to each agent. This cache is based on a hash table indexed by destination agent name that contains the corrresponding security context associated with a destination agent. This cache is not related to connections cache, since the number of connections is limited by the maximum number of file descriptors that Linux allows per process and security contexts would be unlimited (but taking into account available memory restrictions). Therefore, when a connection with an agent is closed, the associated security context is not lost.

Kerberos security contexts expire (they are not valid infinitely), so an agent can discover that a security context is no longer valid when trying to encrypt or decrypt data. Then, a new security context has to be negotiated with his conversation partner.

6   Performance Evaluation

In this section a performance evaluation between normal Magentix versus Magentix with the security infrastructure activated is made. Including security features obviously makes Magentix perform worse, but further study is needed to quantify this performance penalty, to determine whether adding the security infrastructure affects Magentix MAP performance in such a way that it becomes unsuitable for developing MAS requiring high-performance.

As agent communication is provided with integrity and confidentiality when using the security infrastructure, expensive cryptographic computations are required, so message sending performance will get worse with respect to the messaging performance achieved when the security infrastructure is not used. As MAS are distributed systems with a lot of interactions, using the security infrastructure may result in secure but inefficient MAS applications.

We have compared the message sending when Magentix uses its security infrastructure to when this infrastructure is not active. In order to carry out this comparison, we have designed a test. In this test, we launch a sender agent that exchanges messages of 10 bytes with a receiver agent. Each pair exchanges 1000 messages and the total time in the test is measured as the elapsed time (in seconds) between when all the pairs start sending messages until all the pairs have exchanged 1000 messages.

The test presented has been performed using 2 PCs Intel(R) Pentium(R) 4 CPU 3.00GHz, with 1GB of RAM memory, and running the Ubuntu Linux 6.06 OS (kernel 2.6.15). In secure Magentix, Kerberos has been configured to use AES algorithm with 128-bit keys to encrypt and SHA-1 hash function with 96-bit keys to perform HMAC computations.

Figure 3 shows results obtained. It is easily observed that when activating the security infrastructure in Magentix (Secure Magentix) there is an extra overhead,

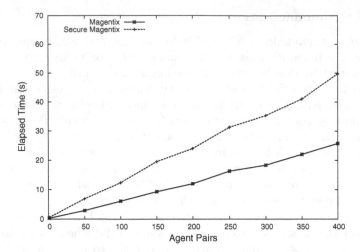

Fig. 3. Magentix vs Secure Magentix

as one could expect. However, this overhead seems to be short enough so that secure Magentix should allow the development of secure MAS with efficiency requirements.

7   Conclusions

This paper presents a security infrastructure based on both the Kerberos protocol and the Linux OS access control in order to secure the Magentix MAP. Kerberos provides the MAP with authentication, integrity and confidentiality, while access control is achieved using Linux OS mechanisms.

Different alternatives are considered to bring authentication, integrity and confidentiality to the Magentix MAP. IPsec is unsuitable for Magentix MAP because it operates at network layer. When comparing TLS to Kerberos, the latter seems to perform better because it is only based on symmetric cryptography (more efficient than asymmetric cryptography) and allows the re-using of security contexts in different connections with the same agent (avoiding security context re-negotiations in each new connection).

A performance evaluation is also carried out in order to validate that even adding the security infrastructure designed, the Magentix MAP remains efficient enough to allow the development of complex MAS, i.e., with a huge number of agents with a lot of interactions with each other and running on a huge number of hosts distributed on a large network. Results presented in section 6 shows that the overhead introduced by the security infrastructure is short enough so that secure Magentix should be a MAP that supports secure complex MAS.

A future work is the definition of a general schema to control access to not only OS resources but also other typical resources for a MAS. For instance, Magentix MAP supports the creation of agent groups, so this general schema would allow the specification of what agents can create groups. What is more, this general schema would allow the specification of what agents can interact with others in the same group, so agent organization hierarchies can be created.

References

1. Cougaar, http://www.cougaar.org
2. Fipa (the foundation for intelligent physical agents), http://www.fipa.org
3. Java agent development framework (jade), http://jade.tilab.com
4. Mit kerberos, http://web.mit.edu/Kerberos/
5. Semoa, http://www.semoa.org
6. Voyager, http://www.recursionsw.com/voyager.htm
7. Alberola, J.M., Mulet, L., Such, J.M., Garcia-Fornes, A., Espinosa, A., Botti, V.: Operating system aware multiagent platform design. In: Proceedings of the Fifth European Workshop on Multi-Agent Systems (EUMAS 2007), pp. 658–667 (2007)
8. Burbeck, K., Garpe, D., Nadjm-Tehrani, S.: Scale-up and performance studies of three agent platforms. In: IPCCC 2004 (2004)
9. Camacho, D., Aler, R., Castro, C., Molina, J.M.: Performance evaluation of zeus, jade, and skeletonagent frameworks. In: IEEE International Conference on Systems, Man and Cybernetics (2002)
10. Chmiel, K., Tomiak, D., Gawinecki, M., Karczmarek, P.: Testing the efficency of jade agent platform. In: Proceedings of the ISPDC/HeteroPar 2004, pp. 49–56 (2004)
11. Coarfa, C., Druschel, P., Wallach, D.: Performance analysis of tls web servers (2002)
12. Cortese, E., Quarta, F., Vitaglione, G.: Scalability and performance of jade message transport system. EXP. 3, 52–65 (2003)
13. Dierks, T., Allen, C.: The tls protocol version 1.0. RFC 2246 (1999)
14. Duvigneau, M., Moldt, D., Rölke, H.: Concurrent architecture for a multi-agent platform. In: Giunchiglia, F., Odell, J.J., Weiss, G. (eds.) AOSE 2002. LNCS, vol. 2585, pp. 59–72. Springer, Heidelberg (2003)
15. Frier, A., Karlton, P., Kocher, P.: The secure socket layer. Technical Report MSU-CSE-00-2, Netscape Communications (1996)
16. Kent, S., Atkinson, R.: Security architecture for the internet protocol. RFC 2401 (1998)
17. Kuo, F.-C., Tschofenig, H., Meyer, F., Fu, X.: Comparison studies between pre-shared and public key exchange mechanisms for transport layer security. In: IN-FOCOM (2006)
18. Mulet, L., Such, J.M., Botti, J.M.A.V., Espinosa, A., Garcia, A., Terrasa, A.: Performance evaluation of open-source multiagent platforms. In: Proceedings of the Fifth International Joint Conference on Autonomous Agents and Multiagent Systems (AAMAS 2006), pp. 1107–1109. Association for Computing Machinery, Inc./ ACM Press (2006)
19. Neuman, C., Yu, T., Hartman, S., Raeburn, K.: The kerberos network authentication service (v5). RFC 4120 (2005)
20. Such, J.M., Alberola, J.M., Mulet, L., Espinosa, A., Garcia-Fornes, A., Botti, V.: Large-scale multiagent platform benchmarks. In: Dastani, M., El Fallah Seghrouchni, A., Leite, J., Torroni, P. (eds.) LADS 2007. LNCS, vol. 5118, pp. 192–204. Springer, Heidelberg (2008)

21. Ugurlu, S., Erdogan, N.: An overview of secmap secure mobile agent platform. In: Proceedings of Second International Workshop on Safety and Security in Multiagent Systems (2005)
22. Vrba, P.: Java-based agent platform evaluation. In: Mařík, V., McFarlane, D.C., Valckenaers, P. (eds.) HoloMAS 2003. LNCS, vol. 2744, pp. 47–58. Springer, Heidelberg (2003)
23. Wray, J.: Generic security service api version 2: C-bindings. RFC 2744 (2000)
24. Xu, H., Shatz, S.M.: Adk: An agent development kit based on a formal design model for multi-agent systems. Journal of Automated Software Engineering 10, 337–365 (2003)

Agent Contest Competition: 4th Edition

Tristan M. Behrens[2], Mehdi Dastani[1], Jürgen Dix[2], and Peter Novák[2]

[1]Utrecht University
P.O.Box 80.089, 3508 TB Utrecht, The Netherlands
mehdi@cs.uu.nl
[2]Clausthal University of Technology
Julius-Albert-Str. 4, 38678 Clausthal-Zellerfeld, Germany
{tristan.behrens,dix,peter.novak}@tu-clausthal.de

Abstract. This paper summarises the Agent Contest 2008, organised in association with ProMAS'08. The aim of the contest is to stimulate research in the area of multi-agent systems by identifying key problems and collecting suitable benchmarks that can serve as milestones for evaluating new tools, models, and techniques to develop multi-agent systems. The first two editions of this contest were organised in association with CLIMA conference series and the third edition was organised in association with ProMAS'07. Based on the experiences from the previous three editions ([16,17,18]), the contest scenario has been changed to test the participating multi-agent systems on their abilities to *coordinate* and *cooperate*. We wanted to emphasise *team work* and *team strategy* issues in a dynamic environment where teams compete for the same resources. Seven groups from Iran, Ireland, England, France, Germany, Poland, and Turkey did participate in this years contest.

1 Introduction

Multi-agent systems are beginning to play an important role in today's software development. In the field of agent-oriented software engineering, various multi-agent system development methodologies have been proposed. Each methodology focuses on specific stages of the multi-agent system development. For example, Gaia [21] and Prometheus [20] focus on the specification and design stages assuming that other stages such as requirement and implementation are similar to corresponding stages of other software development paradigms. Therefore, software developers using Gaia and Prometheus propose models to specify and design multi-agent systems, while ignoring the implementation models.

Moreover, there is a growing number of agent-oriented programming languages and development platforms that are proposed to facilitate the implementation of multi-agent systems [11,15]. These programming languages and platforms introduce programming constructs that can facilitate efficient and effective implementation and execution of multi-agent systems. The development of multi-agent systems requires efficient and effective solutions for different problems which can be divided into three classes: Problems related to (1) the development of individual agents, (2) the development of coordination and cooperation mechanisms to

K.V. Hindriks, A. Pokahr, and S. Sardina (Eds.): ProMAS 2008, LNAI 5442, pp. 211–222, 2009.

manage the interactions between individual agents and team work, and (3) the development of the shared environment in which agents perform their actions.

Typical problems related to individual agents are how to specify, design and implement issues such as *autonomy, pro-active/reactive behaviour, perception and update of information, reasoning and deliberation*, and *planning*. Typical problems related to the interaction of individual agents are how to specify, design and implement issues such as *communication, coordination, cooperation, negotiation*, and *team working*. Finally, typical problems related to the development of their environment are how to specify, design and implement issues such as *resources and services*, agents' access to *resources*, active and passive *sensing* of the environment, and realizing the *effects of actions*.

This competition started as an attempt to stimulate research in the area of multi-agent systems by

1. *identifying key problems in developing multi-agent systems, and*
2. *evaluating state-of-the-art tools, models, and techniques in the field of multi-agent systems.*

While there already exist several competitions in various areas of artificial intelligence (theorem proving, planning, Robo-Cup, Games, etc.) and, lately, also in specialised areas in agent systems (Trading Agent Competition (TAC) [1] and AgentCities competitions [2]), the emphasis of this contest is on the use of existing tools, models, and techniques that are proposed to develop multi-agent systems ([11,10,12,13,14,19]. In particular, we aim at evaluating existing approaches for the development of multi-agent systems where individual agents cooperate with each other to solve a task. In this respect, issues such as team working, team strategy, interaction with dynamic environment, modeling the environment, limited perception, uncertain action effects, reasoning and planning, and learning are essential.

The previous editions of this contest were organised in cooperation with CLIMA and ProMAS workshop series. The scenario from this year is changed in order to put the participating multi-agent systems under a test with respect to coordination, cooperation, and team working issues in a dynamic environment where teams of agents compete for the same resources.

2   Scenario Description

The competition task consisted of developing a multi-agent system to solve a cooperative task in a dynamically changing environment. The environment of the multi-agent system (see also [9]) is a grid-like world where agents can move from one cell to a neighbouring cell. In this environment, herds of cows can appear and move around in the environment showing swarm-like behavior. Participating agent teams are expected to explore the environment, avoid obstacles and compete with another agent team to get most cows. The agents of each team can coordinate their actions in order to control the movement of herds and move as much cows as possible to their own corral. Agents have only a local view on their environment, their perceptions are incomplete, and their actions can fail.

There were seven teams participating in the competition:

- Jason from the ENS Mines of Saint Etienne, France, and University of Durham, UK,
- SHABaN from the Iran University Of Science and Technology,
- Jadex from the Hamburg University of Applied Sciences,
- Bogtrotters from the University College Dublin, Ireland,
- Krzaczory from the, Polish Academy of Sciences,
- KANGAL from the Bogazici University, Istanbul, Turkey, and
- JIAC-TNG from the Technische Universität Berlin, Germany.

Each team competed against all other teams in a series of matches in parallelised tournaments on three servers. Each match between two competing teams consisted of three simulations. A simulation between two teams was a competition between them with respect to a certain starting configuration of the environment. Winning a simulation yielded three points for the team, a draw was worth one point and a loss resulted in zero points. The winner of the whole tournament was evaluated on the basis of the overall number of collected points in the matches during the tournament. In the case of an equal number of points, the winner would have been decided on the basis of the absolute number of collected cows. Details on the number of simulations per match and the exact structure of the competition has been published prior to the Contest on the official Agent Contest 2008 website at http://cig.in. tu-clausthal.de/agentcontest2008/.

2.1 Technical Description of the Scenario

In the contest, the agents from each participating team were *executed locally* (on the participant's hardware) while the simulated environment, in which all agents from competing teams performed actions, was run on the *remote contest simulation server* run by the contest organisers. The interaction/communication between agents from one team were managed locally, but the interaction between individual agents and their environment (run on the simulation server) took place via Internet. Participating agents were connected to one of the simulation servers that did provide the information about the environment. Each agent from each team connected to and communicated with the simulation server using TCP protocol and messages in XML format.

During the initial phase[1] agents from all competing teams connected to the simulation servers, identified and authenticated themselves and got general match information. At the announced start time of the tournament, the simulation servers were on-line and the agents from participating teams were able to connect to it. After a successful initial handshake during which agents identified themselves by their IDs and received acknowledgment from the servers, they waited for the simulation start. The initial connecting phase took a reasonable

---

[1] The contest organisers contacted participants before the actual tournament and provided them the IDs necessary for identification of their agents for the tournament.

amount of time in order to allow agents to be initialised and getting connected (15 minutes).

The simulation servers controlled the competitions by selecting the competing teams and managing the matches and simulations. In each simulation, a simulation server, in a cyclic fashion, provided sensory information about the environment to the participating agents and expected their reactions within a given time limit. Each agent reacted to the received sensory information by indicating which action (including the *skip action*) it wants to perform in the environment. If no reaction was received from the agent within the given time limit, the simulation server assumed that the agent performed the *skip* action. Agents had only a local view on their environment, their perceptions were incomplete, and their actions can fail. After a finite number of steps the simulation server stopped the cycle and participating agents received a notification about the end of a simulation. Then the server started a new simulation possibly involving the same teams.

2.2   Team, Match, and Simulation

An agent team consisted of six software agents with distinct IDs. There were no restrictions on the implementation of agents, although we encouraged the use of approaches based on state-of-the-art tools, methodologies and languages for programming agents and multi-agent systems, as well as the use of computational logic based approaches. The tournament consisted of a number of matches. A match was a sequence of simulations during which two teams of agents competed in several different settings of the environment. For each match, the server 1) picked two teams to play it and, subsequently, 2) started the first simulation of the match. Each simulation in a match started by notifying the agents from the participating teams and sending them the details of the simulation. These included for example the size of the grid, the corral position, the number of steps the simulation will perform, etc. A simulation consisted of a number of simulation steps. Each step consisted of 1) sending a sensory information to agents (one or more) and 2) waiting for their actions, and 3) processing agents' replies and calculating the next state of the environment. As mentioned above, in the case that an agent did not respond within a timeout (specified at the beginning of the simulation) by a valid action, it was considered to perform the *skip* action in the given simulation step.

2.3   Environment Objects

The (simulated) environment was a rectangular grid consisting of cells. The simulated environment contained two corrals—one for each team—which serve as a location where cows should be directed to. Each cell could contain either nothing, an agent, a cow or an obstacle. If a cow entered a corral it was removed. Agents could enter the corrals without effect. All three maps were hand crafted for the particular scenario.

2.4   Actions and Perceptions

At the start of each simulation the agents received the details of the environment:

- simulation ID,
- opponent's ID,
- grid size,
- corral position and size, and
- number of steps the simulation will last.

Agents were located in the grid and the simulation server provided each agent with the following information in each step:

- information about the cells in the visibility range of the agent (including the one agent stands on),
- the agent's absolute position in the grid,
- the current simulation step number,
- the number of caught cows and
- the deadline for responding.

If two agents were standing in each other's field of view, they were able to recognise whether they are enemies, or they belong to the same team. Also, individual cows were identifiable.

All perceptions except for the agent's and the corral's position were subject to be "forgotten" by the server, whereas the server never gave wrong information.

Agents were allowed to perform one action in a simulation step. The following actions were allowed:

- *skip* – the agent does nothing,
- *north* – the agent moves to the north,
- *northeast* – the agent moves to the northeast,
- *east* – the agent moves to the east,
- *southeast* – the agent moves to the southeast,
- *south* – the agent moves to the south,
- *southwest* – the agent moves to the southwest,
- *west* – the agent moves to the west,
- *northwest* – the agent moves to the northwest.

All actions, except the *skip* action, could fail. The result of a failed action is the same as the result of the *skip* action. An action can fail either because the conditions for its successful execution are not fulfilled or because of the information distortion.

2.5   Cow Movement Algorithm

Cows are simple creatures. They tend to move away from cells that they do not like and to move towards cells they do like. Cows want to move away from agents and trees. On the other hand, they are attracted by empty spaces and they want to stay close to other cows, however not too close. Cows have the tendency to form herds, which tend to be tighter in times when the animals are scared by cowboys.

The cows have two fixed visibility ranges. Cows are attracted to other cows that are in the visibility-square and not too close and they are repelled by cows that are too close.

Cows are slower than agents. Each cow only moves every three steps. Our simulation ensures that all cows do not move in the same step using a simple algorithm.

The direction in which a cow will move in the next step is determined by calculating a weighted linear-combination of the distance-vectors to visible cells, with weights respective to the content of the cells. Cows do not move if the resulting vector is zero. See [9] for technical details about cow movements.

2.6   Final Phase of the Simulation

In the final phase, the simulation server sent a message to each agent allowing them to disconnect from the server. By this, the tournament was over.

3   Submission

The participation in this contest consisted of two parts. Participants first submitted the description of analysis, design and implementation of a multi-agent system for the above application. We encouraged the use of existing state-of-the-art multi-agent system methodologies to describe the systems. For the description of the implementations, the participants were asked to explain how the design is implemented. This could be done by explaining, for example, which programming language, platform, tools, and techniques are used to implement the multi-agent system. All teams, except the one from Turkey, provided submissions that are included in this volume.

The second part of the contest was the actual participation in the tournament by means of an (executable) implementation of a multi-agent system. The agents from each participating systems (agent teams) were executed locally (on the participant's hardware) while the simulated environment, in which all agents from competing teams perform actions, was run on a remote contest simulation server. Interaction/communication between agents from one team has been managed locally, but the interaction between individual agents and their environment (run on the simulation server) was via Internet.

3.1   Received Submissions

For the 2008 edition of the Contest we initially received 9 submissions from 7 countries from all around the globe with a majority from Europe: JIAC-TNG [5]

(Germany), Jadex [6] (Germany), SHABaN [7] (Iran), Krzacory [3] (Poland), Jason [8] (France/United Kingdom), Bogtrotters [4] (Ireland), KANGAL (Turkey), FLUX (Germany) and CSIRO (Australia). Shortly before the Contest launch, the teams CSIRO and FLUX withdrew due to technical and organizational issues in the development team, thus leaving finally 7 teams to compete in the Contest. Detailed descriptions of the submissions (except for KANGAL team) are included in this volume.

In comparison to the last editions, in this year's Contest we could observe a rise of using more formal approaches to system analysis and design. Four teams (JIAC-TNG, Jadex, Jason and Bogtrotters) used a state-of-the-art methodology to devise the multi-agent system architecture of their team. One team (SHABaN) used a MAS prototyping language to evaluate their early designs. Finally the teams KANGAL and Krzacory used either ad-hoc design, or their approach was partly based on a utility function optimization technique.

Almost all the teams came up with a design using two generic role types for their agents: *herders* and *explorers*. However, the resulting designs differ in coordination techniques as well as approaches to MAS organisation and role-assignment. According to the agent coordination the approaches can be divided into two groups: those using a rather *decentralised* approach (JIAC-TNG, Jason and Bogtrotters) and teams with a single *centralised* coordination entity/agent (Jadex, SHABaN and Krzacory).

The centralised approaches used the main coordinator/master agent for steering the agents in the teams, however it can be observed that anyway all these approaches left a significant part of the autonomous acting and decision making on single agents (e.g. obstacle avoidance, exploration strategy, etc.). Unlike in the previous Contest editions, this year we did not see a truly centralised approach - a one in which agents lack autonomy and are completely directed by the team managing agent.

The approaches employed by the teams without a centralised control and MAS organisation varied from using auctions for assignment a role in a team to particular agents (Bogtrotters) to sharing intentions among agents in a team (JIAC-TNG).

We observe also an interesting trend in approaches to agent navigation in the environment. It seems that more and more teams employ the A^* algorithm to search for shortest paths in the map of the environment. Thus the navigation in even complex environments is not that much of an issue as we could observe in previous Contest editions.

Another interesting arising trend seems to be employment of MAS recovery monitoring mechanisms to keep the agent team up and running. As this used to be an issue in the previous years of the Contest, the teams JIAC-TNG and Bogtrotters implemented a team recovery technique to restart/recreate a crashed agent as well as to inform the restarted agent about the current status of the team knowledge (note that both teams use a decentralised approach).

4   Technical Infrastructure

In the fourth edition of this Agent Contest, we re-used the technical infrastructure we developed for the previous editions. Briefly, the server's architecture consists of

1. *simulation plug-in*: A replaceable module providing the logics of the environment simulation,
2. *agent session manager*: Responsible for holding the sessions between the server and individual agents and en/de-coding of XML messages of the protocol,
3. *visualization library*: It produced the SVG records from each time frame of the simulation environment state,
4. *contest webinterface*: Providing a public view and interface to the MASSim server, and
5. MASSim core module: Managing the tournament scheme and providing the connection between the simulation plug-in, agent session manager and webinterface.

A more detailed description of the system can be found in the report on the second edition of the Agent Contest [17]. The system is published on the official Contest website: http://cig.in.tu-clausthal.de/AgentContest/.

4.1   Contest Preparation

As in previous editions, before the tournament itself, the Contest organisation went through several preparatory stages. We released the scenario description for the Agent Contest on 18 February 2008 and updated on 18 April 2008. The communication protocol for the simulation scenario was released later on 13 March 2008. The Agent Contest testing phase was launched on 29 April 2008 and ran until the very Contest tournament launch on 26 May 2008. During this period, which lasted more than one month, the participants could freely connect to the testing server and test their agents in a simulated match against our dummy *Bot* agent team. We did not allow different teams to compete against each other as this should happen only during the tournament itself. During the testing phase, few minor bugs in the scenario implementation were discovered and quickly fixed.

4.2   Tournament

The Agent Contest 2008 tournament itself was launched on Monday, May 26th 2008 at about 10:00 CEST (UTC/GMT+2). A few days in advance, the participants received the Internet coordinates of the tournament server together with credentials for their agents. The Agent Contest was served on the three tournament servers called *Agent-Contest1*, *Agent-Contest2*, and *Agent-Contest3* that could be observed via a web-interface at the address `http://agentserver.in.tu-clausthal.de`. We provided also a chat space for participants, what in the course of the tournament itself turned out to be a vital and efficient communication tool.

The teams competed against each other on four successive days and based on three different simulation servers. The time table of these matches are shown below[2]:

Day \ server	Agent-Contest1	AgentContest2	AgentContest3
26th May	Jason vs SHABaN	Jadex vs Bogtrotters Jadex vs KANGAL Bogtrotters vs KANGAL	JIAC-TNG vs krzaczory
27th May	Jason vs Jadex	JIAC-TNG vs Bogtrotters	krzaczory vs KANGAL krzaczory vs SHABaN KANGAL vs SHABaN
28th May	Jason vs krzaczory Jason vs Bogtrotters krzaczory vs Bogtrotters		JIAC-TNG vs Jadex JIAC-TNG vs SHABaN Jadex vs SHABaN
29th May	Jason vs JIAC-TNG Jason vs KANGAL JIAC-TNG vs KANGAL	krzaczory vs Jadex	SHABaN vs Bogtrotters

All results, together with the SVG recordings of all the matches can be downloaded from `http://agentserver.in.tu-clausthal.de`.

4.3 Simulation Instances

The teams competed in matches each consisting of 3 different grid simulations with identifiers *CowSkullMountain*, *RazorEdge* and *Street* (Figure 1). All scenarios are handcrafted labyrinths to challenge agent teams obstacle avoiding and communication approaches.

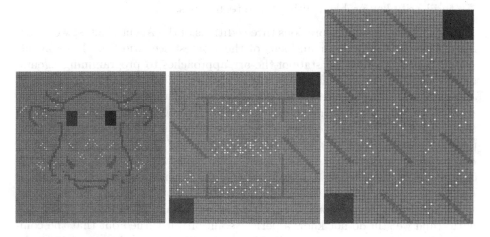

Fig. 1. Initial simulation scenarios *cowskullmountain*, *razoredge*, and *street*

---

[2] The table is fragmented due to the fact that the tournament was originally scheduled for 9 participating teams.

5   Contest Results

The winner of the ProMAS Agent Contest 2008 was the JIAC-TNG team from the DAI-Labor, Technische Universität Berlin, Germany. They gained the highest number of points: 46. The second team was Jadex (Germany) with 42 points followed by the SHABaN team (Iran) with 37 points. The summary of the whole tournament is summarised in the Table 1.

Table 1. Final tournament results

Rank	Team	CowScore	Points
1.	JIAC-TNG team	643	64
2.	Jadex	542	42
3.	SHABaN	373	37
4.	krzaczory	379	26
5.	Jason	393	21
6.	bogtrotters	305	13
7.	KANGAL	32	1

6   Conclusion

As in the previous Contest editions, our main motivations behind this Agent Contest are the following:

- to foster the research and development of practically oriented approaches to programming multi-agent systems, and
- to evaluate the state-of-the-art techniques in the field, and
- to identify key problems using these techniques.

After the success of the previous three editions of the Agent Contest we recognised a need to shift the main focus of the Contest scenario from basic agent-system issues (testing the state-of-the-art approaches to programming agents) more towards a *multi*-agent setting, i.e. coordination and cooperation strategies among agents in a MAS team. For the 2008 edition we devised a new scenario *cows & cowboys*, which turned out to be more challenging and entertaining than the previous *gold miners* scenario. The main emphasis was to construct a competition scenario in such a way that the success of the team *should strongly depend on coordination of several agents*. This was achieved by our design decision, not to allow to push a group of cows in a certain direction by a *single agent*.

Although initially we have been rather sceptical about solubility of the scenario (and we still do not know a perfect solution), it turned out that the competing teams performed rather well. The most difficult scenario turned out to be the *RazorEdge* map 1. To push a group of cows through the narrow opening in the map so that cows do not escape in the wrong direction turned out to require good cooperation abilities of the agent team. In scenarios similar to this we see still a potential for improvement of agent team performance.

Similarly to the previous Contest editions, we collected interesting feedback from the participants. To our pleasure, it turns out that one of the main gains from participating in the Agent Contest tournaments are contributions to testing and debugging of the participants MAS-oriented frameworks and programming systems. Another important aspect seems to be the educational value of the Contest: We seem to attract more and more teams including students on both post-graduate, as well as undergraduate levels.

We run this year's Contest edition in a different organisational structure. We divided the tournament into four sub-tournaments, each ran on a separate day. On each day we executed three parallel contests. This resulted into a significant decrease of the tournament running time and allowed us to use larger maps and more complex scenarios for individual simulations. In the future we want to further follow this line.

Acknowledgements

We are very thankful to the students of the Department of Informatics of Clausthal University of Technology. They worked very hard in order to meet all the deadlines and deliver high-quality code. In particular, our thanks go this year to

- *Jens Dehnert* and
- *Slawomir Deren*

for the numerous hours they have invested to help us get the scenario and the tournament ready in time.

References

1. http://www.sics.se/tac
2. http://www.agentcities.org/EUNET/Competition
3. AC08 system description. In: Sixth International Workshop on Programming Multi-Agent Systems (2008)
4. Dublin Bogtrotters: Agent Herders. In: Sixth International Workshop on Programming Multi-Agent Systems (2008)
5. Herding agents - JIAC TNG in Multi-Agent Programming Contest 2008. In: Sixth International Workshop on Programming Multi-Agent Systems (2008)
6. On Herding Artificial Cows: Using Jadex to Coordinate Cowboy Agents. In: Sixth International Workshop on Programming Multi-Agent Systems (2008)
7. SHABaN multi-agent team to herd cows. In: Sixth International Workshop on Programming Multi-Agent Systems (2008)
8. Using Jason and $\mathcal{M}oise^+$ to develop a team of cowboys. In: Sixth International Workshop on Programming Multi-Agent Systems (2008)
9. Behrens, T.M., Dastani, M., Dix, J., Novák, P.: Technical aspects of the agent contest competition. Technical Report IfI-08-05, Clausthal University of Technology, Dept of Computer Science, 4th edition (to appear) (2008)

10. Bordini, R.H., Dastani, M., Dix, J., Fallah-Seghrouchni, A.E. (eds.): PROMAS 2003. LNCS, vol. 3067. Springer, Heidelberg (2004)
11. Bordini, R.H., Dastani, M., Dix, J., Fallah-Seghrouchni, A.E. (eds.): Multi-Agent Programming: Languages, Platforms and Applications. Multiagent Systems, Artificial Societies, and Simulated Organizations, vol. 15. Springer, Berlin (2005)
12. Bordini, R.H., Dastani, M., Dix, J., Fallah-Seghrouchni, A.E. (eds.): PROMAS 2004. LNCS, vol. 3346. Springer, Heidelberg (2005)
13. Bordini, R.H., Dastani, M., Dix, J., Fallah-Seghrouchni, A.E. (eds.): PROMAS 2005. LNCS, vol. 3862. Springer, Heidelberg (2006)
14. Bordini, R.H., Dastani, M., Dix, J., Fallah-Seghrouchni, A.E. (eds.): PROMAS 2006. LNCS, vol. 4411. Springer, Heidelberg (2007)
15. Bordini, R.H., Dastani, M., Dix, J., Fallah-Seghrouchni, A.E. (eds.): Multi-Agent Tools: Languages, Platforms and Applications. Springer, Berlin (2009)
16. Dastani, M., Dix, J., Novák, P.: The First Contest on Multi-Agent Systems based on Computational Logic. In: Toni, F., Torroni, P. (eds.) CLIMA 2005. LNCS, vol. 3900, pp. 373–384. Springer, Heidelberg (2006)
17. Dastani, M., Dix, J., Novák, P.: The second contest on multi-agent systems based on computational logic. In: Inoue, K., Satoh, K., Toni, F. (eds.) CLIMA 2006. LNCS, vol. 4371, pp. 266–283. Springer, Heidelberg (2007)
18. Dastani, M., Dix, J., Novák, P.: Agent Contest Competition: 3rd edition. In: Dastani, M., El Fallah Seghrouchni, A., Ricci, A., Winikoff, M. (eds.) ProMAS 2007. LNCS, vol. 4908, pp. 221–240. Springer, Heidelberg (2008)
19. Dastani, M., El Fallah Seghrouchni, A., Ricci, A., Winikoff, M. (eds.): ProMAS 2007. LNCS, vol. 4908. Springer, Heidelberg (2008)
20. Padgham, L., Winikoff, M.: Prometheus: A methodology for developing intelligent agents. In: Giunchiglia, F., Odell, J.J., Weiss, G. (eds.) AOSE 2002. LNCS (LNAI), vol. 2585, pp. 174–185. Springer, Heidelberg (2003)
21. Zambonelli, F., Jennings, N.R., Wooldridge, M.: Developing multiagent systems: The Gaia methodology. ACM Transactions on Software Engineering and Methodology (TOSEM) 12(3), 317–370 (2003)

AC08 System Description

Jacek Szklarski*

Institute of Fundamental Technological Research, Polish Academy of Sciences
jszklar@ippt.gov.pl

Abstract. A simple multi-agent system which participated in the Multi-Agent Programming Contest in association with ProMAS 2008 is described. Agents take actions in order to maximize a global utility function from at each step. Coordination is done via the max-plus algorithm or by the greedy strategy.

1 Introduction

The goal of agents in the contest scenario is to collect as many cows as possible into a home corral and, possibly, make it more difficult for opponents to collect theirs own cows. To do this the agents in the described system try to maximize a global utility function U at each step. The value of U depends on the position of observed cows, knowledge of the terrain and relative positions of cows, agents and the corrals. At each step the agents communicate to agree what are the optimal actions they should take, in order to get maximum U in the next step. Bearing in mind that there exists 10s deadline for making the decision, we apply the max-plus algorithm (1; 2) which can be interrupted at any time giving the best solution found so far. Alternatively the greedy strategy is used.

2 System Analysis and Design

The goal of implementing the discussed MAS is to check if this simple approach can actually generate cooperative behavior, and how its performance is compared with more sophisticated methods. The agents maximize a simple mathematical function which describes the observed environment, and any methodologies such as Gaia or Tropos were not used. There are parameters used to calculate U, and some of them are specific to a single agent. Consequently, by using different values for each agent one obtains heterogeneous system in which the agents have different roles. Moreover, if the observed state of the game does not improve for some time, the agents are can modify theirs parameters and take specific actions.

In theory, the system can be implemented as completely independent processes corresponding to a single agent. However, it was more convenient to introduce the master-agent which is used to collect the observed information from all the agents and, after processing, it sends results back to the agents.

---

* Corresponding author.

K.V. Hindriks, A. Pokahr, and S. Sardina (Eds.): ProMAS 2008, LNAI 5442, pp. 223–227, 2009.

3   Software Architecture

For reasons of convenience and simplicity, the system has been programmed with use of Java language. The agents are based on the *AbstractAgent* class which has been supplied by the Organizers of the contest. The agents communicate with the master-agent over TCP/IP. The presented method can be implement without any master-agent by means of all-to-all communication at each step. In that case the vulnerability due to the master agent would be removed, and the system would become completely decentralized (and independent of the number of active agents).

4   Agent Team Strategy

4.1   The Master-Agent

All the agents after perceiving their environment send observed data to the single master-agent. This agent keeps track of all the obstacles, the cows, the enemies and the enemy corral. Since a cow moves only if (step mod 3) equals to its individual randomly assigned (but constant) number, the master-agent can tell if a cow with given id will move in the next step or not. Based on the observations it also guesses possible weights $w(cow), w(agent)$, etc. It also calculates shortest-path distances to the home and enemy corral (if the latter has been observed), and keeps information about knowledge of the environment.

4.2   Utility Function

The global utility function $\mathcal{U}$, which all the agents try to increase, consists of the three components

$$\mathcal{U} = \mathcal{U}_e + \mathcal{U}_c + \mathcal{U}_p,$$

where $\mathcal{U}_e$ is a reward for exploration, $\mathcal{U}_c$ a reward for moving cows in the next step closer to the home corral and further from the enemy corral, $\mathcal{U}_p$ is a reward for an agent being on a proper position (see below). In the current implementation all the calculations of the utility function are done by the master-agent class.

Exploration. If an agent makes a proper observation of a cell (x, y), the master-agent sets $E(x, y) = 1$ (initially $E = 0$ everywhere). Knowledge about the environment decays, such as $E_{t+1} = E_t \gamma_E$, where $\gamma_E \in [0, 1]$ is a constant parameter. When a new action for the agent i is considered, the reward for exploration is calculated as

$$\mathcal{U}_e(i) = \beta_i \sum_{(x,y) \in \mathcal{V}_i} 1 - E(x, y),$$

where $\mathcal{V}_i$ denotes all the positions of newly perceived cells by the agent i, $\beta_i \in [0, 1]$ is a constant number characterizing the agent's exploration character. $\mathcal{U}_e$ is then $\mathcal{U}_e = \beta \sum_i \mathcal{U}_e(i)$, where $\beta \in [0, 1]$ is yet another constant parameter.

Cows. For set of all the observed cows $\mathcal{C}$,

$$\mathcal{U}_c = \sum_{(x,y) \in \mathcal{C}} f[D_h(x,y)] + g[D_e(x,y)],$$

where D_h/D_e is the shortest-path distance from the home/enemy corral. $f(x) = c_1 x^{c_2}$, $g(x) = c_3 x^{c_4}$, and c_i are constant parameters (depending on the grid size as well; c_2, c_4 are negative).

Position. In order to move an agent to a proper position with respect to the cows and the corrals, another reward is provided. The algorithm for finding $\mathcal{U}_p$ is as follows:

$C(x,y) \leftarrow 0$ for all cells (x,y)
for all observed cows j **do**
    Find a vector $\mathbf{v_1}$ directed from the cow j to the home corral *along the shortest path*
    for all cells (x,y) **do**
        Find a vector $\mathbf{v_2}$ directed from (x,y) to the cow *along the shortest path*
        $\alpha \leftarrow$ the angle between $\mathbf{v_1}$ and $\mathbf{v_2}$, $\alpha \in [0, 2\pi)$.
        $d \leftarrow$ the shortest distance between the cow j and (x,y)
        $C(x,y) \leftarrow C(x,y) + \cos(\alpha) \times f(d)$
        Optionally, if $C(x,y)0$ then $C(x,y) \leftarrow 0$
    end for
end for

here $f(x) = d_1 x^{d_2}$. Now, for each agent i at position (x_a, y_a), we calculate

$$p_i(x,y) = C(x,y)g(r), \text{ for } (x,y) \in \mathcal{V}_i$$

and $p_i(x,y) = 0$ for $(x,y) \notin \mathcal{V}_i$, r being the distance along the shortest path between (x,y) and (x_a, y_a), $g(x) = d_3 x^{d_4}$, d_i are parameters. Afterwards interactions with the other agents are handled, and the agent's i payoff is calculated,

$$\mathcal{U}_p(i) = \sum_{(x,y) \in \mathcal{V}_i} \left(p_i(x,y) - \sum_{i \neq j} p_j(x,y) \right).$$

In exactly the same way, but with different parameters, $\bar{\mathcal{U}}_p(i)$ is calculated for the enemy corral.
    Then

$$\mathcal{U}_p = \lambda \sum_i \left(\mathcal{U}_p(i) + \bar{\mathcal{U}}_p(i) \right),$$

λ_i and λ are parameters characterizing the agents.

4.3   Switching Agents to Special Modes

Each agent can operate in one of the two additional modes. These modes significantly improve the overall performance of the team.

Call for assistance. Each agent i can compute its local utility function $\mathcal{U}_L(i)$ based on information *only from its neighborhood*. The values $\mathcal{U}_L$ are then sorted in descending order. The winner, i.e., the agent a with the highest $\mathcal{U}_L$ can call the agent b with the lowest $\mathcal{U}_L$ for help. If the call is accepted (it can be rejected if, e.g., b itself has $\mathcal{U}_L$ comparable with that of a), the agent b in the next steps will travel along the shortest path to a place near the calling agent a. After reaching the destination, b is switched back to the normal mode.

Single cow pushing. If for longer time, about 100 steps or so, the $\mathcal{U}$ does not improve, one of the agents switches itself to a single-cow-pushing mode. This is simply realized by assuming, that the agent sees only single cow, the one which is at the smallest shortest-path distance from the home corral.

4.4   Coordination

Each agent should choose its action a_i from the set of all possible actions $\mathcal{A}$. The goal is to find the joint action $\mathbf{a} = (a_1, \ldots, a_n)$ maximizing $\mathcal{U}$, that is finding $\mathbf{a}^* = \arg \max_a \mathcal{U}(\mathbf{a})$. To do this we apply the max-plus algorithm in which the agents exchange messages until a convergence criterion is met (1; 2).

Alternatively, a much faster simple greedy strategy is used. In this case, the agent 1, as the first one, takes the action a_1 giving the largest payoff, assuming that the others do nothing. Then the agent 2 takes its best action, given that the agent 1 took a_1, etc. Note that the ordering of the agents is predefined.

4.5   The Strategy

The strategy is based solely on the process of maximizing the global utility function *in the next step*, i.e., from step t to $t+1$. There is no long-term planning and, consequently, the approach fails if actions giving reward in the far future are necessary.

Firstly, if there are no cows observed, the agents explore the terrain by increasing the term $\mathcal{U}_e$. If a cow herd has been found, and, say, three agents have taken care about them, the others still are able to explore since they do not get any reward from $\mathcal{U}_c$ or $\mathcal{U}_p$.

The cows are controlled in the following way. First, by increasing $\mathcal{U}_p$, the agents move to proper positions taking into account relative positions of the corrals, the cows and themselves. Each distance is computed along the shortest-path distance for the current known map of obstacles. The parameters are chosen in such a way, that $\mathcal{U}_p$ is more important for the agents than $\mathcal{U}_c$. Nevertheless, if the agents have already proper positions, theirs actions are chosen in a way which maximizes $\mathcal{U}_c$ in the next step, i.e., by pushing the cows towards the home corral and away from the enemy corral.

Action coordination is done via the distributed optimization, i.e., max-plus algorithm, or by the greedy approach. The max-plus algorithm leads often to more logical local behavior with respect to, e.g., three agents taking care about a herd of cows. However, the number of collected cows after many steps is more or less the same for the both methods. Therefore, using here the more sophisticated algorithm gives no improvement. This is not surprising since in the system, the locally made decisions have small influence on the goal in the far future.

Due to the nature of the system design there is no background processing implemented. There exists a simple script handling crash recovery: if a process representing any agent or the master-agent crashes, it is automatically restarted.

5   Discussion

The point of implementing the system and participating in the Agent Contest 2008 was to gain some insight concerning performance of the simple approach, and compare the results with other, more advanced MAS. It is understood that with absence of any long-term planning strategies, the agents are unable to perform well on complicated and tricky maps.

Such poor performance was evident in the map *RazorEdge* (however, it should be noted that this map was problematic for other systems as well). The agents stubbornly tried to push entire herds through a small passage leading to the corridor towards the home corral. However, the nature of the competition was such that, after the first day, the participants knew all the maps. Lacking clauses explicitly forbidding it, the teams were able to make changes in theirs MAS. Therefore, after the second day it was decided to introduce the single-cow-pushing mode discussed above. Due to this modification one agent starts to execute "better something than nothing" strategy, and collects single cows in maps of the *RazorEdge* style. Obviously this idea can be extended to all the agents. This would significantly increased number of the collected cows in such cases, and removed any cooperative behavior at the same time. Note here that in my opinion implementing any hard-coded map-specific rules is absolutely pointless.

The performance in the other maps was much better. The agents were able to cooperate and push entire herds towards the home corral. Moreover, they were able to disturb the enemy and block cows from pushing them towards the enemy corral.

When it comes to the technical approach, there were no problems concerning implementing the MAS. The classes provided by the Organizers worked without any serious problems. Similarly, during the contest itself, everything went fine.

Bibliography

[1] Vlassis, N., Elhorst, R., Kok, J.R.: Anytime algorithms for multiagent decision making using coordination graphs. In: Proc. Intl. Conf. on Systems, Man and Cybernetics (2004)
[2] Vlassis, N.: A Concise Introduction to Multiagent Systems and Distributed Artificial Intelligence. Morgan and Claypool (2007)

Herding Agents - JIAC TNG in Multi-Agent Programming Contest 2008

Axel Hessler, Jan Keiser, Tobias Küster, Marcel Patzlaff, Alexander Thiele, and Erdene-Ochir Tuguldur

DAI-Labor, Technische Universität Berlin, Germany

Abstract. Another essential problem of mankind must be solved in this year's agent contest: cow capturing. We present the JIAC approach to this problem by applying the iterative and incremental JIAC methodology and JIAC tools. The solution will be designed and implemented using the next generation of the JIAC agent framework that provides easier way of agent construction, but that is in early beta state. We admire this contest as an evaluation platform for our developments (like our last year's MicroJIAC team).

1 Introduction

The JIAC TNG (The Next Generation) agent team has been prepared by members of the Competence Center Agent Core Technologies of DAI-Labor at Technische Universität Berlin. We use the new JIAC TNG agent framework, the successor of JIAC IV [1], with accompanying toolkit, which have been created in the course of last year's projects at DAI-Labor. The motivation to participate in the contest was to test the functionality and usability of this framework like our last year's contribution to the competition did with MicroJIAC [2]. In contrast to AC'07, the scenario of this contest is more complex and requires more coordination and cooperation. Thus, we are implementing a multi-agent system which addresses those issues more than our previous contributions [2][3].

2 System Analysis and Design

We follow the iterative and incremental JIAC methodology (see Figure 1): First, we collect domain vocabulary and requirements, structure and prioritise them. For example, class *Cow* has attributes *colour*, *methane output* and *origin*. The overall requirement is to capture and keep as much of these cows as possible. We can find some necessary basic requirements such as the ability to communicate with the competition server as well as with other agents, to sense the world and to walk. The next step is to design the MAS architecture by naming agents that play a role in the scenario. We just skip this step because we follow the design of the organisers who have set a team of six agents into being. Then, we derive an agent role model. Each of our agents must play different roles according to the perceived situation and depending on what other agents, friends and foes,

K.V. Hindriks, A. Pokahr, and S. Sardina (Eds.): ProMAS 2008, LNAI 5442, pp. 228–232, 2009.

do or intend to do. We have found the following roles: *scout*, *herder*, and *smart opponent assistant*. The scout role has capabilities to systematically search the terrain for cows, the herder role is able to direct cows to the corral. The opponent assistant is in itself a complex role. In AC'07 [3], we described our agents as fair, stepping aside when opponents come. This time we concentrated on observing

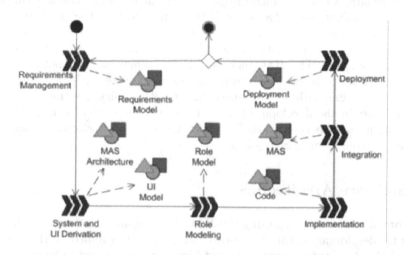

Fig. 1. JIAC methodology - iterative and incremental process model in SPEM [4] notation

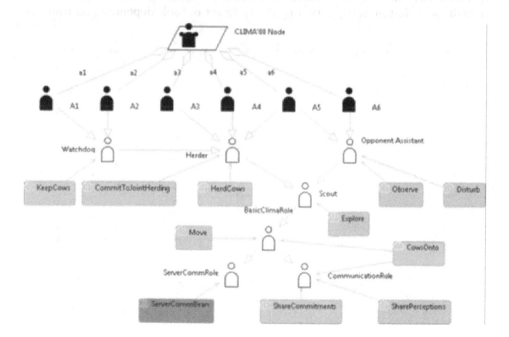

Fig. 2. The agent role model created with the JIAC AgentRoleEditor tool

opponents' behaviour and crisscrossing their plans. The agent role model (see Figure 2) also contains the interdependencies between roles.

Each Agent has its own perceptions, thus developing its own world model over time and also choosing its actions based on this world model. However, we believe that team communication and coordination plays a vital role in solving the contest scenario. Coordination strategies are specified in more detail in chapter 4.

While designing the MAS using JIAC tools, most of the implementation, integration and deployment artefacts are generated from the design, and are immediately ready to get evaluated, in order to generate new requirements or to change the old ones. The JIAC methodology is an agile development methodology with the outcome of real software agent-based systems. It does not iterate theoretical designs without cross-checking it with reality. As the design is an essential part in the development, it will not win the contest alone. When the competition server became available, short iterations and prioritised increments ensured a strong competitive solution.

3   Software Architecture

Our contribution is realised using the JIAC TNG agent framework which we are currently developing as the successor of JIAC IV. It is aimed at the easy and efficient development of large-scale and high-performance multi-agent systems. It provides a scalable single-agent model and is built on state-of-the-art standard technologies. The main focus rests on usability meaning that a developer can use it easily and that he is supported by the right set of tools depending on what he

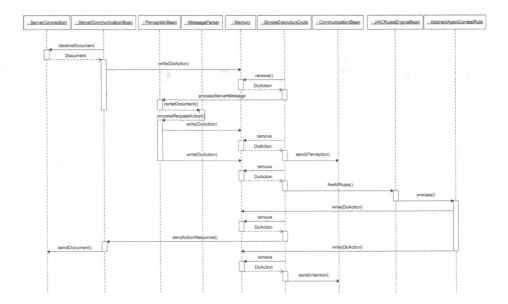

Fig. 3. The single agent control flow realising general cowherd behaviour

is doing. Like its predecessor JIAC IV and its smaller brother MicroJIAC, JIAC TNG is implemented in the Java programming language.

The aforementioned roles are implemented with agent components which are the behavioural structures of the agent. They access and modify the agent's state, generate knowledge and trigger the actions. We also use two sensor/actuator components. One component, the standard communication component of the framework, is used for the information exchange between our agents. The other component gathers the perception messages from and delegates the action messages to the competition server (see Figure 3).

4   Agent Team Strategy

A team is always worth more than the sum of its participants. We assume that this must also hold true for the MAS. We addressed this in several iterations dealing with communication, coordination, and cooperation.

Our approach to communication and cooperation is fully decentralised. Each agent has the capability of finding other agents on the network and communicating to them, no matter where they physically reside. Every agent builds its own world model from what it is told by the server and the other agents. Every agent also plans for itself, by taking the intentions of its teammates into account, and also, of course, what it thinks what opponents intend to do.

Our agents cooperate on a number of levels. First, they share their perceptions. Next, we enabled them to share their intentions (such as "I plan to direct cow C to (X,Y)"). This prevents agents from going to the same unknown field or even exploring the same region of the world and thus wasting precious steps. Every agent can appraise from what it knows if it will be better to leave the team member alone or to take the intention as its own when it is more promising.

We did not investigate different coordination strategies. However, we have observed emergent behaviour concerning herd driving: 3 or 4 agents collectively driving a larger number of cows, just arising from communication of perception and intention.

The agents navigate using the A* algorithm. We identified two different cases for its application. First, if an agent wants to explore the area or come to help, it calculates the path between its current position and the destination. Second, if the agent wants to drive a cow, it calculates the path between the position of the cow and the corral. So it knows where to position itself to be always behind the cows. The navigation algorithm treats opponents as obstacles so our agents will not block them explicitly.

Our agents possess two recovery mechanisms. The agent tries to reconnect, whenever the connection between an agent and the server breaks during the simulation. Furthermore, if an agent crashed and must be restarted, the agent requests other agents after the restart to send their actual world states.

We followed the discussion about unmoral agents and decided to let the agents make their own behavioural decisions. As a matter of fact, they are capable of helping the opponent team scattering the cow herds. Also they avoid the opponents' corral by treating it like fields with obstacles.

5   Discussion

After our success in last year's agent competition we are happy for once more having the possibility to show the maturity of our new agent framework.

Clearly this year's competition was a much greater challenge that it was last year, since now the agents have to cope with "moving targets", making the world a lot more open and dynamic than it was before. There are much more parameters to think of and a greater variability of possible behaviours. When choosing our strategy we tried to consider as much as possible. We also were very curious regarding the other teams strategies.

It is still a challenge and adventurous to use existing agent technology and frameworks. While testing new ideas in this Agent Contest we try to bring forward our understanding of what agents can achieve. And it is always a pleasure to meet up with other teams in a competitive but friendly manner.

6   Conclusion

The JIAC TNG team solved the problem of capturing as much cows as possible. We used the contest as evaluation platform for our new agent framework. The greatest pleasure was the emergent team behaviour, which we did not foresee. It was not clear to us that sharing perceptions and intentions between agents is such a powerful concept. We also appreciate the higher scenario complexity.

References

1. Fricke, S., Bsufka, K., Keiser, J., Schmidt, T., Sesseler, R., Albayrak, S.: A Toolkit for the Realization of Agent-based Telematic Services and Telecommunication Applications. Communications of the ACM 44(4), 43–48 (2001)
2. Tuguldur, E.O., Patzlaff, M.: Collecting gold. In: Dastani, M., El Fallah Seghrouchni, A., Ricci, A., Winikoff, M. (eds.) ProMAS 2007. LNCS (LNAI), vol. 4908, pp. 251–255. Springer, Heidelberg (2008)
3. Hessler, A., Hirsch, B., Keiser, J.: JIAC IV in Multi-Agent Programming Contest 2007. In: Dastani, M., Fallah Seghrouchni, A.E., Ricci, A., Winikoff, M. (eds.) ProMAS 2007. LNCS, vol. 4908, pp. 256–260. Springer, Heidelberg (2008)
4. Object Management Group: Software Process Engineering Metamodel (SPEM) Specification. Version 1.1. Object Management Group, Inc. (2005)

On Herding Artificial Cows: Using Jadex to Coordinate Cowboy Agents

Gregor Balthasar, Jan Sudeikat, and Wolfgang Renz

Multimedia Systems Laboratory,
Hamburg University of Applied Sciences,
Berliner Tor 7, 20099 Hamburg, Germany
Tel.: +49-40-42875-8304
{baltha_g,sudeikat,wr}@informatik.haw-hamburg.de

Abstract. The *Cows and Herders* scenario of the 2008 Multi–Agent Programming Contest provides a challenging testbed for the coordination of intelligent agents. Our first–time participation in this contest is based on a set of BDI agents which share knowledge and coordinate by a centralized planning guidance to cope with the (possibly) hostile environment. The conceived design has been implemented in the *Jadex* system which provides an execution environment for BDI–style agents on the basis of a distributed systems middleware.

1 Introduction

The Jadex system [1] provides an execution environment and development tools for realizing Multi–Agent Systems (MAS) that are composed of *Belief–Desire–Intention* (BDI) agents. According to this agent architecture, the local agent activity is guided by *beliefs*, *goals* and *plans*. The agents' beliefs define the domain-dependent abstraction of their environment as well as internal state. Goals represent agents' desires, typically understood as target states of beliefs. Agents deliberate which goals to pursue and access a library of plans, in order to accomplish intended goals. Developers implement Jadex agents by declaring the structure of agents in XML language and implementing agent plans in the Java programming language. Each agent is represented by a so-called *Agent Definition File* (ADF) which describes the structure of beliefs, goals and plans in XML syntax. The activities an agent can perform are coded in plans, i.e. ordinary Java classes. The modularization of agents is enabled by so-called *capabilities* [2,3]. These are also given as ADFs that are accompanied by plan classes.

In the following we describe the design of a Jadex–based MAS that had competed in the 2008 Multi–Agent Programming Contest. BDI agents control the individual players and their strategic game play is controlled by a centralized agent that maintains the sum of local agent perceptions as a global game view and heuristically allocates agents to herd the identified swarms of cows.

K.V. Hindriks, A. Pokahr, and S. Sardina (Eds.): ProMAS 2008, LNAI 5442, pp. 233–237, 2009.

2   System Analysis and Design

The MAS is subject to incremental development of agent prototypes. Throughout the development *Tropos* modeling notations and tools are utilized.[1] While the *early requirements* activities are inapplicable in the context of this contest, Tropos provides appropriate tools, notations and mindsets to guide the refinement of BDI agents during the incremental development.

The application consists of a homogeneous set of six *Teammates* which have the ability to play a fixed set of roles. The two identified basic roles are:

- Explorer: wandering the environment and report perceptions
- Herder: cooperative guidance of groups of cows

The allocation of Teammates to the herding of cow swarms is decided by a centralized agent (so–called *Herding Officer*). This agent gets continuously informed about the local perceptions of Teammates and decides on the basis of this accumulated knowledge, which agents should cooperatively steer a swarm to the team corral.

Therefore, Teammate agents get allocated to herd swarms when these are identified. If no swarm is available they ask proactively for the allocation to a region of the environment to be examined, thus allowing the coordination of collective map exploration. These roles are carried out autonomously. The movement of the Teammates and the guidance of agents that participate in cooperative herding both utilize an adjusted A^* implementation. The communication with the officer agent takes place via ACL messages. These are supported by the Jadex agent system and enable the exchange of ontology objects, i.e. Java language objects.

3   Software Architecture

The competition team is implemented in Jadex. It provides language constructs for agent oriented programming, i.e. defining the beliefs, goals and plans of BDI–like agents. The BDI agent architecture has been selected, as we found that goal–oriented programming supports guiding the individual agent's selection of the different behaviors to exhibit. The Jadex implementation platform facilitates the realization since it makes no restrictions on the (third–party) programming language libraries to be used within agent plans. Also it provides a set of tools for agent development and debugging.

In addition, the modularization of agent behaviors in capabilities is used to structure the implementation. Each agent is equipped with a capability that encapsulates the interactions with the competition server. The capability offers a goal–oriented interface for the agent to connect to the game server, i.e. issue movement actions. The perception of the environment is also encapsulated by processing the messages that are received from the game server and

---

[1] e.g. TAOM4E: http://sra.itc.it/tools/taom4e/

storing the relevant information in the agents' beliefbase. Agents react on the changes of belief values (environment perception) as well as on receptions of Jadex internal communication from team mates. The behaviors of agents (e.g searching for cows, herding cows, etc.) is modularized to ensure the separation of concerns.

The MAS is composed of a homogeneous set of *Teammates* and the coordinator of the herding behavior (*Herding Officer*). Teammates interact with the competition server, i.e. sense and (inter–)act with the environment. They use MAS internal communication to request assistance from each other and regularly communicate their (local) perceptions to the Herding Officer agent, which provides a central representation of game information, i.e. team knowledge about the environment state. The Herding Officer is also used to visualize the game play. Herding cows is a cooperative effort and movement of the swarms is coordinated by the Herding Officer.

Figure 1 (A) shows the dependency relationships of the identified agent types. The Herding Officer agent depends on the communications of Teammates concerning their perceptions to maintain the information and obtain the ability of centralized planning. The Teammates in turn rely on the Herding Officer to receive the role changing guidance and the exploration guidance as well as the results of the centralized planning. The Teammates interact directly with the Contest-Server. They depend on their local perceptions to be provided by the Contest–Server and issue movement requests.

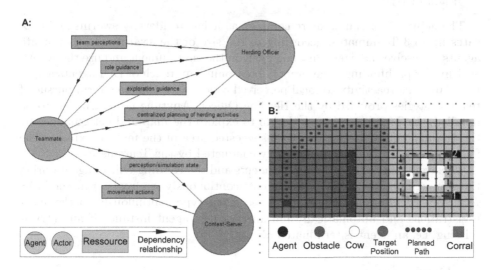

Fig. 1. The MAS Architecture. A: Tropos model for the dependencies between Teammates and the Herding Officer as well as the Contest-Server. B: Edited screenshot of the environment visualization. The dashed line symbolizes the swarm bounding box. Agents are positioned on the corners.

4   Agent Team Strategy

We distinguish the global strategy of the team itself and the local strategies which steer the behavior of agents playing particular roles. The teams global strategy is to move swarms of cows to the own corral as quickly as possible. The game setting permits members of the opposing team to scare away cows herded by agents or to block agents / cows of herded swarms at bottlenecks which are possibly formed by obstacles. These issues are not included in our strategy.

The global effectiveness of the team crucially depends on bringing swarms of cows to the corral. Due to this fact the biggest effort lies on the development of a highly efficient herding strategy. As mentioned before the planning is implemented in a centralized way, done by the well–informed Herding Officer. The results can be requested by the Teammates. The Herding Algorithm works as follows:

1. Once identified swarms are selected by taking their size and their distance to the team corral into account.
2. Paths are generated for each of these swarms by using the A* Algorithm including a preprocessed map. Preprocessing refers to the provision of cells which are next to obstacles, enemy agents or enemy corral cells with higher costs, creating a buffer zone around them to avoid these areas.
3. Regarding the direction of the reversed vector of the first node computed by the A* algorithm, a bounding box is generated around each swarm. Teammates are positioned at the corners of this box to steer swarm movement (cf. Figure 1 (B)).

The actual algorithm is more complex as it has to identify swarms and allocates up to 3 Teammates, according to the size of the swarm. The Teammate agents themselves navigate autonomously in the environment and use the A* Algorithm for pathfinding. The practical reasoning approach of BDI agents allows to balance the reactivity to local perceived events with the long–term pursue of team strategies provided by the Herding Officer. Anytime no swarm has to be handled, the Teammate agents decide to explore the map and get guidance by the Herding Officer in the form of a suggested area of the map to explore. The following exploration is independently conducted by the Teammates.

The availability of the Teammate agents and the Herding Officer agent during the competition is ensured. These agents continuously (re-)register at the MAS *Directory Facilitator* (DF). A dedicated agent type continuously checks agent registrations and automatically initializes a new agent instance if an entry is missing, i.e. an agent is terminated abruptly.

5   Discussion

The chosen strategy of herding cows, using the A* Algorithm to continuously plan the path a swarm should be steered along, works out very well most of the time. This facilitates obstacle and opponent avoidance. A maximum number of three herding agents per swarm is sufficient. Problems are only discovered in the start-up period on maps with large coherent structures of obstacles which are not yet fully discovered. As a consequence, both the greedy-like mechanism for choosing the swarm to be herded next and the A* Algorithm for planning the swarms' path cannot work properly. A solution for the first issue could be the replacement of the Euclidean swarm/corral distance by the length of a calculated path. A solution for the second issue could be the enforcement of an initial map exploration or the selective exploration of unknown map areas to complete path calculations.

The contest itself provides a good testbed in terms of reaction speed and stability for the used framework and the scenario is interesting and challenging.

The *capability* modularization concept [2,3] is particularly useful as it allowes to encapsulate specific functionalities, e.g. the communication with the Contest Server, therefore facilitating the separation of concerns in the agent models.

Finally some suggestions:

- An earlier release of a final scenario description and a public available testbed would provide developers more time to focus on MAS-specific questions.
- In large swarms it can be observed, that cows blocking each other leads to a kind of *crystallization*, which disables swarm movement. We would appreciate an according revision of the cow-algorithm.

6 Conclusion

The first-time-participation in this contest-series has been both successful and informative. Due to the lack of time between the release of the scenario description/ public available testbed and the beginning of the contest a *centralized planning for distributed plans* had to be preferred to a *distributed planning for distributed plans* [4]. Also, BDI features could not be worked out as far as originally planned.

Nevertheless the system works very well for most of all cases and with the gained experiences and the now existing base we facilitate addressing the mentioned issues and more sophisticated strategic game play in future MAS designs. Therefore, we are looking forward to the next–year's competition that will hopefully be as challenging and exciting as this year's.

References

1. Braubach, L., Pokahr, A., Lamersdorf, W.: Jadex: A bdi agent system combining middleware and reasoning. In: Software Agent-Based Applications, Platforms and Development Kits. Whitestein Series in Software Agent Technologies. Birkhäuser, Basel (2005)
2. Braubach, L., Pokahr, A., Lamersdorf, W.: Extending the capability concept for flexible BDI agent modularization. In: Bordini, R.H., Dastani, M., Dix, J., El Fallah Seghrouchni, A. (eds.) ProMAS 2005. LNCS, vol. 3862, pp. 139–155. Springer, Heidelberg (2006)
3. Busetta, P., Howden, N., Rönnquist, R., Hodgson, A.: Structuring BDI agents in functional clusters. In: Jennings, N.R. (ed.) ATAL 1999. LNCS, vol. 1757, pp. 277–289. Springer, Heidelberg (2000)
4. Wooldridge, M.: An Introduction to Multi Agent Systems. Wiley, Chichester (2002)

Using *Jason* and $\mathcal{M}$OISE$^+$ to Develop a Team of Cowboys

Jomi F. Hübner[1], Rafael H. Bordini[2], and Gauthier Picard[1]

[1] École des Mines de Saint-Étienne, France
{hubner,picard}@emse.fr
[2] University of Durham, UK
r.bordini@durham.ac.uk

1 Introduction

This paper gives an overview of a multi-agent system forming a team of "cowboys" to compete in the Multi-Agent Programming Contest 2008 (the 'Cows and Herders' scenario). In the two previous contests, we tested and improved *Jason* [2], an agent platform based on an extension of an agent-oriented programming language called AgentSpeak(L) [5]. The language is inspired by the BDI architecture, thus based on notions such as goals, plans, beliefs, intentions, etc. The participation in previous contests also increased our experience both in using BDI concepts as well as in programming agents with *Jason* specifically. In the 2006 contest, the focus was on the definition of agent's plans [1], leading to rather reactive agents. In the 2007 contest, the focus was on (declarative) goals [3], leading to more pro-active, goal-directed agents.

For the 2008 contest, we were motivated to continue improving the multi-agent programming abstractions, now towards social or organisational agents, using the concepts such as *roles* and *groups*. The system is therefore developed in two dimensions: agents (using declarative goals) and organisation (using groups, roles, and shared goals). Among several organisational models available, we will use the $\mathcal{M}$OISE$^+$ model because it is well integrated with *Jason* [4]. Our objective in participating in this contest was thus twofold: (*i*) to continue to test and improve *Jason* and its integration with $\mathcal{M}$OISE$^+$; (*ii*) evaluate the use of organisational constructs in the development of the team.

2 System Analysis and Design

It is clear, from the description of the scenario, the importance of cowboys working as a coordinated team. It would be very difficult for a cowboy alone to herd a group of cows. We therefore adopted a strategy strongly tied to the notion of group of agents where issues such as spatial formation, membership, and coordination would be emphasised.

The organisational structure of the team is specified in Fig. 1 using the $\mathcal{M}$OISE$^+$ notation. Our team has two types of subgroups: one to explore the environment searching for cows (the *exploration group*) and another one that leads the herd towards the corral (the *herding group*). The team always has three instances of the exploration group, each one responsible for some part of the scenario. The agents enter and leave these groups as the result of their decision to start or stop searching cows. The herding groups are dynamically created as the agents decide to herd a cluster of cows. The number of those

K.V. Hindriks, A. Pokahr, and S. Sardina (Eds.): ProMAS 2008, LNAI 5442, pp. 238–242, 2009.

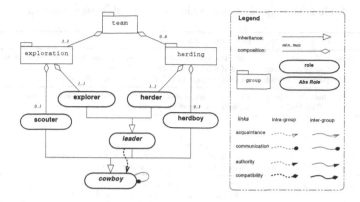

Fig. 1. The Structural Specification of the Organisation

groups and the agents that belong to them depend on the size and location of found clusters of cows. The following roles can be played by agents in the respective groups:

- *explorer*: explores the environment until it detects a cow;
- *scouter*: follows the explorer;
- *herder*: herds the cows detected by explorers until they reach the corral;
- *herdboy*: helps the herder to lead cows to the corral.

The roles *leader* and *cowboy* are abstract and used to specify common properties of their sub-roles. For example, leaders have authority over others cowboys.

The general dynamics of the agents playing the above roles is described with the help of the following scenario. (1-start) At the beginning of the simulation, three exploration groups are created with two agents in each group, on playing the explorer and the other the scouter role. Agents split themselves up so as to cover as wide a range as possible, without necessarily keeping each other in sight. (2-herd) As soon as an agent perceives cows, it informs the members of its exploration group. The explorer of the group creates a new herding group and then changes its role to herder. The scouter also changes its role to herdboy in the new group. After the new group is created, a cluster of cows is assigned to it based on the cows already seen by the agents. The leader then defines the group formation so that the cows are led to the corral. (3-merge) If two herding groups are too near, they are 'merged': one group remains and the other is removed from the organisation. All agents of the removed group change their roles to herdboy in the remaining group. (4-dissolve) Once the corral is reached and the cluster is empty, the herding group is dissolved and the agents create exploration groups returning to the first step (1-start). Table 1 briefly presents the goals that agents are obligated to achieve when playing each of the roles. An agent that adopts the role *scouter*, for instance, is obligated to achieve the goals share_seen_cows and follow_leader.

Although we have some global constraints over the agents' behaviour (based on the roles they are playing), they are *autonomous* to decide how to achieve the goals assigned to them. While *coordination* and *team work* are managed by the $\mathcal{M}$OISE$^+$ tools, the *autonomy* and *pro-activeness* are facilitated by the BDI architecture of our agents implemented in *Jason*. Regarding *communication* (required, for example, for the share_seen_cows goal), we use speech-act based communication available in *Jason*.

Table 1. The Organisational (Maintenance) Goals assigned to Roles

Role	Goal	Goal Description
explorer	find_scouter	find a free agent nearby to play scouter and help in the exploration
	change_to_herding	check if it is best to change to a herding group
	goto_near_unvisited	go to the nearest unvisited location within the group's area
scouter	share_seen_cows	share information about cows with other agents in the group
	follow_leader	follow the leader of the group (an explorer)
herder	recruit	recruit more herdboys depending on the size of the cluster
	release_boys	whenever the group has too many herdboys, release some
	define_formation	compute the ideal location of each member of the group
	be_in_formation	go to the place allocated to the agent in the formation
	change_to_exploring	check if it is best to change to an exploring group
herdboy	share_seen_cows	share information about cows with other agents in the group
	be_in_formation	go to the place allocated to the agent in the formation

3 Software Architecture

To implement our agent team, two features of *Jason* were specially useful: architecture customisation and internal actions. A customisation of the agent architecture is used to interface between the agent and its environment. The environment for the Agent Contest is implemented in a remote server that simulates the cattle field, sending perception to the agents and receiving requests for action execution. Therefore, when an agent attempts to perceive the environment, the customised architecture sends to the agent the information provided by the server, and when the agent chooses an action to be performed, the architecture sends the action execution request to the server.

Although most of the agent code was written in AgentSpeak, some parts were implemented in Java, either because we used legacy code or Java was more appropriate for the task. In particular, we already had a Java implementation of the A* search algorithm, which we used to find paths and calculate distances in the various scenarios of the competition. Also, the computation of the formation of the herding groups requires a lot of vector operations, so best done in Java. These algorithms ware made accessible to the agents by means of *internal actions*.

The organisational interaction is also made available to the agents by means of a custom architecture and internal actions. This architecture produces events when: (1) something has changed in the state of the organisation (e.g., a new group was created); and (2) when the agent has some new obligation based on the roles it is playing. These events may then lead to the creation of intentions to handle them. For example, when some agent adopts the role herder in a herding group, achievement goal events are produced for all obligatory goals of this role (Table 1). An AgentSpeak plan pattern as follows was used to program suitable reactions to those events:

```
+!define_formation[group(G),role(R)]      // plan to handle a goal addition
   <- ... <the code> ...
     .wait("+pos(X,Y,Cycle)");            // wait for the next cycle
     !define_formation[group(G),role(R)]. // achieve that same goal again
```

Note that organisational goals here are maintenance goals: for example, at every simulation cycle the target group formation should be (re)defined. These goals are also annotated with the group and the role that triggered the obligation. This allows us

to code interesting plans such as "`-group(Type,GroupId) <- .drop_inten`
`tion(_[group(GroupId)]).`", i.e., whenever a group is removed (e.g., a herding
group), all the intentions that originated from that group are dropped.

The agents' code is essentially a set of plans to achieve such organisational goals. In many cases, these plans have to decide whether to change the organisation. For example, the goal recruit may trigger a merging of two herding groups; the actions of this plan are roughly: destroy one group and ask their members to change their roles (Algorithm 1). By changing the roles, new goals are automatically defined for the agents. To sum up, decisions are taken at the organisational level (groups/roles), the goals and intentions are a consequence.

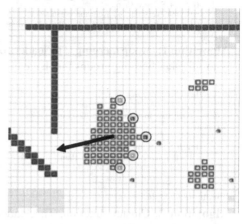

Fig. 2. Team formation in a contest scenario. Cows are yellow and obstacles are black. Green squares inside red circles are target locations for the agents (blue). The arrow indicates the direction of the corral.

The overall performance of the team is, however, also dependent on lower level algorithms. The most important are: (*i*) A* to find good paths; (*ii*) the definition of the cluster of cows for a herding group — the cluster should be the largest the agents can herd (see Algorithm 2); and (*iii*) the definition of the agent formation so that the cows are led to the corral (Fig. 2 illustrated the result[1] of our algorithm).

4 Discussion

The AgentSpeak code for the team is, in our opinion, quite an elegant solution, being declarative, goal-based (or BDI-based), and adequately integrated with an organisational mode. In this paper, we have emphasised the modelling and programming of the team by means of organisational concepts, specially groups and roles. Agents' goals originate from the obligations attached to their roles. This allows us to maintain high abstraction level and good coding style. In some cases, to change the team behaviour we simply changed the organisational specification that was followed by our cowboys. The *Jason* interpreter provided good support for high-level communication, transparent integration with the contest server, use of existing Java code, and integration of organisational programming through $\mathcal{M}$OISE$^+$. As in previous contests, the experience helped us to improve several issues of *Jason*, $\mathcal{M}$OISE$^+$, and their integration.

We had three main difficulties in developing of our team. The first was the lack of an analytical tool to model the organisational dynamics regarding both the changes of agent's roles and the life-cycle of groups. Although the $\mathcal{M}$OISE$^+$ specification language

---

[1] Note that cows stuck to clusters which were difficult to move in the competition simulation (cows behaved differently from the initial scenario description). Thus, even though the formation seems efficient, the best strategy to herd large clusters of cows was to herd them separately.

plan merge(g_i)   // g_i is the herding group of the agent using this plan

forall *herding group* g_j *such that* $g_i > g_j$ **do**
  let S_i be the set of cows of g_i's cluster
  let S_j be the set of cows of g_j's cluster
  if $S_i \cap S_j \neq \emptyset$ **then**
    remove group g_j from the organisation
    ask all agents of g_j to adopt the role *scouter* in g_i

Algorithm 1: Group merging. The leaders of herding groups check a possible merging with all other herding groups that have a smaller ID number.

function cluster(V, m) ;   // V is the set of all seen cows in the group
                                              // m is the maximum number of cows in the cluster
$C \leftarrow \{$ the cow in V nearest to the corral $\}$;   // C is the resulting cluster
repeat
  $add \leftarrow false$
  forall $v \in V$ **do**
    if *some cow in* C *sees* v **then**
      move v from V to C
      $add \leftarrow true$

until $\neg add \vee |C| \geq m$

Algorithm 2: Cluster function. The leaders of herding groups use this function to compute the current cluster of the group.

is used at runtime to *constrain* the dynamics of the organisation (e.g., by the cardinality of roles), it does not help the agents to make decisions about when and what exactly to change. The second problem was the lack of suitable tools to debug the team. Even with the *Jason* mind inspector, communication sniffers, and organisational GUIs, finding bugs take most of the development time. Due to its high abstraction level, BDI and organisational programming require new kinds of debugging tools. These two issue will be the subject of our future work. The third difficulty was due to the various problem-dependent parameters (e.g., perception range, repulsion force, cluster size, herding group size) that influenced the collective behaviour, differing from one scenario to another. This led us to long tuning activities to obtain adequate behaviors, without any automatic learning phase. Such an exploration of the parameter space may be an interesting challenge, but hardly generalisable and outside of our interests.

References

1. Bordini, R.H., Hübner, J.F., Tralamazza, D.M.: Using Jason to implement a team of gold miners. In: Inoue, K., Satoh, K., Toni, F. (eds.) CLIMA 2006. LNCS, vol. 4371, pp. 304–313. Springer, Heidelberg (2007)
2. Bordini, R.H., Hübner, J.F., Wooldrige, M.: Programming Multi-Agent Systems in AgentSpeak using Jason. John Wiley & Sons, Chichester (2007)
3. Hübner, J.F., Bordini, R.H.: Developing a team of gold miners using Jason. In: Dastani, M., Fallah Seghrouchni, A.E., Ricci, A., Winikoff, M. (eds.) ProMAS 2007. LNCS, vol. 4908, pp. 241–245. Springer, Heidelberg (2008)
4. Hübner, J.F., Sichman, J.S., Boissier, O.: Developing organised multi-agent systems using the MOISE+ model: Programming issues at the system and agent levels. Int. J.Agent-Oriented Software Engineering 1(3/4), 370–395 (2007)
5. Rao, A.S.: AgentSpeak(L): BDI agents speak out in a logical computable language. In: Perram, J., Van de Velde, W. (eds.) MAAMAW 1996. LNCS (LNAI), vol. 1038, pp. 42–55. Springer, Heidelberg (1996)

Dublin Bogtrotters: Agent Herders

M. Dragone, D. Lillis, C. Muldoon, R. Tynan,
R. W. Collier, and G. M. P. O'Hare

School of Computer Science and Informatics
University College Dublin
{mauro.dragone, david.lillis, conor.muldoon,
richard.tynan, rem.collier, gregory.ohare}@ucd.ie

Abstract. This paper describes an entry to the Multi-Agent Programming Contest 2008. The approach employs the pre-existing Agent Factory framework and extends this framework in line with experience gained from its use within the robotics domain.

1 Introduction

This paper outlines the approach adopted for the Dublin Bogtrotters entry in the PROMAS Agent Programming Contest. For the purposes of the competition, we adapted the pre-existing Agent Factory (AF) framework [1,2], making use of our previous experience in the area of robotics [3]. As is described in Section 3, we have developed a 2-tier hybrid agent architecture that is loosely based on the SoSAA architecture [3]. This system is implemented using an agile methodology [4], outlined in Section 2, that supports agile modelling and test driven development. Some details on the strategies that were employed in the competition are discussed in Section 4.

2 System Analysis and Design

The system was specified and designed with the SADAAM methodology [4], which supports agile modelling and test-driven development. In this methodology, agile modelling is realised using a combination of Agent UML Protocol Diagrams and customised UML Case Diagrams and Activity Diagrams. As is usual in such methodologies, rather than deliver a comprehensive system design, we used our design notation only as a mechanism to clarify how certain core system features were implemented. SADAAM was chosen because it has previously been used in conjunction with AF to develop agent-based systems.

3 Software Architecture

The overall system architecture (figure 1 is oriented around a core set of herder agents, that are supported by a number of ancillary agents, including: a herd

K.V. Hindriks, A. Pokahr, and S. Sardina (Eds.): ProMAS 2008, LNAI 5442, pp. 243–247, 2009.

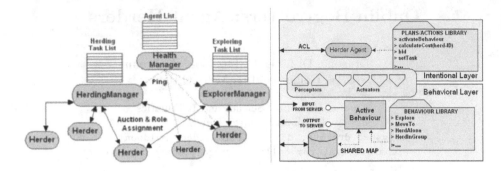

Fig. 1. Bogtrotter System (Left) and Hybrid Agent Architecture (Right)

manager agent that was responsible for creating herders and allocating user-names to them; a health agent, that monitored the health of other agents (see Section 4); and a strategy agent that oversaw potential strategies.

While all of the ancillary agents were implemented using only the Agent Factory Agent Programming Language (AFAPL) [5], the core herder agents were implemented using a hybrid agent architecture that is inspired by the SoSAA robot software framework [3]. This framework advocates the adoption of a two-tier architecture for robotic systems that combines an intentional multi-agent system with a low-level component-based infrastructure. The idea behind this approach is that the upper agent layer enhances the lower-level mechanisms by way of their intentional reasoning abilities and support for multi-agent organisation. For instance, agents can negotiate the use of system resources, and also supervise the low-level communication mechanisms that are used to exchange non-ACL messages amongst low-level components.

For this competition, the framework was realised through a combination AFAPL for the agent level and a simple Java-based architectural framework that provided basic mechanisms that attend to the run-time and data-distribution requirements of lower-level components. Interaction between these layers was facilitated by a clear and standardised interface which was realised through AF platform services. An overview of this architecture can be seen in figure 1.

The AFAPL language models agents as mental entities whose internal state consists of beliefs and commitments. Informally, beliefs represent the agent's current state of its environment, while commitments represent the outcome of an underlying reasoning process through which the agent selects what activities it should perform. In AFAPL, an agent has both primitive abilities, in the form of directly executable actions, and composite abilities, in the form of plans built from plan operators such as SEQ (sequential execution) and FOREACH (plan expansion). Execution of an AFAPL program involves the update of the agent's mental state by repeatedly applying an internal reasoning process that combines: update of the agents beliefs via perception of the environment through a set of auxiliary Java components, known as perceptors; the adoption of new commitments though the evaluation of a set of commitment rules, which map belief states onto commitments that should be adopted should that state arise; and the realisation of commitments through the performing of actions that are implemented through a set of auxiliary Java components, known as actuators.

The rationale for the hybrid architecture was to delegate many of the details of the herders' control to a reactive behavioural system, whose operation was linked to the underlying sensory-motor apparatus. This system consisted of various components that formed the agents primary skill-set, including: simple action patterns (`stop`, `turn`, `move_backward`) and more complex patterns that attempt to maintain or achieve simple conditions between the agent and the environment (`follow_border_obstacle`, `follow_border_herd`, `move_toward_target`, `explore`). Additional components embodying sensor data processing routines were also included, that were used to recognise features in the agent's world model or to signal events generated by the currently active behaviour (`path_obstructed`, `close(target)`). These features and events were passed to the agents belief set via perceptors, where they were used as perceptual triggers for the activation of other behaviours specified by AFAPL plans.

4 Agent Team Strategy

Central to our approach were the herder agents. These agents were responsible for controlling the behaviour of the herders and were organised into teams that were formed to achieve a particular task (e.g. exploration, herding a particular group of cows). Each team was controlled by a team manager agent. Resource allocation was carried out by team managers holding auctions in which the herders would bid using a greedy bidding strategy to join particular teams or cover certain roles. These auctions were intended to have three notable benefits. Firstly, because of the greedy nature of the agents' bidding strategy, the time needed to carry out these auctions was minimal. Secondly, an agent that is most suited to a task was most likely to win an auction (e.g. for a task to explore a particular part of the map, the bidding agent that is closest will win the auction). Finally, it enabled dynamic reallocation of agents' priorities. For example, as more cows were discovered, agents could switch from exploring to teams that engaged in herding, returning to exploring once the cows were gathered.

A key strategy underlying our approach was the use of hybrid communication by combining Agent Communication Language (ACL)-based communication and blackboard-based communication. The ACL-based communication was realised the AF implementation of the FIPA-ACL standards, and the blackboard-based communication was realised through a shared map that was accessible via Java RMI. The shared map exported a distributed update interface to all the agents in the system. Through this interface, each agent could update the server with its own observations and receive in return an update of all the observations collected by the rest of the team.

In each simulation step, each herding agent had a limited time slice to send an action message. The message sent was determined by the agent's current low-level behaviour. For instance if the agent was engaged in a `move_toward_target` behaviour, the next message would be a movement in a direction that aids in the fulfillment of this goal. At all times, however, the higher-level management agents reasoned about their perceived current state of the world in order to optimise the overall strategies of the participating agents. This meant that an agent's active behaviour could change because of an instruction from a team leader, or due to a change in team membership brought about by an auction.

Robustness was a high priority in participating in the contest. Herding agents who were still active but had become disconnected from the competition server needed to be capable of re-establishing that connection. Additionally, a health management system monitored both agents and the agent platforms to detect any failures that may occur. A failed agent was replaced with a new agent of the same type and a failed platform resulted in all the agents formerly residing on it being recreated on other platforms.

5   Discussion

Much of our effort was in designing and implementing the infrastructure framework as this was our first entry in the contest. Unfortunately by the beginning of the contest we had not completed testing and tuning of our functional components to the extent we would have wished. As a result, our behavioural functions occasionally encountered unexpected exceptions that had not arisen during development, and the resource allocation auctions were not optimised in terms of evaluating the costs and the benefits of engaging in the various tasks.

The difficulties with the auction were the greatest limiting factor in our performance. Agents tended to prefer exploration and single-agent herding to the formation of groups to herd larger numbers of cows. Figure 2 illustrates this through a case where a herd of 15 cows were driven through the bottleneck of the "RazorEdge" scenario (a map on which the average score was a mere 5 cows). However, having pushed this herd through the gap, the agents decided to explore for more cows rather than continue pushing this particular herd to the corral. This shows that while the simple agent behaviours were effective, the weighting attached to various scenarios for the purposes of the auctions were sub-optimal.

We believe that this year's scenario was a very useful and well organised attempt to promote multi-agent programming. Since we have now a working infrastructure framework, we are in a position to be more competitive in the next contest, as we will be able to focus our work on adapting our system to the new application scenario and focus on our real interest: multi-agent coordination.

We feel that the slowness of the simulator was a big obstacle to our development plan in this year's first entry to the contest, as it was difficult to run a sufficient number of simulations to test different task and environment configurations. In the future, this would be also an obstacle to the adoption of machine learning techniques that may require substantial amounts of training data.

We believe that real systems need MAS self-organisation techniques that are shaped by ACL-based coordination but that still manage to produce reliable and efficient control. Because of the large time slices allotted between moves,

Fig. 2. RazorEdge Scenario: A herd is pushed through the bottleneck

teams are currently able to make use of computational expensive deliberation phases before transmitting an instruction to the central server. While our system architecture allowed us to produce very fast response in the behavioural layer, we felt that the present organisation of the contest does not place a high value such a feature. We believe that reducing the size of this time slice will force participants to develop solutions that are closer to their real world counterparts.

6   Conclusion

This paper presents an overview of our submission to the ProMAS Multi-Agent Programming Contest. The solution developed employed a hybrid agent architecture, whose upper deliberative layer was realised using AFAPL, and whose lower layer consisted of a reactive architecture. High-level system behaviours were designed using an agile modeling process, and were implemented in AFAPL. These high level behaviours drove the adoption of various lower level reactive behaviours, including obstacle avoidance, herding, and exploring.

References

1. O'Hare, G., Jennings, N.: Foundations of Distributed Artificial Intelligence. Wiley/ IEEE, Los Alamitos (1996)
2. Collier, R., O'Hare, G., Lowen, T., Rooney, C.: Beyond Prototyping in the Factory of Agents. In: Mařík, V., Müller, J.P., Pěchouček, M. (eds.) CEEMAS 2003. LNCS, vol. 2691, p. 383. Springer, Heidelberg (2003)
3. Dragone, M.: Sosaa: An agent-based robot software framework (2008), http://csserver.ucd.ie/
4. Clynch, N., Collier, R.: Sadaam: Software agent development - an agile methodology. In: Dastani, M., El Fallah Seghrouchni, A., Leite, J., Torroni, P. (eds.) LADS 2007. LNCS, vol. 5118. Springer, Heidelberg (2007)
5. Collier, R.: Agent Factory: A Framework for the Engineering of Agent- Oriented Applications. PhD thesis, University College Dublin (2002)

SHABaN Multi-agent Team To Herd Cows

Adel T. Rahmani, Alireza Saberi, Mehdi Mohammadi, Amin Nikanjam,
Ehsan Adeli Mosabbeb, and Monireh Abdoos

Iran University of Science and Technology
{rahmani,a_saberi,mh_mohammadi,nikanjam,eadeli,abdoos}@iust.ac.ir

Abstract. This paper is submitted as the final team description of SHA-BaN[1] team, one of the participants in the Second Multi-Agent Programming Contest in association with the ProMAS 2008 workshop. Here we describe the agent architecture and behaviors to solve a cooperative task in a highly dynamic environment. Our approach consists of evaluating strategies in NetLogo and a raw implementation.

1 Introduction

Multi-agent systems are composed of a number of interacting computing elements, also known as agents. Agents have two important capabilities: the abilities to take autonomous actions and interact with other agents [1].

Agent contest is an attempt to motivate research in the area of multi-agent system development and programming. The scenario this year is about cows and herders. Each team owns six agents, whose duties are to collect cows and guide them to the corral. To this end, we propose a multi-agent system to compete against the opponent through a sequence of rationale actions aiming the cooperation and coordination concepts.

NetLogo [2], a cross-platform multi-agent programmable modeling environment, is used for the simple prototyping and simulation of the strategies. After designing and testing the strategies, a programming language is employed to implement them.

The paper is organized as what follows: next section provides the information on the analysis and design of system. Section 3 illustrates the software architecture of the proposed multi-agent system. In Section 4 we briefly describe the team strategy and some algorithms. A discussion about the Contest is mentioned in section 5. Finally the conclusion remarks could be found in section 6.

2 System Analysis and Design

The SHABaN team is designed as 6 independent agents that communicate with a coordinator. Figure 1 shows the single agent architecture, coordination and monitoring modules. The Communication component connects to the contest simulation server, parses the received information and passes them to the perceptor. The communication component sends back the desired actions and other necessary information to the server.

---

[1] SHABaN is a Farsi name that means shepherd.

K.V. Hindriks, A. Pokahr, and S. Sardina (Eds.): ProMAS 2008, LNAI 5442, pp. 248–252, 2009.

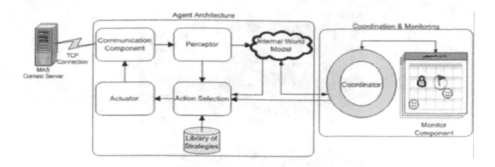

Fig. 1. Agent architecture, coordination and monitoring modules

```
Start Tournament:
  for each agent in team:
    Connect to simulation server using one TCP connection.
    Identify and authenticate yourself and receive acknowledgement
from the server and wait for the match to start.
    Start Match:
      Get match information
      Repeat for a finite number of steps:
        Each agent gets sensory information.
        Process the received sensory information.
        Update the internal world model.
        Each agent negotiates with the coordinator and selects an action
        or autonomously select an action based on its goal.
      Encode and send the actions to the simulation server.
      Once a while, analyze the situation and update the strategy.
```

Fig. 2. Algorithmic description of SHABaN multi-agent team

The perceptor component senses the environment via the received information, and updates the internal world model. Action selection component uses the internal world model, preceptor, coordinator and library of strategies to select the best action. Actually there are two basic roles for agents: exploration and herding. In the exploration mode agents are to explore the environment but in the herding mode they target a cow and try to move it toward the own corral. Actuator prepares the appropriate command due to the selected action and passes it to the communication component.

The coordinator makes the comprehensive world model by using the internal world model of the all agents and a modified BFS algorithm. This comprehensive world model assists agents to find the best path to the corral and the nearest cow. The monitor component uses coordinator information to present a world view during run-time. The main usage of the monitor component is to ease the debugging process.

A high-level algorithmic description of SHABaN is shown in figure 2.

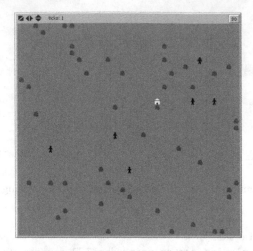

Fig. 3. A sample simulated environment using NetLogo

3 Software Architecture

This section gives an overview of the software tools used for simulation and implementation of SHABaN team.

3.1 Simulation

NetLogo is a multi-agent programming language and modeling environment for simulating natural and social phenomena. It was authored by Uri Wilensky in 1999 and still is under development at the Center for Connected Learning and Computer-Based Modeling [2].

We use NetLogo to implement and evaluate our ideas before detailed implementation. Its simplicity lets us to test our strategies in a multi-agent environment quickly. Furthermore, while contest server was not available NetLogo was utilized as an appropriate simulation environment. Figure 3 shows a sample simulated environment using NetLogo.

3.2 Implementation

For implementation a multi-agent and a non-multi-agent based approach were firstly chosen. As the multi-agent approach, JIAC IV [3] was used. JIAC IV is a framework for development of powerful emergent intelligence and autonomous multi-agent systems. It is built on the basis of compact component architecture and uses a specific agent programming language, JADL [4].

Due to the lack of enough experience with JIAC and the short time before the contest, the JIAC IV approach was set aside after around a month of working with. A simple non-multi-agent based framework was implemented using a Windows platform and the C# programming language. All the algorithms and interfacing protocols were implemented using this language. But for long-term research, such a multi-agent implementation environment like JIAC, which proved to be efficient, is strongly advised.

4   Agent Team strategy

We have defined two different roles for agents: exploration and herding. In exploration mode, agents travel to unknown or previously known areas and try to detect the environment. Once the agent decides to bring a cow home, the agent switches to herding mode. In the both modes once the agent receive the sensory information, it updates the internal world model and consequently the coordinator.

At the beginning of each match the grid is divided into some areas. Then agents in the exploration mode go to the nearest area assigned by the coordinator to explore that area. At each time step agents transfer their percept to the internal world model. After some time steps and exploring sufficient areas required for constructing the comprehensive world model, the coordinator makes agents to switch to herding mode by assigning a cow to herd. Then each agent autonomously tries to herd the specific cow toward the corral using a simple algorithm based on the distance of neighbor cells to the corral.

As it was mentioned before a modified BFS algorithm is used to construct the comprehensive world model. This model contains all grid information based on agent perceptions: cows, trees, corrals and other agents. The BFS algorithm assigns a semi-shortest path for each pair of cells in the environment. It uses an incremental algorithm, such that once a new aspect of the environment is discovered it updates all the previously found paths which could be improved using these newly discovered cells. The comprehensive model is constructed in coordinator based on all agents' perceptions and is reachable by all agents.

In maze-like scenario the blocking strategy can play a leading role, if a bottleneck is available and it can be detected by the agents. The coordinator finds narrowest part of the way to opponent corral as bottleneck and assigns at most two agents to patrol this area. This strategy will be effective if other agents do their best and move cows to own corral efficiently. In order to detect bottlenecks, the cells are divided in to groups based on their distance to opponent corral and the group with smaller members has the chance to be a bottlenecks. Furthermore, it is not necessary to explore the entire map or the opponent corral neighborhoods to detect the opponent bottleneck in symmetric maps. We may find our bottleneck by exploring our corral neighborhoods and estimate the opponent bottleneck location by considering the map symmetry.

5   Discussion

We think that our first attendance in the Agent Contest was successful. Engaging in a time-consuming sophisticated process of developing multi-agent team is very useful as well as nice. We touch all the theoretic challenges in practice and discover our shortcomings. From our point of view the main critic is lack of effective cooperation. Individual behavior of SHABaN agents is acceptable for us but they can not cooperate effectively with each other in exploring the environment and herding.

Although Agents Contest 2008 is successful to serve its purpose to provide a testbed for multi-agent system programming but we argue some suggestions. It will be better if all teams come to a specific place to participate in the contest like RoboCup series. Face to face discussions and observing the design and execution of other teams will be really helpful. With remote online participation, we prefer that all matches in a specific grid take place consecutively and at one session. This approach seems to be much better than what is done in Agent Contest 2008.

6 Conclusion

In this paper we have demonstrated a multi-agent team, including six herders and a coordinator, aiming the goal of collecting cows as much as possible. SHABaN team strategies are first simulated and evaluated using NetLogo. It could usefully help us to extract efficient ideas. The first attempt to participate in this contest, for sure, has been a great experience and will ameliorate us for probable future events. We look forward to participating in Agent Contest 2009.

References

1. Wooldridge, M.: An Introduction to Multiagent Systems. John Wiley & Sons LTD., Chichester (2002)
2. Wilensky, U.: NetLogo 4.0.2, Center for Connected Learning and Computer-Based Modeling, Northwestern University, Evanston, IL (2007),
   http://ccl.northwestern.edu/netlogo
3. Sesseler, R.: A modular architecture for service based interactions between Agents, PhD thesis, Technische Universität Berlin (2002)
4. Konnerth, T., Hirsch, B., Albayrak, S.: JADL-An Agent Description Language for Smart Agents. In: Baldoni, M., Endriss, U. (eds.) DALT 2006. LNCS, vol. 4327, pp. 141–155. Springer, Heidelberg (2006)

Author Index